D0843857

THE CAMBRIDGE
COMPANION TO

KAFKA

Franz Kafka's writing has had a wide-reaching influence on European literature, culture, and thought. *The Cambridge Companion to Kafka* offers a comprehensive account of his life and work, providing a rounded contemporary appraisal of Central Europe's most distinctive modernist. Contributions cover all the key texts, and discuss Kafka's writing in a variety of critical contexts such as feminism, deconstruction, psychoanalysis, Marxism, and Jewish studies. Other chapters discuss his impact on popular culture and film. The essays are well supported by a chronology of significant dates relating to Kafka and detailed guides to further reading, and will be of interest to students of German, Comparative Literature, and Jewish Studies.

JULIAN PREECE is Senior Lecturer at the School of European Culture and Languages at the University of Kent at Canterbury. He is the author (with Waldemar Lotnik) of *Nine Lives: Ethnic Conflict in the Polish–Ukrainian Borderlands* (1999) and *The Life and Work of Günter Grass: Literature, History, Politics* (2001).

OKANAGAN COLLEGE
LIBRARY
BRITISH COLUMBIA

THE CAMBRIDGE
COMPANION TO
KAFKA

EDITED BY
JULIAN PREECE
University of Kent at Canterbury

CAMBRIDGE
UNIVERSITY PRESS

PUBLISHED BY THE PRESS SYNDICATE OF THE UNIVERSITY OF CAMBRIDGE
The Pitt Building, Trumpington Street, Cambridge, United Kingdom

CAMBRIDGE UNIVERSITY PRESS
The Edinburgh Building, Cambridge CB2 2RU, UK
40 West 20th Street, New York, NY 10011–4211, USA
477 Williamstown Road, Port Melbourne, VIC 3207, Australia
Ruiz de Alarcón 13, 28014 Madrid, Spain
Dock House, The Waterfront, Cape Town 8001, South Africa

http://www.cambridge.org

© Cambridge University Press 2002

This book is in copyright. Subject to statutory exception
and to the provisions of relevant collective licensing agreements,
no reproduction of any part may take place without
the written permission of Cambridge University Press.

First published 2002
Reprinted 2003

Typeface Sabon 10/13 pt.   *System* L^AT_EX 2_ε [TB]

A catalogue record for this book is available from the British Library

Library of Congress Cataloguing in Publication Data
The Cambridge companion to Kafka / edited by Julian Preece.
    p.   cm. – (Cambridge companions to literature)
    Includes bibliographical references and index.
    ISBN 0 521 66314 8 – ISBN 0 521 66391 1 (pbk)
    1. Kafka, Franz, 1883–1924.   2. Authors, Austrian – 20th century – Biography.
    I. Preece, Julian.   II. Series.
    PT2621.A26 Z488   2002
        833′.912 – dc21
        [B]   2001043212

ISBN 0 521 66314 8 hardback
ISBN 0 521 66391 1 paperback

Transferred to digital printing 2005

For Pippa,

Marianne, and Gabriel

CONTENTS

CONTENTS

CONTRIBUTORS

ELIZABETH BOA has taught German literature for more than thirty years at the University of Nottingham, where she is now professor. She is the author of *The Sexual Circus: Wedekind's Theatre of Subversion* (1987) and *Kafka: Gender, Class, and Race in the Letters and Fictions* (1996) and (with Rachel Palfreyman) *Heimat – A German Dream: Regional Loyalties and National Identity in German Culture 1890–1990* (2000). She is currently President of the Conference of University Teachers of German in Great Britain and Ireland.

MARTIN BRADY is a visiting lecturer and honorary research fellow in the German Department of King's College London. He wrote his PhD on the early films of Jean-Marie Straub and Danièle Huillet and has published on the history of German film, Straub/Huillet, Arnold Schönberg, Robert Bresson, adaptations of Kleist, and Paul Celan. He is the translator of Victor Klemperer's *Language of the Third Reich. LTI: Lingua Tertii Imperii* (2000) and is active as a visual artist.

IRIS BRUCE is assistant professor of German and Comparative Literature at McMaster University, Hamilton (Ontario). She wrote a PhD on Kafka and the Jewish tradition at the University of Toronto and has since published a number of essays on Kafka and Judaism, Kafka and Nadine Gordimer, and Kafka in popular culture. She is presently completing a book entitled *Dates in Palestine: Kafka's Cultural Zionism*.

DAVID CONSTANTINE taught German language and literature, first at Durham, then at Oxford, before retiring in 2000. He is known as a translator (most recently, *Selected Writings: Heinrich von Kleist*, 1997), a scholar of the German Classical Age (*Early Greek Travellers and the Hellenic Ideal*, 1984; *Hölderlin*, 1988), and a poet. His *Selected Poems* appeared with Bloodaxe in 1991. Since then he has published *Caspar Hauser* (1994) and *The Pelt of Wasps* (1998).

STANLEY CORNGOLD is professor of German and Comparative Literature at Princeton University. He is the author of *The Commentators' Despair: the Interpretation of Kafka's Metamorphosis* (1973), *Franz Kafka: the Neccesity of Form* (1988), a novel entitled *Borrowed Lives* (1991), *The Fate of the Self: German Writers and French Theory* (rev. edn. 1994), and *Complex Pleasures: Forms of Feeling in German Literature* (1998). He has also translated 'The Metamorphosis' and is the editor of the Norton edition of that work (1996). He is currently completing a new study of Kafka, entitled *Lambent Traces*.

BILL DODD, reader in German Studies at the University of Birmingham, is the author of numerous books on Kafka, including student guides to *Der Prozess* (1991), *The Metamorphosis, The Trial, and The Castle* (1995), and *Kafka and Dostoyevsky* (1992). He also has many publications in the field of linguistics and was a co-author of *Modern German Grammar: a Practical Guide* (1996). He has recently been awarded a Leverhulme Major Research Fellowship to investigate 'Sprachkritik, Nazism, and the German Conscience: the Career of Dolf Sternberger'.

OSMAN DURRANI taught German at the University of Durham for twenty-three years before his appointment to a professorship in 1995 at the University of Kent at Canterbury. He is the author of *Faust and the Bible* (1977), *Fictions of Germany: Images of the German Nation in the Modern Novel* (1994), editor of *German Poetry of the Romantic Era: an Anthology* (1986), and co-editor (with Colin Good and Keven Hilliard) of *The New Germany: Literature and Society after Unification* (1995). He has published on Kafka and Harold Pinter and written extensively on modern drama and prose. He is currently working on German popular music and cabaret.

ANNE FUCHS studied at the University of Konstanz, Germany, and is now senior lecturer in German at University College, Dublin. Her research focuses on the self and the other in modern literature, including travel writing. She is the author of *Dramaturgie des Narrentums: das Komische in der Prosa Robert Walsers* (1993) and *A Space of Anxiety: Dislocation and Abjection in Modern German-Jewish Literature* (1999). She has also edited (with Theo Harden), *Reisen im Diskurs: Modelle der literarischen Fremderfahrung von den Pilgerberichten bis zur Postmoderne* (1995) and (with Florian Krobb), *Ghetto Writing: Traditional and Eastern Jewry in German-Jewish Literature* (1999).

ROLF J. GOEBEL teaches German language, culture, and literature at the University of Alabama in Huntsville. In Germany he studied at the University of Kiel, in the US at Brown and Maryland. He is the author of *Kritik und Revision: Kafkas Rezeption mythologischer, biblischer und historischer Traditionen* (1986) and *Constructing China: Kafka's Orientalist Discourse* (1997), as well as recent articles on Walter Benjamin, postcolonialism, and urban discourse. He is currently completing a book on the reconceptualisation of the flâneur in a postcolonial context.

RUTH V. GROSS is the author of *PLAN and the Austrian Rebirth* (1982) and editor of *Critical Essays on Franz Kafka* (1990). She has twice been President of the Kafka Society of America and is a member of the Editorial Board for the *Journal of the Kafka Society of America*. She teaches German at the University of Texas, Arlington, where she chaired the Department of Foreign Languages for seven years and is now Dean of the College of Liberal Arts.

HELEN HUGHES teaches German language, linguistics, and film at the University of Surrey. She wrote her PhD ('The Bureaucratic Muse') on prose style in the works of Adalbert Stifter, Kafka, Thomas Bernhard, and Oswald Wiener. She has published on contemporary cinema, Bernhard, Stifter and Robert Bresson, and the Austrian film-maker and artist, Valie Export.

DAGMAR C. G. LORENZ, a native of the Federal Republic of Germany, received her PhD in German and Master's in English from the University of Cincinnati. She has taught at Rutgers and, for many years, at the Ohio State University. In 1998 she joined the Department of German at the University of Illinois at Chicago. She is the author of *Ilse Aichinger* (1981), *Franz Grillparzer: Dichter des sozialen Konflikts* (1986), *Verfolgung bis zum Massenmord* (1992), and *Keepers of the Motherland: German Texts by Jewish Women Writers* (1997). She is also the editor and translator of *Contemporary Jewish Writing in Austria* (1999) and currently serves as Editor of *German Quarterly*.

ANTHONY DROSTE NORTHEY was born in the US, grew up in Germany and Austria, and studied in Canada. He has been teaching German at Acadia University in Nova Scotia, Canada, since 1970 and since 1973 has been engaged in biographical research on Kafka. He contributed to the *Kafka-Handbuch*, edited by Hartmut Binder (1979), and is the author of *Kafka's Relatives: their Lives and his Writing* (1991), which has been translated into numerous languages, as well as of many essays in both English and German. From 1998 to 2000 he was President of the Canadian Association of German Teachers.

JULIAN PREECE teaches German and Comparative Literature at the University of Kent at Canterbury. His main research interests lie in German culture of the second half of the twentieth century, especially contemporary literature. He is the author of *The Life and Work of Günter Grass: Literature, History, Politics* (2001) and (with Waldemar Lotnik) *Nine Lives: Ethnic Conflict in the Polish–Ukrainian Borderlands* (1999). From 1994 to 2000 he was co-editor of the Bradford Series of Colloquia on Contemporary German Literature.

ACKNOWLEDGEMENTS

Most of the chapters in this Companion were presented and discussed at a meeting of the contributors which took place in Prague in July 1999. We are grateful to the Zentrum Franze Kafky and the Austrian Culture Institute in Prague for inviting us to use their premises and to Kurt Krolop and Josef Čermák for their valuable comments.

Transatlantic collaborations of this sort are rare in German studies but made much easier nowadays by electronic communication. My task as editor has been greatly eased by the spirit of co-operation which has characterised this enterprise from the beginning and I would like to thank the contributors for that. My special thanks go to my colleague Osman Durrani whose contribution to the volume has been far in excess of his own chapter.

ABBREVIATIONS

As one of the primary aims of this volume is to bring Kafka further into the orbit of the non-German speaker, all quotations from his writings are in English translation. Sometimes the contributors have preferred to translate themselves, sometimes they have used well-known published translations, which they have modified where appropriate. This variety of approaches has entailed a large number of cited German and English editions (for further clarification, see chapter 12, 'Editions, Translations, Adaptations').

When reference is made to German, the paperback version of the German critical edition has been used: Franz Kafka, *Gesammelte Werke in zwölf Bänden* (Collected Works in Twelve Volumes), ed. Hans-Gerd Koch (Frankfurt aM: Fischer, 1994):

EL   *Ein Landarzt und andere Drucke zu Lebzeiten*, vol. 1 (A Country Doctor and Other Texts Printed in his Lifetime)

DV   *Der Verschollene*, vol. 2 (*The Man who Disappeared*)

DP   *Der Proceß*, vol. 3 (*The Trial*)

DS   *Das Schloß*, vol. 4 (*The Castle*)

BK   *Beschreibung eines Kampfes und andere Schriften aus dem Nachlaß*, vol. 5 (Description of a Struggle and Other Posthumous Writings)

BB   *Beim Bau der chinesischen Mauer und andere Schriften aus dem Nachlaß*, vol. 6 (The Great Wall of China and Other Posthumous Writings)

ZFG   *Zur Frage der Gesetze und andere Schriften aus dem Nachlaß*, vol. 7 (On the Question of Laws and Other Posthumous Writings)

DE   *Das Ehepaar und andere Schriften aus dem Nachlaß*, vol. 8 (The Married Couple and Other Posthumous Writings)

TB1   *Tagebücher: 1909–1912*, vol. 9 (Diaries: 1909–1912)

TB2   *Tagebücher: 1912–1914*, vol. 10 (Diaries: 1912–1914)

TB3   *Tagebücher: 1914–1923*, vol. 11 (Diaries: 1914–1923)

RT   *Reisetagebücher*, vol. 12 (Travel Diaries)

The editorial situation with the letters is more complicated as only the first of a planned five volumes of correspondence has so far appeared:

B2   *Briefe 1902–1912* (Letters 1902–1912), ed. Hans-Gerd Koch (Frankfurt aM: Fischer, 1999)

The following volumes are also cited:

BF   *Briefe an Felice und andere Korrespondenz aus der Verlobungszeit* (Letters to Felice and Other Correspondence from the Time of his Engagement), ed. Erich Heller and Jürgen Born (Frankfurt aM: Fischer, 1967)

BM   *Briefe an Milena. Erweiterte und neu geordnete Ausgabe* (Letters to Milena. Revised Edition), ed. Jürgen Born and Michael Müller (Frankfurt aM: Fischer, 1983)

B1   *Briefe 1902–1924* (Letters 1902–1924), ed. Max Brod (Frankfurt aM: Fischer, 1958)

Apart from the diaries, which are only available in translations of Max Brod's editions, we have cited published translations which follow the revised critical edition of the fiction:

TT   *The Trial*, tr. Breon Mitchell (New York: Schocken, 1998)

GWC   *The Great Wall of China and Other Short Works*, tr. and ed. Malcolm Pasley (Harmondsworth: Penguin Books, 1991)

TOS   *The Transformation and Other Stories: Works Published During Kafka's Lifetime*, tr. and ed. Malcolm Pasley (Harmondsworth: Penguin, 1992)

M   *The Metamorphosis: Tradition, Backgrounds and Context* (New York: Norton, 1996), ed. and tr. Stanley Corngold

D1   *The Diaries of Franz Kafka 1910–13*, ed. Max Brod, tr. Joseph Kresh (London: Secker and Warburg, 1948)

D2   *The Diaries of Franz Kafka 1914–23*, ed. Max Brod, tr. Martin Greenberg with the co-operation of Hannah Arendt (London: Secker and Warburg, 1949)

LF   *Letters to Felice*, ed. Erich Heller and Jürgen Born, tr. James Stern and Elisabeth Duckworth (New York: Schocken, 1973)

LFFE   *Letters to Friends, Family, and Editors*, ed. Max Brod, tr. Richard and Clara Winston (New York: Schocken, 1978)

CHRONOLOGY

3 July 1883	Birth of Franz Kafka in Prague, capital of the kingdom of Bohemia in the dual monarchy of Austria–Hungary. His parents, the fancy-goods merchants, Hermann and Julie Kafka, name him after the Habsburg emperor, Franz Josef.
1886	Death of Kafka's brother Georg at fifteen months from measles.
1887	Birth of Felice Bauer in Silesia (Germany).
1888	Death of Kafka's second brother Heinrich at seven months from meningitis.
1889	The Panama affair. Jewish financiers are blamed for the collapse of the Panama Canal project. Thousands of French investors lose their money. Kafka's uncles Alfred and Joseph Loewy worked for the Panama Canal Company and feel the brunt of French anti-Semitism.
1889–90	The Dreyfus trial. After Alfred Dreyfus, a captain in the French army, is found guilty of passing military secrets to the Germans, France becomes embroiled in a bout of anti-Semitism, during which the loyalty of French Jews is called into question. The Dreyfus affair echoed through the decades in pre-Hitler Europe.
1889–92	Birth of Kafka's three sisters, Elli, Valli, and Ottla, all of whom will perish in the Holocaust.
1893–1901	Kafka attends the Altstädter Deutsches Gymnasium (German Grammar School) in Prague.
1896	Bar-mitzvah; Theodor Herzl publishes *The Jewish State*, the book which founded the Zionist movement; birth of Milena Jesenská.
1897	Three-day anti-Jewish riots in Prague (the 'December Storm').

1900	Publication of Sigmund Freud's *The Interpretation of Dreams*; death of Friedrich Nietzsche.
1901	Kafka's first foreign holiday – to the German islands of Norderney and Helgoland in the North Sea – on completion of his *Abitur* (school-leaving certificate). Publication of Otto Weininger's *Sex and Character*.
1901–6	Studies at the German University in Prague. After sampling courses in chemistry, art history, and German literature, finally settles on law and is awarded a doctorate after five years of study.
1902	Hugo von Hofmannsthal publishes 'Letter to Lord Chandos', arguably the most important single document in the *Sprachkrise* ('Crisis of language'), where he articulates a loss of confidence in words as a means of communication; Kafka meets Max Brod; correspondence with schoolfriends, Paul Kisch and Oskar Pollak.
1903	Journey to Munich.
1905	Failed revolution in Russia; Kafka spends part of the summer at a sanatorium in Zuckmantel, Austrian Silesia (now Poland).
1905–6	In order to qualify as a civil servant Kafka works for twelve months for no pay at the criminal courts.
1907–8	Employed at the Assicurazioni Generali in Prague.
1907–9	Correspondence with Hedwig Weiler.
1908	First publications of short prose pieces in literary journal; joins the Workers' Accident Insurance Institute, where he is promoted rapidly in his first five years and carries on working until 1922; Austria–Hungary annexes Bosnia–Herzegovina.
1909	The earliest date for surviving diary entries; journey with Brod to Brescia in northern Italy (September); publication of 'The Aeroplane in Brescia'.
1910	Journey with Brod to Paris (October); first journey to Berlin (December).
1911	Hears a lecture by Albert Einstein (May), whose *General Theory of Relativity* was published three years earlier; journey with Brod to Switzerland, northern Italy, and Paris (August/September); meeting with the Yiddish Theatre Troupe from Lemberg/Lwów (September); becomes closely involved with the running of the Kafka family's asbestos factory (autumn).

1911–13   Beiliss affair in Russia unleashes wave of anti-Semitism which, like the Dreyfus trial more than twenty years earlier, washes over the neighbouring Habsburg lands. After the brutal murder of a young schoolboy in Kiev, the 'blood libel' against the Jews is revived once more. Mendel Beiliss is accused of murdering the boy to use his blood for ritualistic purposes. The Tsarist authorities know of his innocence but proceed with the prosecution; Beiliss is finally acquitted.

1912–13   First and second Balkan Wars.

1912   Kafka delivers 'Introductory Lecture on Yiddish' (February); hears lecture by the Czech Social Democrat František Soukup on America and meets his future publishers, Ernst Rowohlt and Kurt Wolff (June); journey with Brod to Leipzig and Weimar (July), first book, *Contemplation*, accepted for publication; meets Felice Bauer (August) and begins correspondence with her (September); writes 'The Judgement', 'The Metamorphosis', and most of *The Man who Disappeared* (September–December).

1913   Meets the Zionist writer and intellectual Martin Buber (January); continues intensive correspondence with Bauer whom he visits in March; announces engagement on his thirtieth birthday; begins correspondence with Grete Bloch; travels to Vienna, Venice, and Riva (September).

1914   Outbreak of First World War after the assassination of the heir to the Habsburg crown, Archduke Franz-Ferdinand, in Sarajevo, the capital of Bosnia–Herzegovina (28 June); Austro-Hungarian troops march east on Russia and south on Serbia, suffering heavy defeats on both fronts; Kafka breaks off engagement with Bauer after acrimonious meeting in Berlin (July); begins work on *The Trial*, writes 'The Village Schoolmaster', 'In the Penal Colony'.

1915   Accompanies his sister Elli to the front in Hungary to visit brother-in-law (April); the German playwright Carl Sternheim donates his winnings from the Fontane Prize to Kafka.

1916   Holiday with Bauer in Marienbad (Marianski Lasne); work on short pieces for *A Country Doctor*; gives public reading from 'In the Penal Colony' in Munich (November).

1917   Bolshevik Revolution in Russia; Balfour Declaration in favour of a Jewish state; writes 'A Report for an Academy'

	(April); begins to learn Hebrew (May); first signs of the tuberculosis which will kill him (August); final break with Bauer; recuperation with Ottla in rural Zürau; work on aphorisms.
1918–19	After the defeat of Germany and Austria–Hungary much of Central Europe is in the grip of revolution; Prague becomes the capital of independent Czechoslovakia; Kafka travels to Schelesen in Bohemia for a further rest cure (November–December).
1919	Divides his time between work in Prague and rest cures in Schelesen; engagement with Julie Wohryzek; meets Minze Eisner, writes 'Letter to his Father' (November).
1920	Rest cure in Merano; correspondence with Milena Jesenská begins (April).
1920–1	Rest cure in Slovakian Matliary; correspondence with Robert Klopstock begins.
1922	Assassination of Walter Rathenau, the German foreign minister, by right-wing anti-Semites; Kafka writes *The Castle* (January–August), 'A Fasting-artist' (May), 'Investigations of a Dog'; retires from the Workers' Accident Insurance Institute on grounds of ill health.
1923	Meets Dora Diamant in Müritz on the Baltic coast (August) and lives with her in Berlin during the great inflation until March 1924; writes 'A Little Woman'.
1924	Writes 'Josephine, the Songstress or: the Mouse People' (March–April); dies in Vienna on 3 June and is buried in the Jewish Cemetery in Prague.

(See Roger Hermes et al., *Franz Kafka: eine Chronik* (Berlin: Wagenbach, 1999).)

JULIAN PREECE

Introduction: Kafka's Europe

Jewish, German, Czech, born a subject of the Habsburgs at 'the heart of Europe' in Bohemian Prague in 1883, died a citizen of Czechoslovakia on the outskirts of Vienna forty-one years later; a speaker of French and Italian in addition to his native German, Czech, and Yiddish, which he learnt as an adult; steeped in both Jewish lore and German literature and surrounded by the sound of Czech for most of his life, Franz Kafka was first and foremost an internationalist and a European. Since his death he has been claimed as one of the foremost Jewish authors of his age, as the greatest modernist prose writer in the German language, and – at least after 1945 – as an icon of both German and Austrian literature. More recently, though with less enthusiasm, he has been hailed in his homeland as a Czech, where his memory helped inspire resistance to Soviet dominance in the 1960s. One thing is certain: in his affiliations and the resonance of his writings Kafka is the most cosmopolitan of all German-language writers.

Yet the Europe which moulded this internationalism has been lost; it was torn at the seams by the First World War and the Versailles settlement which concluded it and then shredded by Hitler. Today Jewish Europe barely exists in the lands Kafka knew and the multilingual Habsburg Europe of Austria–Hungary long ago gave way to largely monolingual nation states. After the Second World War and the Holocaust, which claimed Kafka's three sisters and many of his surviving friends, Prague fell behind the Iron Curtain and Kafka's books were banned not celebrated. After the extermination of the European Jews came the expulsion of the Czech Germans in 1945. The tensions and communal anxieties which fuelled this destruction already shaped Kafka's fiction and autobiographical writing. Establishing Kafka's Europe cannot thus be an act of cultural resuscitation; it is a matter of historical and imaginative reconstruction. But this does not mean that our twenty-first-century world is not linked to his. His images of anxiety and cultural dislocation, his multilayered prose which partakes of a multitude of discourses simultaneously, and his ignorance of ultimate answers still speak to us directly. Indeed, the secret of Kafka's continued appeal is that he has all this time kept so many of his secrets.

Kafka's education at one of Prague's German Grammar Schools, attended principally by German-speaking Jews, followed the classical syllabus whose roots lay in the European Renaissance of the sixteenth century. He learnt Latin and Greek as a matter of course, though not necessarily with joy, which meant he could read his favourite classical authors in the original. He read the German and Austrian classics (Goethe, Kleist, Grillparzer) as part of a cultural canon which was at once his own (as a German) and not his own (as a Jew). The European greats of the nineteenth century belonged indisputably to his understanding of his own modern tradition: Dostoevsky among the Russians; Flaubert from the French; and Dickens from the English. There is no sense in which he read them to savour foreign style or experience; he regarded them as fellow Europeans in a way which is rarer three-quarters of a century after his death.

Prodigious as his linguistic accomplishments may seem to us now, they were not unusual; his supposedly uncultivated father was more or less trilingual. While Kafka's first language and first cultural tradition were German, Hermann Kafka had been brought up speaking Czech at home and German at school. As his own father had not married until the Habsburg laws restricting Jewish marriage had been lifted in 1849, Hermann was a second-generation Jewish migrant. When the family moved from country to city, they transformed themselves from unemancipated, second-class Jewish subjects of the emperor to semi-assimilated bourgeois businessmen. The changes had been rapid and the emerging social and cultural formations which generated identity and underpinned relations within society proved fragile. As the Italian Prague historian, Angelo Maria Ripellino, comments: 'in this tottering boarding house of nationalities Jews were always the most isolated . . . no less alien to the Germans than to the Czechs'.[1] Kafka's diary comments from Christmas 1911 on the status of 'minor literatures', by which he meant specifically Yiddish but also Czech and the other non-German languages of the empire, show how his own sensitivity extended to the collective, cultural sphere. The comments inspired a once fashionable book and in the era of identity politics have lost none of their urgency or incisiveness.[2] Everything in Kafka's Europe appeared in flux and – as history was to show with a barbarism none could have foreseen – consequently under threat. His images of fractured perception, his figures' search for wholeness, and their experience of authority divorced from responsibility are modernist images of Europe on the brink of its most awful hour.

Kafka's Europe extended beyond the borders of the Austro-Hungarian empire of the Habsburgs. As a cultural territory it stretched from the western

Ukraine, home of the Yiddish Theatre Troupe which so impressed him in 1911, to the German coasts of the North Sea and the Baltic where he spent his holidays, to Paris, which he visited twice and where two of his uncles had settled, to Switzerland and northern Italy, which he toured in the company of his friend, Max Brod. When Kafka went to Germany he followed a route through Dresden to Berlin, stopping at Leipzig or Weimar. Vienna, where he attended a Zionist congress in 1913, and Berlin, home of Felice Bauer, are the two other points of his Central European cultural triangle after Prague. His Europe is demarcated too by the locations of the sanatoria and health resorts he visited from his early twenties and where he spent increasing lengths of time in his last five years: Jungborn in the German Harz, where he enjoyed gymnastic exercises *au naturel*; Zuckmantel in Silesia (then Germany, now Poland); Meran, which became Italian Merano in 1918; and Matliary just over the Hungarian border in Slovakia. His natural hinterland, however, was Czech-speaking rural Bohemia, a fact again brought out by the locations where he was sent to convalesce in his last years: Zürau, where he stayed with his sister Ottla after first contracting tuberculosis; or Schelesen, where he wrote his 'Letter to his Father'.

Apart from his first novel, *The Man who Disappeared*, which he set in an imaginary USA he had learnt about from books and lectures (though it was home to some of his relatives), Kafka rarely specified where his fictions took place, but that does not make them place-less, let alone time-less. When he mentions real places in his early stories and sketches (Berlin, Constantinople, St Petersburg) he does not do so for the sake of realism. The Traveller is one of his favourite figures (one thinks of K. from *The Castle*) along with the Stranger or Foreigner, like Karl Roßmann from *The Man who Disappeared* or even Josef K. from *The Trial*, a stranger in his own city. But they are metaphorical itinerants who have ventured out from home into a threatening and puzzling environment. The chapters in the Companion devoted to the three novels bring out these qualities in different but related ways, suggesting not only the unity of the novels but showing too how Kafka was preoccupied by the theme of belonging and non-belonging. Symbolically Russia was one of his most evocative locations, suggesting both personal loneliness in its immense open spaces and the threat of barbarism. 'An Old Manuscript' ('Ein altes Blatt'), a short tale of two pages written during the First World War, narrates the invasion 'from the North' (*EL*: 208) of brutish nomads, who communicate with one another in animal-like noises and who devour flesh from living beasts – even their horses are carnivores. It emerges in the last few lines that the fate of the narrator's unsuspecting and unprepared civilisation is in his own hands and those of his fellow craftsmen and shopkeepers. But they are clearly not up to defending their *Vaterland* against the dreadful force which has erupted in their midst. While Rolf Goebel identifies this short text as one of Kafka's 'Chinese tales', its exposed, land-locked territory could be that of Central Europe.[3]

This was a Europe whose values had been shaken by the writings of Nietzsche, Freud, and Marx, whose revolutions in thought left their mark on Kafka's work. *Fin-de-siècle* decadence and dandyish aestheticism, as discussed by Dagmar Lorenz and Rolf Goebel respectively, German Expressionism, the turn-of-the-century *Sprachkrise* ('crisis of language') articulated by Hugo von Hofmannsthal in his 'Letter to Lord Chandos', as well as nudism, Rudolf Steiner's theosophy, and the cult of Teutonic authenticity in the back-to-nature handicrafts and *Heimat* movement are all contemporary cultural and artistic trends, apparently contradictory expressions of the spirit of the age. In politics this is not only the period of the rise of the 'little nations', the Czechs, the Poles, the Hungarians, the South Slavs of Yugoslavia, all of whom resented rule from the imperial centre of Vienna. It also witnessed the rise of international social democracy, the failed revolution in Russia in 1905 and the Bolshevik takeover in Moscow in 1917, the aborted German revolution in 1918–19 and a similar uprising in Budapest. Of most concern to Kafka was the rise of anti-Semitism and the burgeoning Zionist movement in which he took a great interest. The age was marked by technological innovation, which both fascinated and repelled him, and rapid industrialisation, particularly in Bohemia, the industrial powerhouse of the empire. It is not often appreciated that Kafka worked at the cutting edge of a new industry, workers' accident insurance. Technology and industrial relations, how one set of people – employers – dealt with another set – their employees – were quite literally his bread and butter. His first fiancée, Felice Bauer, worked for a high-tech firm, one powerful reason for his initial attraction to her.

In addition to industrialisation and urban migration, changing cultural identities and class conflict, Kafka witnessed great changes in the status of women during his life time. He liked strong, independent women: Bauer was a pioneer in her profession; Milena Jesenská, his second great correspondent, an alumnus of the famed Minerva Girls High School in Prague, the first *Gymnasium* in Central Europe to teach girls the classical humanist syllabus and one of the first to grant them equality with boys by awarding them the *Abitur*. Kafka supported his younger sister Ottla in her bid to 'marry out' and defy the wishes of their parents. It is little wonder that identity and cultural dislocation, gender and politics feature so strongly in many of the chapters to follow in the Companion.

If Kafka does not name places in his fiction, his rootedness, if that is the right expression, in Central Europe becomes clearer in his correspondence and diaries, which record his journeys. His correspondents' places of origin and residence help define the boundaries and internal borders of this cultural region. Their places of death, often hundreds or thousands of miles away, point to the relationship between geography and history in this region at this time. Felice Bauer was an assimilated Berlin Jew, who fled Hitler to the United States where she died in 1960; her friend Grete Bloch shared her background and profession and perished in the Holocaust after emigrating as far as Italy. Milena Jesenská was a Christian Czech who died in 1944 in the concentration camp at Ravensbrück, persecuted by the Nazis for her politics. Dora Diamant, whom Kafka met in the last summer before his death, was the daughter of orthodox East European Jews. She fled Hitler to die in London in 1953. Kafka's other great love and second fiancée after Felice, Julie Wohryzek, came from a modest Czech Jewish background of the type Kafka's father had escaped through enterprise and hard work. Male and female friends or fiancées thus have much in common, both with each other and with Kafka himself. But if one looks closely there are differences, subtle but significant variations in the nature of their Jewish origins, their attitude to their own Jewishness, or, in Jesenská's case, their straddling of two cultures. Does it seem that in his great affairs of the mind and the heart Kafka was trying out identities or testing himself against them?

The origins and fate of his male friends complement this picture. They were all Jewish, at least by background. Max Brod eluded the Nazis to reach Palestine where he died in 1968; Robert Klopstock, a Hungarian medic from Budapest, died in New York in 1972. Kafka recommended him as a translator of his stories to his publisher, Kurt Wolff, who was also to flee to the US. But two schoolfriends, Paul Kisch and Oskar Pollak, with both of whom he conducted a correspondence which has survived, show possibilities for Kafka himself. Both, in different but related ways, more than flirted with German nationalism: Pollak introduced Kafka to the ideas of the *Kunstwart* journal, an aesthetic but decidedly Teutonic publication. On the outbreak of the First World War he volunteered for the Austrian army and was killed in action on the Italian front in 1915. In the case of Kisch, the brutal ineluctability of ethnic identity becomes clearer. Despite repudiating his Jewishness and signing up completely to the nationalist cause, he perished in Auschwitz.[4]

Migration makes it difficult to disentangle geography and history, as those who move on progress through time as well as space, as Kafka explains in his 'Introductory Talk on the Yiddish Language', which he delivered in February 1912 to introduce a performance of the Yiddish players from Lemberg he had befriended the previous autumn: 'the historical development of Yiddish could have been traced horizontally in the present almost as well as it can be traced vertically through history' (BK: 152).[5] The emancipated Western

Jews who comprised his audience had left behind the milieu of the East European ghetto, still home to the *Ostjuden* ('Eastern Jews') on the north-eastern periphery of Austria–Hungary and, moving further eastwards, in darkest Tsarist Russia. Discovering his parental and ancestral cultural roots, Kafka articulates his own sense of European cultural identity most fully in this short lecture. He presents the subject through a series of antitheses; first he opposes Western Europe, where he and his audience live, and Yiddish, which he calls 'the youngest European language, only four hundred years old' (*BK*: 149), and which originates in the East. With arch irony he declares Western Europe to be 'ordered' and the people, that is its Jewish inhabitants, to 'live in contented harmony', which is why they have little interest in the language of their forebears. Yiddish is the opposite of ordered and harmonious because in its ever-changing variety it has not been rationalised on the printed page; it belongs to the people as a spoken language and the people will not let the grammarians, those repressed codifiers, get their hands on it. In turn, this is a metaphor for the fluidity of Jewish identity. A yet more remarkable facet of Yiddish is that 'it consists only of loan words' (*Fremdwörter*), apparently possessing no identity of its own, as these words remain part of their original languages ('German, Hebrew, French, English, Slavic, Dutch, Romanian, even Latin') which somehow still all exist independently in Yiddish: 'it takes a great deal of effort to keep these languages together in this state' (*BK*: 150). All of Europe seems to be Yiddish and Yiddish all of Europe, united by linguistic difference. As usual with Kafka we have to peel away the textual layers to get at what he is really talking about. Here he is constructing a series of images of what it is like to be a Central European Jew. In his concluding remarks he taunts his audience to admit that they can understand Yiddish after all, even though they think they cannot, because 'in you knowledge and energies and traces of energies are active which enable you to understand Yiddish with your feelings' (*BK*: 152). In short, they will recognise themselves in the exotic performances, which they are about to see and hear from the Yiddish players. Once Yiddish has taken hold of them, they will not be able to understand their earlier contentedness; they will be afraid, not of Yiddish, but of themselves.

There is something of a paradox inherent in this definition of Jewish identity, as Jewishness could also be – and was more often – suffocating in its restrictiveness. If there was one thing which Kafka grew to hate more and more, it was the provincial, the narrowness of family and cultural background. He advises the young Minze Eisner to escape her background: 'the world, the spiritual world above all, is much bigger than the accursed triangle, Teplitz–Karlsbad–Prague' (Nov./Dec. 1920; *B1*: 281). This is why he sometimes hated his own Jewishness; it was stifling because all-encompassing. Against this was a sense of his own family's internationalism, as through his relatives he was connected with much of the rest of the world. His mother's brothers Joseph and Alfred Loewy had worked in Panama and the Congo, China and Canada, before settling in Paris; Alfred worked in Madrid as director of a railway company. As Anthony Northey has argued: 'Both ... offer classic examples of how Jews from modest backgrounds were able to advance themselves at the time of the great capitalist, colonial expansion.'[6] Where did Kafka himself fit in? He once said he was Chinese and also asked rhetorically what he should have in common with the Jews when he didn't even have anything in common with himself. Karl Roßmann in *The Man who Disappeared* reflects on the question of his origins, comparing his new American environment with his *Heimat* or homeland more frequently than any other of Kafka's characters. In the present context it is fascinating that he introduces himself as 'a German from Bohemia' (rather than an Austrian) but that he never refers to 'Germany', instead saying 'Europe' when meaning home. In the United States he is frequently thrown together with his fellow Europeans, including some from the empire, Austrians, Slovaks, Hungarians and Romanians, and others from beyond, French, Italians, and Irish, whose untrustworthiness he has been warned about. While they are clearly distinguished from one another, their shared foreignness in the New World, that is their common cultural experience as Europeans, binds them together.

The Europe which Kafka knew changed once more in 1989 with the fall of Soviet Communism, precipitated in Czechoslovakia by the Velvet Revolution, which in turn led to the split between the Czech Republic and Slovakia. These great upheavals provide one reason for another book about Kafka, the greatest Czech author who did not write Czech. With the end of the Cold War ideologies are said to be in retreat, illustrated by Bill Dodd's tentative considerations of Kafka's own politics in chapter 8. Another reason to consider Kafka afresh is the new critical edition in German which has been appearing since the early 1980s and which has led already to new translations of the novels and short fiction – hence Osman Durrani's chapter on the history of Kafka editions and translations. The chapters on film and popular culture testify to Kafka's living legacy as his works and life are recreated and reinvented in a variety of media. While Anthony Northey debunks some of the myths surrounding perceptions of his life, he shows too what a potent icon or legend Kafka remains. But what I hope the following chapters show is that no justification for yet another book on Kafka is necessary because each new generation will always have something new to say about him. New light is cast on his texts by new trends in literary and cultural theory, just as new research continues to shed more light on his contexts. Kafka proves not only to have something to say on contemporary debates on gender and identity, for instance, but to have already engaged with such questions in ways we are only beginning to appreciate.

NOTES

1. *Magic Prague*, pp. 20–1.
2. Gilles Deleuze and Felix Guattari, *Kafka: Toward a Minor Literature*, tr. Dana Polan (Minneapolis: University of Minnesota Press, 1986).
3. Rolf J. Goebel, *Constructing China: Kafka's Orientalist Discourse* (Columbia: Camden House, 1997), pp. 91–102.
4. Klaus Hermsdorf, 'Kafkas Karten und Briefe an Paul Kisch', *Sinn und Form 40* (1988), 809–17.
5. 'Einleitungsvortrag über Jargon' (*BK*: 149–53). Translated in Anderson (ed.), *Reading Kafka*, pp. 263–6.
6. Anthony Northey, *Kafka's Relatives: their Lives and his Writing* (New Haven and London: Yale University Press, 1991), p. 8.

FURTHER READING

Anderson, Mark M. (ed.), *Reading Kafka: Prague, Politics and the Fin de Siècle* (New York: Schocken, 1989).

Davies, Norman, *Europe: a History* (Oxford: Oxford University Press, 1996).

Heidsieck, Arnold, *The Intellectual Contexts of Kafka's Fiction: Philosophy, Law, Religion* (Columbia: Camden House, 1994).

Magris, Claudio, *Danube: a Sentimental Journey from the Source to the Black Sea*, tr. Patrick Creagh (London: Collins Harvill, 1990).

Kieval, Hillel L., *The Making of Czech Jewry: National Conflict and Jewish Society in Bohemia 1890–1918* (Oxford: Oxford University Press, 1988).

Ripellino, Angelo Maria, *Magic Prague*, tr. David Newton Marinelli, ed. Michael Henry Heim (London: Picador, 1995).

I

DAVID CONSTANTINE

Kafka's writing and our reading

It is not always helpful to know what a writer thinks about the vocation and the act of writing, but in Kafka's case it may be. It may help us to read him better. In letters and diaries he says many things about writing in general and about his own in particular which, illuminating in themselves, may also do a real service. They may alert us to the peculiarity of his novels and stories, and so to how we might best try to read them. Certainly, there is no key to Kafka, but just as certainly there are better and worse ways of reading him. Had I needed a motto, I could have looked to some bleakly courageous little sentences in Beckett's *Worstward Ho*. They are: 'Ever tried. Ever failed. No matter. Try again. Fail again. Fail better.'[1] They seem to me a noble epitaph for Kafka's writing and a good injunction for our reading.

Writing

The premise is necessity. Writers have to write. They are not necessarily people to whom writing comes more easily than to others nor do they necessarily enjoy writing, in any usual sense of the word 'enjoy'. They are people who have to write. Friedrich Hölderlin's friend Christian Neuffer, who certainly thought of himself as a poet and wrote a great deal of verse, all of it bad, told Hölderlin one day that he was taking a break from poetry for a while – 'hanging my harp up on the wall' was his actual phrase. Hölderlin replied: 'And that is fine, if you can do it without pangs of conscience. Your sense of yourself is founded on other worthwhile activities too, and so you are not annihilated if you are not a poet.'[2] Hölderlin knew he was 'annihilated' – *vernichtet*, made nothing – if he could not write poetry. And Tasso (Goethe's at least) said:

> If I am not to ponder things and write poetry
> Then life to me will not be life at all.[3]

He compared himself to the silkworm, spinning the stuff out of his own body, and having no option, even if it killed him. Kafka's was an extreme

9

version of that necessity. And he further developed, to an extreme degree, the unhappy possibility contained in the image of the silkworm: that though life without writing was no life at all – he was *vernichtet* (annihilated) if he could not write – life with writing, in writing, was fatal also.

The premise is: Kafka had to write. And it is important to understand at the outset that the premise is thoroughly paradoxical. For the sake of his very life he had to do something harmful, possibly fatal to his life.

Along with necessity comes bad conscience. But why should you feel bad – blameworthy, guilty – about something you have to do? And yet very often and certainly in Kafka's case writing brings bad conscience with it like its shadow.

There are two main reasons for Kafka's bad conscience about his writing. The first is that whatever he writes and however well he writes it he feels that it could have come out better. He feels he is to blame that it didn't come out better. And the second reason for his bad conscience lies in his always asking himself the question: however good the writing is, what good is it anyway? That question is fundamental. What justifies the activity which for him is a necessity? Being necessary doesn't of itself amount to a justification.

Take the second reason first: Kafka has a bad conscience about his writing, however well he does it, he asks what good it is, because in his eyes much more apparent than any good is an immense harm, to himself and to anyone in close dealings with him. Kafka's diaries and letters document ad nauseam the harm his writing does. He observes with morbid satisfaction the terrible specialization that, for him, being a writer entails: 'Everything that isn't literature bores me and I hate it because it disturbs me or holds me up' (*TB2*: 193). His personality has impoverished itself, to serve one purpose: writing:

> It is easy to recognise in me a concentration on writing. When it became clear in the organism of myself that writing was the most fruitful direction my being could take then everything ran to that point and all my other capabilities, at first directed towards the pleasures of sex, drinking, philosophy, music, they were all left empty. In all those directions I became emaciated. That was necessary, because my powers in their sum total were so slight that only when gathered together could they even half serve the purpose of writing. (3.1.12; *TB1*: 264)

It is like the monstrous hypertrophy of one organ. I leave aside the question – though it needs asking – whether in Kafka it really was that bad and whether he appeared so deformed to other people. The diaries and letters are a sort of trying out the worst about himself, perhaps to exorcise it or as an act of apotropaic magic. But in that version of himself he is a person specialised to the point of deformity and incurable damage by his vocation. And his doubts and bad conscience about that vocation are inevitably nourished by witnessing the damage which, in his view, it inflicts. And inflicts not just on him. Kafka also took satisfaction in the understanding of himself as, for instance, the ruin of Felice Bauer and her family:

> My relationship with the family only makes sense to me in a unified way if I understand myself as that family's ruin. It is the only organic explanation there is, one that quite overrides whatever in my relationship might otherwise be astonishing. (5.XXI.14; *TB3*: 60–1)

If that were true, how good, and of what enormous good, would writing have to be to compensate?

The more obvious reason for Kafka's bad conscience – and commoner in writers, I should say – came from his feeling that his writing could be better and that he is to blame that it isn't. He berates himself for not writing to the limit of his abilities or for not giving himself up to it wholly. For example: 'Have worked since August, in general not a little and not badly, but neither in the first respect nor in the second to the limits of my ability, as I ought to have done' (31.XII.14; *TB3*: 68). He is dissatisfied because he does not have the courage to create the circumstances in which writing could be done with more chance of success. This latter stricture often boils down to the flat antithesis between writing and his job. Kafka at the office, Kafka at his desk, Kafka in dealings with his boss at the Workers' Accident Insurance Institute for the Kingdom of Bohemia in Prague is a richly and blackly funny topic. Having stayed up all night writing 'The Judgement', he sent in a note next morning saying he would be late on account of a little dizzy spell. He wrote to Felice that he looked about him at work with such looks as perhaps had never been seen in an office before (3.XII.12; *BF*: 153). He lived in a contradiction – 'Writing/Office' – that was damaging to him not least in that (so he felt) it demonstrated his failure to assert himself as a writer; thus, his cowardice. Naturally, this proof added itself daily to the piles of proof against him in the court of his own conscience. In October 1914, having taken a week's leave to get on with *The Trial* and having after three days got nowhere, he asked himself: 'Are these three days enough for me to conclude that I am not worthy to live without the office?' (7.X.14; *TB3*: 39). But if he was unfit for life without the office, with it he was living a life that denied his writing its proper chance. 'In the office I answer my obligations outwardly, but not my inner obligations and every one of those not satisfied grows into an unhappiness that stays in me for ever' (28.III.11; *TB1*: 31). He notes against himself every occasion when he fails to give writing its proper chance; when he fails to organise his day so as to have time – and the best time is the hours of the night – in which to write. Whenever he idles, whenever he wastes his hours, whenever he lies on the sofa and instead of sleeping, which would strengthen him for the writing at night, only broods and daydreams, he notes it in the diary against himself. Sleeplessness itself – caused by writing, he says (02.X.11; *TB1*: 43) – becomes blameworthy, sleep something he has ceased to deserve. He writes to Milena that sleep is an innocent thing and for that reason will not visit a man like him (4.V.20; *BM*: 11). On 21 January 1922 (*TB3*: 203–4) he sleeps till 5am, feels himself unworthy of such a blessing, undoes the good effects of the sleep in brooding on his unworthiness. And if he doesn't sleep, the next day will be wasted. The office will exhaust him, he won't be able to write. On many days in his diaries he lays the stigma of his failure to write. Thus here in the summer of 1912: 'Wrote nothing [. . .] Wrote almost nothing [. . .] Today wrote nothing [. . .] For so long now have written nothing [. . .] Wrote nothing [. . .] Nothing, nothing' (*TB2*: 73, 74, 76).

So he fails to write; or he writes and the writing is a failure. And what would success matter? Would it outweigh the damage done by trying? He doubts it.

Kafka's notorious self-loathing is, as he perceives it, in large measure caused by writing: by failing to write, by not writing well enough, by the damage that trying and failing to write causes. And that condition of acute dissatisfaction with himself, largely caused by writing, then often becomes the stuff of the writing itself. It is a vicious circle, peculiarly vicious; and yet at the same time potentially redemptive. Writing is not only the cause of much of the misery and the means of its expression but is also, potentially, the means by which the writer might get free of it. He held out that possibility to Felice Bauer: 'Who knows, the more I write and the more I liberate myself, all the purer perhaps and worthier I shall be for you' (24.XI.12; *BF*: 117). And two years later he set that possibility down as his only hope:

> In utter helplessness wrote scarcely 2 sides. Fell back a great deal today, despite the fact that I had slept well. But I know that I must not give way if I am to get over the lowest sufferings of my writing – writing that the rest of my life is holding down – and come into the larger freedom which is perhaps awaiting me. (1.X.14; *TB3*: 38)

This is an extension of the paradox we began with. Writing is simultaneously the affliction and, potentially, the means by which that affliction can be escaped from and left behind. Josef K.'s 'arrest' works similarly: affliction and opportunity; as does also, perhaps, Gregor Samsa's metamorphosis. Both are – quite bizarrely – liberated as a result of the awful change in their circumstances, which leads in both cases to a miserable death.

If I say that the writing might be redemptive, I mean that the hope is it will do more than merely neutralise the ill effects of the vocation of writing itself; I mean it might enable a breakthrough out of loneliness, out of anxiety, out of guilt and self-hatred into the fullness of life in dealings with others. The fact that Kafka never felt it did do that for him is sad, for him; but not, I think, any proof that the writings might not do it now for others, his readers.

The premise in paradox is worth insisting on. It ought to prepare us for paradox in the work and deter us from saying that things must be this or that. They are more likely, in Kafka, to be this and that, in contradiction.

One unhappy effect of reading Kafka's diaries is that cumulatively they may persuade you that he is indeed as abject as he makes himself out to be. Imagining with pleasure, after an interval of not being able to, the turning of a knife in his heart; assessing where exactly it would be best to insert the point of a knife into his neck; dissolving, as he puts it, in sadness and uselessness; watching himself like his own self-appointed torturer . . . When he gave his diaries to Milena to read, then asked: 'Have you found anything decisively against me in the diaries?' (19.1.22; *TB3*: 202), did he trust her to dismiss all the evidence he had accumulated against himself? The lovelessness depicted in so much of Kafka's writing has its source in his own inability to love himself. 'I have loving people but I cannot love' (29.1.22; *TB3*: 212). Nobody can love in return who will not acknowledge that the person loving him may after all have grounds.

A context and perhaps the grounds for self-hatred come with the ideology (and its practice in familial and social structures) that the victim inherits or succumbs to. Gerard Manley Hopkins in the grip of the Jesuits is an example. The so-called 'Terrible Sonnets' excite not only pity but also regret: that a man should ever allow himself into dealings with such a brutal creed. And one salutary movement in those sonnets, almost a revolt, is the concession that he ought to be kinder on himself. Hopkins writes:

> My own heart let me more have pity on; let
> Me live to my sad self hereafter kind,
> Charitable; not live this tormented mind
> With this tormented mind tormenting yet.[4]

Kafka too, suffering like Hopkins in the grip of forces inimical to life and, like Hopkins, often siding with them against himself, does also from time to time concede the need for kindness towards himself. Thus after some terrible collapse in January 1922: 'Be content, learn (learn, now forty years of age,) to rest in the moment' (18.1.22; *TB3*: 199). He even concedes he may not be wholly lost: 'I admit [. . .] that there are possibilities in me [. . .] that a good-for-nothing can become a decent human being, a decent and a happy human being' (26.11.22; *TB3*: 222). But there are few such concessions, in all the years.

Many writers have had a poor opinion of themselves and their achievements. But the gap in Kafka's case between his own and the world's estimation of him is peculiarly wide. How does a man so persuasively (in the diaries and letters) depicting himself as only fit to die 'like a dog', as Josef K. had it, then in the eyes of the world, if not in his own, redeem himself? The answer is: through fictions; and again the example of Hopkins will serve to illustrate the familiar paradox that a man in a poem lamenting his inability to build, make, create is actually doing just that in the very process of lamenting that he can't. The sonnet 'Thou art indeed just, Lord . . .' concludes:

> See, banks and brakes
> Now, leavèd how thick! Lacèd they are again
> With fretty chervil, look, and fresh wind shakes
> Them; birds build – but not I build; no, but strain,
> Time's eunuch, and not breed one work that wakes.
> Mine, O thou lord of life, send my roots rain.[5]

I have been viewing Kafka's diaries in an unfair light, seeking out the worst. In fact the personal complaints in them are interspersed with and greatly outweighed by bits and pieces (some very substantial) of fiction: the beginnings, the continuations, the fragments of stories. And these are all, each and every one of them, steps in the direction of release and redemption. As is also in the diaries the abundant evidence of close, sustained, and lively attention paid to events and to other people. Day by day Kafka tries to set down exactly what an event and what the interactions of people in it were like. And there are many glimpses of other people, particularly girls and women, on the street. All these accounts, some brief, some quite lengthy, count as writing; they are assessed, like the attempts at fiction, as pieces of writing: good or less good, bad or less bad. Writers write because they have to, and every sentence they write comes with its own criteria for success or failure. All sentences can be written more or less well. All come with an injunction to be written as well as possible. Understood like that, writing, for a writer, is indivisible from life.

Thus we may see not only the fictions and the accounts of happenings and people in Kafka's daily life as pieces of writing all charged with the potential of success or failure, but also the complaints about and the enquiries into his own unhappy condition may be viewed in that same light. The making of sentences, even on the narrow subject of himself, is – potentially – redemptive, because in that exercise, as in all his other writing, he is trying to arrive at truth, clear truth, truth in the form of clarity. And it might be that if on the subject of himself he can arrive at truth, if he can understand the subject ever more clearly, perhaps that truth will set him free.

Perhaps. There are obvious risks. Clear formulation of the problem of himself is not a solution of the problem; at most it is a basis from which to go forward towards one. Indeed, formulating, ever more clearly, truths about himself can become a masochistically self-delighting end in itself. Kafka knew that perfectly well. Hence his grave doubts about the value of his own facility with words.

And another reason why making truthful sentences out of his own misery might not liberate him from that misery is this: he risks doing it so well, so persuasively, that his unfitness to live becomes quite indisputable. The hope must be that the creative charge released in the making of sentences, even on the unhappy subject of oneself, will actually counter the revealed misery of their material; but the procedure is risky. Fictions are a better bet.

The more Kafka turns to fictions, the better. That way hope lies. But the fictions themselves, in his assessment, are constant failures. He thinks of himself as a writer with failing powers. He looks back on earlier work, itself a failure, as achievements beyond his present ability. Was there ever a writer so convinced of failure? All writers are, more or less. Failure is intrinsic in writing. It is there most palpably in the gap between conception and realisation:

> Certainly everything I have already conceived even word for word in a good feeling or perhaps only incidentally but in definite words, at the desk, trying to write it down, it all appears dry, wrong, unmoving, an obstacle to everything around it, anxious and above all full of holes, even though nothing of the original conception has been forgotten.   (15.XI.11; *TB1*: 95)

The conception, or invention, lingers, as an affront to its sorry realisation in the medium of words. But the palpable gap, though deeply disappointing, is that without which the writer would not be driven on and on to write. The gap is the motor of writing: it wants filling. After every failure the imagination lifts itself up, and again the inadequate powers of realisation come struggling after. Precisely through failure comes a sense of superabundance, of the excess of life over art, of life's intractability by art, of life's irreducibility. This may be the despair of the writer at the time, but it is the truth, and writing that constantly comes up against and acknowledges that truth serves life (and our lives) better than any art proceeding in the illusion that it should or could ever master life. The passage quoted above continues, in explanation of the failure:

> The chief reason is of course that I have good conceptions only away from the paper at the time of the uplifting of my spirit – an uplifting I fear more than I long for it, however much I do long for it – but that then the abundance is so great I have to refrain and out of the stream of it take blindly what I can in snatches and by chance so that when it comes to a thoughtful writing down my acquisition is nothing in comparison with the abundance in which it lived and is incapable of fetching that abundance in and is thus something bad and distracting because it tempts me uselessly.   (15.XI.11; *TB1*: 95)

One obvious form of failure is not finishing. Kafka finished none of his three novels and – relatively (relative to the number he began) – very few of his short stories. True, unfinishedness may be viewed not as failure but as a virtue; Romantic poetics makes a virtue of it. The unfinished text is one still under way, in process; unfinishedness is appropriate, truthful. We must come back to that positive view later, but say now that there is no doubt that Kafka wanted to finish his novels, did his level best to, and abandoning them felt he had failed.

And failure is apparent more immediately, in every step of the process itself. A paragraph, a single sentence, often seems to Kafka to be failure manifest. If writing comes out of bodily and spiritual uneasiness, then failure to compose adequate sentences only compounds that unhappy existential state. Failed sentences, when the words won't fit, when they fail to cohere and do not amount to anything, cause their author acute distress:

> Almost no word I write fits with any another, I can hear the consonants rubbing together like bits of tin and the vowels sing along like black slaves up for sale. My doubts encircle every word, I see them sooner than I see the word.
>
> (15.XII.10: *TB1*: 103)

Or he writes a passage, an entity on a particular subject, scrutinises it and decides at once that only a morsel of it has validity. Thus, on 10 and 12 March 1912, what might be the beginnings of two stories: he breaks off and comments on the first:

> Nothing, nothing ...I was involved, and then only feebly, at 'Later he had to...', especially at the word 'tip'. In the description of the landscape I did think, for a moment, that I was seeing something right. (*TB2*: 52)

And on the second: 'Only the billowing greatcoat stands its ground, all the rest is invented' (58).

Thus the whole enterprise is riddled with failure. Single paragraphs perish under his look. The large works peter out.

Insisting so much on failure, Kafka has at the same time a very clear idea of what success would be like. Indeed, his sense of failure is born out of and nourished by his intense imagining of success. After 1912, his most productive and successful year, his *annus mirabilis*, as he thought, the year of 'The Judgement', 'The Metamorphosis', *The Man who Disappeared*, that imagining twins itself with remembering. It seems to him, looking back, that he could do it once, that he did do it, that he had it in him to succeed. He is left with the dreadful anxiety that perhaps he missed his chance: 'Always this chief anxiety: Had I set off in 1912 in the full possession of all my abilities with a clear head, not eaten up by the efforts to suppress my living abilities!' (25.XII.15; *TB3*: 116). Letters and diaries of 1912, needless to say, were littered with self-beratings and harsh verdicts on his achievements.

Typically – because much of what can be said about Kafka's writing is existential rather than literary, that is it concerns a disposition and achievement of the personality, it concerns how a person *is* – typically, his rare exultation, his feeling of success, belongs to the manner of writing as much as or even more than to the produced text. And 'manner' is quite the wrong word, quite inadequate. I really mean the whole bodily and psychic state of the man in the act of writing. The achievement of that state, in which, out of which, successful writing will be more likely to come, is itself cause for exultation or, since he rarely achieves it, for continual fretting after it and self-recrimination that he fails to allow or induce it.

Immediately after the writing of 'The Judgement', almost uniquely in the diaries, there is an entry that is almost self-satisfied: 'I wrote this story 'The Judgement' in one go during the night of the 22nd to the 23rd between 10pm and 6am.' After that night of ability he said: 'That is the only way to write [. . .] with such complete opening up of body and soul' (23.IX.12; *TB2*: 101). The imagery he uses to describe this success is that of birth or the sudden and beneficial breaking open of a wound. Again and again in his injunctions to himself he urges the recovery of a state in which writing would break forth from him, in which he would be borne along by it: 'End of writing. When will it take me up again?' (20.I.15; *TB3*: 73). It is an imagery of going down, of sinking down, of diving:

> There are some connections that I feel clearly but am not in a position to know. It would be enough to dive a little bit deeper, but there the lift is so strong that I could believe myself to be on the bottom did I not feel the pull of the currents under me. Anyway, I look up, to where the light comes from and in its thousands of fragments breaks on me. I climb, and drift around on the surface, even though I hate everything on the surface.
>
> (undated; *TB3*: 12)

Malcolm Pasley speaks of Kafka in the act of writing as 'listening' (particularly to sound and rhythm and punctuating accordingly),[6] and that image might be extended and developed: listening to and attending very precisely and intently to something taking place; a quite peculiarly intense concentration, which is both passive – an opening up of himself to something in the process of occurring – and keenly active in its attending, and in the hand hurrying across the page.

In the subordination of the self to the process of writing the self is, for that time, forgotten. In that primary sense (there are others) writing may be understood as release and redemption.

The preferred ambience for this kind of writing is the night. It is cause for frequent complaint and self-recrimination in Kafka's life that he could not or did not sufficiently well organize the day and so did not have the hours of the night for writing in. For example:

> End of one chapter a failure, and another one, which I began well, I'll scarcely or rather definitely not be able to continue that well, whereas it would certainly have come right back then during the night. (TB3: 37)

And

> Saw again that everything written down in a fragmented way and not in the course of the larger part (or even the whole) of a night is inferior and that by the circumstances of my life I am condemned, precisely, to what is inferior. (TB3: 62)

To sum up so far. Kafka was a writer for whom writing was an existential necessity. It was a cause of guilt in his life because of the damage it did. But it was also his best chance of preserving and asserting himself in the world. He called it 'My struggle for the preservation of myself' (31.VII.14; TB2: 165). It fortified him. He wrote: 'the firmness that the least writing brings about in me is ungainsayable and wonderful' (27.XI.13; TB2: 209). He spoke of 'the great help that writing is' (13.IX.14; TB3: 39), of writing as a 'wondrous, mysterious, perhaps perilous, perhaps redemptive consolation' (27.I.22; TB3: 210). By writing, which might indeed be perilous, which actually risked unfitting him for life itself, he could hope and sometimes believe that he would come through into a greater fullness of life. Successful writing would be for him 'a heavenly releasing and a real coming alive' (3.X.11; TB1: 45). But in practice he was chiefly persuaded not of the possibility of redemption but of the constant presence of failure. He fails to finish, his powers are failing, but he has a luminous sense of what success would be like. The state of body and soul in which successful writing might take place is one of deep concentration on a developing event. Night, at least so long as he is still in employment and especially whilst still living at home, is the most propitious time for the attempt. The writing of 'The Judgement', in the night at one sitting, becomes emblematic of how it should be done. He notes in December 1914 'Yesterday wrote 'The Village Schoolmaster', almost unconsciously' (19.XII.14; TB3: 65); said of 'The Metamorphosis' that it should have been written in at most two sessions (each ten hours long) and thought it irredeemably spoilt when he had to interrupt it with a business trip.

I said earlier that failure, or an intense awareness of the gap between conception and execution, is the motor of writing, but I should add that, of course, so too are the glimpses of success, the exultant moments of achievement. The two conditions may actually be one and the same, turning a different face. And by both the writer is driven on to write.

The efforts to achieve a successful writing are like the endeavours, largely unsuccessful but persistent, of several of Kafka's heroes to reach a goal, get at a truth, arrive at some clarity, stability, state of belonging; which does not mean that Kafka's fictions are *about* writing, but that writing is a means (*the* means for Kafka) of trying to get at truth and often the heroes of his fictions are trying to do just that. They are trying to do what the writing itself is trying to do. The process of writing and its subject are allied. And the third constituent of the whole endeavour is our reading, which must undergo what the writer and his heroes undergo: bafflement and thwarting, hope in glimpses, and disappointment and failure in large measure.

Reading

There are different ways of reading as there are of writing. How should we read Kafka? Bearing in mind how his fictions were written, and what in his case the profession and act of writing entailed, how for the greatest pleasure and profit should they be read?

It is easier to say how not. And I feel some justification in trying that way since definition through the negative, getting some sense of how things are through how they manifestly aren't, is very much the way that Kafka in his fictions tries himself.

Kafka's fiction is, as Robert Lowell said a poem is, an event, not the record of an event.[7] It is in process, it is underway. It is a means by which the clarification of truth may be arrived at and the life of its author and the lives of its readers may be changed. The truth is not in the writer's possession when he starts, his writing is not the recording or recounting of a truth he is already master of; his writing is his laborious struggle towards that truth. Understood thus, the writing requires our participation in that laborious process. Everything about the fiction – its author, its genesis and most importantly (since we might know nothing about its author or its genesis) its manifest workings – absolutely forbids reductive reading. Any reading that supposes, or in its procedure implies, that Kafka, already in possession of the truth, then merely encoded it in the process of writing, so that the business of literary criticism is *decoding* – any such reading must be wrong. Kakfa's fiction is an act of seeking, it is a would-be discovery, invention, engenderer of the truth. Seen thus its unfinishedness is itself expressive. Failure it may be, but in an endeavour very unlikely to succeed. And if the author, sentence by sentence seeking after the truth, fails to arrive, how should the critic?

As an analogy (and perhaps more than that), we might consider the states of guiltiness and anxiety which, as everybody knows, are common in Kafka. Their essence, their peculiar power to harm the individual in their grip, is that they are irreducible. They can't be bindingly ascribed to any particular thing, and so can't be relieved by the removal or the disarming of that thing. Talking to Milena about the anxiety Jews live in, Kafka describes the state as one of always feeling threatened. Threatened by what? 'By threats' (30.V.20; BM: 26). And guilt in Kafka never has the simple relationship to transgression, punishment, and release contained in the root sense of the German word *Schuld*, namely 'debt'. Guiltiness and anxiety are not the whole of Kafka, but they do condition much of his writing and being themselves irreducible they are an expressive analogy of the irreducibility of the writing itself.

Reading reductively is reading acquisitively. The supposition behind it – quite false, in my view – is that the text contains a finished truth, there to be had. But Kafka's texts are laced with indicators that the truth cannot be had. Kafka is one author for the reading of whom mere observation and description of what goes on in the texts may help as much as interpretative criticism. Here a few such observations. They concern motifs in and characteristics of the stories which demonstrate that understanding is, to say the least, a problem and that the search for the truth, though it has to be attempted, is laborious and probably neverending.

Failure to arrive, failure to understand

K. never gets into the Castle; Josef K. gets nowhere in his understanding of his case; Karl Roßmann merely repeats the essentials of his predicament.

Failure even to begin

In 'An Imperial Message', for example, and more than once in the diaries there is an imagery, almost a doctrine, not of progress but of infinite regression. Thus: 'If there is such a thing as metempsychosis then I am not yet at the lowest stage. My life is the hesitation before birth' (24.1.22; *TB3*: 207). And:

> I don't know that anybody's task was ever this hard. You might say it isn't a task, not even an impossible one, it is not even impossibility itself, it is nothing, it is not even as much a child as a barren woman's hope of one. And yet it is the air I breathe, so long as I am to breathe.   (21.1.22; *TB3*: 203)

Reducing a goal or a desired effect almost, but not quite, to vanishing point is very kafkaesque. Bureaucracy is the most developed image of this.

Puzzlement

Often the narrative voice is a puzzled one. A narrator, in the act of narrating, is trying to make sense of an event or a phenomenon. Thus in 'Josephine, the Songstress'. Or again and again in the novels the hero, in his innocence or ignorance, has things explained to him by people who may know better. Altogether, in novels and stories, there is a very great deal of discussion, explanation and interpretation of behaviour.

Exegesis of texts

Letters from Klamm, for example. A letter read in the dark, in the wind, by candlelight, subjected to interpretation.

Parables, supposedly helpful or exemplary stories

Notably 'Before the Law', but Amalia's story in *The Castle* works similarly. Kafka was a collector of such emblematic or exemplary stories. He related one such, concerning Dostoevsky, to Milena, and asked her: 'Do you see how mysterious this story is, how incapable of being penetrated by the reasoning mind?' (April/May, 1920; *BM*: 12). Traditionally, in the New Testament, for example, parables are used to make concretely clear a new or abstract or for some other reason difficult concept. Thus Christ answers the question 'Who is my neighbour?' with the parable of the Good Samaritan. But in Kafka's fictions the stories and parables told are never unambiguous and the difficulty the listener is in may only be compounded by hearing them. The gesture of clarification is belied by its effect. Extending this category or observation, which has to do with the belying or failure of traditional gestures and structures, we can point to the disheartening version of the Quest, in *The Castle*, and of the Damascus Road Experience in *The Trial*. K.'s quest founders, the line of it peters out. And Josef K., stopped in his tracks as surely as Saul, never learns which way to go.

The hero's restricted perspective and limited abilities

In the three novels Kafka keeps pretty strictly to his hero's limited perspective on the world. And Josef K. in particular is very poorly equipped to deal with the onus or opportunity laid on him by his arrest. Unlike the 'man from the country', he never gets even a distant glimpse of the radiance of the Law; he sees the Law as squalid. True, as readers we are not wholly confined within the experience of the hero. We can reflect upon it and seek to enlarge it; but by ill-equipping his heroes and by limiting the narrative perspective to theirs,

Kafka surely indicates the enormity of the whole undertaking of his writing and of our reading.

Those observations – and others might be added – prove that the difficulty of understanding, the laborious enquiry after the truth, is not just a subject of Kafka's texts but is their very warp and weft. If that is the nexus out of which they arise, if that is what they are about, if that is actually what constitutes their most characteristic texture and procedures, then they cannot be susceptible of reductive interpretation. Any such reading goes quite against their grain.

Three larger characteristics reinforce that view.

Lucidity, its failure

Kafka's characters are wonderfully able to hypothesise and set out alternatives and endlessly ramifying possibilities. For example, Titorelli presenting the possible outcomes of a trial; or the *Vorsteher* recounting to K. all the past history of the Castle's interest in employing a land-surveyor. Such characters are pedantically, tiresomely, exact in their accounts. They compose sentences adequate to their complicated tasks. And in so doing they rather prove the futility of this, the best, the considerable best, that they can do. Wherever the truth is, it does not seem reachable by that route. The characters actually demonstrate the inadequacy of the means – their considerable powers of argument, discrimination, definition, speculation – at their disposal. They and their author are well equipped, but with something that will not help them. As readers we participate in the failure of their kind of lucid reasoning.

Disproportion, its fundamentally disquieting effect

I mean especially the disproportion between the transgression and the punishment. Thus in *The Man who Disappeared*, 'In the Penal Colony', 'The Judgement'. There is something unbearably worrying about that relationship in a matter of justice. Either the world is thoroughly unjust; or you have not understood its laws; or both. Yes, the ordering of the world is thoroughly unjust. No, you have not understood its laws. This latter possibility haunts *The Trial*.

The story, what is it really about?

We feel it is not really about what it is ostensibly about. Stories of that kind, for example 'The Village Schoolmaster', shift the mind into an anxiety about its ability to grasp things. Or about the status of the reality it is trying to grasp. What is going on? What is *really* going on? A large part of the total sense of that particular story may actually consist in the uneasy feeling it engenders that whatever it seems to be about it is not really about.

Kafka proceeds through metaphor, not through allegory. Allegory suits a mind already sure of its ideas and chiefly concerned how best to set them down. Between the allegory and the idea you might translate to and fro: translate the idea into an allegory, translate the allegory back into its idea. But no such traffic is possible with metaphor. The idea and its concrete realisation are indissolubly fused. The metaphor is the only way of knowing. We might be glad that there is such a way at all, but, typically, Kafka mistrusts even that sole possibility. Indeed, metaphor seems to him to demonstrate the inherent insufficiency of writing. He notes in his diary a metaphorical usage from one of his own letters: 'I warm myself by it in this sad winter'; and comments:

> Metaphors are one among many things that make me despair about writing. How unindependent writing is, how dependent on the servant girl lighting the fire, on the cat warming itself by the fire, even on the poor old man warming himself. All these are independent and autonomous activities, only writing is helpless, does not dwell in itself, is a joke, is desperation.
>
> (6.XII.21; *TB3*: 196–7)

The crucial question is how to increase the autonomy of writing without decreasing its vital contact with and bearing upon real life. Kafka shifts into fictions that are large, finely ramified and autonomous; he dwells in them in writing, and we must in reading. The hunger artist is very anxious to have witnesses there in the cage with him, to see that he does not cheat. It is an image very close to Kafka's own anxiety that in moving away from mimetic and representational art into the greater autonomy of metaphor he is entering a zone where his criteria for success – which is to say, for truthfulness – are no longer obvious. His truth becomes less and less verifiable by anybody else. His chosen mode brings with it the risk of arbitrariness and dishonesty. For a writer as scrupulous and self-doubting as Kafka, that risk is a terrible burden.

Goethe, weary of being asked or told what *Elective Affinities* was *about*, made a pronouncement that will help in reading Kafka too. He said: 'Once written the thing has rights of its own, and will assert them' (*das Gedichtete behauptet sein Recht*).[8] We cannot reduce a literary work to the criteria already in our possession. The work is actually engendering the criteria by which it might be judged. The successful work corroborates itself. It is then, like the human activities noted above, independent and autonomous; it dwells in itself. That is what Kakfa felt as he wrote 'The Judgement': 'the story confirmed itself as being beyond doubt' (25.IX.12; *TB2*: 103). Elsewhere he says that if a story (any story) truly has a *raison d'être*, if it is *justified*, then like a seed it will contain its total organisation there already at its conception (19.XII.14; *TB3*: 65). It opens then in the act of writing. Invention (*Erfindung*), in the old sense of the word, meant the discovery of something already existent and waiting to be found. The thing is already there, if you can only bring it to the surface. Reading is participation in that invention. It is an entry into, a dwelling in the metaphor being brought by the act of writing into the light. That metaphor does relate – vitally and critically – to our reality, but not as allegory nor as mimetic representation. It is not reducible, not replaceable; nor, since it is not a means to an end, is it discardable. Its relationship to our reality (our lives) is simultaneously enigmatic and indisputable.

Kafka said of 'The Judgement': 'It [the story] is a bit wild and senseless and if it did not have inner truth (which can never be generally established but must on every occasion by every reader or listener be conceded or denied anew) it would be nothing' (4–5.XII.12; *BF*: 156). Kafka thought of his readers as necessary participants in the process of making sense. Our search for the truth of the text, our conceding it or denying it in the course of every reading, is akin to the writerly and existential process he is involved in, body and soul, himself.

Reading is always a dialectical process, and reading Kafka eminently so. Drawn into his metaphors, dwelling in them while the fictions last, we are nonetheless required to assert our right to contradict. Often his texts, in their depiction of lovelessness, in their reduction of human relations to a matter of relative power, cry out for their own contradiction. He tries out the worst, and in so doing, through the negative, through a palpable absence, conjures up the need for a better way of being in the world. The very urgent social injunction in Kafka's writing will only be realised if his readers engage with him in the struggle to make sense.

NOTES

1. Samuel Beckett, *Worstward Ho* (London: Calder, 1983), p. 1.
2. Friedrich Hölderlin, *Sämtliche Werke*, ed. Friedrich Beißner and Adolf Beck, 8 vols. (Große Stuttgarter Ausgabe, 1943–85), vol. 6, pp. 243–4.
3. Johann Wolfgang von Goethe, *Tasso*, lines 3081–87.
4. *The Poetical Works of Gerard Manley Hopkins*, ed. Norman M. Mackenzie (Clarendon: Oxford, 1990), p. 186.
5. Ibid., p. 201.
6. 'Nachbemerkung' to *Das Schloß* (*DS*: 390).
7. Quoted in Seamus Heaney, *The Government of the Tongue* (London: Faber, 1989), p. 129.
8. Letter to Karl Friedrich von Reinhard, 31 Dec. 1809, quoted in Heinz Hartl (ed.), *Die Wahlverwandtschaften: eine Dokumentation der Wirkung von Goethes Roman 1808–1832* (Berlin: Akademie Verlag, 1983), p. 100.

2

ANNE FUCHS

A psychoanalytic reading of
The Man who Disappeared

Kafka's first novel, *The Man who Disappeared (Der Verschollene)*, still better known in the English-speaking world at least under Max Brod's title, *Amerika*, is set against the realist backdrop of the most modern and technologically advanced society in the world, the USA. The America of this novel remains strangely hyper-real, however, in spite of Kafka's careful depiction of various icons of modernity. This strange encoding of reality, both mimetic and anti-mimetic, cannot fully be explained by Kafka's lack of first-hand experience of American life. Rather, it has to do with the way he employs modern America both as the main locus of social contest and as a metaphor. From the outset, the novel is characterised by the citation of cultural myths and stereotypical images of the American dream, such as the description of the Statue of Liberty in the opening paragraph and Uncle Jakob's life story, which seems to validate the all-American 'From Rags to Riches' fairy tale.

Kafka repeatedly evokes the great American myth of boundless opportunities: there is Uncle Jakob's enormous steel residence in chapter 2, which, with its six overground and five underground storeys, its enormous lift and balconies, is a symbol of power and cutting-edge technology. In chapter 5 American architectural and technological modernity is further underlined by the multistorey Hotel Occidental, which contains a buzzing self-service restaurant and operates some thirty lifts. In addition, there is the detailed description of Uncle Jakob's gigantic business enterprise, which, with its mechanical telephone operators, reads like an early version of the modern call-centre.

These descriptive details, however, do not denote the American reality mimetically but rather connote a specifically European version of America. Or, to put it differently, the Statue of Liberty, the traffic in New York city, the vast buildings and interiors are all scripted and perceived from the European perspective of the novel's young protagonist, Karl Roßmann. The opening description of the Statue of Liberty indicates this clearly. Upon entering the harbour of New York, Roßmann sees the Statue as if it were illuminated by a sudden burst of sunshine. The arm holding the sword seems to rise up afresh and, round the Statue, free winds are blowing. Some critics have interpreted the sword-bearing Statue as a symbol of a destructive power, others have read it more positively as an allegory of justice. The point of this distortion, however, is twofold: it not only anticipates the outcome of the novel but also foregrounds perception as one of its prominent themes.

Expelled from his family and home, Karl is a deterritorialised figure who, as this chapter argues, is unable to read what he sees. From the very moment of his arrival in the new world he perceives unstable images and distorted objects which are simultaneously both vivid and blurred, hyper-real and anti-mimetic. Paradoxically, by taking mimesis to its extreme and carefully registering the contradictory sensual impressions of the hero, the narrative mode becomes extremely anti-mimetic. *The Man who Disappeared* does not limit itself to disfiguring the great American myths of wealth and opportunity; it also points the reader to the very forces that underpin what some psychoanalysts have called the 'symbolic order': repression and the exclusion of otherness. According to Jacques Lacan, the symbolic is dominated by the 'law of the father' which requires the child's acceptance of its post-Oedipal position. Lacan argues that through the Oedipal drama the child has to repress its pre-Oedipal attachment to the mother. This alone enables the child to become a speaking subject in the social order. Thus the symbolic is dominated by the imperatives of paternal authority.

The following analysis therefore examines how authority and power are exercised in the novel. Tracing Karl's odyssey through a space which is neither real nor wholly imaginary, I will argue that the novel exposes the power play of a social order which relies entirely on mechanisms of exclusion for its sense of identity. In the last analysis, Karl's degradation at the hands of those who represent the social order reflects the phobic nature of this order itself, which needs to assert its power through repeated gestures of expulsion. As a young immigrant from Central Europe, Roßmann embodies physical and epistemological dislocation. It is essential to establish how we interpret Kafka's treatment of the dynamic of appearance and disappearance, as this structures his novel throughout. As the title suggests, this dynamic eventually causes Roßmann to disappear somewhere in the vast American space.

Unlike *The Trial* and *The Castle* which are set in predominantly imaginary landscapes, *The Man who Disappeared* presents itself at first sight as a piece of realist writing. Kafka refers his reader to geographical locations on the map, such as New York, Boston, the Hudson River, and San Francisco. This apparent realistic tendency was further underlined when Max Brod published it in 1927 as *Amerika*. By choosing this title rather than following Kafka's various references to *Der Verschollene* (which conveys the sense of 'missing presumed dead'), Brod placed the novel squarely in the context of the modern travel narrative which employs the travel paradigm as a tool for social critique. In so doing he unwittingly contradicted what Kafka had written to Felice Bauer: 'The story which I am writing and which seems set to run on endlessly, is called "The Man who Went Missing", to give you a preliminary idea, and it is entirely set in North America' (11.XI.12; *BF*: 86). A relevant example of the American travel narrative is Arthur Holitscher's *Amerika heute und morgen* (America Today and Tomorrow) published in 1911 and 1912 in *Die Neue Rundschau*, which appeared in book form a year later. Since Kafka subscribed to this journal and owned a copy of the book edition, his debt to Holitscher has been given considerable scholarly attention. Thematic links are numerous. Among these are the depiction of unemployment, the critique of the working conditions of industrial labourers and the sheer scale of American life. However, while such thematic similarities undoubtedly help to shed light on one of Kafka's major sources, it is equally important to examine the fundamental differences between the two narratives.

Holitscher emphasises the social consequences of rapid technological change. American society in his account can be analysed rationally and, consequently, reformed. His largely socialist perspective acts as a conceptual filter that allows him to interpret what he sees coherently. It is therefore not surprising that he uses a stable register which maps out the physical and social environment confidently. In contrast, Kafka's America is, as Mark Anderson has rightly pointed out, both recognisable and disfigured.[1] While the Statue of Liberty holds a sword instead of a torch, no other famous New York buildings or streets are identified at all, and the sparse references which are made to real locations tend to be displaced. Although Kafka's descriptions of objects and places appear to be visually exact, they have nothing to do with conventional realism. In Anderson's words, Kafka's novel is an 'anti-tourist guide' which, by distorting well-known American icons, demonstrates the destabilisation of the protagonist's perception.[2] As a result of this, Karl fails to undergo the process of self-formation (*Bildung*) typical of travel writings in the Enlightenment tradition. According to this paradigm, travel, with its pitfalls, dangers and challenges, ultimately allows the self to experience a process of growth. Kafka diverges from this by expelling his hero from home, thus indicating his lack of traditional free will. From the outset his journey consists of repeated acts of punishment which take him down the social scale.

Karl is always punished by male characters (Uncle Jakob, his emissary Mister Green, the Head Waiter, and the Head Porter at the Hotel Occidental). They act as socially graded representatives of the prevailing order and enforce its harsh patriarchal laws. For instance, chapters 2 and 3 reveal that the adoption by his uncle turns out to be conditional on Karl's complete submission to paternal authority. Uncle Jakob's letter of expulsion in chapter 3 spells out the rigid rules by which he lives his life: defining himself as a 'man of principles', he argues that Karl's acceptance of Pollunder's invitation represents a 'general attack' on the very foundations of his life which he cannot tolerate (DV: 97).

Uncle Jakob is the first in a series of male characters who rely on mechanisms of exclusion to form their own power-driven sense of identity. Expelling Karl from his care, he is not at all concerned with the total mismatch between the alleged misdemeanour and his harsh punishment, which casts the now impoverished Karl back to the bottom of the heap. The same scenario is re-enacted when Karl first finds and then loses employment in the Hotel Occidental. Here it is the maternal figure of the Head Cook, the Viennese Grete Mitzelbach, who adopts him by offering him food, accommodation, and a job as lift-boy. However, the interrogation scene in chapter 6 shows that her maternal impulse to protect him is severely hampered by the paternal authority of the Head Waiter who, like Uncle Jakob, exercises his right to punish Karl severely for a relatively minor transgression. The next stage of Karl's gradual degradation is his encounter with Brunelda and the former vagrants Delamarche and Robinson. Enslaved in a seedy world of sado-masochism, he now seems to have plunged to the lowest social depths.

In *The Man who Disappeared*, the suspension of intimacy between self and world, one of the hallmarks of travel writing, only points to the fragility and instability of subjectivity in a largely unreadable and hostile modern environment. The travelling self we encounter in Karl Roßmann is therefore no longer the 'seeing man' who looks at the world in order to possess it.[3] Instead he is a blinded maze-walker whose experience remains disorientating and fragmented.

The novel's opening chapter, published separately as 'The Stoker' in 1913, provides a microcosm for my analysis as it encapsulates nearly all the prominent themes. The chapter carefully builds up a network of associations between the hero's sense of non-belonging and his past which weighs him down. One of the most powerful images of his sense of dislocation is his suitcase which he abandons on the first page in order to search for his umbrella. This search leads him from the Stoker to the Captain's cabin, where he accidentally meets his temporary saviour, Uncle Jakob. At the end of the chapter we see Karl leave with his rich uncle who has the means to offer him a brilliant career. We hear nothing more of the suitcase until Karl receives

Uncle Jakob's letter of expulsion at the end of chapter 3: Mister Green then hands it to him along with his umbrella and a third-class train-ticket to San Francisco. Thus, the narrative establishes a metonymic relation between the suitcase and Karl's homelessness.

When the suitcase is foregrounded again at the beginning of chapter 4, the reader is pointed to Karl's individual history and family background which he carries around with him as an ultimately non-disposable burden. When Karl examines the contents of his suitcase he is afraid that the most precious items might well have disappeared. Initially he is shocked at the great disorder of his belongings, but finds on closer inspection that none of his things has gone missing. All his clothes are there, his money, passport, and his watch, even a Veronese salami that was packed by his mother, as well as a bible, writing paper, and one photograph of his parents. The suitcase now seems to evoke a sense of a caring order that is associated with his parents. However, this impression is deceptive, as a close-up examination of some of the contents will reveal.

The suitcase denotes both the immigrant's otherness and his longing to belong; it evokes a sense of connectedness which it simultaneously denies. From a logical viewpoint absence and presence are clearly defined through a relation of mutual exclusion. While this opposition normally underpins the subject's identity, in Kafka's narrative absence and presence interlock with each other in such a way that the presence of Karl's only belongings always evokes a significant absence. That this absence gives shape to Karl's presence is also alluded to in the novel's title: announcing the hero to be a missing person, Kafka not only prefigures Karl's fate but, more importantly, highlights his and – by implication the reader's – relationship to time past: the title is a figure of inversion which produces Karl Roßmann as a presence in the reader's life. As long as we read about him he has not gone missing. However, on the other hand, this presence is always predicated upon a significant absence, a pervasive lack for which the suitcase is a powerful image.

The passport found in the suitcase is the official document which endorses the immigrant's identity. It attests to his name as well as to his place and date of birth. It should also contain the visa which gives the immigrant official entry rights and entitles him to work and to settle down. The reader first comes across the passport in chapter 1: when asked what his name is, he answers briefly 'Without, as was his custom, introducing himself by means of his passport, which he would have had to search for first: Karl Roßmann' (*DV*: 29). Thus he usually delegates the act of introducing himself to an official document. His reluctance to utter his own name is a first hint of his lack of a proper self. The second, more indirect reference occurs at the beginning of chapter 2 where he arrives at the conclusion that without his uncle's intervention the American immigration officials would probably have sent him straight back to Europe without any regard to the fact that he no longer had a home. The implication here is that his parents dispatched him to the United States without a proper visa. From the very beginning he is thus an unwelcome outsider with neither a stable identity nor secure rights.

Karl's estrangement from his parents is fully brought to the fore when he examines his only parental photograph. Family photographs are an indispensable item in the immigrant's suitcase. In the words of Susan Sontag: 'through photographs, each family constructs a portrait-chronicle of itself, a portable kit of images that bear witness to its connectedness'.[4] *The Man who Disappeared* can be traced back to real-life sources, such as Kafka's cousin Robert Kafka, who was seduced by a family cook at the age of fourteen, or Otto Kafka, his 'interesting cousin from Paraguay'.[5] Northey also reproduces the photograph of Kafka's grandparents, Joseph, the butcher from Wossek, and his wife Franziska, which inspired his description in the scene analysed above. But this 'kit of images' documents a connectedness that is historical and highly elusive, a relic that incites the onlooker to sentimental reverie. While on one level the family photograph authenticates the togetherness of this particular family at that particular place and time, on a second level it does just the opposite. As Annette Kuhn has argued, it 'is also the expression of a lack and a desire to put things right',[6] since it shows that the family is no longer together. Presence once more denotes absence.

In Karl's case the photograph does not really succeed in terms of social rite: instead of furnishing evidence of the family's connectedness it documents Karl's displacement. The photograph follows the formal convention of showing the *pater familias* standing with one arm draped on the back of an armchair and the other on an illustrated book. Karl's mother occupies the armchair. Two iconographic details can be observed in this description: the father's hand is clenched into a fist while the mother appears withdrawn, her posture slightly slumped. Karl's alienation from the sphere of the paternal is further reinforced when he examines the picture more closely but fails to catch his father's eye: no matter how hard he tries, his father's image does not gain life. The family photograph thus represents Karl's painful alienation from the paternal sphere and prompts his corresponding desire to heal this wound. This can be demonstrated with reference to Karl's careful examination of his mother's image which unleashes in him a strong pre-Oedipal attachment and unfulfilled desire. Certain of the secret feelings of his mother in the photograph, Karl is overwhelmed by the desire to kiss her dangling hand. Laden with unspoken Oedipal rivalry, the family photograph

thus presents an image of alienation which is also a blueprint for the family dynamic in 'The Metamorphosis' and 'The Judgement', the two stories
which Kafka considered combining with 'The Stoker' under the title of 'The
Sons'.

At the beginning of chapter 1 Karl's search for his umbrella turns into a
labyrinthine journey through the ship's interior. His sense of confusion is
given grammatical expression in one long sentence whose subclauses lead the
reader and the protagonist into dead ends, up and down short staircases, to
branching off corridors, until both parties are totally lost. Kafka repeatedly
describes Karl's environment as a series of labyrinths which mirrors his sense
of dislocation. During the trial scene in the Captain's cabin he notices the
bustle of the boats and ships on the river. In their perpetual movement,
these reflect a restlessness which, according to the narrative voice, has been
transferred from the sea onto human beings and their works. In chapter 2
Karl gazes down similarly on the constant stream of traffic visible from his
uncle's balcony. Seen from such a vantage point, New York's traffic appears
in perpetual movement, distorted and unclear:

> From morning to evening and in the dreams of the night there was a constant
> stream of traffic on that street which, seen from above, looked like a forever re-
> starting, inextricable mixture of distorted human figures and rooves of all kinds
> of vehicles, giving rise to another new mixture, multiplied and wilder, of noise,
> dust and smells; and all this was enveloped and penetrated by the powerful light
> which, time and again, was dispersed, carried away and strongly reproduced
> by a multitude of objects, and which appeared to the dazzled eye so physical
> as if a glass roof stretching across the street were being smashed into pieces at
> every moment.   (*DV*: 49)

As before, the grammatical structure of this sentence mimics Karl's confusion
as he finds himself confronted with an overwhelming concoction of sounds,
smells, and dust. The resulting 'wild mixture' blurs olfactory, visual, and audible impressions to such an extent that the ability of both central figure and
reader to perceive any object clearly is disrupted. This perceptual confusion
is further heightened by the light, which, as so often in Kafka's writing, does
not illuminate. Instead it disperses the boundaries of the objects until the
human eye is completely dazzled.

This departure from the stable register of naturalism is characteristic of
many texts of this period which explore the city as a space of a newly de-
personalised perception. Another example of the modernist exploration of
the metropolis is Robert Walser's *Jakob von Gunten* (1909) which Kafka
knew and praised. Like Karl Roßmann, Jakob von Gunten is fascinated

by the cinematographic dynamic of the urban space, in this instance Berlin:

> What a crush and a crowd, what rattlings and patterings! What shoutings, whizzings, and hummings! And everything so tightly penned in. Right up close to the wheels of cars people are walking, children, girls, men, and elegant women; old men and cripples and people with bandaged heads, one sees all these in the crowd. And always fresh bevies of people and vehicles. The coaches of the electric trolleys look like boxfuls of figures. The buses go galumphing past like clumsy great beetles.[7]

The juxtaposition of the two passages shows how the city is metonymically construed in both novels. Unlike metaphor, which substitutes one expression for another on the basis of similarity, metonymy takes a characteristic or attribute and substitutes it for the whole. For instance, in Walser's passage the description of the noise of city life replaces the depiction of the moving crowds. This metonymic evocation of the metropolis has a striking effect: it flattens all social hierarchies and distinctions by telescoping everything into a relation of contiguity. By its very nature contiguity disrespects the hierarchical boundaries of the established social order. This danger is clearly perceived by Uncle Jakob who, in a long speech, emphasises the importance of good judgement and explicitly warns Karl not to spend his days on the balcony looking down at the bustle of the city. As Karl's paternal educator, Jakob adheres to a value system which equates good judgement with order, discipline and 'good principles' (*DV*: 46). From this viewpoint, the city therefore appears as a space of disorder and confusion which jeopardises Jakob's plans for Karl's education.

This perception of the city as a transgressive space is also echoed in Joseph Roth's novel *Hiob* (1930; *Job*), where the central character Mendel Singer loses consciousness when, upon his arrival in New York from his Russian shtetl, he finds himself exposed to an overpowering cocktail of heat, smells, and noises. Like Walser and Kafka, Roth describes this moment as one in which the individual is totally overcome by a blend of sensual impressions which he can no longer decode. While Kafka and Walser emphasise the visual and audible, Roth concentrates more on the olfactory sense by evoking the smell of melting tarmac, dust, the stench of sewers, petrol fumes, and fish halls, all of which melt into a hot vapour that overpowers the hero completely. Although Roth and Kafka are very different writers, they both dramatise the total collapse of boundaries as the principal reason their central figures are no longer able to make sense of their environment. For, if making sense depends on one's ability to register and categorise facets of reality with the help of discrete concepts, then both Kafka and Roth highlight the dramatic consequences for the self when such distinctions are abolished: the self's boundaries are violated to such an extent that it can no longer differentiate between the inner and outer world.

In all three novels the metropolis of New York is characterised as a space which de-familiarises all kinship relations. Von Gunten deliberately disowns his aristocratic family background in search of an energy which is associated with the city. At first sight Mendel Singer and Karl Roßmann seem to differ from him in that they do not celebrate the rejection of the kinship principle in the same manner; however, they too experience a failure to recognise their own kith and kin. In Karl's case, kinship was first denied when his parents expelled him from home. But this denial also characterises Karl himself who, in chapter 1, is emotionally quite unaffected by the disclosure that the influential Senator is his uncle. Significantly, chapter 1 finishes with him doubting whether this man would ever be able to replace the Stoker in his affections. This latent rejection of kinship is reciprocated by Uncle Jakob himself when he expels Karl. In the second chapter the failure to recognise kinship is projected onto the vast space of the metropolis where humans appear disfigured. The city as an icon of modernity thus mirrors Karl's sense of displacement.

At the end of chapter 2 Pollunder's car takes a complicated route through the packed streets of New York to the suburbs, where it is further diverted into side streets because the main arteries are blocked by a workers' mass demonstration. As in the scene on board ship, the chaotic quality of the traffic is a symbol of Karl's status as a maze-walker who never quite realises that he makes no progress within the labyrinth. In chapter 3 Pollunder's country house turns out to conceal a nightmarishly complex architectural maze. Finally, Karl encounters another labyrinth when, after his dismissal from the Hotel Occidental, Delamarche drags him through the interconnecting corridors and courtyards of a working-class apartment block.

What is striking about Kafka's labyrinths is the combination of a grammatical precision which mimics architectural complexity, and his hero's sense of confusion. The labyrinth is thus characterised by a fundamental ambivalence: from a bird's-eye-view it is a magnificent design, from the perspective of the maze-walker it is a 'space of anxiety'.

The physical and perceptual disorientation Karl experiences in the ship's interior is suspended when he is invited into the Stoker's cabin where he takes up the latter's invitation to lie down on his bunk. Here he loses all sense of alienation and the feeling that he is on the uncertain boards of a ship, beside the coast of an unknown continent. This sudden experience of feeling at home leads to his eagerness to act as the Stoker's spokesperson. The immediacy with which he adopts this role suggests that he identifies with the Stoker and if this is so, there are two reasons for it: their apparently shared social status and, more importantly, the Stoker's underlying xenophobia. The Stoker's major complaint about his employment on board the transatlantic liner consists in the fact that his superior, a certain Schubal, is of Romanian rather than German origin. He later launches into an inarticulate attack on Schubal, which is described as a 'sad whirlpool' (DV: 24), devoid of any argumentative rationality. The Stoker's language and, in particular, the obsessive repetition of Schubal's name, is reminiscent of a child's anguished attempt at self-defence. Clearly, Schubal is the object of the Stoker's xenophobia which, simultaneously, condenses his fear of all otherness and reveals his powerlessness. The Stoker is an example of the phobic psyche which attempts to maintain its fragile boundaries through mechanisms of exclusion. It is for this reason that the only sense of identity which is available to him depends on the jingoistic notion of a shared Germanness.

This phobia towards all things foreign is echoed in Karl's memory of how he used to sit up at night because he feared that a Slovak fellow passenger would steal his luggage. The same fear resurfaces in chapter 4 where Karl, after introducing himself to Delamarche and Robinson as a German national, worries about Robinson's Irishness. Ironically, whenever the idioms of kinship and home are cited in the narrative, they connote Karl's homelessness.

The Man who Disappeared thus highlights the self's fragile position within the harsh symbolic order. The experience of reality as labyrinth always points to the physical, perceptual, and psychological disorientation suffered by a self that has gone astray, or a maze-walker who cannot assimilate an environment which only heightens his disorientation. Although the effects of industrialisation and urbanisation undoubtedly reinforce his dislocation, they are not, contrary to the claims of some critics, the ultimate cause of the loss of identity in the novel. Kafka explores more than social change, he deals with the underlying mechanisms of the symbolic order as such. Instead of anchoring his hero's plight in metaphysical guilt, he points the reader to the relentlessness of a social order which relies primarily on male rites of expulsion and punishment for its sense of identity. In order to elaborate this aspect which is crucial for many of Kafka's writings, the notion of the 'symbolic order' needs to be briefly explained with reference to its origin in psychoanalytic theory.

Central to our understanding of the way in which the symbolic order is constituted is Freud's Oedipal drama which establishes social relations through the paternal prohibition of incest. According to Freud, the Oedipal drama interrupts the symbiotic mother–child relation by curbing the little boy's demands for unlimited access to the mother through the father's phallic

authority. Realising that the father is an unbeatable rival and potential castra-
tor, the little boy eventually gives up his attachment to the mother in favour
of a pact between father and son which stipulates that if the boy renounces
the mother and takes on the father's attributes he too will ultimately occupy
a position of power. The symbolic order is thus founded on the phallic power
of the father and the repression of desire for the mother. As Elizabeth Grosz
writes, this pact 'founds patriarchy anew for each generation, guaranteeing
the son a position as heir to the father's position in so far as he takes on
the father's attributes'.[8] Lacan speaks of the 'paternal metaphor' to indicate
that it is not necessarily the genetic or biological father but symbolic representations such as the Law, God, economic power, and so on, which instil in
the child this sense of submission. For Lacan, the Oedipus Complex and the
paternal metaphor also explain the centrality of language in the social construction of subjectivity. Without this, he argues, the child would not have
access to a stable identity. Lacan thus views the symbolic order as a system based in language whose primary signifier is the sign of the father, the
phallus. In other words: patriarchal dominance results less from biological
privilege than from a phallocentric socioeconomic and linguistic system.

Like no other modernist writer Kafka is concerned with the symbolic
threats on which the symbolic order is erected. This is the explicit theme of his
'Letter to his Father' which explores his own relationship with his father as an
example of the crippling effects of unbridled paternal dominance. Both 'The
Judgement' and 'The Metamorphosis' also deal with the consequences of the
son's failure to manage the culturally expected internalisation of the symbolic
father's authority: while Georg Bendemann ('The Judgement') appears as
a socially grounded individual who is about to get married (assuming his
position as heir), the ensuing linguistic battle between him and his giant
father highlights the father's unbroken power over the son. Similarly, Gregor
Samsa's transformation into a beetle and his attempt to explain himself to his
family are met with the father's physical attack on him. Hurling an apple at
Gregor, the father wounds him in the back and contributes to his demise. In
Kafka's world the fathers and their delegates do not just punish their sons,
they destroy them in order to reinstate their fragile identity as phallically
empowered fathers. In neither story does the ageing father-figure accept his
son as rightful heir.

Karl Roßmann appears like a younger version of the figure of the unsuccessfully dutiful son which haunts Kafka's writings. Throughout the novel
the male representatives of power perceive him as a threat to a social fabric which relies exclusively on the law of the father for regulating social
interchange. This also accounts for the fact that the only representative of
maternal love – the Head Cook who in a typically maternal gesture provides

Karl with food, a bed, and a job – does not succeed with her intervention on his behalf when he is about to be sacked by the Head Waiter. In Kafka's world the voice of the maternal is always submissive to the authority of the law of the father. Viewed from a psychoanalytic angle, *The Man who Disappeared* can thus be read as a story of non-assimilation in which the social rites of expulsion and rejection are repeatedly enacted in order to protect the power of the symbolic father.

Again this can be demonstrated with reference to chapter 1. After he has made the Stoker's acquaintance, Karl decides to act as his spokesperson. When the Stoker's request to speak to the Head Purser is met with blunt refusal, Karl launches himself across the room, produces his passport, and makes a quasi-judicial speech on the Stoker's behalf. Unlike the Stoker, whose ability to represent himself linguistically is clearly limited, Karl is the master of his language. Essentially, he repeats the Stoker's allegation against Schubal, claiming that the former has a solid track record as a worker. However, by moving from the general to the specific and employing subordinate clauses as well as modal verbs and the subjunctive, he also manages to demonstrate his allegiance to a rhetoric of rationality which governs the norms of social interaction. This impression is reinforced a little later when he reprimands the Stoker for his emotional outburst in the following manner:

> You must tell it more simply, more clearly; the captain cannot pay attention to what you are telling him if you carry on like that. He can hardly know all the mechanics and ship's boys by their surnames, let alone by their first names, so that when you mention so-and-so, he can hardly know immediately who you mean. Order your grievances, begin with the most serious and descend to the lesser ones, perhaps it won't then be necessary to mention most of them at all.
>
> (*DV*: 23)

By asking the Stoker to observe the rhetorical rules of judicial pleadings, Karl makes a demand which his new friend cannot possibly meet. As a phobic self, the working-class Stoker can only express himself through symptomatic linguistic gesturing. Karl appeals explicitly to the stable social code which is governed by collective rules and shared conventions which regulate the symbolic order. But his advocacy of the symbolic order turns out to be feigned since his speech act is based on a lie: 'If one can steal suitcases in America, one can surely also tell a lie now and then, he thought letting himself off the hook' (*DV*: 23). Evidently, the lie undermines the whole purpose of the exercise because it destroys both the propositional content of the speech act and the social relation between speaker and addressee which must be based on truthfulness in order to function. The lie thus allows Karl to feign mastery of a social code which, as the ensuing story unfolds, he does not really possess. His actual position within the symbolic order is extremely fragile.

It is striking when he is expelled from his uncle's care in chapter 3 that he never questions the rationale for such severe punishment. Instead he confines himself to asking Green for his suitcase and umbrella. While this certainly underlines what Manfred Engel has aptly called the *Musterknabensyndrom*, namely Karl's unflinching acceptance of the code of authority,[9] it also demonstrates how, on this journey down the social ladder, his ability to defend himself is gradually undermined. Compare for instance the first chapter with the dismissal from the Hotel Occidental: while at the beginning Karl acts as a strong advocate of the symbolic order and its rhetoric, in chapter 5 he echoes the Stoker's loss of all hope when, even prior to the interrogation by the Head Waiter, he arrives at the pessimistic conclusion that he will be dismissed from the hotel. Recognising that no efforts in self-defence will overcome the interrogators' fundamental lack of good-will, he eventually falls silent. This progression from a seemingly authoritative rhetoric of rationality to moments of total speechlessness shows his growing awareness that his voice is not powerful enough. On the other hand, his stifling also points to the erosion of his status as a subject within the symbolic order. Kafka thus suggests that language is not simply an important tool for implementing a social practice, but that it is the very condition for the constitution of the subject. Accession to the symbolic order rests on one's mastery of language.[10]

There were already hints of Karl's fragile position within the social order in the Captain's cabin when the attendant chases him away 'as if he were chasing a piece of vermin' (*DV*: 20), creating an obvious link to 'The Metamorphosis'. As a bug or 'piece of vermin' (*Ungeziefer*) Gregor Samsa feels disgust at human food, preferring household rubbish and leftovers. This change in his tastes is compounded by the loss of his human voice. When he tries to communicate with his family and the *Prokurist* (the executive secretary of the company which employs him) through the door of his bedroom, to his horror the *Prokurist* hears an animal's voice. At the end of chapter 1, when Gregor is eager to explain his failure to turn up for work on time, he is still unaware of his changed physical appearance and the complete loss of a comprehensible language. But this loss has far-reaching consequences: it amounts to an unconscious renunciation of his participation in the symbolic order. The metamorphosis thus allows him to abandon a social identity which is based on the son's obligation to clear the parental *Schuld*, a term which connotes both financial debt as well as guilt. By repudiating a commonly shared code through the metamorphosis, Samsa revolts against the omnipresent and stifling law of the father by crawling with enjoyment up and down the walls of his room. However, the price to be paid for this attempt to separate himself from the symbolic is his own death. At the end of the story, the maid proudly announces that she will dispose of the 'rubbish next door' (*EL*: 156). The representatives of the symbolic order, in this case the family, view his dead body as refuse that has to be thrust aside in order to make room for life. This image reverberates in one of Kafka's famous letters to Felice in which he explains: 'My life consists and, at bottom, has always consisted of attempts at writing, most of which have been unsuccessful. But when I was not writing, I was lying flat on the floor, fit to be swept out of the house' (1.XI.12; *BF*: 65). Kafka's drastic metaphor spells out that when the process of writing fails, the writer turns into mere waste, a corpse which has to be disposed of. As that which is no longer of use, waste is clearly the other of the symbolic; it thus upsets the mechanisms of referencing and ordering, in short all those relations which establish the signifying system. Without his writing, the writer is waste. Kafka thus disposes of the notion of a subjectivity prior to the act of writing.

Similarly, Karl's increasing inability to participate in the linguistic power games of his superiors highlights his growing distance from the symbolic order. One of the most poignant symbols of the gradual erosion of his status is the name he chooses when signing up for the Theatre of Oclahama (sic): stripped of his suitcase, passport, and his only family photograph he has finally lost all tokens of identity. Enrolling as 'Negro' (*DV*: 306), he now aligns himself with the most stigmatised and oppressed group in American history. But even here in the quasi-utopian world of the 'Great Theatre of Oklahoma', which promises to employ everybody, regardless of the applicant's professional expertise, his acceptance is conditional on his ability to produce *Legitimationspapiere*, papers that legitimise him. His original aspirations are once more evoked when he tries to apply for the post of engineer. However, he is quickly discharged and sent on to the bureau for 'people with technical knowledge' (*DV*: 305), and from there to that for intermediate pupils, where he is again dispatched to an even smaller and humbler booth for European intermediate pupils, situated on the very margins of the theatre's grounds. The bureaucratic enrolment procedure with its hierarchical structures and, above all, the imminent threat that his details will be cross-checked, show that the Theatre of Oklahoma is hardly a paradise regained but that it reads more like a slapstick parody of the Austro-Hungarian bureaucracy which Kafka knew so well. Karl's grotesque categorisation as 'Negro, technical worker' underlines once more the loss of his social status, true history, name, and voice.

Senator Jakob invites his nephew into a world that is defined by authority and power. But before Karl is allowed to establish new ties, the initial act of expulsion is repeated and he finds himself in the company of two other social rejects, the vagrants Delamarche and Robinson. His abrupt expulsion from his uncle's world is, however, not an obscure and unfathomable decision but rather a gesture that underlines the fact that Jakob's allegiance with the symbolic supersedes emotional ties. The precariousness of their relationship is already alluded to in the recognition scene in the first chapter where Karl responds to the revelation that the Senator is in fact his own uncle with a high degree of detached, unemotional formality. This impression is reinforced in the ensuing exchange in which he challenges this offer of kinship on the grounds that Jakob does not carry the maiden name of his mother, 'Bendelmayer' (*DV*: 32). Upon his arrival in America, the uncle relinquished his original name, thus not only cutting off all ties with Europe but also with his first family. In a way, the American myth of the self-made man allows Uncle Jakob to give birth to himself without the aid of a mother. As the embodiment of the American dream he thus represents the price the speaking subject pays for the mastery of its position within the symbolic order: the silencing of the maternal. By inviting Karl to enter his world, he ultimately asks Karl to subject himself to a rebirth which represses the physical and sensual side of life in favour of the rational activity of imposing order:

> The first days of a European in America were comparable to a birth, and although Karl should not be unduly frightened because one got used to it more quickly than if one entered this world from the afterlife, one had to keep in mind that one's first judgements rested on fragile foundations and that one should not let this jeopardise all future judgements which would shape one's life over here.
>
> (*DV*: 46)

Jakob's idea of an orderly rebirth is totally cut off from the painful physicality of the real process of giving birth. Instead he offers a sterile fantasy of a rebirth based on nothing but the cerebral activity of making the right judgement. In his thinking the physical raw material of life, the body with its impulses and energies, requires a regimentation that aims at the repression of all pleasure and, in the last analysis, of all desire. Desire is clearly present in the balcony scene where Karl is totally absorbed by the city's perpetually vibrant movement and its complex traffic pattern. Thus Mark Anderson argues that traffic in the novel connotes not only automobile and pedestrian movement but also sexual traffic, most explicitly in the Brunelda episode.[11] From Uncle Jakob's point of view, pleasure and desire can only corrupt Karl. However, the narrative encodes Jakob's repressive behaviour not just as an example of individual authoritarianism, but rather as the symptomatic expression of the symbolic order as such. Jakob, Green, the Head Waiter, and the Head Porter are all in their own way representatives of the symbolic order whose stability depends on a harsh penal system and the repression of all desire.

Within Kafka's narrative universe, these gestures of expulsion always serve to reinstate the authority of the symbolic which Karl unwittingly challenges by ignoring the rules and boundaries that are its very substance. However, this is not to suggest that *The Man who Disappeared* actually endorses the judgements that are made by the hero's opponents. On the contrary, the novel foregrounds the fictionality of such clear boundaries and divisions.

NOTES

1. Anderson, *Kafka's Clothes*, p. 105.
2. Ibid., p. 105.
3. Mary Louise Pratt, *Imperial Eyes: Travel Writing and Transculturation* (London and New York: Routledge, 1992), p. 7.
4. Susan Sontag, *On Photography* (New York: Farrar, Straus and Giroux, 1989), p. 8.
5. Northey, *Kafka's Relatives*, p. 52.
6. Annette Kuhn, 'Remembrance', in Jo Spence and Patricia Holland (eds.), *Family Snaps – the Meaning of Domestic Photography* (London: Virago, 1991), p. 23.
7. Robert Walser, *Jakob von Gunten*, tr. and intro. Christopher Middleton (Austin and London: University of Texas Press, 1969), p. 48.
8. Elizabeth Grosz, *Jacques Lacan: a Feminist Introduction* (London and New York: Routledge, 1990), p. 68.
9. Manfred Engel, 'Aussenwelt und Innenwelt: Subjektivitätsentwurf und moderne Romanpoetik in Robert Walsers *Jakob von Gunten* und Franz Kafkas *Der Verschollene*', *Jahrbuch der deutschen Schillergesellschaft* 30 (1986), 533–70, here p. 544.
10. Julia Kristeva, *Powers of Horror: an Essay on Abjection*, tr. Leon S. Roudiez (New York: Columbia University Press, 1982), p. 67.
11. Anderson, *Kafka's Clothes*, p. 109.

FURTHER READING

Anderson, Mark M., 'Kafka in America: Notes in a Travelling Narrative', in *Kafka's Clothes: Ornament and Aestheticism in the Habsburg Fin de Siècle* (Oxford: Clarendon, 1992), pp. 98–122.

Emrich, Wilhelm, 'The Modern Industrial World: the Novel *The Man Who Was Lost Sight of (America)*', in *Franz Kafka: a Critical Study of his Works*, tr. Sheema Zeben Buehne (New York: Ungar, 1968), pp. 276–315.

Fuchs, Anne, *A Space of Anxiety: Dislocation and Abjection in Modern German-Jewish Travel Narratives* (Amsterdam and Atlanta, GA: Rodopi, 1999).

Hermsdorf, Klaus, 'Kafka's *America*', in Kenneth Hughes (ed. and tr.), *Franz Kafka: an Anthology of Marxist Criticism* (Hanover and London: University Press of New England, 1981), pp. 22–37.

Northey, Anthony, 'The Discovery of the New World: Kafka's Cousins and *Amerika*', in *Kafka's Relatives – Their Lives and His Writing* (New Haven and London: Yale University Press, 1991), pp. 51–68.

Politzer, Heinz, '*Der Verschollene*: the Innocence of Karl Rossmann', in *Franz Kafka: Parable and Paradox*, 2nd edn (Ithaca, NY: Cornell University Press, 1966), pp. 116–62.

Rüsing, Hans-Peter, 'Quellenforschung als Interpretation: Holitscher und Soukups Reiseberichte über Amerika und Kafkas Roman *Der Verschollene*', *Modern Austrian Literature* 20 (1987), 1–38.

Sandberg, Beatrice and Ronald Speirs, '*The Missing Person*', in *Franz Kafka* (Basingstoke: Macmillan, 1997), pp. 29–62.

3

ROLF J. GOEBEL

The exploration of the modern city in *The Trial*

The tribulations of Josef K., the protagonist of Kafka's second novel *The Trial (Der Proceß)*, revolve around the clash between the inaccessible court's unspecified accusation and K.'s insistence on his own innocence. This irresolvable conflict forces K. to embark on an exploratory journey through the 'phantasmagoria' of the modern city, a space defined by surfaces, theatrical scenarios and unreadable representations. The novel stands clearly in the tradition of modernist city narratives, where urban space supplies the location for the disappearance of the alienated individual in the lonely crowd. Situated outside 'mainstream' German culture, the Prague Kafka knew is a particularly suitable backdrop and many readers have felt they have recognised it in *The Trial*. The city's tragic history, marked by national and social conflicts, reached into the present of its crooked streets and impenetrable courtyards and is reflected in a literature filled with madmen, eccentrics, cripples, prostitutes, and pimps.[1]

How does Josef K. situate himself in this unstable, shifting space? One critic has seen him, unlike Karl Roßmann in *The Man who Disappeared* and K. in *The Castle*, as neither a traveller nor a foreigner but a socially successful and ambitious urban citizen. By contrast, another maintains he is Roßmann's close relative because he finds himself, as it were, in exile in his own hometown.[2] Alienated, arrested by an unknown but powerful authority and fearing punishment, suffering the intrusion of the faraway court into his private sphere and finding himself expelled into some quasi-foreign territory, K. shares many predicaments with real exiles. In order to mediate between such strictly *literal* and self-consciously *metaphorical* interpretations, I want to offer a new reading of *The Trial* by going back once more to one of Kafka's earliest and most insightful commentators, Walter Benjamin.

In his commemorative essay on the tenth anniversary of Kafka's death, Benjamin argued that the patriarchal and corrupt court of *The Trial* uncannily evokes a world of arbitrary power myths that date from a time before the era of written laws.[3] But there is another, unexplored connection between

Benjamin and Kafka, one that draws *The Trial* into the orbit of Benjamin's seminal analysis of urban modernity. In the *Arcades Project* (*Passagen-Werk*), his unfinished *magnum opus* on Paris as the capital of the nineteenth century, and in his related essays on Charles Baudelaire, Benjamin portrays what could be seen as the historical precursor to the hapless Josef K. This figure is the Baudelairean *flâneur*, the leisurely stroller who inhabits the fashionable shopping arcades and teeming streets of Paris. Viewing the evanescent and elusive multitude of minute details – faces, architecture, traffic, merchandise – through the urban melee, the *flâneur* experiences the city as a dreamlike, even surrealistic 'spectacle'. Paris emerges as what Benjamin calls a phantasmagoria of capitalist culture, typified by the spectacular World Exhibitions held in 1855 and 1867, by luxury and fashion and an entertainment industry that turns manipulated and alienated human subjects into commodities.[4] This is the *flâneur*'s privileged territory although his activity is by no means limited to the Paris of the Second Empire. As cultural critics and sociologists have argued recently, the *flâneur*, while originating in a specific time and culture, can be reconceptualised as the quintessential representative of urban modernity, and as such he is of considerable interest for a new reading of *The Trial*. K. is the archetypal modern city dweller whose attempt to penetrate the obscurities of the legal system turns into an obsessive, futile, and often comical process of observing, deciphering, and journeying through the surrealistic, dreamlike spectacle of his city.

The *flâneur* is in fact both a model for and a counter-figure to K. To be sure, K. does not display the genuine *flâneur*'s intoxication with fleeting urban images for their own aesthetic sake; instead, he roams the streets of his hometown with a decidedly utilitarian purpose in mind: to find out the court's location and intentions. Nor does he share the *flâneur*'s artistic productivity, although he does decide to write a petition to the court in the form of a self-exculpating memoir, which will address every detail of his life. This autobiographical text promises to be a thorough examination of his *inner* self and thus does not emulate the *flâneur*'s project of turning impressions of *external* street life into literary texts. However, in many other crucial ways, Kafka's portrayal of K. includes a series of striking allusions to the *flâneur*, which Kafka, in a move typical of his ironic attitude towards traditions, partly preserves and partly disfigures, parodies, and even reverses. To approach Kafka's novel in this way is to invite scepticism; for is not the motif of the *flâneur* too limited, even obscure, to serve as a key to such a notoriously complex novel? The motif's apparent marginality, however, can be turned into a strategic starting point for a new interpretation. For instead of adding yet another general reading of Kafka's masterwork to the excellent ones already available, I intend to use the trope of *flânerie* to approach

The Trial from a deliberately strange, provocative, and literally eccentric angle in order to elicit new meanings by de-centring and de-familiarising this all-too canonical text.

While Paris and later Berlin (in texts by Benjamin, Siegfried Kracauer, and Franz Hessel) are privileged sites of *flânerie*, Vienna and Prague also figure prominently in this tradition. In a sketch by Peter Altenberg, for example, the Austrian capital's Praterstraße appears as a space, not of summer pleasure and distraction, but of the *flâneur's* unhappiness and (self-)marginalisation. He imagines that he and other passers-by have 'failed the examination of life' itself. While they can only dream of a happy recreational life in the country, the Praterstraße disintegrates into a multitude of visual details which reflect the fragmented existence and loss of coherent meaning typical of urban modernity:

> Eight o'clock at night. Like nothing but stores on both sides. Peaches next to pickled herrings. Basketwork. Seaside hats. Blackened radishes. Bicycles gleaming everywhere [. . .] Electric lights ambitious to resemble firebugs don't make things any better. Summer misery brought to light.[5]

Tracing K. back to such borderline cases of the classical *flâneur* allows us also to connect him with figures from Kafka's early fiction, especially the pieces collected in *Contemplation (Betrachtung)*. As Peter-André Alt has shown, these brief narratives are filled with lonely strollers, curious observers, and mistrustful eavesdroppers.[6] In 'Absently Gazing Out' ('Zerstreutes Hinausschaun'), the observer does not walk in the street and enjoy the dynamic spectacle of public life; instead, he is confined to his place at the window, mixing desire and distraction as he watches the momentary encounter between a young girl and an older man at sunset. In 'The Way Home' ('Der Nachhauseweg'), the casual, impressionistic pleasure of viewing petrifies into the 'march' of a conceited first-person narrator. He is overwhelmed by his own achievements and believes his speed of walking matches the speed of the street, feeling 'rightfully responsible' for all the disparate fragments of urban life around him – for people knocking on doors and tabletops, for toasts, for lovers in their beds, in dark alleys, or on the ottomans of bordellos – in an orgy of perceptual domination. And in 'The People Running By' ('Die Vorüberlaufenden'), a nightly walk turns into a hallucinatory fantasy of persecution, possible murder, and isolated people engrossed in their own pursuits who know nothing of others. Here we encounter Josef K.'s precursors, the lost denizens of the big city, self-absorbed and self-aggrandising people who project their own subjectivity onto an external world in which they cannot participate. Instead of continuous experiences that would make life meaningful, they can only have the most fragmented and disjointed encounters, very similar to those shocklike moments that, according to Benjamin, assault human consciousness in the innumerable overlapping relationships typical of modern metropolitan life, a condition Benjamin sees reflected paradigmatically in Baudelaire's poetry.[7] The territorially disoriented figures in Kafka's early fiction demonstrate the ways in which *flânerie* is perverted, even threatened with extinction, amid the traffic, the incomprehensible surface appearances, and manipulative power mechanisms that for Kafka are typical of early twentieth-century urban modernity.

What links K. on the most basic level to these endangered *flâneurs* is his persistently observational gaze, a conspicuous leitmotif of the novel. According to Baudelaire, the classical *flâneur* can be likened to a mirror as vast as the crowd itself; or to a kaleidoscope gifted with consciousness, responding to each one of its movements and reproducing the multiplicity and the flickering grace of all the elements of life.[8] To some extent, K.'s subjectivity and the city's reality, too, mirror each other mimetically. The petty-bourgeois conventionality of his lodging house, the strict hierarchy in operation at his bank, the many sexualised scenarios, the crowded proletarian streets in the suburb, and the court's labyrinthine corridors and overcrowded chambers are all the 'objective correlatives' or outward manifestations of K.'s inner world, his narrow-mindedness and social pretensions, his emotional self-oppression and legal delusions. But whereas Baudelaire's *flâneur* marvels at the 'eternal beauty' and 'amazing harmony of life in the capital cities, a harmony so providentially maintained amid the turmoil of human freedom',[9] K.'s subjectivity cannot forge the city into a meaningful totality or coherent narrative. According to Friedrich Beißner, Kafka's 'mono-perspectival narration' (*einsinnige Erzählweise*) presents virtually all external reality through the protagonist's own perceptive apparatus and horizon of consciousness.[10] For *The Trial*, though, this term may be not entirely appropriate. K.'s subjective perspective is frequently interrupted and supplemented by what can either be identified as a superior narrative consciousness or as K.'s own self-distancing, reflexive insights. Moreover, *The Trial*'s urban reality cannot be confined and unified into one singular meaning by K.'s perception as the term *einsinnig* ('of one sense') suggests. Although apprehended through K.'s eyes, many of its locations, his lodging house, the suburban slums and working-class tenements which house the court offices, the lawyer Huld's residence, the court painter Titorelli's atelier, the cathedral, and finally the execution site, are described with a hallucinatory abundance of sharply edged details. Yet they do not constitute a unified topography with clearly interrelated locations. This holds true even if Hartmut Binder has been able to identify a number of Prague localities which served Kafka as the basis for his fictionalised space, especially the walk to the execution site. As Antony Johae notes, K.'s anonymous city 'has a topography without a recognisable relief. It is received as a traveller enters a foreign city for the first time without a map: so strange does everything seem that it is as if the traveller were dreaming.'[11]

Similarly, all the counter-figures and counter-voices in *The Trial* – the bank employees, K.'s boarding – house neighbour Fräulein Bürstner, Huld and his nurse Leni, Titorelli, the priest, the executioners – continually subvert K.'s monologic, and therefore unsuccessful, attempt to force the city's multitude of meanings into conforming to his own world view, as determined by his profession of innocence, legalistic rationality, and moral superiority. Thus, whereas the Baudelairian *flâneur* experiences an aestheticised harmony between himself and the city's significations, K.'s gaze expresses his fundamental estrangement from his surroundings. His decision, during the initial inquiry, 'to observe more than speak' (*TT*: 43) is but one of the many instances where K. prefers to be the detached, coolly analytic, and at times ironic spectator. Titorelli cautions K.: 'You don't seem to have a general overview of the court yet' (*TT*: 150). But K. pretends that he has established useful contacts with the lower bureaucracy representing the inaccessible Office of Prosecution. He imagines that he is almost joining the ranks of the court's subordinate members like the painter himself, thus obtaining the same improved overview as they have. But his alienated gaze produces merely the illusion of one day attaining a perspective that would yield more than the most fragmented and partial understanding of the legal system. K.'s gaze, moreover, is continually deflected by conspicuous counter-gazes that are every bit as powerful, constraining, and unsettling as his own. His arrest is witnessed from across the street by an unusually curious old lady, who is soon joined by an even older man whom she embraces, and by another man with an open shirt twisting and turning his red goatee. Beginning with this strangely voyeuristic scene, K. the observer will himself be continually scrutinised wherever he goes – in the slum streets, at his first hearing, during his consultations with Huld, or at Titorelli's studio which is swarming with curious children. Josef K. conforms in this respect also to Benjamin's definition of the *flâneur* 'who feels himself viewed by all and sundry as a true suspect'.[12]

The uncanny constellation of mutual gazes locked in relations of power, subjection, and suspicion contributes to the novel's consistent theatricality. It was Benjamin who first noted that 'Kafka's world is a world theater. For him, man is on stage from the very beginning.'[13] Indeed, K. experiences the city as a tragicomic scenario of stage tableaux, actorlike inhabitants, and grotesquely exaggerated situations, a strangely performative territory that he gazes at without being able to attain understanding or acceptance. As one of the two guards notifying him of his arrest points out, K. is ignorant of the law but nonetheless claims to be innocent. Such ignorance leads to high tragedy and carnivalesque farce. Observed by his neighbour-spectators and lying in bed, K. has his breakfast routine interrupted and his stern trust in the moral order of the legal state shaken by the guards who confiscate his nightgown and underwear while consuming his food. The conversation between the guards, the inspector, and their victim is a masterpiece of pompous self-assertions, misunderstandings and non-sequiturs, pitting K.'s confusion, fear, and even thoughts of suicide against what he calls the 'idle talk of these lowly agents' (*TT*: 9) and their 'intellectual limitations' (11). In his view, the entire arrest seems a 'crude joke' perhaps staged by his colleagues at the bank on the occasion of his birthday, a 'farce' (7) which he is reluctantly willing to join, and a painful series of 'ridiculous formalities' (11).

In the evening, K. imitates this farcical and even sexualised performance even more outrageously when telling the self-confident, emancipated, and theatre-loving Fräulein Bürstner of the day's events. Although K. had called the three neighbours watching his arrest 'obnoxious, thoughtless people' (*TT*: 16), he assigns the tired but sympathetic Fräulein Bürstner the same role when staging the scene of his arrest in her own room with great panache and obvious delight. Underscoring the persistently theatrical nature of K.'s trial, this parodic repetition of the original arrest scene also brings out his own repressed sexuality. He is suddenly overcome by ludicrously adolescent desire, kissing Fräulein Bürstner all over her face and throat 'like a thirsty animal lapping greedily at a spring it has found at last' (33), and leaves her room quite satisfied with his behaviour. During his first hearing, K. recapitulates the arrest yet again before an apparently attentive audience. Again the performative nature of his legal plight is clearly expressed when K., taking up an ancient rhetorical gesture, professes his humility and incompetence as an orator (47), only to launch into yet another lengthy, heated, and excessively theatrical account of how he was arrested.

If seen in the context of *flânerie*, observation, and theatricality, the apparent conflict between viewing K. as an urban native or exile can be mediated dialectically: K. is the dislocated stranger in his own phantasmagoric hometown, travelling its streets, suburbs, law offices, and dusty attics in frantic search of settlement, justice, legal resolution, of a closure that, until his eventual execution, remains forever deferred and denied. The themes of both spatial and interpretive movement characterise the novel from its first pages. One of the guards, for instance, wears a tight black jacket resembling a traveller's outfit (*TT*: 3). Although K. finds it inexplicable, the guard's suit suggests that the court literally and figuratively arrives from faraway to invade the most intimate terrain of K.'s private life. Conversely, K.'s *arrest* does not mean confinement but paradoxically sets him in perpetual *motion* to venture through urban space in search of the court. When K. gets dressed to face the inspector, he selects a black suit with a well-tailored waistline, not coincidentally of similar colour and cut as Franz's outfit. If the court literally travels to K. to assert its peculiar power, which is attracted by the very guilt of the accused, K. must mimic the court's forays by becoming a traveller to the city's periphery, to the edges or limits of urban bourgeois conventionality, in order to face the legal institution.

When meeting the merchant Block in Huld's apartment, K. himself alludes to his status as a foreigner in his own city. Doubting that Block, a fellow client, has given his real name, K. feels a sense of freedom that, as he tells himself, one otherwise experiences only when talking to lowly folks in a foreign country (*in der Fremde*). There one reveals no personal details about oneself and talks indifferently about the subordinate person's interests (*TT*: 168). This estrangement marks K. as a counter-figure to the classical *flâneur*, for whom, as Baudelaire points out, 'it is an immense joy to set up house' in the teeming streets.[14] By contrast, K. feels not at all at home in the streets of his city; nor does he actually have a permanent home, for he lives, somewhat curiously for a bank official, in a single room in a crowded boarding house without much comfort and privacy.

Taking inordinate pains to dress elegantly, going for strolls alone or with some of his acquaintances, and participating in occasional automobile excursions with the bank director, K. displays some typical aspects of the *flâneur*'s outward habits, his public facade, and self-stylisation. But put more precisely, K. signifies what Benjamin clearly recognised as the very *end* of this type in advanced modernity. With the increasingly hectic traffic and dense crowds, the demolition of the shopping arcades and the rise of anonymous department stores, the habits of the leisurely connoisseur of urban impressions became increasingly anachronistic. Traces of this social change appear in Kafka's novel when, on the Sunday following his arrest, K. is summoned to his initial inquiry. Despite a hangover after a late night in the tavern, he rushes to his destination, where he finds that the court's offices are housed in a squalid, working-class tenement building. But while K. is afraid of being late (even though he has not been given a time for his appointment), he does not take the readily available electric tram. This only makes sense if we consider K. a would-be *flâneur*, whose business, after all, is not to take public transport but to walk and see. And indeed, Kafka mentions specifically that K. has 'little time to look about'. To his surprise, he encounters the three bank clerks who had been present at his arrest. Two of them, Rabensteiner and Kullych, are riding a tram that crosses K.'s path, while the third, Kaminer, sits like a *flâneur* on the terrace of a coffeehouse, peering out. All three, K. feels, are watching him curiously as he hurries along, while he assures himself that he has refused to take the tram simply out of spite and stubborn self-reliance in all matters related to his trial. In Kafka's city, then, *flânerie* falls victim to capitalist mechanisation as well as, and more devastatingly, to the legal obscurities, territorial remoteness, and enormous psychological pressures of the anonymous court bureaucracy. For Benjamin, the *flâneur*'s lifestyle, although alienated, 'still conceals behind a mitigating nimbus the coming desolation of the big-city dweller'.[15] After his arrest, K.'s increasingly disconsolate existence loses any such transfiguring aura.

As Walter Sokel has pointed out, K.'s investigations take him from the centre of his seemingly secure metropolitan life and the conventions of his own bourgeois existence to the suburban periphery, where the strange and the foreign reside in the midst of social misery, poverty, and the filth of the slums. Resembling Georg Bendemann's friend in 'The Judgement' ('Das Urteil') or the ethnographic traveller who observes the torture scenes in 'In the Penal Colony' ('In der Strafkolonie'), K. experiences a kind of social exile.[16] He encounters a mixture of proletarian vitality and social deprivation: men relaxing at the windows; women going shopping; a fruit vendor offering his wares; shouts across the streets; a blaring gramophone; children playing everywhere. The naturalistic accumulation of minute details pushes the description from realism to surrealistic dream. These scenes are part of the urban spectacle which would merit a *flâneur*'s interest were he to venture from the fashionable shopping arcades to the proletarian outskirts of his urban milieu. Still, K. echoes the typical *flâneur*'s obsession with visual signifiers for, 'contrary to his normal habit, he was taking close note of all these surface details' (*TT*: 39).

One may object that the traditional *flâneur* moves through the outside spaces of the city, whereas except for streets scenes like these, K.'s search for the court takes place inside, in apartments, hallways and offices, as well as bedrooms, kitchens and the cathedral. But as Benjamin points out, *flânerie* is the art of inhabiting the streets as if they were an interior. It transformed the districts of Paris into a continuous set of apartment rooms without separating thresholds,[17] while the shopping arcades, the preferred haunts of the *flâneur*, are ambiguous spaces of (self-)display, located halfway between street and interior. Similarly, in Kafka's city, streets and houses fuse into one continuous labyrinthine space. In the house where the court hearing is supposed to take place, the colourful array of proletarian street life outside blends seamlessly into the life inside the narrow rooms, their doors open and their beds crowded with women, children, and sick people. The endless maze of hallways, attics, and court chambers, filled with noisy onlookers or humiliated defendants, standing with their backs bowed and knees bent, 'like beggars in the street' (*TT*: 69), constitutes a confusing interiority that corresponds to the hectic traffic, disorientation, and disturbed communication typical of the modern city's public spaces. Kafka's suburban scenes, despite their occasionally idyllic touch of proletarian life, essentially share the strangely mechanical, manic, and dehumanised appearance that Benjamin in his interpretation of Edgar Allan Poe's *The Man of the Crowd* finds typical of modern urban crowds. The leisurely act of *flânerie* cannot flourish under these circumstances.[18]

K.'s excursion from the metropolitan centre to the unfamiliar periphery also parodies the journey of the (colonialist) ethnographer searching for authenticity in the local community. This he imagines to be held together by shared values and traditional social bonds, a territory whose strangeness alienates him from his origins and customary surroundings. *Flânerie* shares this ethnographic desire, for, as Benjamin notes, it allows distant countries and times to intrude into one's own space and time.[19] Although K. ventures into the exotic space of proletarian life, his self-consciously social difference and his legal preoccupations prevent him from participating or empathising with this 'Other'. Bothered by the children playing on the staircase of the grimy tenement building, he tells himself that next time, he ought either to bring some candy to win them over or a cane to beat them. K. treats foreign reality as something to manipulate and exploit rather than to understand, an attitude more akin to colonialist ideology than to the *flâneur*'s gaze.

In this situation, K. must become the detective who, persistently if in vain, seeks to impose rationality, logic, and legal analysis on a court world whose ambiguities and seemingly arbitrary authority defy any such manoeuvres. Faced with the speedy life of the modern metropolis, the *flâneur* must be interested in legitimising the social merits of his leisurely way of viewing the city. He needs to present his indolence as a deceptive pose that masks the 'riveted attention of an observer who will not let the unsuspecting malefactor out of his sight'.[20] Confronted with his own arrest and trial, Kafka's protagonist can no longer feign indolence; instead he must become the detective of his own case, pursuing his opponent, the court, with as much logic as he can muster. Since K. is convinced of his own innocence, it does not occur to him, except as we shall see, in the final scene, to investigate himself as a potential culprit by engaging in serious moral self-reflexion about his superficial way of life, his social snobbery, chauvinistic attitude toward women, and other such shortcomings. Instead, he directs his detective-like attention solely at the court which keeps forever outside the grasp of his reasoning. Like Benjamin's *flâneur*-detective, K. seeks to maintain a detached pose of observation, but as the trial proceeds, he realises that action, not contemplation, is called for. Dissatisfied with his advocate's apparent incompetence,

K. decides to take matters into his own hands. As long as he had entrusted his defence to the advocate, he reasons, his trial had actually not affected him very much. Now that he has decided to get more directly involved in his own defence, he will be exposed dangerously to the court, if only temporarily and for the sake for his eventual release.

K.'s detective-like gaze, however, is ill-equipped to decipher the illegibility of the city's signs. If for Benjamin Paris resembled a vast book to be read, a multilayered assemblage of signs which the *flâneur*'s sympathetic eye read as expressions of rich cultural traditions, reminiscences, and historical echoes, the machinery of the court presents itself to K. as a textualised labyrinth. He can only accuse it of corruption, immorality, and illegal persecution. Kafka repeatedly alludes to this textual character of the court world – a variant of the novel's pervasive theatricality – through self-reflexive reference to books, images, and other representational forms. The soiled, pornographic books that K. finds on the examining magistrate's desk in chapter 3 reflect in his eyes the overwhelming moral depravity of the court's hierarchy. K. himself, of course, is not above using women – Fräulein Bürstner, the court usher's wife, and later Leni – as pawns in his fight. But unlike the traditional topos of the world as book, the court world refuses to yield any deeper significance behind its dimly lit corridors, dusty chambers, and self-important bureaucrats. K. himself shows neither the desire nor the ability to comprehend the legal mechanism on its own terms, if indeed this is possible. Merely wishing to ascertain 'that the interior of this judicial system was just as repugnant as its exterior' (*TT*: 72–3), he remains trapped in the closed circuit of surface signs and mere conjecture.

The court's theatrical self-presentation as a mechanism of power, which K. finds both attractive and repulsive, cannot be kept away from his seemingly clean, orderly, and respectable world. As the 'flogger' episode shows, it infiltrates even the bastion of bourgeois-capitalist security, K.'s bank. In a junk room near his office K. discovers three men engaged in a gruesome ritual among discarded old documents and empty ink bottles, which are again signs of the court's archaic, unreadable, and estranged textuality. The two guards who had arrested him are being flogged because K. had complained about them to the examining magistrate. It is especially the confiscation of K.'s fine underwear that has led to the men's punishment. The victims have been stripped naked before the flogger, a wild-looking man clad in a dark leather garment that leaves his neck, chest, and arms exposed. The court's sexual perversity turns K. into a spectator who is at least as voyeuristic as the three neighbours who had watched his arrest. Deeply offended, K. tries to bribe the flogger into letting the guards go, but refuses to sacrifice himself and his position at the bank for these men. He argues that had he intended to do this, it would have been easier to strip in order to offer himself to the flogger as a substitute. But of course, K. cannot let himself give in to what may be a secret masochistic desire to identify with the tortured victims. While he might persuade himself that the flogger would never have accepted this offer, the real reason may be that the voyeur is not interested in getting involved in reality but only wants to register stimulating signals. Next day, K. discovers that the flogging scene is still going on, all the participants at their places, quite unchanged from the day before. Vacillating between desire and revulsion, the voyeur cannot help but return to the scene of his former oppressors' victimisation and punishment. He is unable, however, to face its terrifying implication: that his own trial may be as repetitive, torturous, and utterly surrealistic as this. The only winner in this parodic game of *fin-de-siècle* decadence and perversity is the supremely ironic author, who seemingly enjoys staging these horrific punishment rituals in great detail.

Theatricality, sexual performance, and deceptive mimetic displays also characterise the next chapters. Here again, the strongly visual character of the scenes corresponds to the *flâneur*'s attraction to images, to the physical or corporeal surface significations of urban life, even if K.'s encounters take place, as usual, in interiors rather than in the public space of the boulevard. A large painting in Huld's study depicts a man in a judge's robe sitting on a high, golden throne and seeming to be about to leap up at any moment to make a decisive statement or to pass a sentence. As Leni explains, this picture dates from the judge's youthful days; the portrait does not resemble him at all any more. He is actually quite tiny but has himself painted in this awe-inspiring manner because he is as vain as everybody connected to the court. Even the chair is actually not a throne but a simple kitchen stool covered with an old horse blanket. Although the picture clearly demonstrates the court's tendency to self-aggrandisement, Leni's deconstruction of its representational illusion is of little concrete help to K. Instead K., always in the habit of instrumentalising women for his cause through his sexual power, responds to Leni's erotic desires, hoping to attain help from her in his trial. After being kissed by K., she urges him to confess and rely on her legal advice. She also claims that she has become a substitute for K.'s mistress Elsa. In a way, however, she also takes on the role of K. himself. Personifying the mythic prehistory that so fascinated Benjamin in Kafka's writing, she has an amphibian tissue connecting the middle and ring fingers of her right hand. This defect adds to the sinister way in which she bites and kisses K.'s throat and hair, thus repeating the K.'s similarly vampire-like assault on Fräulein Bürstner.

Even more illuminating than the picture in Huld's study, if no less inconsequential in terms of legal action, is the art of the court painter Titorelli. Fraudulent, opportunistic, and dilettantish, it nonetheless sheds light on the court's self-obfuscating tactics. Titorelli lives in a suburb located on the opposite side of the city from the court offices K. had visited earlier. The area is even poorer; the houses are darker, the streets full of dirt; Titorelli has a ramshackle atelier under the roof of a rat-infested tenement building. Like K. during his arrest, the painter is dressed in his nightshirt. And while K.'s arrest took place under the scrutinising gaze of his curious elderly neighbours, each move during his visit to the artist is observed by rather obnoxious girls, in whose faces K. discovers a 'mixture of childishness and depravity' (*TT*: 141). Even in Titorelli's house there are court offices; indeed, his studio is part of them. As he points out, they can be found in every attic in the city, thus confirming the court's all-encompassing sphere of power.

Titorelli shows K. one of his paintings which resembles the judge's portrait in the advocate's study. But this picture is not yet finished, and the very process of painting reveals the uncanny connection between legal power and representational falsity. Here K. may learn more about the court than through the painter's exhaustive but inconsequential lecture on three sorts of possible releases: 'actual acquittal', 'apparent acquittal', and 'protraction' (*TT*: 152–62).

For Benjamin, the *flâneur*'s alienated, melancholic gaze allegorises the city; abandoning the hope to interpret things according to their secret interconnections, the allegorising strategy takes them out of their contexts so that the *flâneur* may ponder the significance of each individual fragment. K. shares this preference for allegory for he is unable to decipher the entire court machinery in its elusive totality, focusing instead on isolated representations of the legal system. Titorelli, too, is engaged in allegorising. He is working on an emblematic figure behind the threatening judge's throne which is supposed to be the personification of justice. But K. observes that the figure combines the traditional blindfold and scales with a pair of wings attached to her heels, as if she were running. As Titorelli claims, the figure's purpose is to signify Justice and the Goddess of Victory in one. Again, the allegorical details do not form a unified whole. K. objects, quite reasonably, that this is not a good combination because Justice ought to be at rest for a just sentence to be passed. But the artist admits frankly that everything in the painting is pure invention, depicted to order. The judge's festive pose panders to his vanity, while the pastel colours will please the lady who will receive the painting. Proceeding to finish his work, the painter adds a kind of aura to the allegorical figure, which in K.'s eyes now takes on the appearance of the Goddess of the Hunt. Thus, while the painting eludes the hermeneutic desire to establish a determinate, coherent meaning, it does, in terms of K.'s subjective projections, reflect his innermost, almost paranoid fear of persecution, punishment, and defeat.

Representing the uncanny resurrection of mythology in bureaucratic modernity that fascinated Benjamin, Titorelli's painting at the same time undermines the late nineteenth-century *art for art's sake* ideal. Cynically complicit with power and its vain self-display, art loses its aesthetic autonomy as well as any claim to authenticity, verisimilitude, or truth. All his other paintings, three of which K. decides to buy, depict nothing but the same landscape, a heath with two frail trees standing wide apart in the dark grass before a richly coloured sunset. In these pictures, the aura of originality and uniqueness surrounding the classical work of art gives way to the spread of infinitely reproducible mass products. By flaunting their inauthenticity and non-mimetic techniques, all these pictures suggest what K. has been fearing all along. There may indeed be no substance, no legal justice or moral truth behind the court's pitifully self-important representatives and their (pseudo-)legal, endlessly proliferating arguments.

The deciphering of human portraits extends to the reading of actual human faces, an activity that again links K. directly to the *flâneur*, whose leisurely observations of people, as Benjamin argues, is closely related to what the French call *physiologies*. These portraits of typical denizens of the Parisian streets assume that one can read profession, character, biographical descent, and lifestyle from faces. The harmless, friendly images contributed to the phantasmagoric appearance of Paris. They falsely suggested that knowledge of the human condition helped cope with the disquieting life in the modern metropolis, which was characterised by increasing traffic (together with the reduction of human communication to anonymous visual encounters), competition, and other factors of the capitalist market economy. If Benjamin calls the physiological method the 'phantasmagoria of the flâneur',[21] Kafka similarly suggests that the trust in the readability of surfaces is highly deceptive and suspicious. The merchant Block explains that many people waiting in the court's chambers claim they can predict the outcome of the trial in the defendant's face, especially in the contours made by his lips. According to this view, K.'s lips suggest that he will definitely and very soon be convicted, while another defendant even thinks that he detected the sign of his own sentencing. Examining himself in a pocket mirror, however, K. cannot see anything special in his lips; he and Block agree that the theory is pure superstition.

Huld gives the physiological reading an even more ambiguous twist. He tells K. that Leni finds all defendants beautiful. Although he cannot help agreeing with her aestheticisation of the defendants' plight, he argues that this phenomenon is not simply a sign of guilt. After all, some of the accused may actually not be guilty. Nor is beauty an indication of the impending punishment, as not all will be punished. Rather, it is the legal case itself that results in the defendants' various shades of beauty. Quite reasonably, K. believes that this theory only diverts his attention from the more urgent matters of his defence. Like the judges' pictures in Huld's study and Titorelli's studio or the contorted bodies of the guards in the flogging scene, the enigmatic beauty of the defendants' faces is a physiognomic surface sign. K.'s allegorical gaze must read it as an oblique reference to his own plight without being able to decipher it conclusively. In a world where any metaphysical truth remains hidden or absent, where grand hermeneutical master-narratives prove futile, even the concrete details of the persecuted but strangely transfigured bodies of the defendants, including K.'s own, remain shrouded in ambiguity, not offering any real enlightenment about his trial.

In terms of physiological appearance as well as in other respects, the Italian business associate visiting K.'s bank is of particular interest because he turns out to be the *flâneur* that K. cannot be. The businessman wants to see some of the local art treasures and K. is assigned the tedious task of acting as his guide on the grounds that he knows a few Italian phrases. He also possesses some knowledge of cultural history, and is a member of the Society for the Preservation of Municipal Works of Art. The Italian fits the stereotype of the perfect dandy-*flâneur*. Presenting himself as a decadent *fin-de-siècle* aesthete, he laughs and talks a lot, strokes his bushy, grey-blue, and enticingly perfumed moustache with a nervous hand, and is elegantly if ostentatiously dressed in a short, sharply tailored jacket. He speaks French in addition to his local southern Italian dialect, but K. finds both languages hard to understand. As if to allude again to the deceptive physiological reading method, this problem is compounded by the fact that the Italian's moustache covers his lip movements, whose open display might otherwise have helped K. to comprehend him.

Although pressed for time because of his business obligations, the visitor really seems more interested in the city's artistic treasures. In short, this *flâneur* is the reverse of K. He is a traveller who puts shining surface appearances and an indulgent lifestyle of aesthetic pleasures above the analytic mind-set and bourgeois-capitalist work ethic that dominate K. Having just returned from a business trip with a terrible headache, K. prefers to attend to his banking duties than to show the Italian visitor the cathedral, especially because he is worried his position at the office will be harmed if he absents himself. When Leni calls him on the telephone, she unexpectedly connects K.'s visit to the cathedral with his trial: 'They are hounding you' (*T*: 205), she says, and K. agrees. Thus it seems that in Kafka's world, even the *flâneur* belongs to the court; the Italian aesthete, claiming to pursue pure artistic pleasures, may actually be a secret intermediary between the court and its victim.

In the cathedral, as in Huld's study and Titorelli's studio, art loses its autonomy, serving instead – or so it appears to K. – as a representation of the court. While K. waits for his guest, who in the end fails to show up, he discovers that the altar paintings are barely visible in the dark. One of these panels depicts a tall knight in armour with a sword who attentively watches an event that supposedly takes place directly before him. Again, for K., art is not the object of religious or aesthetic contemplation but a cryptic allegory of unspecified menace and power. As he muses, what would happen if he himself, like the Italian, were a foreigner who had entered the cathedral merely to do some sightseeing? Although this seems to be what K. is doing, *flânerie* is in fact not at all the reason he is here; instead, he must listen to the priest's explanations of what finally appear to be the hermeneutic underpinnings of his entire trial. As prison chaplain, the priest is yet another intermediary between K. and the court; like the others, he offers K. partial insight into what governs the trial without showing him an actual escape route from the trial's sphere of influence.

The famous legend of the doorkeeper and the man from the country (better known as 'Before the Law', which Kafka published separately in his lifetime) takes up the dialectic of travelling and frustrated inquiry that structures K.'s trial. Constructed around questions of legitimacy, power, and deceit that arise from the man's desire to enter the Law, the exegetical dialogue between K. and the priest about the parable's many implications recapitulates the positions and counter-positions that endlessly prolong K.'s trial. 'The correct understanding of a matter and misunderstanding the matter are not mutually exclusive' (*TT*: 219), the priest tells K. He never offers him final answers as to the meaning of the parable, but claims to be 'just pointing out the various opinions that exist on the matter'. K. is not to pay too much attention to interpretive options, for the text of the parable is 'immutable' and the various 'opinions are often only an expression of despair' (220) over this fact. And finally, 'you don't have to consider everything true, you just have to consider it necessary'. K. desperately rejects this seemingly cynical view of the relation between power and knowledge: 'A depressing opinion [...] Lies are made into a universal system' (223). I have simply listed these statements without mentioning the specific points of the parable to which they refer in order to highlight their increasingly fatalistic implications. K.'s legal battle has reached an argumentative dead end.

Indeed, the concluding chapter, perhaps one of the most poetic pieces Kafka ever wrote, comes with inescapable urgency. It summarises the novel's conjuncture of parodic *flânerie*, comic theatricality, and legal inevitability. On the eve of his thirty-first birthday, one year after his arrest, two court executioners arrive at K.'s lodging. The walk through the night city reads like the final performance of three dandies, the executioners pale and fat, dressed in waistcoats and top hats, K. likewise in an elegant black suit. Their outward appearance stands in brutal if comic contrast to the gruesome purpose of the excursion. 'They've sent old supporting actors for me', K. muses, sad that 'they want to finish me off cheaply'. Walking between them while they hold his hands 'with a well-trained, practiced, and irresistible grip', he tries to keep his dignity before these disgustingly polite gentlemen, who look like tenors with thick double chins and revoltingly clean faces (*TT*: 226–7). The theatrical metaphors again convey those persistent surfaces and appearances that K. cannot read; his question why it was they who were sent to pick him up remains, like all his other queries, unanswered.

Surprisingly, a woman who may or may not be Fräulein Bürstner, appears from a narrow lane ahead of K. and his executioners. Conducting herself as the emancipated 'New Woman', she is seen walking unaccompanied through the city at night, perhaps to go to the theatre or to meet a male acquaintance. Whatever her reason, she may well represent the type of the female *flâneur*, who, as Anke Gleber has shown, transgresses the traditional roles of women in the streets – prostitute, bag lady, or house wife running errands – always governed by moral convention and determined by fear of masculine assault. The female *flâneur*, a figure half obscured by the canonical literature about and by the male *flâneur*, sets out to enjoy her own independent mode of gazing in public spaces. She tries to be the active subject collecting urban images rather than the oppressed object of the male gaze.[22] This is why it is not important to K. whether the woman in front of him is really Fräulein Bürstner; rather, her mere appearance lets him realise the futility of putting up any resistance to his fate. Instead of assaulting her with his erotic desire as he had done earlier, K. now merely wishes to follow her from a distance, 'not because he wanted to catch up with her, and not because he wanted to keep her in sight for as long as possible, but simply not to forget the reminder she signified for him' (*TT*: 227–8). Here, then, the failed male *flâneur* voluntarily surrenders his traditional sexual and scopic power over the woman. It is the *flâneuse* who acts as the catalyst of K.'s final self-examination. He vows to 'keep [his] mind calm and analytical to the last'; while he always wanted to interfere in the world's business with 'twenty hands' for an entirely un-justifiable purpose, he now does not wish to appear as someone who has failed to learn anything from his year-long trial (228). Thus the lesson of K.'s trial is not the acceptance of a specific legal guilt or moral failure, but the recognition that his arrogance and selfishness have somehow determined a manipulative involvement in a reality that is so strange that it refuses to be mastered by K's moral rectitude, legal knowledge, and sexual desire. If interference proves fatal, the terrible problem is, of course, that the opposite stance, the coolly detached analytic reason, is equally ineffective in K.'s world of bureaucratic terror, legal harassment, and other inescapable acts of domination. This dilemma seems irresolvable, for a third position, the *flâneur's* aesthetic pleasure of enjoying the fleeting images of urban modernity without necessarily getting involved in the existential situations they represent, is not available to K. Only characters like Kaminer sitting in his café and the Italian businessman enjoying the city's monuments without K. can take this option.

Ironically, K.'s final walk through the beautifully moonlit cityscape – with a bridge, a small island, masses of trees and shrubbery, and steeply rising side streets – both imitates and mocks the very *flânerie* that he cannot pursue. Arriving at a deserted stone quarry, the killers try in vain to find a comfortable position for K. to lie down that is not 'quite forced and implausible' (*TT*: 230). But this disavowal of artificiality cannot conceal the incomparable mixture of operatic pathos and second-rate horror-movie style in which the execution takes place, complete with repulsively polite rituals and a long, thin, sharp butcher's knife. During K.'s final moments, an insubstantial-looking human being appears dramatically at a window of an adjoining apartment building, leaning forward with stretched-out arms. Perhaps a friend, perhaps a good person sympathetic to his plight, this spectator, the last in the series of observers before whom K.'s trial has been performed, figures as the supreme allegory of all the unanswered questions about the denied help and the unknown judge K. has never met. And thus, as the executioners' knife plunges into his heart, he dies 'like a dog' while 'it seemed as though the shame was to outlive him' (231).

As seen through K.'s *flâneur*-like eyes, the city's topography evokes the hidden, suppressed or half-forgotten underside of Benjamin's spectacular world exhibitions, elaborately decorated bourgeois apartments, and all the 'dream houses of the collective: arcades, winter gardens, panoramas, factories, wax museums, casinos, railroad stations'.[23] These edifices contributed to the 'dream city' of Paris[24] at a time when capitalism in Benjamin's eyes appeared as a seemingly 'natural phenomenon with which a new dream-filled sleep came over Europe, and, through it, a reactivation of mythic forces'.[25] In Benjamin's Paris, these quasi-mythic forces are sustained by the endless circulation of commodities that appear to be ever-new but are actually repetitive and interchangeable. The critical consciousness of the present (informed by historical materialism) initiates the state of awakening from this remembered, dreamlike past. In Kafka's novel, the nightmarish labyrinth of mythic force masquerading as legal justice shares the apparently 'natural' inevitability of ideology, but lacks the promise of awakening that Benjamin still discovered in nineteenth-century Paris. What K. learns to accept shortly before his execution is that his self-righteous trust in analytic inquiry and the rule of law cannot dispel the bad dream of a society whose bureaucracy seems to be set up only to deny the efficacy of rationality. This inescapable negativity is, ultimately, the reason why K. must imitate the *flâneur*'s exploratory journey through urban space without being able to emulate his visual exhilaration, his feeling of being at home in the midst of urban crowds, and his ability to make sense of the kaleidoscopic images he encounters.

NOTES

In addition to the works cited, I have found the following useful for the writing of this chapter: Joseph Vogl, *Ort der Gewalt: Kafkas literarische Ethik* (Munich: Fink, 1990); Peter Beicken, *Der Proceß* (Munich: Oldenbourg, 1999).

1. This is the Prague explored and celebrated by Angelo Maria Ripellino, *Magic Prague*, tr. David Newton Marinelli, ed. Michael Henry Heim (London: Picador, 1995).

2. Ralf R. Nicolai, *Kafkas 'Process': Motive und Gestalten* (Würzburg: Königshausen und Neumann, 1986), p. 9; Sandra Schwarz, *'Verbannung' als Lebensform: Koordinaten eines literarischen Exils in Franz Kafkas 'Trilogie der Einsamkeit'* (Tübingen: Niemeyer, 1996), pp. 189–215.

3. Walter Benjamin, 'Franz Kafka. On the Tenth Anniversary of his Death', in *Selected Writings*, vol. 2: *1921–1934*, tr. Rodney Livingstone and others, ed. Michael W. Jennings, Howard Eiland, and Gary Smith (Cambridge, Mass: The Belknap Press of Harvard University Press, 1999), pp. 794–818.

4. Walter Benjamin, *The Arcades Project*, tr. Howard Eiland and Kevin McLaughlin (Cambridge, Mass.: The Belknap Press of Harvard University Press, 1999), pp. 3–13 and pp. 416–55.

5. Peter Altenberg, *Sonnenuntergang im Prater: Fünfundfünfzig Prosastücke*, ed. (with afterword) Hans Dieter Schäfer (Stuttgart: Reclam, 1968), pp. 53–4.

6. Peter-André Alt, 'Flaneure, Voyeure, Lauscher an der Wand: zur literarischen Phänomenologie des Gehens, Schauens und Horchens bei Kafka', *Neue Rundschau* 98:1 (1987), 121–39, here p. 122.

7. Walter Benjamin, 'Some Motifs in Baudelaire', in *Charles Baudelaire: a Lyric Poet in the Era of High Capitalism*, tr. Harry Zohn (London: New Left Books, 1973), pp. 107–54.

8. Charles Baudelaire, 'The Painter of Modern Life', *The Painter of Modern Life and Other Essays*, tr. and ed. Jonathan Mayne (New York: Da Capo Press, 1964), pp. 1–40, here p. 9.

9. Ibid., p. 11.

10. Friedrich Beißner, *Der Erzähler Franz Kafka und andere Vorträge* (Frankfurt aM: Suhrkamp, 1983).

11. Johae, 'The City, Light, Air', p. 19.

12. Benjamin, *Arcades Project*, p. 420.

13. Benjamin, 'Franz Kafka', p. 804.

14. Bandelaire, 'The Painter', p. 9.

15. Benjamin, *Arcades Project*, p. 10.

16. Walter Sokel, *Franz Kafka: Tragik und Ironie* (Frankfurt aM: Fischer, 1976), pp. 159–60.
17. Benjamin, *Arcades Project*, p. 422.
18. Benjamin, 'Some Motifs in Baudelaire', pp. 126–31.
19. Benjamin, *Arcades Project*, pp. 419–20.
20. Ibid., p. 442.
21. Ibid., p. 429.
22. Anke Gleber, *The Art of Taking a Walk: Flanerie, Literature, and Film in Weimar Culture* (Princeton: Princeton University Press, 1999), pp. 171–213.
23. Benjamin, *Arcades Project*, p. 405.
24. Ibid., p. 410.
25. Ibid., p. 391.

FURTHER READING

Anderson, Mark M., 'The Physiognomy of Guilt: *The Trial*', in *Kafka's Clothes: Ornament and Aestheticism in the Habsburg Fin de Siècle* (Oxford: Clarendon, 1992), pp. 145–72.
Boa, Elizabeth, 'The Decaying Law: Discourses of Gender, Class, and Race in *The Trial*', in *Kafka: Gender, Class, and Race in the Letters and Fictions* (Oxford: Clarendon, 1996), pp. 181–242.
Dodd, W. J., *Kafka: Der Prozeß* (Glasgow: University of Glasgow French and German Publications, 1991).
Johae, Antony, 'The City, Light, Air and Illness in Kafka's *Der Prozeß*', *Journal of The Kafka Society of America* 20 (1996), 19–29.
Marson, Eric, *Kafka's Trial: the Case against Josef K.* (St Lucia: Queensland University Press, 1975).
Heinz Politzer, 'The Trial against the Court', *Franz Kafka: Parable and Paradox*, 2nd edn (Ithaca, NY: Cornell University Press, 1966), pp. 163–217.
Robertson, Ritchie, 'The Intricate Ways of Guilt: *Der Prozeß* (1914), in *Kafka: Judaism, Politics, and Literature* (Oxford: Clarendon, 1985), pp. 87–130.
'Reading the Clues: Franz Kafka, *Der Proceß*', in *The German Novel in the Twentieth Century*, ed. David Midgeley (Edinburgh: Edinburgh University Press, 1993), pp. 59–79.
Sandberg, Beatrice and Ronald Speirs, '*The Trial*', in *Franz Kafka* (Basingstoke: Macmillan, 1997), pp. 63–103.
Sussmann, Henry, *Franz Kafka: Geometrician of Metaphor* (Madison: Coda Press, 1979).
Tester, Keith (ed.), *The Flaneur* (London: Routledge, 1994).

4

ELIZABETH BOA

The Castle

Something which appears to everyone in childhood and
where no one has ever been: Heimat.

Ernst Bloch[1]

Modernity and community

The modern Western subject, the citizen-individual, is emancipated from the
milieu of his birth, he sets his own values, and he exercises rights freely negotiated in the social contract. K., the hero of Kafka's third novel *The Castle*,
lays claim to such rights, saying shortly after his arrival: 'I want always to be
free' (*DS*: 14). He has left his place of origin, his 'little home town' or 'old
home' (*DS*: 17), he has travelled as a free agent to take up a post in a new
place, and asserts the right to negotiate terms: 'I want no grace and favours
from the castle but my rights' (*DS*: 93). The German word he uses is Heimat,
meaning home town or homeland, which designates a physical place, or social space, or bounded medium which links the self with something larger
through a process of identification signified by a spatial metaphor. Since
no single English word could convey the many associations, I shall use the
German term. But if K. is a modern subject, he seems to have arrived at
the wrong destination. In contrast to Kafka's first novel with its New World
setting and to *The Trial* set in a modern city of banks and proletarian suburbs, in *The Castle* only electric light and the telephone disrupt the otherwise
vaguely feudal atmosphere of a village located under the shadow of a castle.
The modern hero has arrived in a premodern world. Yet having once arrived,
K. remains tenaciously determined to find a place in the village and to force
the castle to recognise his right to stay and his status as official land surveyor.
Why should a self-assertive man with a strong sense of his own worth stay
on in face of the humiliations and failures K. encounters? He could go back
home or continue on to the wider world of the city, or even, as his sweetheart
Frieda suggests: 'If need be we can emigrate, what is there to keep us here

in the village?' (*DS*: 116) These questions open up one path towards reading *The Castle* as a response to the modern condition: a modern subject seeks to underpin his sense of self through integration in a local community.

To explore the possibility of grounding autonomous selfhood through community Kafka transplants a modern hero, emancipated from traditional ties and pieties, into a village tale. The incongruous elements are mutually estranging. K. does not understand the village ways and the villagers find K.'s behaviour baffling. The castle too remains mysterious to K. and to the villagers, for all their claims to superior understanding. Even the castle bureaucrats turn out to be frightened of direct confrontation with ordinary mortals of whose concerns they show little comprehension. Such bafflement among the characters is repeated at the level of the text, for this generically hybrid novel adds onto the basic incongruity of village tale with modern hero such further disparate ingredients as Gothic romance, classical myth, religious allegory, and social satire. Just as the castle buildings present different aspects depending on who is looking at them, so the reader, confronted by the competing signifying systems of realism, allegory, myth, and a host of fleeting intertextual allusions, will find different meanings depending on choice of interpretive strategy. The artistry of *The Castle* lies in the binding together of hybrid elements to make a parallel world, more seamlessly unified than in *The Trial*, which tantalisingly promises yet refuses ultimate, unitary meaning: *the* meaning. But the reader constantly enjoys moments of illumination limited to one strand in the weave – satirical mockery of bureaucracy, for example, or expressive evocation of existential isolation, or critical unmasking of male pretensions and of authoritarianism in K.'s dealings with women and with the assistants, or covert, often comic autobiographical fragments. Yet such moments also contribute to readerly frustration in the quest for *the* meaning, since their limitations are all too evident. Moreover the passages producing the illumination are often overdetermined, full of other meanings that belong to a different picture in the weave. With these provisos, I want now to embark on one path of partial enquiry: why does K. as a modern subject so stubbornly seek admission to a such conservative community?

First, a brief sketch of the historical context. Kafka began writing in the new century when scientific advance, modern transport and communications, and the spread of democratic ideals seemed to herald progress towards ever greater control over nature and towards emancipation in a new urban, cosmopolitan culture. As the rural populace diminished and the cities grew, 'the ancient mechanisms of social subordination were', as Eric Hobsbawm comments, 'often clearly breaking down'.[2] The new, enterprising individual, no longer defined by rank or tied to his place of birth like a serf, enjoyed the social and geographic mobility to realise his potential, as K. seeks to do.

But the modernising process also meant rural populations flooding into city slums and class injustice under the industrial division of labour. The sheer pace of change unleashed a widespread sense of threat to psychological integrity and social stability as the old bases of identity rooted in birthright, custom, and religion were displaced by competitive individualism. These are troubles reflected in *The Trial*, Kafka's novel of city life. Moreover, given the uneven pace of change, the very promise of emancipation unleashed conflict as subaltern peoples sought to overthrow imperialist domination. Kafka lived most of his life in Prague, before the First World War the capital of Bohemia, a province in the dual monarchy of Austria–Hungary, and after the war the capital of Czechoslovakia. The conflicts in the dual monarchy, as the many nationalities fretted under German hegemony, provided the tinder which ignited the First World War and also turned the Jews into scapegoats for the warring nationalities and the ruling Germans alike. In the Bohemian census, by which political representation was determined, the Jews had to identify themselves as either German or Czech and were perceived as shifting sides in accord with self-interest, so contributing to the anti-Semitic stereotype of the grasping rootless Jew. As the sharpening of identity politics made assimilation a less attractive prospect, some intellectuals were drawn to the ideal of a Jewish nation, whether within the mixed communities of Austria–Hungary or the more radical solution of a homeland in Palestine. But in postwar Czechoslovakia, before the German invasion of 1938 heralded the genocide of Czech and European Jewry, a moment of new hope came. The first president of Czechoslovakia, T. G. Masaryk, long sympathetic to Zionism, granted the same recognition to the Jews as to other peoples, a step which, following an anti-Semitic flair-up in 1920, brought a new harmony in Czech–Jewish relations. Such new hopes may account for a mellowing of Kafka's vision in *The Castle* compared with *The Trial*. At the same time, the destruction of faith in an abstract ideal of universal humanity, which had been hastened by the slaughter in the First World War, may account for the tenacity of K.'s pursuit of recognition both of his unique identity yet also of integration in a bounded community.

Heimat old and new

Early on, K. compares his first sight of the castle with his home town where he had long not set foot. In contrast to K.'s memory of the tapering church spire rising above the huddled mass of houses, the highest point of the castle is a crumbling round tower and the village church is just a barnlike chapel with no soaring spire at all. That K.'s memory of home is idealised is signalled, however, by an obtrusively rhetorical tone, suggesting sentimental self-deception on his part: there may not be much to choose, so the reader suspects, between the castle and the village or between the little town K. came from and the village he has arrived in. The castle, which on closer inspection appears to K. as 'a really miserable little town assembled from village houses' (*DS*: 17), is perhaps no more than a heightened reflection of the village; the village no more than an estranged repetition of home, allowing the normally invisible because unconscious structures which underlie communal relations to be shown forth under the eye of a stranger. The castle, the realm of order and meaning, may be simply the ideological reflection of village practice; old and new may be all the same and change or progress mere illusion.

The evocation in memory of an idyllic home town (Heimat) stands in the ambit of a discourse which had been widely disseminated in German-speaking culture since the turn of the century. As a surrounding medium, Heimat protects the self by stimulating identification whether with family, locality, nation, folk or race, native dialect or tongue, or whatever else may fill the empty signifier to fuel a process of defining and buttressing of iden-tity. The arrival of a stranger in a village initiates a search, which is driven by the longing for a utopian harmony of self and other, for a communally sustained yet autonomous identity. Under the stress of rapid change, Heimat discourse around 1900 set country against city, province against metropo-lis, tradition against modernity, and local or familial loyalties against cos-mopolitanism and egoistic individualism. In the sociological terms of the time (coined by Ferdinand Tönnies), it valued *Gemeinschaft* ('organic com-munity') over *Gesellschaft* ('mechanistic society'). At its most reactionary, it expressed rejection of the modern world. At its most dynamically imperialis-tic, it conveyed the colonist's claim to dominate and domesticate strange terri-tory through cultivation. In more conciliatory mood, the Heimat movement sought to counteract urban alienation by fostering communal values and, like green politics in our day, to ameliorate the effects of modernisation on the natural and human environment. The sociologist Anthony Giddens uses the word 'disembedding' to characterise modernisation, namely 'the "lifting-out" of social relations from local contexts and their rearticulation across indefinite tracts of time–space'.[3] Heimat signifies the aspiration to re-embed.

The text by Kafka closest to the Heimat mode is a late fragment of 1924, 'I Have Returned' ('Ich bin zurückgekehrt', *DE*: 162–3). An anonymous speaker tells of his return to his father's farm. He walks across the farmyard, past a lurking cat, old broken-down farm implements, and a torn cloth once wound round a stick in a childhood game. But the text takes back its opening statement of return, for the speaker fails to enter his childhood home, and instead remains hesitating on the threshold, 'I hear, or think I hear, only the faint chiming of a clock sounding across from childhood days' (*DE*: 163).

The figure of the would-be returnee and some of the detail in Kafka's sketch are oddly similar to motifs in a pamphlet of 1918 on the theme of Heimat. The author, Paul Krische, evokes the type of the restless modern man no longer rooted in native soil, yet in whom memories of the household goods of his childhood remain potent:

> And should he once return to his old parents and see the old furniture and hear the ticking of the clock familiar from his childhood days, then the Heimat feeling awakens in him and he feels how alive the things which accompanied him through childhood and youth and which he had thought long dead still are.[4]

Kafka's returnee is more sceptical: 'It is my father's house, but the pieces stand coldly next to one another, as if each were busy with its own affairs which I have half forgotten, half never knew' (*DE*: 162–3). In contrast to such alienation from old things, Krische's modern man feels how the communal things (*Gemeinschaftsdinge*) of childhood remain potent in his subconscious. He allows for modern mobility, although he regrets the loss of millions of Germans through emigration. (K. too rejects emigration.) But he pleads against xenophobia and praises the exceptionally intense fabric of Jewish family life as the expression of the Heimat instinct. (The first village household K. sees evokes the intense fabric of family life but proves less than welcoming to the stranger.) Alongside the material link to a native heath, Krische identifies an imaginary sense of Heimat which comes from literature and the arts. Schools rather than the family, he suggests, mediate the imaginary Heimat. (For K. the school turns out to be the scene of a humiliating failure to set up home.) An especially powerful imaginary Heimat, constituted in textual representations rather than through material connection, is the Jewish Promised Land of the Fathers, which Krische contrasts with the real physical Heimat of the Jewish family household. (The exclusively male domain of the castle and the village where powerful women predominate has something of such a culture divided between male guardians of texts and female guardians of the household; the schoolmistress Gisa is here a modern figure.) The strength of Jewish family life, according to Krische, is produced by the Heimat instinct which, deprived of the original community between man and soil (*Scholle*), seeks a substitute. Such a view comes perilously close to the racist stereotypes of the rootless Jew who contrasts with the German anchored in blood and soil, but in Krische's liberal text the Jews are paradigmatic of modern man in general while simultaneously exemplifying stabilising family values.

If 'I Have Returned' undoes the dream of return to an imaginary rural *Heimat*, *The Castle* is more ambiguous in not only showing the impossibility of simply going back but also exploring whether a new Heimat is possible. A central trope in Heimat literature is topography. The Heimat is often connected to an arterial road running past it by an umbilical link road. Here there is the bridge which K. crosses when he turns off from the main road. (The link road is a key image in Edgar Reitz's film, *Heimat*.) The village thus appears as a deviation from the historical highway. But the bridge K. crosses also signals a metaphorical connection between the world he enters and the unseen world he is leaving behind, just as the reader finds in the represented world a condensed metaphor for the real world. Bounded externally, the Heimat is internally segmented by local paths, like the alleyway turning off from the village street in the opening sequence of *The Castle*. Literary Heimat locations always have a defining central or high point imbued with symbolic value such as a well, or a tree, or the eponymous cross in Clara Viebig's *Das Kreuz im Venn* (The Cross on the Heath, 1908). In Kafka's novel the eponymous castle is the geographical high point, but the most frustrating topographical feature is the lack of any connecting route leading to it from the village. As a land surveyor, K.'s expertise lies in those infrastructural works like road-building which underpin the human transformations of nature into culture, so creating the narrower Heimat, but also leading on into the wider regions of nation and civilisation. K. has, however, left the extensive world behind in order to probe the community he has entered more intensively, but he is frustrated by the lack of a road to the centre.

As a modern subject who has left home, K. seeks to to re-establish a strictly limited rootedness in a community by setting up not a traditional extended family – as a stranger and a man this would be both impossible and undesirable – but a modern nuclear household. (Women may be expected to live with in-laws in an extended household under the rule of a mother-in-law, but not men.) The first household K. sees demonstrates that there is no simple way back. The Lasemanns appear at once as intensely private to the outsider peering in, yet the insiders lack all privacy. K. observes naked men bathing together in a huge tub, while one woman is suckling a baby and another washing clothes and looking after children. Nothing intensifies an outsider's isolation more than the sight of insiders enclosed together in such enveloping, steamy, smokey, hazy twilight. Tanner Lasemann's first-person plural is exclusive. It offers no opening to draw the stranger in: 'We don't need guests' (*DS*: 22). Such a household signifies an archaic Heimat to which there is no return for a modern subject. According to one anecdote, Kafka responded with the word 'Heimat' to the sight of a Hassidic Jew with his grey garb and side-locks.[5] That some of the detail in the Lasemann household is reminiscent of Eastern Jewish customs suggests, however, that Kafka saw no way back into the enclosed ethnic community of the ghetto or schtetl, where exclusivity was intensified by the status of the Jews before emancipation as themselves an excluded minority.[6] Rather, the episode conveys a painful nostalgia for such enclosure which to a man like K. would actually be intolerable. It turns out in any case that this first vision is misleading in veiling inner tensions between men and women and between generations: the young mother has been transported from the castle to a village household of in-laws, – the Brunswick family – and was not in fact at home when K. first saw her. Nor does she feel at home anywhere and finds a champion in a rebellious son, young Hans, who tries to enlist K. as liberator. Thus the enclosed household with no place for strangers is full of inner fissures and is especially oppressive to women in their role as tokens of exchange between fathers and husbands and to young men fretting to be free from paternal law.

As Krische notes, however, rather than women moving between the fixed households of fathers and husbands as in premodern rural society, modern men move around and make a second or even third Heimat by investing labour and emotional engagement in new places, often marrying into their wife's community. K.'s marital status is obscure. He may have a wife and child back at home, as he at one point claims, but he behaves more like a bachelor than an errant husband. A common figure in late nineteenth- and early twentieth-century literature, the bachelor reflects a transitional stage in modernisation. Janus-faced, he represents a happy state of freedom from ties, yet an unhappy state of exclusion from comforts which a passage in Kafka's diary from the period he was working on *The Castle* conjures up. Kafka contrasts the endless, deep, warm, redeeming joy of sitting next to one's child's cradle and across from the mother and feeling that it is not all up to you unless you want it to be, with the very different feeling of the childless man who knows that, whether he likes it or not, it is always up to him, in each nerve-racking moment through to the end, up to him, but without any result. 'Sisyphus was a bachelor' (19.1.22; *TB3*: 201), he asserts, comparing his own repeated failure to marry with the mythological figure condemned to roll his boulder to the summit again and again only to watch it tumble down each time. In blackly comic mode, K.'s efforts to overcome bachelorhood and to reach the castle prove equally Sisyphean. The two endeavours at once hinder yet contaminate each another, for whether K. wants Frieda as a way of reaching Klamm and the castle or whether he wants to reach Klamm to legitimise his relations with Frieda and hence his place in the village is unclear.

Bachelors had populated Kafka's fiction for a decade before he wrote *The Castle*. The bachelor is also a frequent figure in Heimat novels. Whether as newcomer, returnee, or insider, often an artist or an intellectual, he tries to strike roots yet frets at limitations and defends his integrity against local pressures to conform. The tension between communal and emancipatory values is often gendered: on the one side, there is the relatively unchanging female realm of home, which contrasts to the changing world of the male historical agent who yet by the same token suffers alienation. Thus the unhappy bachelor seeks the way back home through woman as the embodiment of Heimat. Krische offers good advice to the incomer to integrate into his wife's community, if only for the sake of the children. But K. soon finds Frieda's intrusive local connections intolerable. To be sure, he successfully seizes her away from Klamm, the patriarch who sits unseen except through keyholes in the Herrenhof inn, the liminal place of contacts between village and castle. And he keeps her from Gardena, the matriarch of the Brückenhof inn, the threshold to the village from the outside world. The pair set up home independently between these two crossing points. But located in the school, the domain of bossy propagators of local rules and regulations, their household proves endlessly open to intrusions, especially from the assistants, one of whom even ends up between K. and Frieda in bed one morning.

The assistants are ambiguously associated both with K.'s old home and his new Heimat and have a special relationship with Frieda, the home-maker. Another passage in the diary of January 1922 suggests that these comically uncanny figures embody both subconscious memories of the childhood Heimat and the desire to strike new Heimat roots. Kafka imagines himself pressing forwards on a lonely road in the snow, unfit for company, amazed at the sight of cheerful people or parents and children, feeling isolated not only in this lonely place but also in his own 'Heimat', Prague, deserted not only by people, but crucially 'by himself in relation to people' (*TB3*: 212). He has gone too far, been expelled, yet because he is human and the roots need nourishment, he has his representatives ' "down below" (or above)', 'miserable, inadequate comedians, with whom I can only make do [...] because my main nourishment comes from other roots in another air, these roots also miserable yet more capable of life' (*TB3*: 212–13). The passage suggests self-division between earthly roots which need nourishment and more vital air-fed roots. The assistants are K.'s doubles, the alienated representatives (*Vertreter*) of the sociable instincts which the ideal of Heimat answers. But precisely the need to feel at home interferes with the aspiration to press on further. Illogically, K. wants Frieda to sever her village connections lest they distract from his quest to reach the castle with a view to confirming his position in the village. Thus the quest risks preventing the very outcome the quester seeks. K. certainly wants no truck with children, whom the childish assistants at times fleetingly recall. But transmogrified from his first appearance as young fellow into ageing bachelor, Jeremias will settle with Frieda and be looked after by her like an elderly baby. *Junggeselle*, the word for bachelor, literally means 'young-fellow'. Jeremias will thus escape the miserable *contradictio in adjecto* afflicting the *alter Junggeselle* or old young-fellow in Kafka's sketch of 1910, 'Das Unglück des Junggesellen' ('The Bachelor's Misfortune'). But whether K., hero of an unfinished fragment, will find a home this side of the grave the reader never learns.

The matriarchal household in the patriarchal Heimat

The transformation of a jolly, youthful assistant over the course of a day or so into an ageing miserable bachelor whom compassionate Frieda will take on as husband-baby exemplifies the subterranean wit informing an extended subtext on the theme of romantic love, sexuality, and marriage. The accelerated transformation of Jeremias, cutting out development over time, produces a cartoonlike effect in juxtaposing images of youth and age, like advertisements showing before and after. Similarly, a game with names juxtaposes stages in life by cutting out intervening temporal development. Thus Frau Brunswick, surrounded Madonna-like by an aureole of pale snowy light, suckles a baby called Frieda and her son, heroic young Hans, shares a name with the hen-pecked husband of massive Gardena, the surrogate mother who seeks to steer a grown-up Frieda into marriage. Doubly trapped into their husbands' gloomy domain by the patriarchal exchange of women and the deceptive lure of romance, young mothers are eventually rewarded by swelling into matriarchs, so much more dominant than the husbands into which young heroes like Hans will dwindle. The matriarch will guard young women from predatory young men to ensure their entrapment by dreams of romance which, having fulfilled their function, are put aside in favour of the prosaic duties of home-making, though the dreams return to haunt the matriarchal memory. Matriarchy appears here as a subdominant system sustaining a dominant patriarchy which prevails irrespective of the personal qualities of actual, often puny men and seemingly powerful women who are yet subject to an imaginary power. For Gardena a romantic encounter with Klamm remains the high point of her life, just as Frieda, married to poor old Jeremias, will no doubt remember her encounter with K. whose affinity to Klamm is signalled in a shared initial.

As K. of the castrated name peers through a keyhole at Klamm or waits for him outside in the snow, so the assistants peer at K. through the window and catch flu outside in the snow. For K. Frieda initially has the aura of association with Klamm, the personification of the power to deny or to grant his desires: in Freudian terms Klamm is the Father. Frieda similarly has the aura of association with K., who to the assistants seems to have the power to grant or deny their desires. As K. seizes Frieda from Klamm, so the assistants are transformed in K.'s jealous imagination into beasts stalking

Frieda, a ludicrously unconvincing image given the charming young men and the pathetic ageing Jeremias the reader otherwise encounters. In first making love with Frieda, K. feels transported to 'an alien place in which even the air has no particle of the air of home' (DS: 55). Yet in that very moment of stepping across into a strange land of terrible enchantments (*unsinnige Verlockungen, DS*: 55), K. draws back when he obediently passes on Klamm's indifferent summons to Frieda. This moment sets the romantic enchantment of erotic desire in opposition to Heimat. But the promise proves illusory: like the road which always curves back away from the castle, the lovers turn back from the strange land to return into the prosaic everyday of coupledom in a community governed by patriarchal ground rules and a matriarchal household order. K.'s and Frieda's return is marked by K.'s passing on Klamm's summons and by Frieda's refusing it. In refusing the call which in memory still enchants Gardena, Frieda opts for the role not of enchantress but of home-maker, while in passing on the summons K. turns back from enchantment and returns to the paternal order. Thus romantic love and sexual passion draw lovers together away from familial ties and workaday projects only to usher them back into the communal order. In this negotiation Klamm plays a double part: the imaginary phallic power he wields comes both from the sexual drive *and* its ordering. Thus Klamm signifies at once the erotic lure of romance which Frieda follows then rejects in favour of marriage and the paternal order which K. obeys. But K. soon takes up his quest again along a different path and it is one of the assistants, representative of the sociable instincts, who sets up with Frieda.

Identity and difference, self and other

The assistants who first appear marching briskly in rhythm along the road are oddly anticipatory of a leitmotif in the later genre of Heimat films which dominated the German film industry in the 1950s. These are the vagabond-musicians who mysteriously pop up along the road, like spirits of the locality, travellers who belong nowhere in particular but who are more at home in the landscape than the dull householder. The assistants are described as boon travelling companions (*gute, aufmunternde Wegbegleiter, DS*: 20) or comrades-at-arms perhaps (they later remind K. of his happy days in the army). They have no inwardness and do not seem to belong in any household. Passed off by K. as his old assistants from home, they also seem to be locals. Associated with the road, they have an affinity with travelling apprentices, in German *fahrende Gesellen*, young men in the premodern guild system who before settling down went on their travels, here following their master, K. In Germany today one still sees young travelling men in the handsome black moleskin costume of waistcoat and trousers with silver buttons. The assistants too display such young man's dandyism with their trimmed beards and close-fitting clothes. As travelling companions they have a utopian aura in integrating the seeming opposites of freedom (of the road) with belonging (in the landscape). They also have affinities with figures from the Jewish theatre of travelling players who wandered from village to village;[7] the circus and fairground entertainers in some of Kafka's stories are further such travellers as are the denizens of the nature theatre of Oklahoma in Kafka's American novel. (Affinities between Heimat films and the Western have often been noted.) But Kafka also shows the fragility of these emanations from a dream of freedom yet belonging. Driven out into the cold by K., the assistants lose their happy-go-lucky air and take on the vulnerability of those excluded from hearth and home. That they are excluded by K., himself a stranger seeking access, compounds the nastiness of the assertion of a would-be settler's rights through their denial to others.

K. asserts mastery of his household by excluding others. That the others are an unrecognised aspect of himself suggests the propensity of human beings to establish their identity both through setting themselves off from others and through suppression of aspects of themselves which are threatening to the ego ideal, to use a Freudian term, and which are then projected on to a despised or hated other. The assistants exemplify the literary device of the double who uncannily represents the return of such repressed elements of the self externalised in an *alter ego*. Thus repression, far from securing identity, sets up psychic conflicts which endanger the integrity of the self. Such doubles assume a much more uncannily threatening aspect in *The Trial* – in the whipper scene, for example, or in the executioners who finally give Josef K. the *coup de grace*. That in *The Castle* the uncanny modulates into dark comedy rather than horror signals a protagonist more able to acknowledge his contradictory desires. K.'s attempted exclusion of the assistants can be seen as the repression, in the interests of a supposed 'higher' purpose, of his own 'lower' needs and sociable instincts which finally return in the shape of a poor old fellow wrapped in a shawl who needs looking after (the fate which befalls Jeremias also befell Kafka, ending his quest to complete *The Castle*). The assistants thus convey the theme of self and other at the psychic level.

The Barnabas story, a substantial subplot in its own right, develops a similar theme at the social level in exploring how communal identity crystallises around the process of excluding scapegoats who become 'the others' against whom the community defines itself. The biblical scapegoat was loaded with the sins of the people. The scapegoat's difference is thus constituted by desires or envies projected onto it as onto a screen. Exclusion then serves to assuage the fears, jealousies and repressed lusts of a community. Kafka underlines the point by showing the transformation of paradigmatic insiders into pariahs whose difference is imaginary not real, for before their exclusion the Barnabas family had been one of the leading households in the village. People absolutely alike come to perceive themselves as absolutely different from their anathematised neighbours. Racism may be directed by colonial powers against exotic peoples in other continents. But internal racism in the form of anti-Semitism or other enmities between racialised ethnic groups is as endemic. Internal racism is stoked by the mixing of people and ideas under empire so that competing belief systems help to perpetuate perceived differences between neighbours (Moslems and Orthodox Christians in the Balkans, for example, or Protestants and Catholics in Ireland). By showing a fall from grace of insiders, the Barnabas story conveys how fear lest lightning strike again intensifies the readiness to exclude. There is no evident mediation between castle law and village executors, no official order to the villagers to punish Amalia's transgression. Rather, the villagers act in accord with what they imagine the castle will demand, suggesting that the castle is simply an externalization of customary village practice and its imaginary heightening in village minds to the status of law. Thus Frieda whose tender heart is touched when the assistants are left out in the cold is also the spokeswoman of a punitive spirit of conformity which demands the exclusion of the hated Barnabas sisters, the virgin and the whore who in their different ways do not conform to local sexual mores. Kafka here offers a hard insight, namely that it is not just racist or fascist activists but ordinary, nice people like Frieda who collectively create the conditions for communal ganging up against those perceived to be different. As she whips Klamm's brutish servitors into line, Frieda polices sexuality according to a law which virginal Amalia refuses to recognise and whorish Olga flouts. In the microcosmic parallel world of *The Castle*, macrocosmic wars and internecine conflicts are absent. But a local culture which sets rules, heightened in imagination into absolutes, as to who may or must have sexual congress with whom, who may or may not consort with whom, does cast an oblique light on the wider world where still today the ordering of sexual relations bears a weight of symbolic meaning which can be the flashpoint for communal conflicts. This dark side of the Heimat ideal, communal self-definition through the exclusion of others with sexuality as a key transmission point of tension, would become more and more overt in the course of the 1920s and 1930s.

Mythic moments

Besides illuminating how communal identity crystallises around exclusion of scapegoats, the Barnabas story also illustrates the tensions accompanying modernisation as 'ancient mechanisms of subordination', to use Hobsbawm's phrase, were weakening, for the act of rebellion initiating the exclusion is Amalia's refusal to submit to the patriarchal order of things. K., by contrast, has a more ambiguous attitude. As a newcomer, K. claims the right to negotiate with the castle over his position in the village. To negotiate is to recognise the body with which one negotiates; to demand recognition of a right implies that such recognition has value. The discourse of rights which has held such sway in liberal, modernising societies thus holds a delicate balance between individual emancipation and institutional power. Whether, as may be hoped, might follows from right – power from legitimacy – or, as is to be feared, right is but the ideological reflex of might, is often obscure. K. differs from the villagers, however, at least in his own self-perception, in confronting the castle as an equal and critical partner, not an unquestioning subordinate obedient to hallowed custom. Thus K. at once claims his rights as a patrimony from a power he recognises, while also seeking to reform an arbitrary, crumbling system: the castle should recognise the land-surveyor whom it summoned and who will measure and redefine prevailing relationships. K.'s behaviour towards the assistants does not bode well for a new, rational order, however, which may well turn out less benign than the old. K.'s harsh exclusion of unwanted assistants compares badly with the castle's almost kindly indifference as to whether a redundant land-surveyor goes or stays. Such a contrast between ruthless K. and an arbitrary yet relatively benevolent, older order might lead the reader to locate *The Castle* in the conservative camp of anti-modern Heimat literature. Much will depend on how the reader evaluates Amalia's radicalism. For whereas K. seeks accommodation with power and finds allies in Barnabas and Olga, Amalia's rejection of the castle bureaucracy is non-negotiable.

The episode of Sortini's ill-fated wooing of Amalia brings a castle official and a villager face to face. In the Barnabas subplot as narrated by Olga, it compares in significance with the face-to-face meeting between K. and Bürgel in the main story. Both episodes are imbued with mythic import. I shall come back shortly to K.'s encounter with Bürgel and the mythic turn in modernist literature, but want first to look at Amalia's encounter with Sortini at the fire-brigade festival in the context of Heimat discourse. The turn-of-the-century prophets of Heimat who railed against the cities set great store by folk rituals and festivals.[8] The nationalities in the dual monarchy likewise expressed their sense of identity through folk dance and costume, and musical composition had long been infused by folk influence. Smetana's opera *The Bartered Bride*, first performed in Prague in 1866, still today has the status of a nation-building work expressing the spirit of the people. Under communism too folk music and dancing served to complement socialist internationalism with loyalty to the local Heimat. In Kafka's youth, best-selling Heimat novels by Gustav Frenssen or Clara Viebig mixed naturalist evocation of the rural milieu with climactic scenes of popular folk ritual and mythic moments of encounter with field spirits or sylvan gods. Rudyard Kipling's *Puck of Pook's Hill* of 1906 or the meeting with the Great God Pan in Kenneth Grahame's *The Wind in the Willows* of 1908 exemplify a similar trend, as does the English folk-song revival. The appeal to folk identity and to the mythic underpinnings of folk culture ranged from harmless whimsy, though the nation-building mythologies of oppressed minorities, hardening into irrationalist fascist and National Socialist appropriation of classical, Germanic or Nordic myth and reactionary volkish ideology.

Where do the folk ritual and mythic moments in the episode of Sortini's wooing of Amalia at the village fire-brigade festival stand in all this? The voluntary fire brigade played – and in Central Europe still plays – an important role in rural life in promoting male bonding, as local men formed a fellowship devoted to the communal good and were rewarded by regular, well-deserved drinking bouts. The womenfolk too would join in at the annual festival with music, dancing, and feasting. Czech film director Milos Forman's hilarious film, *The Fireman's Ball*, made at the height of the Prague Spring in 1967, shows that such customs survived under the communist regime. In a central episode local girls parade in a beauty competition in front of ogling, beer-swilling party officials, just as in Kafka's novel a local maiden is eyed up by a less than erotically electrifying castle official. In Olga's telling, the festival was to be a rite of passage for Amalia in the role of the virgin to be exchanged in accord with the ancient tradition at the very roots of human culture.[9] The antiquity of the fertility rite is signalled in the grandeur of the musical instruments which the castle provides: not humble bucolic bagpipes or fiddles, but trumpets will sound at this rite of spring. Amalia wears a necklace of Bohemian garnets, almost the only geographically specific reference in the whole novel. *Granat*, meaning garnet, also means pomegranate, the fruit associated with the rape of Persephone by Pluto, the god of the underworld.[10] In the myth, the earth goddess Demeter was forced to accept Pluto's seizure of her daughter, but could negotiate her return for half of each year because in Pluto's dark kingdom Persephone had eaten only six pomegranate seeds. The myth integrates life and death in the regenerative cycle of the seasons as Persephone returns each springtime, and conveys, if not reconciliation, then at least a truce between patriarchal and matriarchal powers. In *The Castle*, although village women such as Gardena or the village superintendent's manipulative wife Mizzi are not powerless, it is male castle officials who produce texts, suggesting that the symbolic order is inscribed and transmitted through time by men. The mythic texts subordinating mothers and daughters descend from an archaic patriarchy which still shapes the modern imagination.[11] Thus Klamm dominates over Gardena. But Amalia, a latter-day Persephone, rejects the age-old matriarchal collusion which justifies rape in the name of fertility. That the garnets came to Amalia via Olga, but ultimately from Gardena, a latter-day Demeter, signals the necessity of accommodation to the ritual. It is this necessity which Amalia rejects. Her heroic dignity is enhanced by the author's merciless mockery of the male players in the ritual, the father who lovingly strokes the fire-engine hose (*Spritze*, the term Kafka uses, also means ejaculation), the grotesque lover who, in his eagerness to reach Amalia, jumps over the shaft of the fire-engine (the German word *Deichsel* also means erect penis).[12] In jumping over the shaft, Sortini jumps out of the textual realm of the castle to become embodied in the village: the symbolic Phallus is turning back into a mere penis. Sortini is depicted in realistic detail as a puny little man, a head shorter than Amalia. But the realism is supplemented by emblematic decoration in his strange wrinkles which, instead of running across his forehead, fan out from the root of his nose. Abstract concepts like justice or nationhood are often personified by female goddesses; thus the social powerlessness of women finds imaginary compensation in the mythic powers of goddesses. Here the reward of emblematic power compensating for actual powerlessness goes to a man. For Sortini's wrinkles which emblematically signify intellectualism also, as Richard Sheppard suggests, evoke the horns of a goatish satyr.[13] Satyr's horns turning into wrinkles mockingly travesty what is nowadays called phallogocentrism, the combined power of the phallus and the logos (word). Mastery over words is here shown to be but the petty power-brokering of bureaucrats and the mighty phallus to be but the penis/pen of a letter writer. Letter writer Sortini is one of various bachelors who woo maidens in the novel and through whom Kafka has covertly engaged in wry self-mockery. (Kafka's longest work was his letters to Felice Bauer.) Sortini's stiff legs at once suggest a less than athletic, desk-bound bureaucrat, but also evoke a goat's stiff shin and hoof in contrast to the flexible human ankle. The shadow of the great god Pan when cast by a stiff, wrinkly pen-pusher effects not an epiphany of chthonic powers but an unmasking of ludicrous pretensions. In Homeric epic gods and heroes inhabit the same space. The intrusion of the symbolic in the shape of a hybrid bureaucrat/god into the naturalistic village is, by contrast, a comic transgression of modern generic boundaries between realism and myth. Thus, far from heralding the return of archaic myth in accord with the more reactionary tendency within Heimat discourse, Sortini's wooing of Amalia subverts folk ideology and travesties its mythic underpinnings, the effect of travesty coming from the incongruous mixing of emblematic, mythic, naturalistic, and symbolic moments.

To journey not to arrive

Fascist or National Socialist recourse to mythology and folk ideology buttressed claims to imperial power and racial superiority. Amalia's taciturn heroism contradicts the nationalistic cult of heroic masculinity and the grandiloquence of racist ideologues. But the mythic turn in modernism was not only associated with right-wing reaction. It can express the longing to overcome alienation, to retain wholeness of vision, or to find transcendent meaning in a secular age. Nietzsche had proclaimed the death of God and attacked the fragmentation of knowledge into partial specialisms. Kafka's recourse to classical myth, to mythicised religious figures such as angels, and to the invention of new mythic figures tantalisingly promises yet withholds meaning. The mythic figures resist simple decoding, whether because travesty subverts the source meaning or because the masterplot from which allegorical meaning could flow remains unknown. Thus the key to understanding names such as Erlanger or Galater which are drawn from disparate sources remains unknown.[14] When K. first sees Barnabas he seems like an angelic messenger, but it turns out that he has never been in the castle. Angels cross borders to bring messages from the transcendent to the earthly sphere. But in Kafka's story of 'An Imperial Message' ('Eine kaiserliche Botschaft') the distance is too great, the messenger never arrives, and the waiting addressee only dreams of a message. So it is in *The Castle*. Early on, the telephone seems for a moment to be a magical modern device which could jump across the great distances and the borders which defeat the angelic runner in 'An Imperial Message'. But the telephone fails to make the connection between on high and down below. Pressed against K.'s ear, the shell-like receiver (*Hörmuschel*, literally 'hearing-shell', *DS*: 30) emits a humming as of children's voices, then a sound as of distant singing. A shell pressed to the ear makes a sound like the sea, and the distant collective voices which come together into an ever more penetrating single sound recall the mythic Sirens whose song promises a godlike knowledge of past and future and a paradisiac existence. (In 1917, Kafka had written an ironic reworking of this episode of *The Odyssey*, 'The Silence of the Sirens'.) In the *Odyssey* the Sirens' enchanted isle is first described as a bone-strewn realm of death and then as a flowery meadow. Such a double aspect perhaps means that paradise and absolute knowledge are inaccessible to mortal human beings, yet remain in the human imagination as a utopian dream of sensuous and spiritual harmony. Though Homer's Odysseus listened to the Sirens' song, bound to his mast he did not allow himself to be deflected from his journey back home to Ithaca to restore a patriarchal order which demands sensuous repression and bans illicit knowledge. Thus the archetypal wanderer, the symbolic hero of Western culture, travels in order to reach home. More confused than his great predecessor, K. already is where he wants to be, but determines to continue on past the Sirens, whose terrible enchantments beckon in his first love-making with Frieda, in order that he might reach then return from the castle to make a new order at home in the village. Or so seems to be his muddled purpose. The movement in *The Castle* is thus switched over compared with 'An Imperial Message': K. does not sit waiting for a message, but sets off himself to reach the source of meaning. The closest he gets is his meeting with Bürgel, a rather lazy, bed-bound angel. But K. falls asleep, so missing the utopian moment of presence face-to-face, and like the man at the window merely dreams. Bürgel's voice reaches K. as a murmuring in his ears, like the earlier Siren sounds from the telephone. And like his love-making with Frieda, the dream is another erotic encounter, this time, however, in homo- rather than heterosexual mode. Greek love is a utopia which Kafka comically travesties in the mildly obscene butting and puffing of wrestlers, so subverting the contemporary ideal of male bonding which turned the naked, athletic body into an icon. As the novel comes to a stop, not an end, it looks as if K., far from reaching utopia whether in heterosexual romantic, or in homo-erotic classical, or in the communal folkloristic guise of a village Heimat, may be driven to shelter in the maids' room. Full of envious malice and obsessed with trivia, the figure of Pepi risks perpetuating the misogynistic stereotype of the feminine as the negation of creative man with his cultural projects and unique identity. Endless exposure to Pepi's inane chatter might well seem a fate worse than death. The younger hero of *The Trial* did indeed prefer death over ending up in the maid's room like ageing Kaufmann Block. Whether older K. will creep into the maids' room in order to survive we never learn.

At the dawn of Western civilisation Homer's Odysseus travelled in order to return home where he restored, with the utmost violence, the patriarchal order. The hero of *The Castle* too travels to find a home. The novel tracks how his utopian aspirations threaten to destroy the very values of self-discovery through sociability and love which the hero seeks to realise. As covert autobiography, the novel is a confession that writing threatened the very relationships of friendship and love which fuelled the author's work, an insight also threatening to his sense of its value.[15] Yet the journey continues if with no outcome. *The Castle* might be said to take back the *Odyssey* in its refusal to allow its hero to arrive home. (The violent restoration of order in Botho Strauss's play *Ithaka*, written in response to the restoration of a unified German Heimat, is utterly remote from Kafka's vision.) It also undoes in Amalia's revolt against Sortini that foundational opposition in Western thinking between transcendental (male) spirit and (female) nature which Odysseus and the Sirens mythically prefigure. In Zionist discourse, the Promised Land hovers between being an original and a future homeland, just as in secularised mode, the communist utopia promises the return of an original human wholeness. Kafka's masterpiece resists appropriation by either of these discourses in refusing K. any prospect of arrival. Nor does *The Castle* belong in the Heimat mode, which I have used in this essay as a foil, whether in its conservative, reactionary, or dynamically imperialistic versions. At most, Heimat is here a direction not a place, a never-to-be-reached utopia in the sense Ernst Bloch proposes at the end of his monumental *The Principle of Hope*, which supplied the epigraph at the start of this chapter. Utopian thinking has recently come under attack for having promoted intellectual collusion with oppressive regimes. *The Castle* conveys in K.'s ruthless tendency the dangers of the lust for power which utopianism can serve to mask. But *The Castle* also shows the necessity of dreaming dreams if human life is not to decline into meaningless chatter. Kafka's village tale remains necessary reading for our new century.

NOTES

1. Ernst Bloch, *Das Prinzip Hoffnung*, 3 vols. (Frankfurt aM: Suhrkamp, 1977), p. 1628.
2. Eric Hobsbawm, *The Age of Empire: 1875–1914* (Harmondsworth: Penguin, 1989), p. 104.
3. Anthony Giddens, *Modernity and Self-Identity: Self and Society in the Late Modern Age* (Cambridge: Polity Press, 1991), p. 16.
4. Paul Krische, *Heimat! Grundsätzliches zur Gemeinschaft von Scholle und Mensch* (Berlin: Gebrüder Paetel, 1918), p. 28.
5. I am grateful to Anthony Northey for this anecdote recounted in 'Die Kafkas: Juden? Christen? Tschechen? Deutsche?', in Kurt Krolop and Hans Dieter Zimmermann (eds.), *Kafka und Prag. Colloquium im Goethe-Institut Prag 24–27 November 1992* (Berlin: Walter de Gruyter, 1994), pp. 11–32.
6. See Robertson, *Judaism, Politics and Literature*, pp. 266–7.
7. See ibid., pp. 264–6 on the assistants as a Hassidic image.
8. See Fritz Lienhard (a leading proponent of Heimat), 'Oberammergau' and 'Heimatkunst', in *Neue Ideale: gesammelte Aufsätze* (Leipzig: Georg Heinrich Meyer, 1901), pp. 139–53 and pp. 188–200.
9. Claude Lévi-Strauss, *Les Structures élémentaires de la parenté* (Paris: Mouton, 1967), pp. 549–70, presents the exchange of women as a 'language' which structures culture.
10. See Sheppard, *On Kafka's Castle*, p. 156.
11. On the mythic in gender ideology, see Simone de Beauvoir, *The Second Sex*, tr. H. M. Parshley (Harmondsworth: Penguin, 1983), pp. 171–292.

12. According to Franz Kuna, *Kafka: Literature as Corrective Punishment* (London: Elek, 1974), p. 176, the phrase is a rural metaphor for sexual excitement derived from the behaviour of yoked cattle.
13. Sheppard, *On Kafka's Castle*, p. 155.
14. See Robertson, *Judaism, Politics, and Literature*, p. 227 on the mysterious names.
15. For a more cynical view of the erotic appeal of writing over sex, see Detlev Kremer's witty study, *Kafka. Die Erotik des Schreibens. Schreiben als Lebensentzug* (Frankfurt aM: Athenäum, 1989).

FURTHER READING

Boa, Elizabeth, 'Feminist Approaches to *The Castle*', in *Kafka: Gender, Class, and Race in the Letters and Fictions* (Oxford: Clarendon, 1996), pp. 243–86.

Boa, Elizabeth and Rachel Palfreyman, *Heimat – A German Dream: Local Loyalties and National Identity in German Culture 1890–1990* (Oxford: Oxford University Press, 2000).

Bloom, Harold (ed.), *Franz Kafka's 'The Castle'* (New York: Chelsea House, 1988).

Dowden, Stephen D., *Kafka's Castle and the Critical Imagination* (Columbia, SC: Camden House, 1995).

Heller, Erich, '*The Castle*', in *Kafka* (London: Fontana, 1974), pp. 107–38.

Robertson, Ritchie, 'The Last Earthly Frontier: *Das Schloß* (1922)', in *Kafka: Judaism, Politics and Literature* (Oxford: Clarendon, 1985), pp. 218–73.

Rollins, William, *A Greener Vision of Home: Cultural Politics and Environmental Reform in the German Heimatschütz Movement, 1904–1918* (Ann Arbour: University of Michigan Press, 1997).

Sandberg, Beatrice and Ronald Speirs, '*The Castle*', in *Franz Kafka* (Basingstoke: Macmillan, 1997), pp. 104–35.

Sebald, W. G., 'The Law of Ignominy: Authority, Messianism, and Exile in *The Castle*', in *On Kafka: Semi-Centenary Perspectives*, ed. Franz Kuna (London: Elek, 1976), pp. 42–58.

Sheppard, Richard, *On Kafka's Castle* (London: Croom Helm, 1973).

5

RUTH V. GROSS

Kafka's short fiction

In a letter to Felice Bauer Kafka writes about the venue of his writing, explaining that his letter 'is no longer written from the office, for my office work defies my writing to you; that kind of work is completely foreign to me, and bears no relation to my real needs' (29.X.12; *LF*: 18). He refers in other letters to the 'particularly awful' and 'voracious world' (7.XII.12; *LF*: 96) of his office life, where his 'depressing office desk' (17/18.XII.12; *LF*: 109) 'is littered with a chaotic pile of papers and files; I may just know the things that lie on top, but lower down I suspect nothing but horrors' (3.XII.12; *LF*: 84). We know all too well from comments like these how troubling he found it to balance his 'day job' with his need to write the works for which he became famous.

While the 'Kafkaesque' experience is one in which the everyday becomes uncanny, weird, and anxiety-ridden, for Kafka, the everyday meant going to an office job he hated. It meant dealing with business matters that made him want to run away and at one point even to contemplate suicide. It meant living a double life, one during the day, the other during the night. But for Kafka day time was the dark side of existence. Only at night did he have the hours to write what was important to him, to do his own 'work' and to live the existence he felt was the only real one for him:

> My mode of life is devised solely for writing, and if there are any changes, then only for the sake of perhaps fitting in better with my writing; for time is short, my strength is limited, the office is a horror, the apartment is noisy, and if a pleasant, straightforward life is not possible then one must try to wriggle through by subtle manoeuvres. The satisfaction gained by manoeuvring one's timetable successfully cannot be compared to the permanent misery of knowing that fatigue of any kind shows itself better and more clearly in writing than anything one is really trying to say. (1.XI.12; *LF*: 21–2)

In the world of late nineteenth-century bourgeois Europe, work was more than an economic necessity – it became a way of defining individuals in modern society. As one sociologist has remarked: 'Others react to us on the basis of their assumptions about our work. Sooner or later this impacts our self-concept, our perception of who we are [and] contributes to feelings of self-esteem.'[1] The office may have been a horror to Kafka, but, having grown up in the bourgeois environment of his native Prague, work he had to perform to earn money (the *Brotberuf*) was necessary for his self-esteem. Despite all his lamentations to the contrary, we must believe that Kafka, as a young man at the beginning of the last century, needed to think of himself not only as the writer he wished to be but as the successful official that he was. His first employment with the Assicurazione Generali was not a happy experience, but the Workers' Accident Insurance Institute for which Kafka finally worked, or to give it its full German title, the Arbeiter Unfall Versicherungsanstalt für das Königreich Böhmen in Prag, was a lively and important government agency concerned with rapidly rising accident rates in the era of growing machine production. Insuring workers was a complicated legal, economic, and human problem. Kafka's superiors at the Institute were seemingly quite absorbed and fulfilled by their work. Not so Kafka, and yet he made use of his literary abilities in writing annual reports and drafting lectures and evaluations. They quickly discovered that he was excellent at letter writing, a talent which probably led to two promotions in the space of a year and a half. In March 1913 he was promoted to vice-secretary, making him a *Prokurist* (like Josef K. in *The Trial*); during his tenure there he worked carefully, wrote articles, and was responsible for many of the most complicated and unpleasant matters. Entrusted with a special duty, accident prevention, he articulated rules that were crucial for the Taylorist and Fordist practices of modern industry – the models of efficiency. The ideas in Kafka's official writings are always clearly arranged and his language shows an exact knowledge of the technical terminology of insurance. His essays also reveal the flair more often associated with his literary writing, for example, this passage from his essay 'Measures for the Prevention of Accidents':

> the work was done in the knowledge of constant danger that could not be avoided. A supremely careful worker could perhaps see to it that one of his knuckles did not jump over the object he was machining during the work, but danger mocks all carefulness. Even the hand of the most careful of workers had to get into the gap between the knives when there was a slip or – which often used to happen – when the wood was thrown back.[2]

He was, in fact, what we call today a technical or professional writer, a crucial figure in the modern business enterprise who articulates the rules and regulations that govern all activity. Accident prevention, Kafka's particular speciality, was important to the emergent industries of the early twentieth century, as it defined the rules for efficient production.

Kafka always believed work problems to be solvable, which is ironic, given the unanswered questioning in his fiction. There was a concreteness to the problems of work safety that did not exist for him in his own world of literature. But then, life at work is a regulated life, and the regulations protect life itself. While working everyone leads a regulated life, and Kafka, as author of the regulations (which he does not invent, but must articulate, like the guards and clerks in his novels), produces regulations for a living. Method is how all problems can be solved. Yet it is clear from his letters to friends that he remained unenthusiastic about his tasks. He told Felice:

> I am desperate, like a caged rat, insomnia and headaches tearing at me; how I get through the days is quite beyond description. To be free from the office is my only possible salvation, my primary desire [...] It's not that I'm afraid of life outside the office; the fever that heats my head day and night comes from lack of freedom, and yet as soon as my chief begins to complain that the department will collapse if I leave [...] I cannot do it, the conditioned official in me cannot do it. (March 1916; *LF*: 462)

His description of himself as 'the conditioned official' is reminiscent of many of his characters – Poseidon in the brief tale of that title, the officer in 'In the Penal Colony', and the narrator of 'My Neighbour' ('Der Nachbar'), to mention only a few.

Kafka's expressions of frustration at not having the time to write are numerous in his correspondence and diaries. He saw the world of work as keeping him from his true calling and thus denying him any satisfaction. And yet, from what we know about his jobs, Kafka was just as much a writer by day as by night. He lived in a divided world; the obviously divided world of business and art, but also the divided world of aesthetic modernism in which writing as a form of creativity had both horrific and redemptive qualities. From Kafka's many tales which focus on the world of work it becomes clear that he recognised the problems inherent in the modernist division of the world and repeatedly tested it as an outlet for his own frustration. If, in modernity, the world is divided between work and art, then there must be a huge difference between the bureaucrat and the artist. But, in Kafka's world, there is often a subtle transformation: one turns into the other. As a modernist, Kafka had to think of work and art as two completely separate areas. This was the aesthetic solution to the issue of alienation. But both Kafka's work and his art involved writing and world-creation; the boundary was never as clear as it ought to have been. Consequently, he became a divided self in which one side was always colluding and colliding with the other. This is never clearer than in the short fiction which deals with work as a major theme.

If we get back to the idea of work as calling (*Beruf*), then Kafka's work problems must also be problems of writing, for just as his work at the office often consisted of writing, as we have seen, so Kafka also defined his writing as work. But if *Beruf* or *Berufung* is a calling, then for Kafka, writing was the 'anti-*Beruf*'. In 1903, he wrote to his friend Oskar Pollak: 'It's this way with me: God doesn't want me to write, but I – I must. So there's an everlasting up and down, after all, God is the stronger, and there's more anguish in it than you can imagine' (*LFFE*: 10). The calling comes from inside him, not from above. Thus the work of writing – in this case, literary writing – is a declaration of independence from the realm of the Father as he characterised it in 'Letter to his Father' when he refers to his writing as 'an intentionally long-drawn-out leavetaking' from his father.[3] For Kafka, writing was akin to a religious experience, but in a religion without a church. His sense of *Berufung* becomes clear ten years later in a letter to Felice's father where he explained that his 'whole being is directed toward literature; I have followed this direction unswervingly until my thirtieth year, and the moment I abandon it I cease to live' (28.VIII.13; *LF*: 313). Office work continued to take time and energy away from his literary writing and thus it became increasingly loathsome to him, despite his real expertise and considerable success in his position at the Institute. Writing as work thus happened both at the office *and* at home which meant that in many ways his *Beruf* and anti-*Beruf* were one and the same. The world of work which he portrays in his literary writings becomes the ultimate expression of grappling with his 'self' as a writer and with the perceived division between work and art. Despite his lack of enthusiasm for the office, the world of insurance provided stimulation for his literary work. As a Czech critic recently argued: 'From there he drew the knowledge of the self-motion and inertia of things, there signatures turned into mighty weights that determine fates, there, in files of unfinished business, lurked the ghosts of applicants.'[4]

Again and again, the office or workplace becomes a place of drudgery, paranoia, and insurmountable problems. Often the main characters in these stories (as in the later fiction in general), do not have names, but are designated by their function, by their job, the 'Hunger Artist', the Chief Clerk, the Trapeze Artist, the Emperor, the Messenger, the Gatekeeper, and so on. To be sure, Marthe Robert is correct in her comment that Kafka's reluctance to name characters derives from no set principle,[5] but it is also certain that Kafka himself would have been distressed to think of himself *only* in his work function, as the insurance safety officer. He needs both worlds – the day world and the night world.

In many ways, Poseidon, in the short tale of that title, carries the burdens of the modern bureaucrat (*GWC*: 116–17). His life seems to be determined by his job at the office; but could one not also say that his job at the office is determined by his being Poseidon, the god of the seas? At any rate, he can be nothing more than the bureaucrat. The first line shows the preoccupation with occupation: 'Poseidon sat at his desk, going over the accounts.' In its own way this opening is every bit as astonishing as the often quoted first sentence of 'The Metamorphosis', since until now the name Poseidon would never have brought to mind desks, accounts, or office-related matters. After all, Poseidon is the earth-shaker, the god of the seas, brother of the mighty Zeus. But in Kafka's world, he has been assigned a job, which is nothing more than 'employment' and not very satisfactory employment at that. The word that Kafka uses for his work is *Amt*, an office in the sense of bureaucratic position. It turns out that Poseidon is really nothing more than a prisoner of his status; 'the great Poseidon could hold only a superior position', as 'he had been destined to be God of the Seas since time immemorial, and that was how it had to remain'. The job is like a life sentence; he cannot escape even for a brief moment. The only hope for him is the end of the world, when, perhaps, 'having gone through the last account, he could still make a quick little tour' of his domain, which he had never really seen. Poseidon's only hope for a way out of his office work offers him a glimmer of freedom before the finality of destruction and even this hope is expressed in the subjunctive – 'there might come a quiet moment'.

Poseidon has nothing from his life but worry and work – 'endless work', as we are told. He does his job well, because he takes it seriously, 'very seriously', but, 'it cannot be said that he enjoyed the work'. He must deal with employees, unsympathetic employers, and office gossip. He has job security, but that seems little comfort given the annoyances and monotony that prevail. His problem is that he has no time to be Poseidon because of his job. And that takes us back to square one, because the reason he has this job and must perform its duties so meticulously is because he is Poseidon. Caught in a situation in which his identity determines his being and his being determines his identity, he depicts the perfect Kafkaesque trap. He rules the seas because he is Poseidon, while he is Poseidon because he rules the seas – but ruling means nothing more than 'going through all the accounts'. But if he were to be the best possible Poseidon, he would be a god, not a bureaucrat. Thus the work-Poseidon has no time to be the art-Poseidon, but he would not be the work-Poseidon if he were not the art-Poseidon. The same tension that confronted Kafka takes place in Kafka's ruler of the seas.

This dilemma of identity is replicated in Kafka's writings again and again. In 1911, he had been pressed by his father to become a silent partner in an asbestos factory in Prague that was owned by his brother-in-law, Karl Hermann. During Hermann's absences, he was supposed to look after the factory. At the moment he was preparing for his epic correspondence with Felice and a month after he had written 'The Judgement' in a single nocturnal sitting, Kafka tells Brod of his feelings about being in charge for even a period of two weeks:

> I realized with perfect clarity that now only two possibilities remain open to me, either to jump out of the window once everyone has gone to sleep, or in the next two weeks to go daily to the factory and to my brother-in-law's office. The first would provide me with the opportunity of shedding all responsibility, both for the disturbance of my writing and for the orphaned factory. The second would absolutely interrupt my writing – I cannot simply wipe from my eyes the sleep of fourteen nights – and would leave me, if I had enough strength of will and of hope, the prospect of possibly beginning again, in two weeks, where I left off today. (7.X.12; LFFE: 89)

Watching the factory for two weeks would take Kafka from his writing, a situation worrisome enough for him to consider suicide. Kafka, like Poseidon, is prevented from assuming his godlike image – that of the writer – because he must perform his workday responsibilities. In Poseidon's case, the character cannot admit even privately that he would be undermining himself if he took time off, and so he spins out his justifications which only reinforce his slavery to the identity that destiny has given him. Work prevents him from realising himself. But Poseidon, unlike Kafka, has no clear-cut idea of what that self-realisation could be. By remaining the 'conditioned official', the sea god represses his godlike or artistic side which leads to his daydreaming at work and a sense that liberation of that other side would be the end of the world, quite literally.

In 'My Neighbour' (GWC: 73–4) Kafka presents additional problems at work. While Poseidon's assistants were of little help to him, and, from time to time, he had to deal with a supervisor (Jupiter) who always puts him in an ill temper, the narrator of 'My Neighbour' is his own boss, which of course creates problems of a different nature. The success of his venture rests with him, which can lead to stress and paranoia in the most extreme forms. Without any real action, this tale is a *tour de force* of speculation and suspicion. In the narrator's mind, his neighbour and possible business rival is working against him. 'I' sees this as his neighbour's only goal in life. Since all that we readers have is 'I's' perspective, we must, on one level, believe he is correct, and yet, on another level, we might consider his rantings nothing more than paranoia. As a self-employed businessman 'I' must take responsibility for his actions or inactions. In the second of two paragraphs, he recounts how his hesitation at taking on the extra space next door, which now his neighbour has rented, may have laid the way for his undoing. It was thus his fault that the neighbour, who turns out to be called Harras, opened an office right next door, a fact that causes him great anguish. As he is his own boss, 'I' believes that he is responsible for everything, asserting at the beginning that 'My business rests entirely on my own shoulders.' After allowing Harras to assume the space, he becomes obsessed with his mistake. Harras is a mystery, since there are few clues as to his character or business. A sign on his door, 'Harras, Bureau', leaves the narrator none the wiser, but after making inquiries, he finds out it is a business similar to his. From this point the narrator believes that Harras is obsessed with him and his business, whereas it seems to us to be the other way round. Who is harassing whom?

In business, speculation is always risky by definition; in this particular case, it is catastrophic. Although the narrator hardly sees his neighbour, he is sure that the man is listening through the walls to all his telephone conversations and as a result is undermining his deals by pursuing his contacts before the narrator has even hung up the telephone. The narrator laments the construction of his office: 'These wretchedly thin walls, they betray the man engaged in honest activity but for the dishonest they provide cover.' The walls not only allow for dissimulation, they symbolise a terrifying loss of identity. Who is the honest, who the dishonest man? The walls and the telephone become the tools of business espionage, but are they real or imagined? Although the neighbour may be unethical and may be spying on 'I', 'working against' him, as he believes, from 'I's' point of view, it is clearly his own fault, and the fact that he is at fault may even be the cause of his paranoid fantasy. But perhaps his fault is really that he is not a particularly effective businessman:

> I have trained myself not to mention the names of my customers on the telephone [...] Sometimes, goaded by anxiety, I dance round the telephone on tiptoe with the receiver at my ear, and still I can't prevent secrets being divulged. This means of course that when I'm on the telephone I become unsure in my business decisions as well, my voice begins to quaver.   (GWC: 74)

At the beginning of the tale, words like 'foolishly' and 'minor misgiving' conveyed the narrator's sense of frustration with himself and his assumption of fault, but he turns this round so that now Harras is to blame. If the responsibility for the business rests with him, then, in a very real way, the narrator is being dishonest to spin this tale of Harras and his tactics to account for his own inadequacies. The narrator ultimately does something that Kafka himself was not able to do in real life – deny his own responsibility.

The feeling of being responsible for everything permeated Kafka's soul. In a letter to Max Brod, dated mid November 1917, around the time he wrote this story, three months after contracting the tuberculosis which would kill him and as he finally terminated his second engagement to Felice, Kafka says:

> What I am doing is simple and self-evident: in my relations to city, to family, to profession, to society, to love (you can put this first, if you like), to the existent or prospective community of our people, in all these relations, I have not acquitted myself well, and moreover, I have failed in such a fashion – I know from close observation – as no one else around me. At bottom it is only that child's idea; 'No one is as bad as I am', which later, when corrected, only produces a new pain. But here we are no longer dealing with badness and self-reproach, but with the patent psychological fact of not acquitting oneself. (*LFFE*: 166)

By focusing on Harras and the menace he presents, the narrator of 'My Neighbour' can shift all responsibility for his failings on to another whose talents and abilities become demonic. Thus Kafka has found yet another solution for the divided self. Creating a *Doppelgänger* is a way of bringing two sides of a personality into focus. Naturally, the businesses in this story are similar, just as writing at work was still writing – desk, pen, paper, blotter are all essential elements to both technical and literary writing. The protagonist in 'My Neighbour' cannot help divulging secrets to his competitor because the two sides are never clearly separate. For Kafka, the dayside and the nightside of writing were competing for the same existence, and he clearly felt that the one was always out to undermine the other. The totality that Kafka claimed to be responsible for is hopelessly divided, although neither side is clearly distinct from the other. That is the problem. For this reason, he can neither acquit himself well, nor claim that the family business, for instance, had nothing to do with him. In 'Letter to his Father' he even feels responsible for his father's business misdeeds.

The travelling salesman has other woes than those discussed above, and yet, they play into the same web of responsibility and identity in Kafka's world. Kafka went on record as being dissatisfied with the ending of 'The Metamorphosis', which he blamed on his having had to go on a business trip and not having been able to give it the proper time. Time is the commodity that he craved throughout his brief life, which is reflected in his fiction dealing with the world of work. Was it not the case that Poseidon had no time to peruse his realm until the end of the world? Was the neighbour's neighbour not beating him at his own game because he could scurry – ratlike – and get to customers more quickly? It is not surprising, then, that Kafka should write a tale about time at work: 'An Everyday Occurrence' ('Ein alltäglicher Vorfall', *GWC*: 99).[6]

The premise of this tale is that on some working days time passes in a flash and on other days the tedium of work makes the working day seem endless.

Written in 1917 (one year after Einstein's *General Theory of Relativity* was published in a final and accessible form), 'An Everyday Occurrence' might be seen as the businessman's vision of modern physics, where nothing is what it seems to be and repetitions of events do not happen. But Kafka's world of business is even more troubling than Einstein's universe. The principles appear similar until we recall Einstein's comment that God does not throw dice with the universe. In Kafka's universe, God does exactly that: nothing is predictable.

The tale begins: 'An everyday occurrence: the enduring of it a matter of everyday heroism' and proceeds to tell of character A who has to meet a character called B for a business transaction. On the first day A's trip to B's town of H takes ten minutes. But the next day, 'although all the attendant circumstances, at least in A's opinion, are exactly the same as on the previous day, this time it takes him ten hours to get to H'. As a result of A's lateness, A and B never get together: they have missed the opportunity of being in the same place at the same time. The business deal fails because there is no common space in time for both of them. A and B, sketchy as they are, have very different personalities. A is a family man who feels 'anxious about the deal' which seems to cause him to act rashly in the belief that speed can supplant substance. We know he boasts of the speed of his trip to his family and are told that 'he *hurries* home', covering the distance '*in no more than an instant*' (my emphasis). The problem once he gets home:

> he is informed that B had actually arrived there early in the day, even before A's departure, indeed that he had met A on the doorstep and reminded him about the deal, but A had said he had no time just then, *he had to go off at once on a matter of urgency.* (GWC: 99)

A then '*rushes* upstairs'. It is almost as if A sees speed as the purpose of business, but that can only lead to dismal failure. B, too, is impatient, but always seems more focused on the deal than poor A. After all, it is B that reminds A of the business for which A has no time and it is B who stays to wait for A in the hope that they will meet. But finally B's annoyance at A's absence turns into 'violent rage' and he vanishes 'for good'.

Travelling for business is an unhappy experience. We have only to remember Gregor's lament in 'The Metamorphosis':

> 'O God', he thought, 'what an exhausting job I've chosen! On the move day in, day out. The business worries are worse than they are on the actual premises at home, and on top of that I'm saddled with the strain of all this travelling, the anxiety about train connections, the bad and irregular meals, the constant stream of changing faces with no chance of any warmer, lasting companionship. The devil take it all!' (TOS: 77)

What A encounters in 'An Everyday Occurrence' is 'the trouble of constant travelling'. Finally, the means become the end, and the absurdity of that reality becomes the focus of this tale about the world of work.

To succeed in business is to make the deal, which in turn requires a meeting of the minds and a meeting of bodies (linguistically, physically, temporally). Both of these are always at hand, close by, but somehow also just out of reach. The writer's problem, finding the right word and phrase (an obsession Kafka shared with his forebear Flaubert) mirrors the tradesman's problem, simply getting together with the customer. Writing is thus akin to commerce and shares its frustrations. Kafka had no time to be both A and B, or both the narrator and the neighbour. He did not have enough time to lead two lives, and so what he had feared does indeed come to pass: B disappears and never returns. This would be the art side of Kafka's writing, the side which A longs for when he suffers his 'sprained tendon' sprinting up the stairs to make the appointment. In German the word for tendon (*Sehnen*) also means yearning or longing and carries with it a multitude of associations with Romantic poetry in particular. A *Sehnenzerrung* is a sprain of A's longing for a different life. Without finding space and time, the literary Kafka would disappear, like B. Once again, the anxiety of the divided self has played into a story about work and its frustrations.

In the discussion so far, I have touched upon stories in which the workplace is the setting and the problems at the office are the focus. In much of Kafka's fiction, however, there is a point at which characters refuse to or become unable to go to work, to the 'common place', thus answering Kafka's unspoken but obviously underlying query – what would happen if I didn't go to the office? The answer is that a new creature appears, one who leads a new kind of life, but this creature is rejected and dies. This indicates a breakdown in the system: the tension between the work writer and the art writer and the (necessary) collusion between them disappears catastrophically.

Gregor Samsa turns into an enormous vermin in order to avoid having to face the unpleasantness of going to his job. Much of the first part of 'The Metamorphosis' establishes the unhappy conditions which have been part of Gregor's professional life. According to Gregor, travelling 'day in, day out' and getting up early every morning can drive anyone round the bend. The boss is a tyrant who sits high at his desk and talks down to his employees, whom he believes are at best 'scoundrels' (*TOS*: 81), and at worst lazy or even embezzlers. Some critics have even seen Gregor's inability to return to his job as the underlying psychological motivation for his transformation.[7] The change in his body is the only escape from his mind-deadening existence. Although Gregor has the satisfaction of knowing that by working he is providing his family with a good life and 'a beautiful apartment', they have taken him and the money he brings home for granted. The promise of family respect and honour he so desires in return for sacrificing his happiness will come to him only after he becomes a real sacrifice – after his death. As the sister states: 'Then we wouldn't have a brother, but we'd be able to go on living and honour his memory' (*TOS*: 120). Gregor will be memorialised and appreciated only when he ceases to exist – not unlike Kafka the writer. In Gregor's case the escape from work becomes a horrifying alternative rather than the dream of writing that Kafka envisioned in his letters and diaries. In a sense, however, it is the alternative that Kafka later encountered in real life, when the only escape from work came when he got sick and was ultimately physically incapable of going to the office.

Josephine, in Kafka's last story, 'Josephine, the Songstress or: the Mouse People' ('Josephine die Sängerin oder das Volk der Mäuse'), also wants appreciation: 'public recognition of her art, a recognition that is unambiguous, that outlasts all ages, and far surpasses anything known hitherto' (*TOS*: 232). She, like Kafka, has two kinds of work: the work involved in 'gaining her daily bread' (*TOS*: 231) and her artistic career, which is singing. She believes she should be relieved of her day job because of her gift, arguing that:

> the strain of work adversely affects her voice, that while the strain of work is admittedly a mere trifle by comparison with the strain of singing, it still makes it impossible for her to get sufficient rest after singing [. . .] so that she [. . .] can never, in these circumstances, rise to her very highest achievements.
>
> (*TOS*: 231)

Like Kafka's writing, Josephine's singing is far more strenuous than the daily grind, but it is the artistic career which fulfils her and which provides her with her true sustenance. In her battle to get out of her day job, she is inexhaustible. But, in pursuit of her desire to free herself from work, she miscalculates in her tactics.

Josephine could be a case for Kafka, the safety officer: 'The other day, for example, she claimed that she had hurt her foot at work, so that it was difficult for her to stand up while singing; but since she was only able to sing standing up, she would now actually have to cut short her songs' (*TOS*: 234). Her first attempt to shirk responsibility is not noticed much, since she still carries out her work (singing) with enough expertise, but she finds that even this is too arduous for her, and so she takes a second tack:

> she pleads exhaustion, dejection, feeling faint [. . .] Behind Josephine we see her supporters in the background, begging her and imploring her to sing. She would be happy to do so, but she cannot [. . .] Finally, weeping tears that defy interpretation, she relents; but then, when she intends to sing, evidently at the

end of her powers, enfeebled, her arms not spread wide as usual but hanging limply at her sides, [...] when she then intends to strike up, no, it is no use after all, a reluctant shake of the head tells us as much and she sinks down before her eyes. (*TOS*: 235)

Even with the near breakdown, Josephine manages to sing and, in so doing, seems to regain some of her stamina. But having seen that halfway measures will not suffice to cast off the burden of the day job, she decides to chuck it all. Finally, 'Josephine has vanished, she refuses to sing, she will not even accept an invitation to sing, this time she has deserted us entirely' (*TOS*: 235). This vanishing act is Josephine's big miscalculation; what she did not understand was that when she ceased to sing, she would cease to be. Without her art, she ceases to exist not only for others but for herself, and the paradox, according to the narrator, is that she will reach the height of redemption by being forgotten – precisely the opposite of her desire. By vanishing, she accomplishes her goal of escaping her daily job, but at the cost of her artistic life, and more importantly, by extension, of her existence. She exists only as long as she is in the minds of her people, and because her art is ephemeral in the days before recording studios it cannot outlast her, unlike Kafka's texts outlasting him. Thus, in a strange way, Josephine's daily work is necessary for Josephine's production of art in the environment of the mousefolk. By withdrawing from the world, she has withdrawn her art from the world and is thus forgotten.[8]

Unlike Josephine and Kafka himself, who had to reconcile the work by which they made their living (their *Brotberuf*) with the artistic work that brought them satisfaction, the hunger or fasting artist combines the two elements in one ('A Fasting-Artist'; 'Ein Hungerkünstler'). He lives by and from his art alone, his only *Beruf*, but the irony of the situation for him is that the closer he comes to perfection in his art, the closer he comes to death. Achieving perfection in hunger artistry is death. It is a *Brotberuf* that eschews bread or any physical sustenance. The sustenance is purely spiritual – the satisfaction of being the best at one's calling: 'Just try to explain to someone what the art of fasting is. No one who does not feel it can be made to grasp what it means' (*TOS*: 218). 'A Fasting-Artist' raises various issues about the nature of art as work, of art as necessity, of art as both sustenance and entertainment. The fact that the art in this story is also the *Beruf* makes it central to our discussion.

When we talk of job satisfaction, there is no question about who should be satisfied: clearly it is the individual doing the work. But we also understand that without the satisfaction of the employer or the customer, work will cease to be 'a living' because a dissatisfied employer can dismiss his employee. In

'A Fasting-Artist' the reader learns that only the artist himself 'could be at the same time the completely satisfied spectator of his own fast' (*TOS*: 212). Knowing this, we are not surprised that 'the interest in professional fasting has markedly diminished', as we are told at the beginning of the story. There is no market for an artist who cannot really satisfy an audience. Soon his 'work' will be forgotten and, as he and his work are one, he will be forgotten himself. The irony is that he is to be forgotten just at the point where he is close to perfecting his art. He has hungered so well because people have ceased to pay attention to him. Thus the only way he could accomplish what might satisfy him is by being forgotten:

> and so the fasting-artist did indeed go fasting on, as he had once dreamed of doing, but no one counted the days, no one, not even the fasting-artist himself, knew how great his achievement was, and his heart grew heavy. (*TOS*: 218)

At the point at which he works honestly, he cannot attain the reward, which is to set a record which will be his memorial. Thus, like Josephine, the fasting-artist, will 'rise to the heights of redemption' and be forgotten.

The complete disappearance of the other side is worked out in these last two stories. They lead to a unified self, which has catastrophic consequences, indeed is catastrophic in itself. Josephine and the fasting-artist are living through their own divided selves. Josephine's revenge on her people for forcing her to work turns out to be an act of self-destruction. Kafka too recognised somehow the necessity of the horror of work to his own literary writing. The only happy resolution of the divided self, that is, the only figure who earned his bread with his art in seemingly perfect satisfaction, is the fasting-artist. His body, however, cannot be sustained by the bread he earns because rejecting all food which he works for is, artistically speaking, his work. Here, unlike with Josephine, disappearance is the goal, not an unintended consequence, of the presentation of a unified self of work and art. But the unified self achieves neither the recognition and fame his art deserves, nor the time to reach perfection of his art, because the closer he gets to perfection, the less time remains to him in life. It is the opposite of Zeno's paradox of Achilles and the tortoise: that if the tortoise halves the distance between itself and the finishing line with each movement then it will never cross the line. For the fasting-artist the last interval can be crossed, but when it is, the fasting-artist is dead. So we must conclude the perfectly unified self would be an unattainable state in life. As much as it was his desire, Kafka realised that it could not really be achieved in the real world.

It is not irrelevant that when Kafka became more and more ill during the last few years of his life, more than once, he wrote that it was 'the office' that had helped him keep his balance. He wrote to Brod two and half years after the diagnosis of his illness:

> Consider that the office is not in the least responsible for my illness, that it has had to put up not only with my illness but with the five years in which it was developing, in fact that the office kept me on my feet when in my unawareness I was only staggering through the days. (11.III.21; *LFFE*: 266)

And the following month to his sister Ottla, 'the office kept the illness in check' (April 1921; *LFFE*: 278). Clearly, having the dayside existence, even with all its 'horrors', seems to have tied Kafka to the world. In the end, although he could not eat and had great difficulty swallowing, his reality was less that of the hunger artist and more that of Gregor, inasmuch as the time left to him was not meant for perfecting his art and giving his all to writing, but rather to wasting away and having less strength day by day for any kind of productivity. Speculation is risky for business people, less risky for scholars; so I will venture a concluding remark: had Kafka not been a divided soul, he could never have produced the haunting and remarkably prophetic literature that is his œuvre. Kafka's greatness, in a significant way, developed from his constant struggle to balance his *Brotberuf* with his *Beruf* – the two sides of his calling as a writer.

NOTES

1. Dana L. Dunn, 'Sociological Dimensions of Economic Conversion', in L. J. Dumas (ed.), *Socioeconomics of Conversion: the Theory and Practice of Conversion* (New York: Sharp, 1995), p. 23.
2. Cited in Jan Hançil, *Kafka in Prague* (Prague: Franz Kafka Publishers, 1991), p. 15.
3. 'Letter to his Father', in *Wedding Preparations in the Country and other Posthumous Writings*, with Notes by Max Brod, tr. Ernst Kaiser and Eithne Wilkins (London: Secker and Warburg, 1954), pp. 157–217, here p. 181.
4. Hançil, *Kafka in Prague*, p. 17.
5. Marthe Robert, *As Lonely as Franz Kafka*, tr. Ralph Manheim (New York: Schocken, 1986), p. 19.
6. Due to a transcription error this was first published as 'Eine alltägliche Verwirrung' ('A Common Confusion') and can still be found under that title.
7. Walter Sokel, 'Education for Tragedy', in Stanley Corngold (ed. and tr.), *Franz Kafka: The Metamorphosis* (New York: Bantam, 1981), pp. 169–86, here p. 174.
8. Cf. Erich Heller's 'Introduction', in *The Basic Kafka* (New York: Washington Square Press, 1979), p. x, in which he compares Kafka's wish for Max Brod to destroy his unpublished works with Josephine's quest for 'the height of redemption' – being forgotten.

FURTHER READING

Anderson, Mark M., 'Sliding down the Evolutionary Ladder? Aesthetic Autonomy in *The Metamorphosis*' and '"Jewish" Music? Otto Weininger and "Josephine the Singer"', in *Kafka's Clothes: Ornament and Aestheticism in the Habsburg Fin de Siècle* (Oxford: Clarendon, 1992), pp. 123–44 and pp. 194–216.

Bloom, Harold (ed.), *Franz Kafka's The Metamorphosis* (New York: Chelsea, 1988).

Boa, Elizabeth, 'The Body of Literature: Kafka's Artist Stories', in *Kafka: Gender, Class, Race in the Letters and Fictions* (Oxford: Clarendon, 1996), pp. 148–80.

Corngold, Stanley, *The Commentators' Despair: the Interpretation of Kafka's Metamorphosis* (Port Washington: Kennikat Press, 1973).

Fuller, Roy, 'A Normal Enough Dog: Kafka and the Office', in *The World of Franz Kafka*, ed. J. P. Stern (London: Weidenfeld and Nicolson, 1980), pp. 191–201.

Kempf, Franz R., *Everyone's Darling: Kafka and the Critics of His Short Fiction* (Columbia: Camden House, 1994).

Nabokov, Vladimir, 'Franz Kafka, *The Metamorphosis*', in *Lectures on Literature*, ed. Fredson Bowers (London: Weidenfeld and Nicolson, 1980), pp. 251–84.

Norris, Margot, 'Sadism and Masochism in "In the Penal Colony" and "A Hunger Artist"', in Mark M. Anderson (ed.), *Reading Kafka: Prague, Politics and the Fin de Siècle* (New York: Schocken, 1989), pp. 170–86.

Pascal, Roy, *Kafka's Narrators: a Study of his Stories and Sketches* (Cambridge: Cambridge University Press, 1982).

Rolleston, James, *Kafka's Narrative Theater* (University Park and London: Pennsylvania State University Press, 1974).

6

STANLEY CORNGOLD

Kafka's later stories and aphorisms

Despite the immense amount written about Kafka's work, a number of the stories (and parables and fragments) composed during the last years of his life have gotten too short shrift. These pieces, produced in the years after 1915, following Kafka's abandonment of work on *The Trial*, include diary entries, the aphorisms of 1917/18 that Max Brod entitled 'Reflections on Sin, Suffering, Hope, and the True Way', and lengthier stories like 'The Great Wall of China', 'The Investigations of a Dog', 'The Village Schoolmaster', 'The Little Woman', and 'Josephine, the Songstress or: the Mouse People'. Their relative neglect may be due to the fact that, to employ Martin Greenberg's useful distinction, they are 'thought' stories rather than 'dream' stories, the reflections of a narrator absorbed in exquisitely refined 'research'.[1] A piece like the unfinished 1922 story 'The Researches' [or, more commonly, Investigations] of a Dog' ('Forschungen eines Hundes') exemplifies this late style.

The inquiries of such narrators address a matter that often falls short of visual realisation. 'The Village Schoolmaster' ('Der Dorfschullehrer', 1915), also known as 'The Giant Mole' ('Der Riesenmaulwurf'), for example, begins with the report of a giant mole:

> Those, and I am one of them, who find even a little ordinary-sized mole dis-
> gusting, would probably have died of disgust if they had seen the giant mole
> that was observed a few years ago, not far from a small village which gained
> a certain passing notoriety on that account.   (*GWC*: 1)

In fact, however, no reader of this story will be in even the slightest danger of suffering a fatal revulsion, since the image of the giant mole, like the village it was sighted in, 'has long since sunk back into oblivion'. The story develops, rather, as an account of the tortuous dealings of the narrator with the village schoolmaster, who was once important for having written a pamphlet on the incident. The passage in the narrative from the 'sensate world' of the mole to a space of speculation on traces left by it in the learned world rehearses a major thrust in these late pieces – a thrust that might be called Kafka's 'Gnostic verve'. I refer to Kafka's readiness to lend his stories the tension of the Gnostic world view, in which the created world consists of debased images of a transcendent source that has nonetheless left lambent traces in the mind.

An aphorism composed in January 1918 crystallises Kafka's Gnostic leanings: 'There is nothing other than a spiritual world [*geistige Welt*]; what we call the world of the senses is the evil in the spiritual world' (aphorism 54; *GWC*: 87). Kafka means to explode the pseudo-solidity of the empirical world; in the late work, the physical world is juxtaposed to the spiritual world, from which the writer might hope to snatch and focus a few gleams, since 'With the strongest of lights one can dissolve the world' (aphorism 54; *GWC*: 87). As a result, these stories are hard to decipher, being without sustained empirical reference, and hence trackless, bent chiefly on introducing, into more or less probable-seeming narratives, a transcendent aura, an aura of the immutable and the abysmal that has something to do with the truth. They have the glint of another light. 'Slanting through the words there come vestiges of light', Kafka wrote in a posthumously published fragment.[2] The late pieces are full of delicately staged invocations of 'the heavens' and also mockeries of this passion, such as 'The Coal-scuttle Rider' ('Der Kübelreiter', 1917) in which the heavens figure as 'a silver shield against anyone looking for help from there' (*TOS*: 196), a delusive glitter with the power to hurt.

Kafka requires a metaphysical orientation, which posits a division between this life and a higher life, all the time he demonstrates the impossibility of surveying the line between them. For instance: 'The joys of this life are not this life's joys', but our fear, he wrote, 'of rising up into a higher life; the torments of this life are not this life's torments, but our tormenting of ourselves on account of this fear' (aphorism 96; *BB*: 244). In this sense, the goal of Kafka's writing is to probe the division between these two spheres, to worry and complicate it, and even to risk crossing over it. He will 'assault' 'the last earthly frontier' (16.1.22; *D2*: 202), press against the divide between the flighty self and what it calls 'the heavens', even when the difference between the two seems a gulf so huge that it might in the ordinary sense be senseless to want to imagine this other world, in whatever form, let alone cross over to it. Kafka, however, insists on this adventure, with a view, above all, to the right customs of approach, the right *practical* logic.

This adventure is the task of writing: to force pathways from the empirical self toward that being which Kafka is pleased to call, in a diary entry, 'the pure, the true, and the immutable':

I can still have passing satisfaction from works like 'A Country Doctor' ... But happiness only if I can raise the world into the pure, the true, and the immutable [*die Welt ins Reine, Wahre, Unveränderliche heben kann*]. (25.IX.17; D2: 187)

To do so would be to sustain all connections to the other world at the highest tension, by an act of 'raising up' that necessarily preserves the difference between these orders – a difference that often comes to be represented in the later stories as the difference between the world of the *living* and that of the *unborn* or the *dead*, between the *new* and the *ancient*, between the *filial* and the *patriarchal* (the dead, the ancient, and the patriarchal being possible metaphors of the eternal). For Kafka, it is a matter of inventing rites of intercourse between the daily and the eternal (in its metaphors: the said-to-be-*dead*, said-to-be-*ancient*, said-to-be-*patriarchal*), a series that can be extended to include all those pertinent forms of the not-self which, for Kafka, have a better claim on the infinite and eternal, abysmal and perpetual than the empirical person he is. He wrote: 'In the struggle between yourself and the world, second the world' [literally, 'be the world's second'] (aphorism 52; *GWC*: 87). So add on, from Kafka's standpoint, those figures of other persons to back as representatives of the higher world: the woman, who he is not; the judge of himself, who he is not; the mythic figures from antiquity, like Ulysses and Alexander the Great's war horse Dr Bucephalus, who he is not ... The list can be extended.

With a view, then, to clarifying Kafka's practical logic – a logic informing the practice of life, life being, after all, something to *do* with the truth – we can take our cue from an early diary entry. Here Kafka declares that his writing has pre-empted in him all the other joys of life:

When it became clear in my organism that writing was the most productive direction for my being [*meines Wesens*] to take, everything rushed in that direction and left empty all those abilities which were directed toward the joys of sex, eating, drinking, philosophical reflection, and above all music. I atrophied in all these directions ... My development is now complete and, so far as I can see, there is nothing left to sacrifice. (3.I.12; *D1*: 211)

Thereafter, Kafka does not think of writing as a type of philosophical reflection; instead, it constitutes 'a way', a practical orientation. It is possible that writing might lead to the one goal that matters: 'to become a good man and answer to the Highest Court'. Yet it might also subserve a baser practice – as, 'quite to the contrary', it contents itself with a philosophical survey of mankind, striving 'to know the entire human and animal community, to recognize their fundamental preferences, desires, and moral ideals, to reduce them to simple rules [or laws] [*Vorschriften*]'. As he wrote to Felice Bauer on 30.IX/1.X.17, this entire effort is undertaken with another view in mind:

> that this way I should become thoroughly pleasing to all, and, to be sure, (here comes the jump) so pleasing, that, without sacrificing this general love, I might finally, as the sole sinner who will not be roasted, parade the meanness that dwells in me, openly, before all eyes. (*LF*: 545, tr. modified)

Note that even in the worse case, this human 'law' (a matter of various *Vorschriften*) consists of 'preferences, desires, and moral ideals' – of what we *want* and *do* and not of what we know. There is no mention here of perceptions, discriminations, and judgements as contributing to one's case at law, whether before the highest court or only that of men, 'the court of Man'.

This position is developed in Kafka's late aphorisms of a plainly theological kind: it was in this series, entitled by Max Brod 'Reflections on Sin, Suffering, Hope, and the True Way', that we encountered Kafka's Gnostic view of 'the sensate world'. A second aphorism concerns the knowledge of good and evil given with the Fall.

Kafka's reflections on the Fall belong to an ancient tradition of biblical commentary but also to a German-language reinterpretation of scripture that comes to the fore in the periods termed Classicism and Romanticism. This master narrative tells how the acquisition of the knowledge of good and evil spurs human perfection through the continuous exercise of reflection and judgement on things good and evil. It is sometimes called the 'triadic' view of ethical man and has been associated with Schiller, Hölderlin, Kleist, and Novalis. The narrative describes the passage from an original state of innocence into one of self-reflecting reflection – and hence of division, a sort of evil – en route to a wholeness of being and reflection at a higher synthetic order, to be achieved through a heightening of this very reflectiveness. Kafka's position, however, is the clearest possible *adversary* position, and it is in fact a good deal more radical than one which simply denies the concept of an 'end', of 'closure', to such a development. In Kafka's words, 'It is only on the far side of this knowledge that the real differences begin' (aphorism 86; *GWC*: 93).

What distinction is Kafka pointing to? The differences that matter – the 'real differences' – lie not between the conceptual work one does and the conceptual work someone else does in producing judgements of an ethical kind. The real differences lie between this pervasive and deficiently *conceptual* way of putting to work the knowledge of good and evil and the demand imposed by the acquisition of that knowledge. The first way, the way of experience, accumulates knowledge – perverting the commandment and evading its charge, assembling the images, simulacra, and logical phantasms or connectors Kafka calls *Motivationen* ('justifications' in Malcolm Pasley's translation).

So, what is the right response to the demand that comes with the Fall? It is, says Kafka, to do what one knows is required, act in the name of the good; for 'no one', he continues, 'can be satisfied with the mere knowledge of good and evil but must strive to act in accordance with it' (aphorism 86: GWC: 93). An injunction not easy to obey. Once we hear its siren-call, Kafka concludes, we will be obliged to destroy ourselves out of the awareness that we do not otherwise have the strength to act in conformity with the knowledge of good and evil.

Let us step back, for a moment, to review the stations of Kafka's itinerary of moral consciousness as they are set down in aphorism 86. The first is the difference between conceiving distinctions of principle between good and evil and acting in accordance with the knowledge of these principles. There follows the impossibility of so acting – an awareness that must provoke in us, Kafka says, the decision to destroy ourselves. Finally, however, the strength to destroy ourselves is not given to us any more than the strength to act in accordance with the knowledge of good and evil. Think of Josef K., at the end of *The Trial*:

> K. knew clearly now that it was his duty to seize the knife as it floated from hand to hand above him and plunge it into himself. But he didn't do so; instead he twisted his still-free neck and looked about him. He could not rise entirely to the occasion, he could not relieve the authorities of all their work; the responsibility for this final failure lay with whoever had denied him the remnant of the strength necessary to do so. (*TT*: 230)

Moreover, unlike K., we shrink back from even the effort of conceiving its necessity. And it is this shrinking back that is the actual thrust of what is called aesthetic and intellectual culture, whence Kafka's (Gnostic) account of the work of art: 'Our art consists in being dazzled by the truth; the light upon the grotesque mask as it shrinks back is true, and nothing else' (aphorism 63; GWC: 89). Taking aesthetic pleasure 'with the various flourishes I might have talent for ... ringing simple, or contrapuntal, or a whole orchestration of changes on my theme' (19.IX.17; D2: 184, tr. modified), is part of his effort to undo the demand laid on the writer by the knowledge of good and evil. 'But', Kafka continues:

> what has happened cannot be annulled, it can only be blurred [*getrübt werden*]. It is for this purpose that the justifications [*Motivationen*] arise. The whole world is full of them, indeed the whole visible world is perhaps no more nor less than the self-justification of man in his wish to find a moment of peace. An attempt to distort the fact that knowledge is already given, to make knowledge a goal still to be reached. (aphorism 86; GWC: 93)

The reader may recognise this as the moment from Nietzsche's *The Birth of Tragedy* that contests the Socratic–Euripidean goal of wanting to turn everything into 'concepts, judgments and inferences',[3] a moment famously paraphrased by Norman O. Brown as 'the great, and really rather insane tradition that the goal of mankind is to become as contemplative as possible'.[4] Kafka's Gnostic verve is not, or does not stop at, contemplation. The stake is redemption, which is not an affair, as in the 'triadic' scheme, of heightened reflectiveness. It is less Kafka than the German Idealist philosophers, who, in Walter Benjamin's phrase, compose 'fairy tales for dialecticians'.[5]

We have been examining Kafka's version of an Enlightenment-critique. The knowledge of the Fall is ethical, yet not as an effort of deciphering and supplying 'justifications' – the constructions that people invent to account for the way they act or fail to act in alleged ignorance of the law. Knowledge is an affair of feeling the imposition of a command: *do the right thing*. Yet we are sooner inclined to forget this command or – what is the same thing – to do the work of culture. Maurice Blanchot observed that, for Kafka, writing could amount to the promise of a kind of salvation as long as 'the community was nothing more than a phantom and because the law which still speaks through the community is not even the forgotten law but the feigned forgetting of the law'.[6] Culture is a prolonged denial, a slow, eccentric path to self-extinction never properly grasped. Its images, signs, and representations are simulacra in the sense of the excuses Kafka surprisingly calls *Motivationen* (justifications).

So much, for the moment, for the question of the right, the practical logic of exploration of *the higher world*, a practice in accordance with 'the law' regulating such intercourse.

By what literary means does Kafka experiment with the rule of metaphysical division, the line dividing the physical from the metaphysical world? It will be interesting to observe the patterns of argument through which his late stories conjure – and erase – the impression of transcendent reference.

This process can be identified in two major moments. The first presents this other space–time (the metaphysical or spiritual world) as devoid of morally interesting pathos, feature, or agency; it is unpromising and readily susceptible to negative interpretation, in the register of what's mute, futile, duplicitous, vacuous, and so forth. It can appear as that 'everything' of the aphorism that begins 'All is fraud...' and concludes that 'the Good is defrauded in any case' (aphorism 55: *GWC*: 88). It can appear in a parable, as in the aphorism of the crows: 'The crows maintain that a single crow could destroy the heavens. There is no doubt of that, but it proves nothing against the heavens, for heaven simply means: the impossibility of crows' (aphorism 32;

GWC: 84). More tangibly, this first moment is the corruption emanating from alleged intercourse with the metaphysical or spiritual world. In 'Investigations of a Dog', for example, the seven dancing dogs, who 'from the empty air conjured music', soon appear ridiculous in their nakedness – 'indecent' and 'revolting' (*GWC*: 147).

The second moment, often connected to the first, invokes the other world with a positive-seeming aura. That such a moment might be worth looking for up and down the length of Kafka's work is suggested by at least one other passage from 'Investigations of a Dog'. Here, the narrator, recollecting his researches into dogdom, describes an earlier trancelike moment. As a consequence of prolonged fasting, he has seen and talked to a splendid hunting dog – is it an 'angeldog'? – who suddenly begins to sing. The investigator recalls:

> Today, of course, I deny all such acquisitions of true experience [*Erkenntniße*] and attribute them to my excessive sensitivity at the time; but even if it was an error, nonetheless it had a certain magnificence – it is the only, even if merely seeming reality that, during the time I fasted, I rescued and *brought over into this world* [my emphasis]; and it shows at least how far we can get when we are completely out of our senses [*bei völligem Außer-sich-sein*].
>
> (*GWC*: 175, tr. modified)

Both moments – negative and positive, the latter even as a magnificent error – are presented by techniques essentially thematic or essentially formal. *Thematic* moments occur when someone in a story, including the narrator, explicitly acknowledges them as belonging to a quest for transcendent experience, as in the case of 'Investigations of a Dog' or the aphorism of the crows or, most famously, 'A Fasting-artist' (1922). On the other hand, *formal* feints toward transcendence produce an aura of the abysmal by means of the rhetorical or logical *negation* of a series of conceptually articulated states of affairs. This movement of deconstruction, demythification, or disarticulation may go unreflected by persons in the story but is presumably perceptible to the reader. We shall examine this moment in such a story as 'The [Spinning] Top' ('Der Kreisel', 1917–23) and in the late self-reflecting 'On Parables' ('Von den Gleichnißen', 1922–3).

Thematic moments have their own logic of evidence that is manifested and then as swiftly disappears. One such movement occurs through the quick, accelerated passage from the private case to the communal, as in 'The Village Schoolmaster'. The story conjures a vastly idealised picture of community, having an aura of the fabulous and the archaic that functions as an allusion to the transcendent. The old schoolmaster, who has written an account of the sudden appearance of a giant mole in 'one of our villages', imagines his pamphlet achieving a giant success through the support of his patron, 'a noble benefactor in the city' (*GWC*: 10). The schoolmaster now sees himself at the centre of a procession, accompanied by waving, welcoming, 'chirping' crowds, but his vision evaporates: it had the air of a compensatory daydream, though not one that he acknowledges as such. Like 'every discovery [it] is at once absorbed into the great universe of scientific knowledge, and with that it ceases in a sense to be a discovery' (13). The schoolteacher's imagination of community vanishes, but not before inducing in him an obdurate, inexplicable silence, as if it would take an eternity of reflection for him to absorb the shock of its disappearance. The outcome is an abandoned utopia, a virtual fullness never to be encountered here and now. This is a dreamlike moment buried in a 'thought' story, having an archaic analogue in the scene of festival that, according to the officer in 'In the Penal Colony' (1919), accompanies the illumination of the prisoner being tortured to death, another exemplary bearer of truth. 'How we bathed our cheeks in the glow of this justice' (*TOS*: 141), declares the officer, but that moment, too, is no more.

The story called 'A Little Woman' (1923) offers a related moment of totalisation that then vanishes, though this total being suggests transcendence not as a festival but as a heightening of the whole of existence into a single negative. The narrator tells how very much a certain little woman is furious with him, so furious that even thoughts of improvement that occur to him seem useless, since the merest suggestion of his readiness to reform will only drive the little woman to new heights of fury. According to the speaker – and we have only his account to go on – there has never been a relationship of any sort between 'the little woman' and himself. Her fury is gratuitous; it is real only as a private construction. Nor is she bent on changing things between them: 'She does not even care about my getting ahead', writes the narrator; 'she cares only for her personal interest, that is to say: avenging the torment which I cause her' (*TOS*: 203). And he repeats this point in order to persuade himself that their quarrel does not deserve to be brought before the public.

What is especially striking here is the extreme heightening of the stakes of a rather ordinary-seeming quarrel by a process that can be called 'ontologisation'. By that I mean that the psychological aspects of a personal dispute turn into fundamental issues of human being (with its longing for transcendent peace). The change proceeds as the transformation of a *quantum* – the magnitude of the woman's rage – into a *quale* – the quality of an eternal imprecation that her rage becomes. All reality is contracted to the space of this tribunal and the time without end in which her charge recurs. The entire detail of life is absorbed into the all-governing principle of the woman's fury and the interminable delay of the crisis, which will never come.

The speaker endures the brute, factlike existence of his being-hated, which suggests that the whole of existence is only this: a 'Being-hated-to-death'. The quarrel with the little woman becomes the punishing truth of existence. And then, as swiftly, the quarrel becomes almost nothing at all, for 'if only I keep this little matter just lightly concealed with my hand I shall remain free for a long time to go on living my life as hitherto, untroubled by the world, despite all the raging of this woman' (*TOS*: 209). We are acquainted from 'The Village Schoolmaster' with this moment of the vanishing of a heightened world. In 'The Little Woman', the story evokes, by means of a double negation, a sweet reclusive peace, in which the sufferer waits patiently for heaven: the abysmal pitch of suffering to which an ordinary life is brought is suddenly negated by a simple gesture of the 'hand'. An absolute is evoked in the mind of a suffering character and then allowed to fall into oblivion.

Recall, too, 'The Village Schoolmaster', where the discussion addressed not the giant mole but the manner in which the alleged sighting of the giant mole had been recorded and circulated and then the airy motives of the discussants themselves. The visible outlines of the giant mole get lost in the story, as Gnostic verve informs it. We noted earlier the same movement at the outset of 'Investigations of a Dog', when the object of the investigations (dogdom) turned swiftly into 'investigation' as an object of scrutiny in itself. Interpreters, in the poet Hölderlin's words, can also '*fall* upward'.[7] Such 'skyey', recursive flights that take leave from an initially posited subject matter are Kafka's Gnostic signature.

In other thought stories, aphorisms, and fragments, moments of self-dissolution arise under the pressure of relentless speculation. To the extent that they go unacknowledged by the narrator, they may be termed formal. In 'Josephine, the Songstress or: the Mouse People', thought-projects occur and dissolve: the narrator offers exquisite reflections on the great question of whether or not Josephine actually sings, which, left unanswered, flow into still more exquisite questions on time and death until they too, like Josephine herself, pass into oblivion. As with 'Investigations of a Dog', in the case of the investigations of the mouse people without a history, 'are we not entitled to say that on this occasion nothing whatever occurred?' (*GWC*: 148). Yet such refined hypothesising leaves behind the virtual reality of implicit answers, tribute to Kafka's facility in turning apparent fact or proposition into a vacant surmise and then back again into a world absent but felt. As in Wallace Stevens's 'Snow Man', Kafka's narrator,

> Nothing himself, beholds
> Nothing that is not there and the nothing that is.[8]

The formal device in Kafka's late work most apt to generate the aura of the transcendent (in both positive and negative senses) is a type of deconstructive logic that works through what may be called 'chiastic recursion'. In such a pattern, each new term, consisting of elements syntactically and conceptually parallel to those of a previous term, arises by means of an inversion of these elements. This strategy of figural transposition gives Kafka the swiftest approach to another world abysmally open and beckoning. Observe the workings of chiastic recursion in the story 'The [Spinning] Top'. A philosopher is convinced that mastery of a single event would lead assuredly to mastery of the whole, so he attempts to seize hold of the secret of the top that the children whip into movement. It is his seizing hold that kills the movement. At the close, 'the screaming of the children...chased him away', whereupon, 'he [the philosopher] reeled off like a top under a clumsy whip' (GWC: 134).

The properties of the first-named object (the top) revert to the first-named subject (the philosopher), whereupon a second-order subject comes alive, prompted by 'the screaming of the children'. This new subject operates a new, figurative whipping, whose object is the former subject, the philosopher. But now that the hare of recursion is running, it cannot be stopped: the movement conjures, in turn, another virtual, higher-order flagellation, in which the new subject, who wields a whip, himself turns into the object of another's frenzy. Of course, it is the author's hand that wields this not-so-clumsy whip, under which the virtual second-order whipper becomes, in turn, the object of his assault. But to what extent can this subjectivity – the author's, the master's – claim to be, unlike the philosopher's, something more than only another stage in the dizzy movement under the whip belonging to an unknown master? Borges wrote:

> God moves the player, he in turn the piece,
> But what god beyond God begins the round,

adding, with a pathos foreign to Kafka:

> Of dust and time and sleep and agonies?[9]

Yes, indeed – and what god beyond the god that starts the round?

Kafka is fertile in such transpositions and recursions. In the story 'The Great Wall of China' ('Beim Bau der chinesischen Mauer', 1917), a wall is being built to keep out the nomads of the North. The question arises, however: how can a wall afford protection when it is not built continuously? 'Indeed, such a wall can not only not protect; it is itself in perpetual danger.' For who will protect the protector? And now the clincher:

These blocks of wall, left standing in deserted regions, could easily be destroyed time and again by the nomads, especially since in those days, alarmed by the wall-building, they kept shifting from place to place with incredible rapidity like locusts, and so perhaps had an even better picture of how the wall was progressing than we who were building it.　　　　　　　　　(GWC: 38–9)

The key to the wall is its design which is incomprehensible, except, perhaps, to the nomads whom it exists to ostracise. This fact, taken strongly, means that the builders are dependent on the beings from whom it is their entire purpose to obtain independence. At this point an abysmal paradox opens up.

The deconstructive movement can also advance to the metaphysical moment which, while positive – even alluring – still falls short of being 'redemptive'. It is nonetheless marked by features assimilable to doctrine. 'On Parables' begins with the famous complaint about the uselessness of parables. After all, all parables do is allude to 'some fabulous Yonder' (irgend ein sagenhaftes Drüben) but succeed only in saying: the Incomprehensible is incomprehensible.

> One man then said: 'Why do you resist? If you followed the parables, then you would become parables yourselves, and thus free of your daily cares.'
> Another said: 'I bet that is also a parable.'
> The first said: 'You have won.'
> The second said: 'But unfortunately only in parable.'
> The first said: 'No, in reality; in parable you have lost.'　　　(GWC: 184)

The argument brings to the fore the recursive moment – the perpetual postponement, in principle, of what seems in every case to be the final claim. Indeed, there is nothing here to prevent the second speaker – or the reader who speaks in his name – from answering, 'I bet that is also a parable.' The parable, however, also contains an allusion to a victory of sorts, especially in the redemptive figure posed along the way: the man-become-parable, the body become the paradox of a 'truthful' writing.

The conjunction of the recursive parable and a truth achieved by the embodied self is plainest in the aphorism that has guided the entire argument of this essay – the supreme paradox found in Kafka's last diary entry. How is the recursive field of rhetorical deconstruction related to the writer who, in obedience to the moral law, seeks a truth higher than this field? Answer: he must first wander this field, immerse himself in the formally destructive element, in the experience of recursiveness, in the verbal but not only verbal phenomenon of feints towards an end that appear to track only the failure to arrive at this end. Or does it do more?

Kafka's last diary entry reads:

More and more fearful as I write. It is understandable. Every word, twisted in the hands of the spirits – this twist of the hand is their characteristic gesture – becomes a spear turned against the speaker. Most especially a remark like this. And so ad infinitum. The only consolation would be: it happens whether you like or no. And what you like is of infinitesimally little help. More than consolation is: You too have weapons. (12.VI.23; D2: 233)

The fearful twist of the hand turns a spear against the speaker with the same gesture that informs Kafka's chiastic sentences: they turn back on their thrower, like the seeker of the spinning of the top who, in his failure and his hope, is spun like a top. These sentences tend to produce little parables of non-arrival.

And yet, says Kafka, something happens – 'it' happens. What is 'it'? It might be 'every word', and it might be 'infinity'; but neither referent taken alone gives the right force to the pronoun. What happens is *this movement*, which appears at first to be a play of language and logic finishing in the absence of an end. And yet this movement – chiastic and apparently self-cancelling – is, on the strength of another intuition, which Kafka means to place outside this series, an event. The event is the sign that a mark has been hit, that something has taken hold, 'whether you like or no'.

In a posthumously published aphorism, Kafka wrote of the possibility of an approach to the truth: 'Contemplation and activity have their apparent truth; but only the activity radiated by contemplation, or rather, that which returns to it again, is truth' (dated 22.11.18; *Wedding Preparations*, p. 111). One could adapt this aphorism to speak of the truth of a certain act of writing – the necessity of its recursiveness – as an event 'radiated' by the contemplation of it. This event is then necessarily 'returned' to (further) contemplation. The existence of at least this one necessity – that recursive writing happens – rewrites the ground rules of existence. Kafka thinks of the acknowledgement of this necessity as a 'weapon'. To have this weapon means to write with the strength of the flow between 'contemplation' and 'activity', contemplation and event.

The consequences of this realisation are formidable. An experience of the phenomenon of recursiveness results in an event having practical effect. Consider the conditions of this happening of truth: first, the setting into play of chiastic reversals; second, a contemplative, will-less attending on the event; finally, the emergence of this recognition with the force of an event. This pattern informs Kafka's late fictions. He mimes in language the recursive feints of a move on 'the heavens'. His words provoke the coming to light of the necessity of their own deflection. But the consciousness of such necessity in and through his fictions heightens his power to act, to struggle, giving him something to *do* with the truth. Kafka does the right thing in taunting recursiveness – he writes it into being – and perceiving its necessity, achieves a power that has something to do with the *truth*.

I want to stress, as I conclude, that the event happens to an embodied self – it happens as experience. The writer's words are physical ('twisted in the hands of the spirits'), and he has hands to swing his weapons. Through the fullness of his immersion in this phenomenon of recursiveness, he comes, in a sense, to embody this parabolic thing: he becomes the sensate space where its action can be felt as necessary. The fact that this recognition occurs, whether or not Kafka 'likes' it, is exhilarating; it provokes, he implies, the happiness that comes from his acquiring one more way to take measures against his fear (he possesses 'weapons' – 'weapons' in the plural).

The event is deeply felt. Kafka makes this point in a late series of aphorisms called *He*:

> Thus if he wants to get down to earth, he is choked by the collar of heaven; if he wants to get up to heaven, by the collar of the earth. And despite this he has every possibility and is aware of the fact; indeed he refuses to attribute the whole thing to a mistake in the original chaining.   (aphorism 60; *GWC*: 60)

This feeling gives power, according to another aphorism he wrote in his diary:

> Everything that he does seems to him extraordinarily new, but at the same time, because of this unbelievable spate of novelty it seems extraordinarily amateurish, scarcely even tolerable, incapable of finding its place in history, breaking the chain of the generations, putting off at its most profound source the music of the world for the first time, which before then could at least be divined.   (13.01.20: *TB3*: 175; *GWC*: 105)[10]

At the end of this passage Kafka turns to speak from the standpoint of the world: 'Sometimes in his arrogance he has more anxiety for the world than for himself.' This is the point of his power. 'History', 'the generations', 'the music of the world', for their part, have no room for the eventuation in the writer of the ascetic, world-resisting movement of the parable in him, but this truth is more than a consolation for the writer's existence: it is proof of his formal necessity.

Let this sequence of notions stand for a moment as we reflect that there are many precedents for them in Kafka's thought. To the point that Kafka might be one in a bodily sense with his consciousness of recursiveness as a certain crazy syntax of words, consider, generally, his readiness to identify himself physically with his texts. Early in his life he recorded his craving to write himself immediately into the paper: it is an exemplary case of his words arriving at their goal, the outcome of his desire:

> to write all my anxiety entirely out of me, write it into the depths of the paper just as it comes out of the depths of me, or write it down in such a way that I could draw what I have written into me completely.   (8.XII.11; *D1*: 173)

'If I were ever able to write something large and whole', he confided to his diary:

> well shaped from beginning to end, then in the end the story would never be able to detach itself from me, and it would be possible for me calmly and with open eyes, as a blood relation of a healthy story, to hear it read [aloud]...
>
> (5.XI.11; *D1*: 134)

Kafka's drive to identify himself with written things lays down in his work a whole network of images of hybrid beings – part-text/part-man – textual man, man-into-text. Recall 'The Metamorphosis', as the transformation of man into his metaphor ('This man is a louse'); recall 'In The Penal Colony', in which the prisoner is said to 'decipher' the text of his sentence with his wounds. The 'eleven sons' of the story of the same name – 'Eleven Sons' ('Elf Söhne', 1917) – are, according to Max Brod's recollection of Kafka's own remark, 'quite simply eleven stories I am working on this very moment'. Note the letter-like, stick-figure self-portraits that populate Kafka's notebooks, which are at once verbal marks and bodily images. Finally, the fragment 'A Dream' ('Ein Traum', 1917) depicts K. in his grave, ecstatic at contemplating the inscription of his name on his gravestone. A great contentment arises from this moment.

We have been observing how Kafka's diary entry – 'Every word, twisted in the hands of the spirits' – contains the possibility of his becoming, so to speak, one with his own parables: the parable of the eternal recursiveness of his words. This turning and returning of words as an experienced event places Kafka more in the lineage of Schelling and the later Hölderlin than, predictably, of Kant and Hegel: the first principle of the former line is not conceptual reason but a pre-reflective sentiment of being. This event founds Kafka's feeling of being-a-writer, for which he actually has the word *Schriftstellersein*.

What is finally so important about this experience is that it instantiates a going over from the writing self, an intellectual-artistic being, to the practical self bent on justification. This movement comes as an answer to the dilemma that haunts all of Kafka's late stories and parables: the problem of justifying a life spent in writing in light of the command to act in accordance with the knowledge of good and evil, a command that Kafka understands as requiring his orientation towards the spiritual world. The difficulty might be pictured as follows: Kafka is acquainted with two columns of his personality, the pillar of the constructed artistic self, which, in his view, is as often as not quite splendid; and the pillar of his ethical personality, which lies about him in ruins. The artistic pillar was constructed by the intellect, and the intellect, once stimulated, must return to it and contribute to its building. What delight to be building: how much better than to be supinely, mutely, fearfully lost in the contemplation of one's ruin!

The disturbing surmise, the defeat, however, would be to conclude that the two buildings are forever separate, that no amount of artistic-intellectual construction could ever succeed in erecting a moral personality that is any better proof against judgement than before – a moral being 'where I have the strength to recognise as my own nature what previously was something alien to myself that refreshed me, satisfied, liberated, and exalted me' (dated 7.11.18; *Wedding Preparations*, p. 104). In Kafka we see the severest bifurcation of an intellectual-artistic writing self and a moral self tormented by the command that it must destroy itself (for its strength is lacking). Kafka is free of this anguish only when absorbed in the practice of writing – for which he must find a justification.

And so the key question continues to resonate for Kafka. Could more, or more whole-hearted, artistic experience (experience oriented away from the visible world) ever constitute a support for his broken, anxious moral self? The answer is found in Kafka's last diary entry: the strength he needs arrives as an event of artistic knowledge going over to the moral personality as a being disposed to write. If this movement could be maintained, it would amount to 'more than a consolation', it would supply him weapons suited for 'an assault on the last earthly frontier'. Interesting for more than our contemporary theoretical concerns (read 'deconstruction'), this power turns out to be achievable only by enduring the necessity of chiastic recursion.

NOTES

1. For the categories 'dream story' and 'thought story', see Martin Greenberg, *The Terror of Art: Kafka and Modern Literature* (New York: Basic Books, 1968).
2. Dated 22.11.18. *Wedding Preparations in the Country and other Posthumous Writings*, with Notes by Max Brod, tr. Ernst Kaiser and Eithne Wilkins (London: Secker and Warburg, 1954), p. 287.
3. Friedrich Nietzsche, *The Birth of Tragedy*, in *Basic Writings of Nietzsche*, tr. Walter Kaufmann (New York: Random House, 1968), p. 97.
4. Norman O. Brown, *Life Against Death* (New York: Vintage, 1959), p. 8.
5. Walter Benjamin, *Illuminations*, tr. Harry Zohn (New York: Harcourt, Brace & World, 1968), p. 117.

6. Maurice Blanchot, 'The Diaries: the Exigency of the Work of Art', tr. Lyall H. Powers, in Angel Flores and Homer Swanders (eds.), *Franz Kafka Today* (Madison: University of Wisconsin Press, 1958), pp. 195–220, here p. 198.
7. Friedrich Hölderlin, '[Reflexion]', *Sämtliche Werke und Briefe*, vol. 1 (Munich: Hanser, 1970), p. 855.
8. Wallace Stevens, 'The Snow Man', *Harmonium* (New York: St Martin's Press, 1975), p. 24.
9. Cited in Arturo Pérez-Reverte, *The Flanders Panel*, tr. Margaret Jull Costa (New York: Bantam, 1996), p. 1.
10. Not included in Brod's edition of the diary.

FURTHER READING

Bernheimer, Charles, *Flaubert and Kafka: Studies in Psychopoetic Structure* (New Haven: Yale University Press, 1982).

Corngold, Stanley, *Franz Kafka: the Necessity of Form* (Ithaca, NY: Cornell University Press, 1988).

Gray, Richard, *Constructive Deconstruction. Kafka's Aphorism: Literary Tradition and Literary Transformation* (Tübingen: Niemeyer, 1987).

Karl, Frederick R., *Franz Kafka: Representative Man: Prague, Germans, Jews, and the Crisis of Modernism* (New York: Ticknor and Fields, 1991), esp. pp. 509–13 (on 'The Village Schoolmaster') and pp. 729–31 (on 'A Little Woman').

Koelb, Clayton, *Kafka's Rhetoric: the Passion Of Reading* (Ithaca, NY: Cornell University Press, 1989).

Politzer, Heinz, *Parable and Paradox* (Ithaca, NY: Cornell University Press, 1962).

Sokel, Walter, 'Between Gnosticism and Jehovah: the Dilemma in Kafka's Religious Attitude', *The Germanic Review* 60:2 (1985), 69–77.

Triffit, Gregory B., *Kafka's Landarzt Collection: Rhetoric and Interpretation* (New York: Lang, 1985).

7

JULIAN PREECE

The letters and diaries

The letters complete the œuvre, like a map makes the world complete. We, the unbelievers, who are not satisfied with miracles and need tangible explanations, look for clues and logical reasons.

Milena Jesenská[1]

Letters can cheer me up, move me, or arouse my admiration, but they used to mean much more to me, too much for me to see in them now an essential form of life. I have not been deceived by letters but I deceived myself through them; for years I warmed myself in the warmth they would produce when the whole lot got thrown on to the fire.

Kafka to Robert Klopstock (January 1922; *B1*: 369)

For long bursts of his intensively creative life, from the autumn of 1912 until his death less than twelve years later, Kafka appears to have written every single day. He had been busy before this 'breakthrough', though much writing in the forms of both diaries and fiction he apparently destroyed. His last piece of writing is a letter – to his parents on the subject of his various ailments – which he composed less than twenty-four hours before his death in the hospital at Klosterneuburg on the edge of Vienna. Typically, he wants to put off a proposed visit by them, arguing that he is in an unfit state to be seen; typically too for his last years, he downplays the seriousness of his condition with self-deprecating humour. There are other familiar stylistic characteristics and thematic preoccupations: he straightaway gets down to the point, dispensing with preliminaries, as he invariably does in letters and postcards, though there is perhaps a weariness to the businesslike 'now about the visits'.[2] The second sentence echoes his habitual fretting over a routine matter: 'I have been thinking about it every day.' There then follows a lyrical, not remotely mawkish passage on past moments of family harmony. He has had a glimpse of happy 'togetherness', although perhaps it was just 'once a few hours in Franzensbad', which correspond to idyllic childhood recollections of drinking beer in the company of his father, that ogre of legend.

Life occasionally granted Kafka such epiphanies, which often he appears to have realised only in retrospect. One family point emerges from the letters addressed to his youngest sister, Ottla: Hermann Kafka, the self-made entrepreneur who had little understanding for what interested his son, has an unduly bad press if only 'Letter to his Father' is taken into account.

The letter is thoughtfully, even artfully constructed: his second paragraph details the reasons the parents should not come to Vienna after the first had held out high hopes of what their visit could be like. It opens with a rhetorical turn: 'That and much else speak for the visit, but there is also much which speaks against it.' The way he suggests that they would prefer not to come when he means he would prefer their not coming is typical of the narrative style in his fiction, where his figures invariably show awareness of such doubled nuances, meaning both what they say and its opposite. This is why he gives his physical appearance ('I am still not very pretty, not even worth looking at') and his inability to talk properly as reasons for the concerned parents to stay away from him. If those two comments make one think of Gregor Samsa from 'The Metamorphosis', then the reasoning in the long sentence which begins 'Everything is beginning for the best' is reminiscent of the logic of *The Trial*.

A few hours after writing this letter, Franz Kafka was dead; the last words are scribbled by his companion and lover of the last nine months, Dora Diamant.

The earliest substantial texts by Kafka which have survived are also letters, to two schoolfriends, Paul Kisch and Oskar Pollak. It is remarkable that while in fiction Kafka did not find his mature voice until 'The Judgement' in 1912, his letters evince his characteristic wit right from the start. What is more, they explore themes which will preoccupy him in his maturity. The advice the nineteen-year-old gives to Kisch, for instance, on a story Kisch has sent him anticipates much of the artistic soul-searching in his diaries written in the years ahead:

> A little tremor, a little mood, a little life (not little, but made little) wrapped up nicely in honourable German syntax nowhere hammered out of necessity – I don't have to write, but I'm writing – nowhere lived from the inside.
>
> (4.II.03; B2: 20)

Six months earlier he had written to Pollak that 'a letter is like a leading ram in a flock of sheep, soon twenty more letters will follow in its tracks' (24.VIII.02; B2: 12), which Felice Bauer among others would understand all too well. Kafka's at times pained sense that real communication by letter was impossible – because the gap between what he meant and what he could say (in language, on paper) was too wide – is revealed in his first letter to

Pollak to have its roots in the *Sprachkrise* ('crisis of language') of the turn of the century (04.11.02; *B2*: 10–11), associated with Hugo von Hofmannsthal's 'Letter to Lord Chandos'. The multiple ways he reflects on the medium of writing in his letters, and on letter writing in particular, is of course distinctly literary, which is one reason for considering the bulk of his letters alongside his fiction.

Kafka often appeared to prefer the disembodied act of communication by letter to an encounter in the flesh, however. Seeing Milena Jesenská for a second time was a drab but anticipated disappointment, which he had struggled to put off. It is the turning point (for the worse) of their epistolary relationship which had held out the prospect of happiness. His endlessly putting off Felice, the excuses for not coming to Berlin to see her, for not staying long if he did come, for not seeing her at all or only for a few minutes, are, though one can imagine the torment it causes her, a comic high point. And he was aware of that comedy, desperate though it made him too.

If the notion of a 'crisis of language' was a commonplace at this time, then Kafka's interest in the mechanics of the postal system, on which communication by letter depended, in collection and delivery times, in rates of postage and the relative speeds they denoted, in short the acts of sending and receiving written text, is all his own. It begins too in the first letter to Pollak. The occupations of his three most important correspondents should be borne in mind in this respect. Max Brod was an executive at the Prague Post Office. If Milena translated his texts from German into Czech, which was the reason she approached him in the first place, Felice declared on their first meeting that she liked nothing better than typing up manuscripts, an apparently subordinate feminine role. She worked moreover for a company which produced 'parlographs', the forerunner to the dictaphone, transforming speech into text. There is a pattern to Kafka's choice of correspondents.

The letter writer must sometimes overcome practical obstacles. He knows his missive can fall into the wrong hands or get lost in the post, as Felice's second letter to him apparently did. It can cause the addressee anguish or embarrassment if secrets are revealed, as happens at that exquisite moment five weeks into the correspondence with Felice when Kafka's mother finds one of Felice's letters and writes to Felice herself to warn, to explain, and to ask for help. In particular she is worried about her son's health and implores Felice to ask him about his eating and sleeping habits in the hope that her solicitude will encourage him to change. This sort of thing happened more than once and both Kafka and his correspondents made efforts to prevent it happening again by using false names and *postes restantes*. Kafka wrote to Brod as Martin Salvat. His sudden change from *Du* to *Sie* – from the warmly intimate to the distantly formal – in the letter to Milena cited below, which stands in such contrast to the gradual increase in intimacy culminating in the original change from *Sie* to *Du*, is not explained by encroaching frostiness or the gap of fifteen months since the last letter. Kafka just knows that her husband might be reading. The letters to Felice teem with the hidden presences of others.

Kafka knew that his parents would read any letter he sent to his sister Ottla unless he took steps to prevent them. At one point he imagines, from what she wrote back to him, his father's reaction to his earlier request for sugar to be sent to him in Merano. Sugar was rationed in 1920; he needed it to make lemonade which would help to put on weight:

> Very clear in your letter how our father read my card for the second time, this second reading, when he grabs for something to read after the game, anything which might be lying around on the table, is so much more important than the first reading. As long as one always remained aware of the responsibility as one writes... 'There you have your dear son. What sort of seedy establishment has he crept into now? They don't even have sugar there.'   (17.IV.20)[3]

Two letters later he gives his parents some purely factual information on the weather and the length of his sick leave before turning to Ottla, indicating to them that the rest of the letter is meant for her eyes only. His tone alters instantly. Most of these family letters, including the small collection addressed to his parents, which was discovered in Prague in 1986, are useful as biographical documents, sources of information on Kafka's life, which does help us understand his fictions, but which is, as he documented and dramatised himself to such a degree and to such great effect, of legitimate interest in itself.

Felice's responses and non-responses can be imagined; imagining them in fact makes up one of the joys of reading his letters to her, not to mention the letters to and from others about one or the other of them, which are included, quite rightly, in the volume entitled *Letters to Felice*. What the brief and relatively few letters by the others about him show is how unusual and precious, or, in the case of his mother, perverse, others thought him. As well as Grete Bloch and Kafka's mother, both Brod and his sister are involved; Felice appeals to Brod for help and receives one of the two most revealing pen-portraits of his friend Franz – the other is by Milena, who was also in touch with Brod, another detail which makes us think we might be reading novels. The reader of the published edition of *Letters to Felice* is sometimes in the position of the cleverer reader of *The Trial*, knowing more than the epistolary protagonist. Kafka finds out only later that his mother has written and that Brod and Felice have exchanged letters. These touches add to the literary value of the collections and to the sense that we are witnesses to his inner struggles which he fought within a domestic context we can visualise.

Kafka complains to Hedwig Weiler, with whom he conducted his first and inconclusive love affair in letters, 'What little use is an encounter in letters, it is like two people separated by a sea splashing from the bank' (28.VIII.07; B2: 57–8). As he was writing to Weiler he was working on *Wedding Preparations in the Country*, as well as the short pieces which would make up his first published collection, *Contemplation*. But if they are barely a prelude to the extraordinary work which followed, the Weiler letters offer a little more than a foretaste of the epistolary obsession with Bauer which fed his fiction and upon which his fiction in turn depended – in a manner the word 'inspired' quite fails to capture. Kafka wants to know all about what Weiler did one evening, what time she arrived, what time she left, what she was wearing, where she sat, whether she laughed and danced a lot, whose eyes she looked into for a quarter of an hour, whether she was tired at the end and whether she slept well (11.IX.07; B2: 60). In his second letter to Felice she is asked to keep 'a little diary' which will tell him 'the thousand things about whose existence and possibility I know nothing' (28.IX.12; BF: 46). This evidently frightened her (he has pounced, come to the point, a little too soon) because their correspondence all but spluttered out before it had begun.

Weiler turned out not to be the right partner at all. She does not understand his simile about splashing in a sea and took offence. She then objects to him asking all these questions, which causes him to backtrack. He teases her in response, replying to her wish to reimburse him for the expense he had incurred in advertising for a job for her that the sum was too trivial to mention, but that she would be welcome to pay for the champagne he had drunk to her health the previous evening (24.IX.07; B2: 65). He has been warned off, he is not ready for the assault: the next time, some five years later with Felice, it will be different.

The appearance of daily literary production is deceptive. There were much longer fallow periods, when, for reasons of ill-health or mental indisposition, Kafka wrote nothing at all or very little. At other times, the autumn of 1912 is the most explosive, he wrote on two fronts at once, producing a letter or two per day to Felice, as well as 'The Judgement', ' The Metamorphosis', and most of *The Man who Disappeared*. This left, understandably, little time for his diary, whose function, what Hartmut Binder calls 'mastering' or 'coming to terms' with himself (*Selbstbewältigung*), was taken over by letter writing.[4] Not being able to write becomes at other times the main subject in his diary and the subject of writing preoccupies him in letters too. At least from 1910 when he began writing in it systematically, the diary became essential preparation for the production of fiction: half the three volumes cover the years 1910 to 1912, the other half the whole of the following decade. This intensive diary writing clearly laid the foundations for his first burst of mature fiction writing. Apart from the phenomenal autumn of 1912, he devoted himself to one project, one genre at a time, which is one reason neither diaries or letters contain much information on how he produced so much of his fiction. Yet the diary entries for January 1922, a mixture of sketches, reflections, images, and aphorisms, are ultimately far more revealing of his state of mind as he began *The Castle* than any number of whimsical musings, let alone a blow-by-blow account of how he wrote each chapter. What he gives us instead is an idea of how the images began to explode in his mind and where he felt they were trying to take him. We get them in what is more or less a raw state but what he does not tell is how they were translated into the prose of *The Castle*. It is clear, however, from Malcolm Pasley's examination of the manuscripts, that he sometimes polished up what he wrote in his diary, that there was a 'gap between impression and diary-account, or between an initial idea and its development as a diary-meditation'.[5] This makes diary writing, like letter writing, very much a literary form.

The two modes of writing are thus linked in numerous ways. His talent for observation is revealed in both: in reply to Felice wondering whether he took much notice of her at their first meeting, which pre-dated his first introductory letter by five to six weeks, he responds with several pages of description, which she would have found overwhelming and intimidating. His first letter to Robert Klopstock, a young medical student he had befriended at the sanatorium in Matliary, is in a slightly different vein, detailing the strokes of good fortune thanks to which he had procured a seat on the train back to Prague. It is a highly entertaining anecdote which Kafka narrates perfectly and – so it seems – quite effortlessly. The narrative ingredients and his own perspective on the events have all the hallmarks of the Kafkaesque: the series of mistakes (getting back into the wrong carriage at a stop), chance encounters (with a woman he knew by sight from the sanatorium), the woman's determination to overcome adversity by locating seats in a first-class compartment, the subsequent need to persuade the conductor to change the status of the compartment from first to second class, which engenders the offence and consequent departure of the other passengers who had paid for first-class tickets. While the woman and her two friends are just forceful individuals not prepared to take no for an answer in such a situation, Kafka is amazed at the 'mass of dream-like interconnected coincidences' (2.IX.21; *B1*: 348–9) and stands back to observe them. He is also convinced of his own lack of importance, mentioning that the women did not know his name. The one he recognised could not even remember when she first spoke to him (whereas he remembers *her* very well). The diaries too are full of vignettes from everyday life, but, as Binder stresses, all of them are noted for a reason, making it imperative to know the precise context, in his mental or intellectual preoccupations.[6] In reporting on his own experiences, relating and dissecting what has happened to him, or observing scenes in public between individuals, he is practising a highly literary talent.

Most of Kafka's daily writings, however, are letters, which, in sheer volume, are approximately twice as long as his collected fictions – his novels, stories, fragments, and aphorisms – and three times as long as his diaries. He wrote to male friends, most notably Brod (1904–24), Pollak (1902–04), and Klopstock (1921–4), to family, especially his sister Ottla, to editors and publishers, and to women, most notably Felice Bauer (1912–17) and Milena Jesenská (1920–3), but also Grete Bloch (1913–14) and Minze Eisner (1919–23) and before them all, in a bizarre dress rehearsal for the epistolary dramas to follow, to Hedwig Weiler (1907–9). These letters are both the most intimate texts Kafka wrote and, paradoxically, among the most public. We know for a fact – if they were sent – that he intended at least one person to read them (and to read them in that form), which is not necessarily the case with his unpublished fiction. Even his diaries were never entirely private, as he read extracts from them to friends, and he handed them, together with 'Letter to his Father', to Milena so that she could understand him better. Even the most intimate form of writing is always an act of potential communication. Doubts over their status as private or public documents is another point the letters and diaries have in common with the fictions.

'Letter to his Father' never reached its addressee. It thus did not serve its intended purpose of explaining Kafka's point of view to his father in the row over his choice of fiancée number two, Julie Wohryzek, in 1919. More than any other single piece of his autobiographical writing, however, this 'letter', which Brod first published in a volume of fiction, has helped generate a powerful component of the Kafka myth: his subordination in classic Freudian manner to an overbearing father. 'Letter to his Father' is a hybrid literary document, a piece of rhetorically heightened autobiography. It reveals a poetic truth expressed with an equally poetic licence and, as Walter Müller-Seidel has recently argued, it portrays a small-minded personality whose views are fuelled by resentment, prejudice, and insecurity, in what was to prove a lethal and all too common mixture in Europe at that time.[7] The father of 'Letter to his Father' is a satirical send-up: the boorish uncomprehending patriarch, forever comparing his son's easy life with the hardship he had endured in his own youth and the hard work which he never left behind. One of the keys to understanding the letter is to appreciate that Kafka junior was a second-generation migrant, whose views and self-understanding were invariably radically different from those of his parents. There are worlds which separate them. The memorable phrasing and the bitter humour are not the letter's only literary features: the narrative perspective is carefully handled. Kafka explains his whole life, his upbringing, relationship with his sisters and mother, his schooling and choice of career, his writing, his religion, his place in society, exclusively through his relationship with his father, while deliberately ignoring all other factors. That this is a rhetorical ploy is clear not only at the end when he imagines his father's response and thus interrupts his own narrative perspective with another. It accounts for why he believes both of them to be both innocent and guilty, innocent from their own point of view, guilty from that of the other. This is ultimately a literary rather than a private truth.

Letters are in the first place personal, of course. Things are said in them which only the recipient is meant to read – and the way Kafka changes his tone according to correspondent makes us hesitate to take any of them at face value. They are never unadulterated, purely factual, biographical sources, even though Kafka critics had used them primarily as such until quite recently. Kafka's tone to Pollak differs from that to Brod, as he engages with the different personalities of the two men.[8] The presence of his addressee can always be felt; there is always a dialogue between the two, which meant writing to Kafka could never be a dull experience. He wanted responses and in return reacted to what was said to him. Changes in tone on the same day give the lie to any notion that he was, in the correspondence with Felice, for example, in the grip of a debilitating passion, which the quantity of his writing to her might lead one at first to assume. He is in control, the master of phrasing. Indeed, possibly the most remarkable thing about the letters to Felice and to Grete Bloch, when she for a while superseded her friend in his epistolary affection, is that they do not document a love affair, they constitute it. We do not read to find out about what happened: the letters themselves are what happened. Similarly, it is wrong to say, though that does not reduce the frequency with which it is said, that Felice somehow 'inspired' 'The Judgement' (it is dedicated to her).

It is, however, when we get to the gaping holes in the texts, that the two great letter collections, to Felice and to Milena, resemble the fictions most closely – not only on account of their physical incompleteness. The greatest entrance in *Letters to Felice*, what makes them assume the quality of an epistolary novel rather than a collection of biographical materials, is that of Felice's friend, Grete Bloch, whom Felice sought to employ as an intermediary and to whom Kafka transferred his attentions. This move makes him vulnerable to charges of bad faith in his dealings with Felice, whose own person and personality, wishes, feelings, aspirations, are so often of no consequence to him. Felice has been in fact an empty space; she could be, if not quite any woman, like the Fräulein Bürstner figure in the last pages of *The Trial*, then any one of a large number of women. She is someone he latches on to in order to play out his doomed fantasies about marriage, someone whose image he needs in order to write. A woman can never have been *used* in quite this way before.

While the letters which he sent are at least complete in themselves, the *collections* of letters, are, like the three novels, like the diaries, like the collections of unpublished short fiction, incomplete. Fragmentariness is an essential component of the Kafkaesque. Individual letters written by Kafka himself have got lost and, except in Brod's case, very little that others wrote to him has survived. While he must have received fewer letters than he sent, as he invariably responded immediately and at length and complained about not getting answers, he must have been far more casual or destructive with the writings of others than he was with his own or they were with his. For biographers this appears frustrating because they have to reconstruct mentally the other side's responses and point of view. For Milena this has been done as thoroughly as it probably can be: she has inspired three biographies, her collected newspaper columns have been translated into German and some into English.[9] There is even an edition of her letters to others, pointedly entitled *Letters from Milena*.[10] The revised edition of Kafka's letters to her includes her obituary of him, her letters to Brod about him, and a newspaper article by her which they discussed. In contrast, Felice was not a published writer and played no public role except that of Kafka's fiancée. A biography of her would, forty years after she died, probably be impossible (though one of Dora Diamant, whose grave in East London has recently been identified, is in preparation). This led to an under-estimation of Felice's role, personality, and professional status; only in the last decade or so have critics recognised the newness of her professional independence and her business success. Whatever she was, she was not, as Josef K. says of Fräulein Bürstner, 'a little typewriter woman who would not put up resistance to him for long' (*DP*: 252). In the end Felice resisted him by doing the one thing which frustrated him the most: not answering his letters. For this reason Klaus Theweleit calls her 'one of the first career women in an industrial company': 'she is neither stupid nor as empty as Kafka diagnoses her face at their first meeting (and as most critics have sought to represent her: hopelessly inferior to Kafka; inappropriate for him etc)'.[11] Felice's silences drive Kafka to distraction.

The order in which the letters are presented inevitably affects our reading, as entirely different narratives are constructed: *Letters to Felice* has all the trappings of a novel not least because some of the letters are not to her at all – but all are somehow *about* her. The critical edition, on the other hand, arranges all Kafka's letters chronologically, which quite shifts the emphasis at the beginning of the correspondence with Felice. It also excludes, quite rightly given its purpose, those written by others. But it generates new insights. Ten pages before his overture to Felice we read his foreboding remark to Brod after sharing with him (so is the manner of men) the full text of a postcard from a young woman he had recently met on their trip to Weimar. Amazed at the discrepancy between her actions in his presence, which had radiated indifference, and her warmly affectionate written words in response to his, he exclaims: 'If it were true that one can bind girls with writing!' (13.VII.12; B2: 160). Nine days later there is a further sign of what is to come in another letter to Brod. This time the reference is not to women but to the activity Kafka associated with his relationship with them: 'What I have written has been written in a lukewarm bath, I have not experienced the eternal hell of real writers, with the exception of a few bouts' (22.VII.12; B2: 163). The extraordinary drama which is about to unfurl is to have writing and women – one particular woman – at its heart.

Letters to Milena, more compact and more mature than *Letters to Felice*, are about the possibility of communication – of two people understanding one another completely. He is seductive, but not emotionally manipulative. Near the end of their correspondence, after a fifteen-month break, after in effect his failure to reach her, he writes of his hatred of letters because they can only increase the distance between two people, who can never express the truth to one another in writing:

> How can anyone come to the idea that human beings can relate to one another through letters! One can think of a human being who is far away and one can touch a human being who is near, everything else goes beyond human strength.
>
> (End of March 1922; BM: 302)

Kafka has a little over two years to live when he makes this comment and was half way through writing *The Castle*. There are signs in the early, irresistibly charming letters to Milena that he might have wanted to repeat this pattern with her. But she was made of different stuff and Kafka himself had matured by 1920. There is every sign that this was a match of equals; Kafka is dismayed by what she writes to him, she unsettles him, and he has to respond to her.

Coming from these letters one might easily think that he could not write to a woman without flirting, that writing to women was a form of calculated flirting, but this is not so. The letters to Minze Eisner, the young student he met at Schelesen, reveal a quite different side. Kafka behaves towards Eisner as an older friend, never moves from *Sie* to *Du*, and advises her on her chosen career as a horticulturalist, her training, and then marriage plans without a touch of condescension. He encourages her above all to break out of her provincial rural milieu, to be independent and get out into the world. Kafka repeats this role of mentor with the young Robert Klopstock and showers his sister Elli with advice on the right choice of school for her son, which she did not take.

Brod is the third of Kafka's great correspondents. There is no time when they were not writing to each other; Brod, in immediate recognition of his friend's unique talent, preserved every scrap of paper, letter or postcard from the time they met. The revised edition of these letters, which, uniquely for editions of Kafka's correspondence, includes some of Brod's own responses, underlines that Kafka wrote to Brod each year from 1904. In the first letter he gets himself into a tangle over apologising for his absence at a ball; a fortnight before his death in June 1924 he thanks Brod for a book and makes another apology, this time for his wretched physical state on Brod's last visit to Klosterneuburg. Many in between are classic pieces of prose which have made episodes in Kafka's life into literary events. These letters to his closest male friend, a busy successful writer, show Kafka in one of his most positive roles: not the importunate son veering between resentment and feelings of inadequacy, not the elder brother dispensing advice, and not the would-be or would-be-not lover. In this man-to-man encounter, he appears to repress or ignore his feelings. Emotional outpourings, expressions of despair and self-loathing, are few. The tone is more informative and to the point. If anything it is Brod who confides his feelings, about his marriage, his sexual dissatisfaction with his wife, and his philandering, little of which meets with Kafka's approval.

The bulk of the letters to Brod, nearly two-thirds, were written in the last third of the time covered by their correspondence (1904–24), in the last seven years, from 1917 onwards. The reason is simple: after coughing blood in the night of 12/13 August 1917, an episode he describes with macabre insight in letters to several different people (Ottla, Felice, Milena) and which he viewed, partly with relief, as a confirmation of his inner difference and as a fair conclusion to his five-year 'struggle' to marry Felice, Kafka left Prague for a series of 'cures' in Central European sanatoria or rural retreats. If the letters to Brod and to the family were the only biographical sources we possessed, Kafka's last seven years would amount to nothing as much as another *Magic Mountain*, chronicling physical and medical details, the opinions of specialists, news on diet and body weight, reports on exercise, rest, and fresh air. Finance is an increasing problem and Ottla is often charged with getting letters to his employers translated into decent Czech or with visiting his Director herself to discuss his sick leave or the possibility of retirement. In his last winter in Berlin, hyper-inflation wreaked havoc with his financial arrangements and he was dependent on money sent by sisters and parents.

Like the diaries, letters give some indication of the extent to which he noticed or was affected by current events, items which caught his eye in the newspaper, for instance, or great upheavals, like the First World War. In his diary he wrote several entries on the war, which belies the notion that he shut himself completely away from what was going on in the world. This is the time he was writing *The Trial* and 'In the Penal Colony'. On 6 August 1914 he is scornful of the flag-waving:

> These processions are one of the most repellent aspects of the war. Deriving from Jewish tradespeople, who have been one minute German and another minute Czech, admit as much to themselves, but are never allowed to shout out so loudly as they are now. Naturally they carry lots of others with them.
>
> (*TB2*: 167)

From the pen of a Gentile this would smack of anti-Semitism, from a Jew it shows awareness of what other Jews do in order to be accepted by the dominant German-speaking Austrians. It shows his awareness of how individuals and groups of individuals compete for favour and advantage, a major insight in his fiction, is by no means untouched by historical reality, as critics are sometimes tempted to argue.

References to the war continue. On 13 September he compares his worrying about Austrian defeats, which he had first thought would prevent him from writing, with his old worrying about Felice. On 4 November Pepa (Josef Pollak), his brother-in-law, is back from the front, 'screaming, excited, quite out of control' with tales of death, near escapes, and brutal punishments. On 24 November Kafka is helping Max and Elsa Brod distribute blankets to Jewish refugees from Galicia, with whom he has regular contact. Towards Christmas he writes of 'the defeats in Serbia, the senseless leadership' (*TB2*: 65). In April 1915 he travelled to the Hungarian front with his sister Elli to visit her husband, which gave rise to some of his best travel observations, a genre he had practised in competition with Brod on two journeys the friends undertook before the war.

But the phenomenon associated with current events which absorbed him the most was undoubtedly anti-Semitism and his Jewish identity. If this is a question of self-discovery before 1914, after 1918 it is more a matter of self-defence. Writing to Brod from Planá at the end of June 1922 he shows a rare grasp of a recent event. This was the assassination of the German Foreign Minister, Walter Rathenau, who was hated by the Nationalists on account of his talent, his business success, and the responsibility they imputed to him (quite falsely) for the unnecessary negotiated end to the war – unnecessary because Germany was undefeated in the field. Needless to say, Rathenau was of Jewish descent. Correctly decoding Brod's allusion to 'terrible political news', he responds:

> Do you mean anything other than Rathenau's murder? Incomprehensible that they let him live so long, the rumour of his murder was doing the rounds in Prague 2 months ago, Prof. Münzer was spreading it, it was so credible, was so much a part of Jewish and German fate and is described in your book exactly. – But I have said enough already, the whole matter extends far beyond my circle of vision, even the circle of vision in front of my window is too big for me.
>
> (30.VI.22)[12]

He briefly opens the window to the world or glances quickly through it only to shut it quickly again or pull the curtains. But that does not mean he was unaware of what was going on outside.

The Jewish theme takes up some of the most delicate but also amusing and sometimes trenchant passages in the *Letters to Milena*. In the letters to Brod he returns to the way he is treated as a Jew in Matliary and elsewhere. Allegiance and identity were all-consuming preoccupations at the time when the multilingual, multicultural Austro-Hungarian empire was broken up, and the little nations, which had been subjects of the Kaiser, the Emperor, or the Tsar, formed themselves into states. In letters to Brod and Ottla from Matliary, he dissects the demographic make-up of guests and inhabitants – Slovaks, Hungarians, German-speakers, Jews. The break-up of the empire affects the plan to meet Milena for a night and a day in the border town of Gmünd, when suddenly arrangements for passports and border crossings in the new frontier town become symbolic of their difficulties in communicating with one another. In other respects current affairs or world events indeed bothered him very little. The link between Kafka and his times, which is similar to that between his literary work and his biography, has to be found elsewhere. It is surely located in his unique talent for observation, his ability to interpret gestures, comments, appearances to give them social, psychological, and metaphorical meaning.

His diaries, sometimes the sketchpad for his fictions, sometimes an outlet for his feelings, a private vehicle for self-expression, are less voluminous and take second place to his letters or literary writing. Often he uses the diary notebook for a fictional narrative, which possibly shows how the diary and the fictions went together, or it shows, more prosaically, that the diary notebook was the first paper he had to hand when he wanted to write. Whether in letters or in diaries, he seems to be always reporting on his dreams which he has a knack for remembering completely. There are themes and figures, images and situations, animals, which recur in the diaries' mini-narratives and fragments of narratives. We cannot know how Kafka would have prepared them for publication had he wanted to do so and had he lived. They are raw and in the wrong order because he used two or more notebooks at any one time for reasons which are not always apparent – and why should they be? Does an editor put them into chronological order and make a readable book out of them, as Brod did? If some readers get impatient with the uneven quality and eclectic nature of the entries and Kafka's inconsistent approach, others will see perfection in the imperfection. We get a glimpse not just of his private preoccupations but insight into how his creative mind works. The sequence which includes the first mention of Josef K. on 29 July 1914 shows him groping towards something after the dramatic bust-up with Felice in Berlin in the middle of the month. Suddenly one of the towering figures of twentieth-century literature makes his entrance on the printed page.

The letters' survival and their publication history mirror those of the more famous fictions too; Kafka's momentary destructive wish, which he had ample opportunity to carry out himself, applied to the letters with equal force. Readers had to wait until the 1980s for reliable editions of diaries and fictions and are still waiting for the five-volume critical edition to be completed, which will supersede Brod's 1958 volume. While some of Kafka's correspondents went to considerable lengths to ensure that his letters survived, they themselves often did not: Felice kept hers after she married and emigrated to the United States; she also looked after those given her by Grete Bloch, who was killed in the Holocaust; Milena, who died too in a concentration camp, gave her letters to Willy Haas, who published most of them shortly after the war; Ottla preserved everything in her possession, while other members of her family took no such care. Ernst Weiss, the best writer next to Franz Werfel, among his côterie of friends, took his own life the day after German troops occupied Paris in June 1940. His letters from and to Kafka, whom he accompanied to Berlin to visit Felice and break off the engagement, have not survived. Neither have Werfel's. Hartmut Binder lists several others.[13] The fate of these correspondents, which mirrors the interrupted publishing history of Kafka's works, enhances the appeal or mystique of all Kafka's writings in a way which has not necessarily helped understanding of them. Brod began his task of posthumous publication at a time when Kafka's world was already under threat; he completed the job after that world had been obliterated. One result of this is that posterity came to know the autobiographical writings at the same time as the novels and stories, or not much longer afterwards. Only Letters to Felice (1967) and the Letters to Ottla and the Family (1974) were delayed in a more normal way. The fact remains that the circumstances of reception have rarely determined the reception to quite this degree: biographical mythologising infects the mythologising of the fictions.

In the second of the unsent instructions to Brod, Kafka writes 'most of the addressees you obviously know, it is mainly a question of Frau Felice M, Frau Julie (née) Wohryzek und Frau Milena Polak' (29.XI.22; *Eine Freundschaft*, vol. 2, p. 422). Felice and Milena long ago became silent heroines in twentieth-century literary legend, but Julie Wohryzek, who he met in the Bohemian mountain village of Schelesen in spring 1919, was the truest of the trio. Not a word he wrote to her has been passed down. If the correspondence was worth destroying, there seems little reason to think that Kafka's relationship with her, which after all gave rise to 'Letter to his Father', was much less dramatic or the letters it produced much less exciting. Yet because the letters no longer exist, it is almost as if she never did.

What does all this writing tell us about the novels and stories, which despite interest in the life have to remain the focus of interest? Sometimes he comments on individual stories, most notably on 'The Judgement' and 'The Metamorphosis', and such comments always add something to the understanding of a literary text. They are, however, relatively rare and have been quoted to death. Another more rewarding avenue is to work out how ideas and motifs which form the substance of the fictions recur elsewhere, either pre- or post-dating the fictions. Another approach is to say that the drama of his inner life powered his writing and that his other textual out-pourings helped him concentrate, getting his thoughts and ideas straight. Given the emotional mess that he lived in and expressed so forcefully, it is surprising how he could somehow block it out while he wrote his fiction, distance himself from the turmoil, control it to produce exquisitely crafted works of art. Looked at in this way, his work is anything but autobiographical. A further approach is to view Kafka's life as one of his greatest narratives, which is certainly what has happened in some more popular reception. There are key episodes and well-known formulations which have become part of Kafka-folklore, explored most recently in Robert Crumb and David Mairovitz's comic-book for students, *Kafka for Beginners*. Writing 'The Judgement' through the night is as famous a topos as any in the story itself. It has the status of myth or legend and the idea that it represents a breakthrough obscures the fact that he had already had work accepted for publication. Other passages have become famous from repeated quotation in different contexts. Kafka does, after all, play roles in both his letters and his diaries. *Letters to Felice* ingrain his daily routine in a reader's imagination, his long mornings in the office which ended around 2pm, a time-table he prized because it gave him freedom in the afternoon and energy for other activities in the evening, his double life, which began with evening writing continuing into the small hours. His letters to Felice are his way of talking to a partner at the end of a long day; the couple lived together in his mind during the long period of stability from the end of November 1912 to February 1913.

But what makes the letters unique is Kafka's talent for writing; what enhances their readability is their cumulative effect. The opening sequence of the *Letters to Felice* could hardly be bettered in an old-fashioned epistolary novel. In the first the hero (F.K.) has reason to believe his beloved will barely remember him, that she has spent precious few moments thinking about him since they parted after one evening together, spent for the most part in the company of others. His excuse for writing to her now, which necessitated some determined detective work to get hold of her address, as she makes him tell her in his next letter, is a plan they hatched, though clearly with no seriousness on either part, to travel together to Palestine, already a destination for Zionist immigrants and still part of the Ottoman empire in 1912. Having reminded her of this intention, Kafka stresses in a second paragraph the need for detailed preparations, which they will make, presumably, by letter. His third paragraph then begins: 'One thing I must confess, however bad it sounds and however badly it fits in with what I have just said: I am an unpunctual letter writer' (20.IX.12; *BF*: 43). This is the first mention of either 'letters' or 'writing' and is of tangential relevance at best. As a rhetorical and imaginative leap the statement reveals the letter writer's real intentions: to engage in intimate correspondence with a woman. Typically, the statement takes the form of an admission of a failing which is designed to engage the addressee emotionally and put the writer of the letter at the centre of attention. It is manipulative. His next sentence qualifies his failing whimsically, by saying that of course the typewriter helps him, in order to end with a paradox which counterposes mind and body, the material with the spiritual, in a way which appears clever but which possibly does not mean anything.

He continues with another statement which is soon disproved, to the effect that he does not mind if his correspondent does not write back promptly. His use of *erschrecken* (to frighten or terrify) is calculated to bring his reader, the unprepared Fräulein Bauer, up with a jolt: the word does what it means. This whole paragraph turns out to be all about writing and communicating, as he now returns to the practical business of putting a new piece of paper (impersonal headed writing paper from the Workers' Accident Insurance Institute) into his typewriter. In the next sentence, the most complicated and complex of those we have so far had, he half takes back what he has just said, admitting 'that I have perhaps made myself out to be much more difficult than I am', referring to his creation of this impression as a mistake which he deserved to make. The second main clause of the sentence is part self-dramatisation and more importantly one of those ambiguous rhetorical questions without a question mark. The fourth and final paragraph begins by blaming again the material conditions of writing – the unaccustomed typewriter – for his having wandered off his ostensible subject. The list of words to attach to 'travel', first the innocuous 'companion', followed by the ambivalent 'leader', culminating in the wholly inappropriate but in the circumstances prophetic, 'tyrant', is calculated to disconcert, to intrigue, to arouse pity once more by making himself small immediately after predicting future inappropriate qualities. He ends by getting very neatly to the point he had in mind all along by asking her – not for a dance, not to go with him to see a film or to have a meal – but to start a correspondence with him. It is one of the most beguiling and mildly threatening requests in world literature.

This opening letter is rhetorically perfect, teasingly ambiguous, charming and intimidating all at the same time, moving masterfully to its goal after beginning so casually. That he wrote it after office hours but in the office and on office paper signals that his private and professional lives are not as easily compartmentalised as he would have us think. He is presumably telling the truth when he says in his next letter, written eight days later, immediately on receipt of her reply: 'How often! – not wanting to exaggerate, I will say on ten evenings – did I put that letter together before dropping off to sleep' (28.IX.12; BF: 45). Ten days of uncertainty and indecision, an inability to transfer the words, which he said were 'put together in ordered form', from his mind to paper because 'within each sentence there are transitions, which have to stay in suspension before being written down'. As we saw, he eventually managed these transitions with great skill, but he was well aware that he could be saying one thing and meaning both the opposite and something slightly different at the same time. Kafka has something of the stalker, the voyeur, the controlling flirt in these early letters.

A letter from near the beginning of the correspondence with Milena shows great discrepancies. The last of the undated letters from May 1920 starts with what is presumably a response to a comment from her – '(yes, the [letter] heading is becoming tiresome)'. The brackets help to give it the immediacy of speech, an impression sustained by the grammar and punctuation of the whole of the first paragraph. What we can effectively call the main clause, 'I have never lived among German people' (BM: 17), conveys a personal and cultural loneliness, amplified in the rest of the first half of the letter which is about communication between two people. Milena's switch to her native Czech has brought her closer to him because the language is closer to her; with him, we are invited to visualise her – 'the movements of your body, your hands, so quick, so decisive', in an effort which approximates to a physical meeting. But it is only 'almost an encounter'. And only writing letters has brought her this close to him. The winding sentence takes a turn on 'anyway' (*allerdings*) when he tries to look her in the face: 'anyway when I try to raise my eyes up to your face – what a story this is – fire breaks out in the course of the letter and I can see nothing but fire'. In his second letter to her, before she had replied to him, he had added in a postscript 'that I cannot in fact remember your face in any particular detail' (April 1920; *BM*: 5). Readers coming straight from *Letters to Felice*, which evolved so seamlessly into 'Letters to Grete', can be forgiven at this stage for thinking that the identity of the woman correspondent is not going to matter. As he lifts his gaze, the blazing that he sees, an image which recurs in these letters in similar circumstances, is ignited by the thought of intimacy – not really sexual: beyond that – with a woman. The next paragraph is a little cryptic as it evidently refers, once more, to comments Milena has made to him. It is worth saying that in replying to them he treats them with respect, that he appears to show insight into her character and the advice that he gives shows sympathy but not a trace of condescension. He gives encouragement and wants to strengthen her resolve to continue doing what she has decided to do, while, from a more experienced position, holding out the prospect that her travails will end. The tone is delicate, understanding, apparently genuine: even the potentially hackneyed expression, 'all one can do is silently kiss your hand', is invested with meaning. He still retains the distanced formality appropriate to the *Sie* form of address, however. His own feelings are kept in check, under control. There is perhaps an intimation that this will not always be the case and that the two of them are preparing for an experience or for an attempt at a relationship. There will be joy in getting to know her but 'testing himself' is greater than that joy. But does he mean the joy of knowing her will not be as great as the joy of self-testing or does he mean that self-testing, with or without joy, is greater? His grammar obscures the distinction. There is confidence that he will be able to tell whether or not she is withholding herself from him in her letters by not telling him everything or by painting a rosy picture of other things. There then comes the first, ever so slightly coquettish, reference to his own emotion: 'it would cause me twice as much pain'. The third of his three possibilities, which is that which the two of them try to take, is light years ahead of his preying overture to Felice. They will try to do it together.

That the experience of writing to Milena was ultimately no more satisfying than writing to Felice is not in dispute. The reasons both correspondences foundered in personal terms and yet generated precisely formulated texts (the letters themselves, *The Trial*, with Felice; *The Castle*, with Milena) are similar. The impossibility of reaching the object of a quest or finding out the truth in the novels is matched by the failure in the letters. Seen in this light the letters belong with the fictions, they are works of literary art.

NOTES

1. Milena Jesenská, 'Briefe bedeutender Leute' (1920), in *Alles ist Leben: Feuilletons und Reportagen 1919–1939*, ed. Dorothea Rein (Munich: btb, 1999), pp. 21–4. First published 1984.
2. Franz Kafka, *Briefe an die Eltern aus den Jahren 1922–1924*, ed. Josef Čermák and Martin Svatos (Fischer: Frankfurt aM, 1993), pp. 80–2.
3. *Briefe an Ottla und die Familie*, ed. Hartmut Binder and Klaus Wagenbach (Frankfurt aM: Fischer, 1974), p. 79.
4. Hartmut Binder, 'Die Tagebücher', in *Kafka in neuer Sicht: Mimik, Gestik und Personengefüge als Darstellungsform des Autobiographischen* (Stuttgart: Metzler, 1976), pp. 34–116, here p. 110.
5. Pasley, *Kafka's Diary*, p. 90.
6. Binder, 'Die Tagebücher', p. 104.
7. Walter Müller-Seidel, 'Franz Kafkas Brief an den Vater: ein literarischer Text der Moderne', *Orbis Litterarum* 42 (1987), 353–74.
8. Gerhard Kurz, 'Schnörkel und Schleier und Warzen: die Briefe Kafkas an Oskar Pollak und seine literarischen Anfänge', in Gerhard Kurz (ed.), *Der junge Kafka* (Frankfurt aM: Suhrkamp, 1984), pp. 68–101.
9. By her daughter, Jana Černá, *Kafka's Milena* (London: Souvenir, 1987), tr. A. G. Brain; by her friend in Ravensbrück, Margarete Buber-Neumann, *Milena: the Story of a Remarkable Friendship* (New York: Schocken, 1977), tr. Ralph Manheim; by Alena Wagnerová, *Milena Jesenská: 'Alle meine Artikel sind Liebesbriefe'* (Mannheim: Bollmann, 1994); and Mary Hockaday, *Kafka, Love and Courage: the Life of Milena Jesenská* (London: Deutsch, 1995).
10. *'Ich hätte zu antworten tage- und nächtelang': die Briefe von Milena*, ed. Alena Wagnerová (Mannheim: Bollmann, 1996).
11. Klaus Theweleit, 'Gespensterposten. Briefverkehr, Liebesverkehr, Eisenbahnverkehr. Der Zug ins Jenseits. Orpheus 1913 in Prag', *Buch der Könige. Orpheus und Eurydike* (Basel: Stroemfeld/Roter Stern, 1988), pp. 976–1045, here p. 976 and p. 999.
12. Max Brod/Franz Kafka, *Eine Freundschaft*, 2 vols., ed. Malcolm Pasley (Frankfurt aM: Fischer, 1989), vol. 2, *Briefwechsel*, p. 372.
13. Hartmut Binder, 'Briefe', in Binder, *Kafka-Handbuch*, 2 vols. (Stuttgart: Kröner, 1979), vol. 2, pp. 505–18.

FURTHER READING

Anderson, Mark M., 'Kafka's Unsigned Letters: a Reinterpretation of the Correspondence with Milena', in Anderson (ed.), *Reading Kafka: Prague, Politics and the Fin de Siècle* (New York: Schocken, 1989), pp. 241–56.
Binder, Hartmut, 'The Letters: Form and Content', in Angel Flores (ed.), *The Kafka Debate: New Perspectives for Our Time* (New York: Gordian, 1977), pp. 223–41.

Boa, Elizabeth, 'Letters from a Bachelor: Kafka's Letters to Felice Bauer' and 'An Intercourse of Ghosts: Kafka's Letters to Milena Jesenská', *Kafka: Gender, Class, and Race in the Letters and Fictions* (Oxford: Clarendon, 1996), pp. 45–77 and pp. 78–106.

Canetti, Elias, *Kafka's Other Trial: the Letters to Felice*, tr. Christopher Middleton (London: Caldar and Boyars, 1974).

Kittler, Friedrich A., *Gramophone, Film, Typewriter* (Stanford, Ca: Stanford University Press, 1999), tr., with intro. by Geoffrey Winthrop-Young and Michael Wutz.

Osborne, Charles, 'The Letters and Diaries', in *Kafka* (London and Edinburgh: Boyd, 1967), pp. 16–31.

Pasley, Malcolm, 'Kafka's Diary: Some Clues to its Mode of Composition', *Oxford German Studies* 17 (1988), 90–6.

Siegert, Bernhard, *Relays: Literature as an Epoch of the Postal System* (Stanford, Ca: Stanford University Press, 1999), tr. Kevin Repp.

Zilcosky, John, 'The Traffic of Writing: Technologies of "Verkehr" in Franz Kafka's *Briefe an Milena*', *German Life and Letters* 52 (1999), 365–81.

8

BILL DODD

The case for a political reading

One of the images of Kafka propagated by Kafka criticism, and supported by a much-quoted remark Kafka made in his diary, is of the solitary writer whose subject matter is his own 'dreamlike inner life' (6.VIII.14; D2: 77). Occasionally Kafka's diary entry on the outbreak of the Great War four days earlier is cited as proof of his distance from the political world: 'Germany has declared war on Russia. – Swimming in the afternoon' (D2: 75). But the interpretation sometimes placed on these words, that they belong to a writer far removed from the great events of his time, warrants investigation. Do they or do they not articulate emotional or intellectual distance, unconcern, even aloofness? In contrast, another diary entry, from the previous year: 'Don't forget Kropotkin!' (15.X.13; D1: 330) has attracted relatively little critical attention, even though Max Brod recalls that the memoirs of this nineteenth-century Russian anarchist were amongst Kafka's favourite books. Where it has been commented on it has often been played down. Here, too, the elliptical form of the diary entry itself does not help us make up our minds. What are we to read into these words: an intellectual or emotional commitment, a special indebtedness – or simply a note on an overdue library book?

Setting out to write about 'Kafka's politics' one is reminded of a famous piece of advice from Kafka himself: 'Give it up, give it up!' (GWC: 183). However, an attempt at a systematic study of Kafka's relation to politics has recently been published in German.[1] The very notion that he is in any sense a political writer, let alone a writer offering a radical critique of social institutions and conditions, is still somewhat contentious in Kafka scholarship. There are two major problems. First, to pose the question in the case of a writer like Kafka effectively means asking what we mean by 'the political', and how political interpretations of his work can legitimately be arrived at. He is obviously not a political writer in the way Bertolt Brecht and Heinrich Mann are. He never wrote anything of a campaigning nature, with a message, a programme for change; Kafka's writing in contrast to Brecht's and

Heinrich Mann's is not underlain by an ideology. Neither his writings nor what we know about his biography provide us with much evidence of political commitment, let alone a set of political beliefs. The second problem is that it is very unlikely that we can talk about Kafka's position on political issues without differentiating between the different phases of his life and literary production. Political readings rarely engage with Kafka's works produced before 1912, for example, thus helping to reinforce the idea that 'The Judgement' marks a major turning point in his work.

'Political' readings of Kafka need to take into account the particular qualities of his poetics and especially his relationship to realism, or at least to the ethical and social concerns of the realist tradition. At a key conference on Kafka held in Liblice in Communist Czechoslovakia in 1963 Roger Garaudy pleaded for a redefinition of the then orthodox Marxist definition of realism in literature, which, he claimed, was blinding Soviet Bloc critics to the powerful social criticism and hence underlying critical realism of Kafka's work. It is worth recalling Garaudy's words:

> Kafka is not a revolutionary. He awakens in people the consciousness of their alienation; his work, in making it conscious, makes repression all the more intolerable, but he does not call us to battle nor draw any perspective. He raises the curtains on a drama, without seeing its solution. With all his might he hates the apparatus of repression and the deception that says its power is God-given.[2]

Garaudy's argument, which would have made Kafka accessible to Marxist criticism, was seen as a heresy by the Soviet cultural establishment, and was crushed along with the Prague Spring of 1968 in which it participated. Meanwhile, critics in the West were already working out similar approaches, in their case in opposition to a different critical orthodoxy, that of the religious, metaphysical, solipsistic Kafka. Today, some would actually go beyond Garaudy's cautious statement that Kafka 'does not call us to battle nor draw any perspective'. Enlarging our sense of 'the political' is for these critics a task comparable to the enlarged sense of 'realism' which Garaudy called for then.

In the traditional 'left/right' political model, Kafka has often been perceived by those who read him 'politically' as a writer with underlying strong sympathies for the political left. There is some biographical evidence to support this view, though it is disconcertingly slight and fragmentary. The reliability of some of it has also been questioned, and some is almost certainly fabricated. What is certain is that Kafka's diaries and letters register his awareness of socialist and 'anarchist' figures such as Lily Braun, Alexander Herzen, Peter Kropotkin, and František Soukup. A sketch in the notebooks from 1918, 'The Propertyless Working Men's Association' ('Die besitzlose Arbeiterschaft'), has attracted particular attention from those interested in establishing his left-wing and even anarchist sympathies. Most intriguing perhaps are Kafka's remarks on the Bolsheviks in letters to Milena Jesenská from 1920, which suggest his strong approval for their cause. However, controversy surrounds his alleged attendance at meetings of the radical-anarchist *klub mladych* in Prague between 1909 and 1912, evidence for which is provided principally by one of its members, Michal Mareš. His testimony influentially shapes Klaus Wagenbach's biographies of Kafka and much of the secondary literature on Kafka's putative sympathies with radical politics,[3] but has been dismissed as a fabrication by Hartmut Binder and Ritchie Robertson.[4] To muddy the waters even further, Mareš's version of events appeared to find independent endorsement in Gustav Janouch's second edition of his *Conversations with Kafka*, but it is now widely accepted that this second, 'enhanced' edition contains fabrications.[5] Thus, some of the most promising biographical evidence in support of Kafka's sympathetic interest in the radical politics of his time needs to be handled with caution. These doubts concerning certain witnesses may have dented the case for a radical political reading, but they do not necessarily invalidate Wagenbach's broader conclusions. Other evidence (such as Kafka's remarks on the Bolsheviks) remains to be explained. In any event, one might argue, it is to Kafka's *texts* that one should look for the real evidence.

The evidence of the works themselves is, predictably, given Kafka's literary method, far from straightforward. Here, 'political' readings often appear to compete with other interpretive approaches, and must justify themselves by the quality of their insights, their compatibility with the biographical evidence, and most importantly, their fidelity to the text. There is a perhaps inevitable temptation on the part of critics to find what they set out to look for. Kafka criticism abounds with hobby-horse interpretations which fail to do justice to the structural complexity and semantic and semiotic richness of the fiction, reading into it excessively partial religious, existential, psychoanalytic, and other frames of meaning. It would be surprising, therefore, if the same did not hold for 'political' readings. Historically, much of this 'political' reading of Kafka has been engaged in the task of rescuing him from the aura of a *homo religiosus* with which Brod influentially announced him to the world, and with establishing his credentials as an author of critical enlightenment who belongs to the liberal canon. Recent feminist criticism, however – for example, Elizabeth Boa's study – has begun to ask searching questions which are beginning to modify this rather comforting consensus.

Of all Kafka's fictional works, it is those composed in 1912 which most obviously contain a substantial vein of social and political critique. One reason for this is that the religious and metaphysical themes prominent in later works are less pronounced in 1912. *The Man who Disappeared* precipitates Karl Roßmann, a Prague adolescent, as an innocent abroad into the world (from the perspective of Prague in 1912, a futuristic world) of laissez-faire American capitalism. This is encapsulated in the working conditions at the Hotel Occidental, the tragic story of the orphaned Therese (who seems to have stepped out of Dickens's London), the bewildering scale and pace of the modern metropolis, the radical division of labour under the modern Taylor System with its resulting alienation of workers from the products of their labour, the erosion of the distinction between workers and machines, all juxtaposed with the opulent life of the leisured, capital-owning class. Kafka himself noted the Dickensian template underlying this novel, in a remark which points up an indebtedness to Dickens's basic picaresque structure (8.x.17; *D2*: 188). But there is also a good case for seeing a strong vein of Dickensian social criticism in the novel. In the opening chapter Karl's disembarkation is delayed when he is drawn into the case of the stoker whose semi-articulate claims of injustice degenerate into incoherence and confusion when he nervously tries to put his case in the captain's quarters. Alfred Wirkner's study of Kafka's sources demonstrates his borrowings from the account by the Czech radical thinker (an 'anarchist', in some accounts) Dr František Soukup, whose lecture on America Kafka attended in June 1912.[6] Amongst the illustrations in Soukup's book on this subject, which presumably also featured in his lecture, there is a schematic cross-section of an ocean-going steamer. This shows the structure of the ship to be a microcosm of the social hierarchy. The well-heeled passengers occupy the spacious first-class quarters with their dining and recreation facilities on the uppermost decks. Beneath these are the cramped steerage quarters, and further down still, in the keel, the boilers fuelled by stokers in shirt sleeves. At the very top of this structure is the bridge, the captain's domain. Kafka picks up this symbolic topography and develops its implicit social critique in an evidently sympathetic way to depict the absolute gulf, in social class, in language, and perhaps also in standards of justice, between the world of stokers and the world of captains. Karl's future in the New World seems to be symbolically in the balance between these two extremes. It turns out that he is extremely well connected; rightly or wrongly, however, he sides instinctively with the stoker in his ill-defined but strongly felt sense of injustice, and it is the fate of the stoker which foreshadows his own. Though set on the other side of the globe, it seems reasonable to infer that the novel also works as a futuristic projection of the social and economic conditions in industrialising Bohemia as Kafka encountered them in the course of his work for the Workers' Accident Insurance Institute.

'The Metamorphosis', although it pointedly breaks with a realist aesthetic in its famous opening sentence, in many ways continues this social critique. The narrative focuses in great detail on the material conditions in which the Samsa family live. The affinities between Kafka's fictionalised world and Marx's analysis of capital find only occasional reference in the critical literature, and even then tend to be dismissed or played down. Robertson, for example, remarks that 'the analysis of Gregor's work and its effect on him is certainly unsparing, but would not be easily accommodated in a conventional Marxist view'.[7] Remarks such as these give the impression that the juxtaposition of Kafka and Marx is a critical taboo. One of the few critics to take the notion seriously is Walter Sokel, who finds the correspondences 'exact': 'Gregor's profound self-alienation corresponds, with uncanny precision, to Marx's definition of the "externalisation" of work under capitalism.'[8] That the alienation at the centre of 'The Metamorphosis' is discernibly material and social, and intimately connected with the nature and conditions of employment, is indisputable. The case for a material reading of alienation at any rate seems much stronger than that for a religious or metaphysical interpretation. Indeed, Gregor's half-articulated resentments concerning his job clearly reveal the emotional and psychological damage his economic bondage has inflicted, and, despite moments of what Marxists would call false consciousness ('He felt restored to human company', *TOS*: 86) are not without a certain analytical power – for example his description of his situation as one of 'the constant stream of changing faces with no chance of any warmer, lasting companionship' (77).

If the essentially sympathetic adaptation of Marxian and 'anarchist' social perspectives is a feature of *The Man Who Disappeared* and 'The Metamorphosis', it is less obviously central to 'The Judgement'. This story seems constructed rather on Freudian themes such as the return of the repressed, and the Oedipus complex, and it is to Freud, 'of course', that Kafka acknowledges a debt here (23.IX.12; *D1*: 276). A 'political' reading of this story, such as that advanced by J. P. Stern, takes power as the story's underlying theme and views it as a study in the workings of psychological domination. Stern argues that in this story Kafka 'endows a partly arbitrary ("subjective") law with the validity and power of a wholly objective law, *and shows that this is what he is doing*' (Stern's emphasis).[9] This is a crucial point. Kafka is a critical observer and exposer of power, not a helpless, passive, unreflecting victim; his fictions are designed to have an effect on us, his readers. Stern is essentially stating a point which unites most critics who see Kafka as a 'political'

writer, namely that his texts are not unreflecting expressions of disorientation and despair, but finely observed critiques of power which are presented
in an understated, yet provocative manner which in principle affords the
reader the possibility of critical orientation. The unobtrusiveness of Kafka's
method should not blind us to its ultimately provocative intent. His poetics
make particular demands on us, his readers, to read attentively. As Herbert
Kraft, one of the more controversial perhaps of the political readers, stresses:
'the decisive role is intended for the reader'.[10] In making this point, Kraft is
merely elaborating Kafka's own programmatic declaration to Oskar Pollak
in 1904 on what literature should be: a 'blow on the head' of the reader, an
'axe for the frozen sea inside us' (27.1.04; *LFFE*: 16).

If there is a respectable and familiar case for a socially engaged edge to
Kafka's writing in 1912, this case is somewhat harder to sustain for the later
works, and here the argument for a 'political' Kafka becomes more subtle. The mounting urgency of religious and metaphysical questions in the
works written in 1914 certainly poses considerable problems of interpretation for 'political' readings. Undeniably, religious, existential, psychological,
and biographical readings of *The Trial* and 'In the Penal Colony' need to be
acknowledged, though it is a moot point whether the religious motifs in these
works qualify them as religious. Brod's notion of Kafka as a religious writer
effectively precludes socially critical interpretations – witness Brod's hostility to the early political 'misinterpretations' of *The Trial*, for example by
Siegfried Kracauer.[11] Seeing him as a religious or metaphysical rebel, on the
other hand, has a quite different effect. It is important to see that a 'radical'
reading depends on a particular understanding of Kafka's literary method,
and in particular on the role of irony and travesty, which 'political' readings
tend to argue characterise the implicitly religious or metaphysical elements
in these two works. The extreme point of a political reading of *The Trial*
is the thesis, argued for example by Gilles Deleuze and Felix Guattari, that
Kafka is engaged on a radical questioning of idealist metaphysics, that the
novel is engaged in 'the dismantling of all transcendent justifications'[12] for
the Law that condemns and ultimately executes (or, as Kraft insists, murders) Josef K.[13] On this reading, any claims to a 'higher' truth, religious or
ethical, which the Court may appear to have are actually exposed during
the novel as the psychological and ideological tools of a secular power, and
its central theme is not guilt, or sinfulness, or conscience, but injustice and
oppression, the social psychology of power. A more differentiated view is
put forward by Peter Beicken, who argues that the novel is constructed as
a naked, degenerated power struggle between two antagonistic principles,
equating to indictment and justification, without a clear victor emerging.[14] A
similar debate surrounds 'In the Penal Colony'. An example of a materialist,

political reading is that by Roy Pascal, who relates the story, despite its exotic tropical setting 'half a world away', to the moral dilemmas posed for liberal intellectuals – such as Kafka – by the Great War in Europe, and specifically to the 'ideas of 1914', the unquestioning, xenophobic celebration of 'Gott, Kaiser, Vaterland'.[15] Pascal's 'political' reading of this story proceeds from a fine-grained study of the narrative perspective, and was also amongst the first to insist that the central, problematical, figure in this story is not the officer, but the traveller, whose vacillations in the face of such brutality and fanaticism provide the 'painful element' to which Kafka famously referred in a letter to his publisher Kurt Wolff (11.x.16; *LFFE*: 127). That Kafka's interest in penal settlements is also not purely as a source of exotic metaphor but as exemplars of real political phenomena such as colonialism, terror, and repression (with undertones of a possible Austrian solution to the 'Jewish problem') is argued forcefully by Walter Müller-Seidel in his study of Kafka's sources for this story.[16]

Certain interpretive approaches have tended to compete with this kind of political reading, and the debate about what might be called the referential value of Kafka's fiction (the nature of the reality, or experiences, with which his texts engage) continues. Some strands of criticism seem to point us away from an engagement with the outside world, towards an introverted meaning system, and can produce good evidence in support. Malcolm Pasley has pointed out the existence of 'semi-private' references in some works, such as 'Eleven Sons', which refer to Kafka's own works or to the act of writing.[17] This self-referential dimension has been developed especially by critics who see the act of writing itself and Kafka's reflections on his position as a writer as major underlying themes of his fiction. Pasley argues, for example, that 'the metaphor *horse* for story, and *horse-rider* or *horse-trainer* for writer, run through the whole of [Kafka's] writing'.[18] Other commentators have shown particular interest in references to writing implements such as the writing machine in 'In the Penal Colony'. The demonstrable existence of such veins of meaning in Kafka's writing appears, as I have said, to point towards an introverted meaning system, and thus to question the notion that Kafka engages in some substantial way with an external, social world. Taken to an extreme, this can suggest a picture of Kafka as a solipsist, and some critics tend to endorse this view by reading, for example, *The Trial* and 'In the Penal Colony' substantially as extended metaphors for the trials of writing in general, and writing the work in question in particular. Stanley Corngold's discussion of both these works and Mark Anderson's treatment of 'In the Penal Colony' seem to me examples of this tendency.[19] The impatience of some critics at this line of argument is exemplified by J. P. Stern's dismissal of it as a 'less than riveting' explanation of *The Trial*.[20] If this is the key to

Kafka's work, Stern implicitly asks, why should it be worth reading? One answer to this question could be that the metaphor of writing translates into an array of objective correlatives with which readers can identify: the search for truth or at least an understanding of one's situation, the quest for a form which is one's own, the struggle for control of experience, the sacrifices and moral dilemmas involved in such effort. But even so it is difficult to imagine such an interpretation of the work in which engagement with a particular, empirical world of experience plays no part. And logically, there is no reason why 'self-referential' and 'political' readings should not complement one another as part of a comprehensive interpretation. To admit this possibility is to open oneself up to the complexity and richness of Kafka's fictions, and to a certain extent to the arbitrariness of the division between 'interior' and 'exterior' worlds. For example, it is possible to see in 'In the Penal Colony' elements of Kafka's agonising over his private crises and a profound contemplation on the Great War and the ambivalence of intellectuals like himself in their response to it. The private and the public are closely intertwined, and Kafka criticism needs perhaps to focus more on the interconnectedness of these worlds, taking its lead from Kafka's own remark to Wolff on the painfulness of 'our general and my particular time' (11.X.16; *LFFE*: 127).

Mention has already been made of Kafka's work as an insurance assessor in the Workers' Accident Insurance Institute, and its possible role as a source for his imaginative fiction. Indeed Brod thought it self-evident that, as he put it, 'whole chapters of the novels *The Trial* and *The Castle* derive their outer covers, their realistic wrappings, from the atmosphere Kafka breathed in the Workers' Accident Institute'. He also recalls Kafka's anger at the meekness of workers mutilated in avoidable industrial accidents, who approached the Institute as supplicants instead of storming it and smashing it to bits.[21] To this we might add Kafka's experiences of the family businesses, the fancy-goods store owned by his father and the asbestos works in which he was for a time a partner. Undoubtedly, these provided him with first-hand experience of industrial relations, practices, and conditions. In 'Letter to his Father' Kafka recalls Hermann Kafka's 'tyrannising' way with his employees, whom he regarded as 'paid enemies', to which Kafka adds that his father was in turn their 'paying enemy'.[22] In his diary he expresses his sympathy for the women in the asbestos factory whose work threatens to turn them into dehumanized, exploitable objects before they escape at the end of each shift (5.XI.12; *D1*: 231). His professional duties brought him into contact with industrial enterprises in and around Prague, with the devious ways of employers unwilling to pay the appropriate accident insurance premiums for their workers, and often with the complicity of workers themselves. And he was himself, of course, also an employee, familiar with the uncertainties and frustrations of his class. It has only recently been realised that, in 1912, as Anthony Northey reports:

> Kafka the insurance agency employee was also involved in the creation of an Association of Officials of the Workers' Accident Insurance Institute, the closest these white-collar workers could come to forming a union: Kafka was treasurer of the Association for a brief period. Thus, Kafka occupied the two conflicting positions of factory-owner and union leader at the same time.[23]

He was evidently underpaid for his level of qualifications, and as a Jew was lucky to find employment at the Institute – he happened to know the President in 1908, Dr Otto Přibram, himself a converted Jew. In 1917, Kafka wrote to Brod that the Institute was now 'closed to Jews' (13.XI.17; *LFFE*: 165). His professional experiences undoubtedly inform his fictional presentations of technology, for example in *The Man who Disappeared* and 'In the Penal Colony'. They are also reflected in the detailed attention to conditions of employment imposed on K. in *The Castle*. Andrew Weeks has traced the parallels between this novel and the protracted struggle of Habsburg civil servants (the white-collar 'trade union' to which Kafka belonged) for a code of service, illuminating the connections with a class struggle very close to Kafka's heart.[24] Issues of status, of autonomy and dependence, are already present, for K. at least, 'between the lines' of the letter which seems to confirm his appointment as the Castle's land-surveyor, but in which he perceives a threat to reduce his existence to 'life as a worker. Service, foreman, work, conditions of pay, duty, worker, the letter was swarming with it' (*DS*: 35). K. is fearful that such a life, planned for him by the Castle, will be one of subjugation, effectively nullifying the threat he poses, in his own mind, at least, to the established order.

One of the texts which has often been cited by 'political' readers is 'Die besitzlose Arbeiterschaft' (translated as 'Guild of Workmen without Possessions' and 'The Propertyless Working Men's Association').[25] However, this is not a revolutionary tract in the conventional sense. It consists of a balance sheet of 'rights' and 'obligations' for some hypothetical community of labourers and workers. Written in 1918, it dates from a period when Kafka had begun to immerse himself in Jewish culture and history, in Zionism and the possibility of emigrating to Palestine (following the Balfour Declaration of 1917). As Binder points out, the immediate context is Jewish, not party political.[26] In drawing up a balance sheet of the rights and obligations of the members of what is clearly a commune of some kind (of no more than 500 *men*, be it said), Kafka focuses on the ethical dimensions of membership, stressing that the relationship between worker and employer is a 'relationship of trust' which should never be regulated by the courts. That comment is found, interestingly, under the 'obligations'. Under 'rights' Kafka notes that working life should be 'a matter of conscience and faith in one's fellow man'. There is also provision for a 'council' to negotiate between the commune and the 'government', and recognition that 'capitalist enterprises' also exist. As Binder remarks, this does not read like a socialist pamphlet. However, it arguably does reveal the ideological affinities between the utopian strain of Zionist social philosophy and utopian or Romantic anarchist thought – one thinks of Kropotkin's anti-Darwinian invocation of the natural principle of 'mutual aid', which Kafka very probably knew.[27]

This interest in a politics and social order based on ethical rigour, self-discipline, and commitment to one's fellow human beings, evident in this later phase of Kafka's life, may also explain his forthright praise of the Bolsheviks in two letters to Milena in August and September 1920. He sends her a newspaper article by Bertrand Russell on the situation in Russia. Russell praises the selfless commitment and industriousness of the communist 'who genuinely shares the Party's belief that private property is the root of all evil' and who lives a life of self-denial, working long hours even though he is in a position of power. Russell compares Lenin to Cromwell, saying that both men were driven by a combination of religious faith and democracy, but that military dictatorship forced both to sacrifice democracy to the imperatives of the religion. The article ends with some expressions of concern that these high principles will be corrupted by power. Kafka writes, however, that he has torn off this conclusion, as it contains 'accusations [. . .], which do not belong in this context' (*BM*: 238). In a subsequent letter, he returns to the article and tells Milena: 'What the author expresses reservations about is for me the highest praise possible on earth' (*BM*: 257). Kafka's comments are sufficiently cryptic to leave scope for speculation on how they are to be interpreted. On a certain reading, though, they challenge the comforting consensus of political readings which claim him for the liberal canon.

References to major political events of Kafka's lifetime are sparse in his diaries and letters and difficult to detect in his imaginative fiction. One finds little or nothing, for example, on the Balkan war of 1912, the founding of the Czech state in 1918, or the Balfour Declaration in favour of a Jewish state of 1917. The latter, however, may provide a useful context within which to read some of the short prose pieces from 1917, such as 'Jackals and Arabs'. Seeing the political events of the time reflected in Kafka's fictions is an inherently speculative, but fascinating exercise. As noted above, some critics have traced echoes of the Great War, and particularly of the debate over the 'ideas of 1914', in 'In the Penal Colony'. Links between 'The Judgement' and a *cause célèbre* of the time, the anti-Jewish Beiliss affair (1911–13) have also been traced, suggesting that pogrom may be a subtext in the story. Mendel Beiliss had been accused of the murder of a schoolboy found in a cave on the outskirts of Kiev in the spring of 1911. He was accused, as Jews in Christian Europe had been since the Middle Ages, of using the blood of a Christian child for Jewish ritual. He was eventually acquitted but not until a frenzy of anti-Semitic feeling had been fomented by the Russian authorities, who brought him to trial after the identity of the true culprits was publicly known.[28] The turbulence in Russia is linked in 'The Judgement' to revolution, but also to the figure of the priest on the balcony in Kiev who cuts a cross into the palm of his hand and holds it up to the crowd. There is also a brief reference to the Russian Revolution (of 1905, presumably) in the story.

A more substantial, though oblique, reference to revolutionary Russia may be detected in 'The Great Wall of China', which was written only weeks after the February 1917 uprising. In a passage subsequently deleted in the manuscript, the narrator in this story recalls an episode from his childhood in which a beggar from a neighbouring country passes through his native province distributing revolutionary pamphlets. The beggar is ridiculed and sent on his way, but not before he has made a lasting impression on the young boy:

> And although – so it seems to me in recollection – the gruesomeness of the living present was irrefutably conveyed by the beggar's words, we laughed and shook our heads and refused to listen any longer. So eager are our people to obliterate the present.[29]

In the context of a story in which the narrator sets out to be an 'incorruptible observer' of the mechanisms by which the ideology of nationhood is constructed (for which the Great Wall is a metaphor), it is plausible to suggest that this episode reflects, however obliquely, on the political culture of the Habsburg monarchy of which Kafka was a subject and the myths with which it sustained itself, albeit by 'obliterating the present'. Read self-reflectively, this passage could even be a coded reminiscence of youthful encounters with revolutionary pamphleteers from this turbulent neighbouring state.

Perhaps the most influential critic to insist on Kafka's radical credentials was Theodor Adorno. His essay from the 1950s rejects the religious or existential reception of Kafka as a comfortable artifice 'which knowingly dispenses with the very scandal on which his work is built'. Adorno locates this 'scandal' in the material mechanisms of society: most of Kafka's writing, he observes, is 'a reaction to unlimited power', power which is at once patriarchal and socioeconomic; and the 'shabbiness' of Kafka's work is an astute stratagem:

> the cryptogram of capitalism's highly polished, glittering late phase, which he excludes in order to define it all the more precisely in its negative. Kafka scrutinises the smudges left behind in the deluxe edition of the book of life by the fingers of power.[30]

Dismissing Brod's version of Kafka's religiosity, Adorno insists: 'Kafka's prose sides with the outcasts, the protest of his friend notwithstanding.' Adorno's view is now substantially represented in the critical literature, and a secular focus on power as his enduring theme is now axiomatic. Elias Canetti regards Kafka as 'the greatest expert on power',[31] and Herbert Kraft, in a comment which echoes Garaudy, reads the law in Kafka's work not as a metaphor but literally, as codified social reality, as a way of depicting the workings of hegemony (*Herrschaft*). According to this reading, it is not divine justice and grace which are symbolised in the Court and the Castle; rather, these structures epitomise hegemony and expose its deeper workings.[32]

Recent studies of the historical contexts of Kafka's work have adopted the perspectives of critical discourse analysis and have begun to add important detail to our understanding of the political import of his work. A view is beginning to emerge of Kafka's work as an oppositional discourse which absorbs, reflects, and subverts the dominant political discourses of his day, including those of gender, ethnicity, and Social Darwinism as the prevalent model of economic organisation. Mark M. Anderson has suggested how the polysemous concept of *Verkehr*, which means both 'intercourse' (social and sexual) and 'traffic', the multitude of ways in which words and goods are exchanged between people, enables Kafka to engage critically with the dominant forms of social interaction in economic and sexual life. Sander Gilman's study on the 'pathological Jew' as an ideological stereotype of Kafka's time surveys the interconnections between Kafka's life and work and contemporary maxims about race, gender, and disease. He points out that 'the Jew' was invariably constructed in this public discourse as both male and pathological, while the intellectual was ideologically feminised and thus marginalised within the dominant patriarchal ideology. Gilman suggests how Kafka's writing is entangled in these repressive discourses and is an attempt to control and counter them, albeit in parabolic and ironic fashion. For example, he believes that Kafka was highly sensitive to the charges of (homo)sexual excess, miscegenation (cross-racial sexual union), and ritual murder commonly made against 'the Jew'. He points to the Beiliss trial in Kiev and the Tisza–Eszlar trial in Hungary (both concerning charges of Jewish ritual murder) as important moments impelling Kafka's writing. Gilman also draws parallels between another Jewish *cause célèbre*, the Dreyfus affair, where a French army captain of Jewish extraction was put on trial and sentenced to banishment for (allegedly) passing secrets to the Germans, and an array of themes in *The Trial*, 'In the Penal Colony', and 'The Metamorphosis'. He sees Dreyfus's fate echoed in the transformation of Gregor's body from 'the confident anatomy of the proud military man to the scarred and withered body of the stigmatized outcast'. Recontextualising these painful discourses in an ostensibly non-Jewish, 'universal' discourse, namely West European modernism, Gilman argues, was Kafka's way of confronting and controlling their power over him.[33]

Recent feminist studies have adopted a similar discourse approach to the ideological contexts of Kafka's writings. Elizabeth Boa places Kafka within a tradition of literary modernism which is itself a symptom of 'a crisis in a militaristic age of decaying traditional patriarchy in which masculinity assumes a sado-masochistic character'.[34] Thus, Kafka lived and wrote in an age when established patriarchal structures (the social and sexual superiority of the male, the Judaeo-Christian religious tradition) were already fragmenting, and his own alienation was articulated in part in an anti-patriarchal, feminised discourse, which provided him with an oppositional perspective and rhetoric. She sees *The Trial* as a radical deconstruction of this problematical masculinity, though it is in *The Castle* that women characters take centre-stage and gain an authentic voice. Indeed, Boa finds a self-critical note in this novel in that K.'s claims to being a revolutionary are shown to be bogus – he is actually a patriarch in waiting – while it is Amalia who mounts the only genuine challenge to the power of the Castle. She pays the price too in being ostracised by both the patriarchal Castle and the other women, whose position of power within the patriarchal order is also threatened by her rebellion. It is his capacity for self-criticism and irony, Boa remarks, which marks Kafka out from the misogynistic discourses of his time. However, as Stephen Dowden has pointed out, feminist studies of Kafka are perhaps the only area of critical debate in which the idea of Kafka the exemplary liberal is treated sceptically.[35] Boa, whilst according Kafka 'a feminine core of critical marginality', also notes marked patriarchal and misogynistic features in the letters and in some at least of his works, such as 'The Silence of the Sirens'. Nor is this the only paradox she detects. She sees his writings as a way of escaping from the world of real gendered relations (real women) to a world in which he could exercise immense and arbitrary power over them. The later Kafka, however, from 1916 onwards, appears more mellow and contemplative in his (self-)critiques of the dominant discourses on gender, ethnicity, and nationhood. In his later works, in which he explores his own position as an outsider and artist, he shows increasing sympathy for the female voice, and adopts a female persona for his last story, 'Josephine, the Songstress or: the Mouse People'.

A discourse on the Jews was of course also conducted within the Jewish communities, and Giuliano Baioni has placed Kafka's work within the complex demands of the Jewish cultural politics of his time, resistant to both Brod's separationist politics (Zionism) and Martin Buber's romanticising myths of Judaism. Kafka, Baioni believes, jealously defended his outpost of isolation as the 'most Western of the Western Jews', caught, as Kafka wrote to Brod in 1921, with his hind quarters stuck in the glue-trap of his Jewish ancestry while his forelegs found no footing in modernity (*LFFE*: 289). Baioni's reading of 'The Great Wall of China', for example, follows other critics in seeing it as a parabolic essay on Jewish identity, but he reads it as a rebuttal of Brod.[36] Kafka's fictions, he argues, the products of and motivation for his willed isolation, leave open the question of whether his life's work was marked by ethical rigour (the dog narrator of 'Investigations of a Dog') or diabolical narcissism (the prima donna starvation artist in 'A Fasting-artist'). In resisting both wings of Jewish cultural politics, Kafka reserved for himself the dubious 'privilege of traversing the world of the lie and soiling himself with all the dirt of the assimilation culture – in a word, of being the salvation of mankind in the "Western Jewish time"'.[37]

These approaches to Kafka's texts as refractions of and (subversive) responses to oppressive historical discourses and ideologies have added importantly to our understanding of the way his writings engage with the 'political' themes of his time, though there is clearly still plenty of scope for different emphases and even disagreements within this paradigm, as indeed there was in the intense debate between Bertolt Brecht and Walter Benjamin in the 1930s. Brecht, though he regarded Kafka as a great writer, could not 'accept' him, regarding him as a 'failure', an exemplar of the petit-bourgeois class 'caught under the wheels', whose writings were characterised by 'mystification'. Benjamin, however, whose reading of Kafka combined political, Jewish, and mythological perspectives, noted:

> it is necessary to clarify Kafka, that is to say to formulate the practicable suggestions that can be extracted from his stories. It is to be supposed that such suggestions *can* be extracted from them, if only because of their tone of superior calm.[38]

Brecht's view reflects in essence the Marxist orthodoxy which still prevailed at Liblice in 1963. In contrast, Benjamin's conviction that practicable suggestions *can* be extracted from an analytical Kafka now looks modern, initiating a lineage of political readings with their intellectual roots in the Frankfurt School, of which Adorno's is the most eminent. Herbert Kraft is arguably the most adventurous of the more recent critics belonging to this lineage, insofar as he argues for a criticism which relates Kafka to our present, on the grounds that our age has now caught up with Kafka's imaginative projections. Kraft insists that in order to read him correctly we must move beyond the standardised reception of the canonised, 'important' texts, and explore the smaller, less well known texts. In doing so we will see the 'major' texts afresh. His study of the fragment 'Der Unterstaatsanwalt' ('The Assistant Prosecutor'), for example, which has chronological and thematic ties with *The Trial*, demonstrates Kafka's dismantling of the notion of the unpolitical conservative, and provides contextual support for critics who see in *The Trial* a critique of right-wing ideologies such as phrenology and its applications in the criminology of Kafka's day.[39] According to Kraft, short texts such as 'The Problem of our Laws' and 'The Helmsman' are transparently political tracts on the nature of power, the former exposing 'how "the Law" is only the euphemistic formulation for "hegemony"', the latter documenting the mechanism of a *Machtergreifung* ('seizure of power').[40]

In rejecting what might be called the 'religious fallacy' inherent in Brodian readings, secular and political readings must also answer the charge that they are guilty of an equal and opposite simplification of Kafka, the creation of a 'political fallacy'.[41] Making Kafka into a socialist or some other kind of party-political activist on the strength of these insights, no matter how persuasive they are, will simply not do, and the question remains how seriously Kafka's writings should be taken as social and political critiques. On the whole one would not turn to these critics for an appreciation of the profound and hilarious qualities of Kafka the visual and verbal humorist, though his humour is often barbed with social implications (as in the lookalike lodgers and the elements of farce and slap-stick in 'The Metamorphosis'). Also, the fact that clothes are important in Kafka, on which Anderson bases his perceptive study, had gone unregarded, not worthy of note, it seems, by 'political' and 'metaphysical' commentators alike, who in their different ways had assumed that a 'serious', 'major' writer could not be interested in such 'superficial' themes.

Yet the wide-ranging political import of much of Kafka's writing, and the nuanced way in which it engages with major ideological battlegrounds of his time, has been well demonstrated by critics like Pascal, Kraft, and Gilman. It is now no longer possible to take seriously the notion that his writing does not engage in profound and urgent, though subtle and parabolic ways, with a recognisable social reality. The 'political' Kafka who has emerged from these readings is an important and necessary corrective to the picture of the *homo religiosus* or introverted existentialist which tended to dominate his early reception. The question facing Kafka criticism today is not whether political readings are admissible, but how they are to be integrated into an appreciation of his work as a whole. This requires a sophistication and sensitivity equal to the work itself, with its multiple, shifting refractions of meaning, its playfulness and deadly seriousness, its perspectival subtleties and ambiguities, its private and public resonances. Perhaps Peter Beicken's view of *The Trial* points to the possibility of such an adequate reading, suggesting that Kafka's imaginative fiction is shaped by a poetics of attrition between antagonistic points of view which fight out an unresolved battle. Beicken suggests a way of acknowledging an engagement with and interaction of the religious and the secular, the private and the political, accusation and justification, in a way which preserves the ideological complexity of Kafka's work and refrains from 'taking sides', as a critic, in the ideological debates themselves. Such an approach might have much to commend it as a general approach to Kafka's œuvre. But critics like Adorno, Deleuze and Guattari, and Kraft would presumably view this as a compromise and itself an ideological construct which continues to deprive readers of the true import and historical significance of Kafka's work. The essential point is that in the critical debate all schools of interpretation need to justify their findings with reference to the aesthetic, semiotic, and rhetorical features of Kafka's texts, since these appear to be designed to replicate the surface confusions and perspectival tensions of actual experience.

To sum up: Kafka's declared dedication to writing his 'dreamlike inner life' should not prevent us from seeing the ways in which his imaginative fiction also engages critically with a historical, empirical social reality. Those who read him 'politically' make a good case for seeing him as a critical receptor and reflector of social forces, an observer of secular power, a radical sceptic in religious issues, whose imaginative fictions are driven by an iconoclastic, though insidious and oblique, critique of historically real power structures and their discourses. In particular, once we accept that irony and travesty are part of Kafka's treatment of religious themes, it becomes possible to conceive of the social and political dimensions of his critique of metaphysics. Crucially, however, his fictions are composed as intellectual and moral challenges to the reader, offering us the *potential* of analytical insight and radical perspective which it is for us to activate. Seen in this way, his works are constructed as provocations, invitations to see into the mechanisms of power through the 'smudges', as Adorno says, which they leave behind on the surface of conventionalised reality. Kafka was certainly familiar with, and appears to have been sympathetic to, radical political theory of the left, but neither his biography nor his fiction suggests that he subscribed to a conventional political philosophy or programme, with the possible exception of ethical anarchism, which indeed may overlap with the social-ethical programmes of Zionism that he encountered in the latter stages of his life. His critique of patriarchy and other forms of power is at once subtle and capable of self-irony. But the exact extent of these 'political' dimensions to his work is ultimately a matter for interpretation within an overall interpretation of his life and work. It will in all probability remain contentious.

NOTES

1. Dušan Glišović, *Politik im Werk Kafkas* (Tübingen: Francke, 1996).
2. Roger Garaudy, 'Kafka and Modern Art', in Hughes (ed./tr.), *An Anthology of Marxist Criticism*, pp. 104–10, here pp. 109–10.
3. See Klaus Wagenbach, *Franz Kafka in Selbstzeugnissen und Bilddokumenten* (Reinbek bei Hamburg: Rowohlt, 1964), pp. 64–71; Lee Baxandall, 'Kafka and Radical Perspective', *Mosaic* 3:4 (1970), 73–9 and 'Kafka as Radical'; and Tom Morris, 'From Liblice to Kafka'.
4. Hartmut Binder, *Kafka-Handbuch*, 2 vols. (Stuttgart: Kröner, 1979), vol. 1, pp. 361–4; Ritchie Robertson, *Kafka: Judaism, Politics and Literature* (Oxford: Clarendon, 1985), p. 140.
5. Gustav Janouch, *Conversations with Kafka*, second, enlarged edition, tr. Goronwy Rees (London: Village Press, 1971). This includes material from the second, expanded German edition, the veracity of which has been doubted.
6. Alfred Wirkner, *Kafka und die Außenwelt: Quellenstudien zum 'Amerika'-Fragment* (Stuttgart: Klett, 1976), pp. 46–51 and pp. 91–104.
7. Robertson, *Judaism, Politics and Literature*, p. 85.
8. Sokel, From *Marx to Myth*, p. 107.
9. J. P. Stern, 'The Judgement', p. 123.
10. Herbert Kraft, *Kafka: Wirklichkeit und Perspektive* (Bebenhausen: Rotsch, 1972), p. 74.
11. For an English translation of Kracauer's review, see W. J. Dodd (ed.), *Kafka: The Metamorphosis, The Trial and The Castle* (London: Longman, 1995), pp. 88–91. For Brod's response, cf. p. 87.
12. Deleuze and Guattari, *Toward a Minor Literature*, p. 51.
13. Kraft, *Someone Like K.*, pp. 33–85.
14. Peter Beicken, *Franz Kafka: eine kritische Einführung in die Forschung* (Frankfurt aM: Fischer, 1974), pp. 283–4.
15. Pascal, *Kafka's Narrators*, pp. 60–89.
16. Walter Müller-Seidel, *Die Deportation des Menschen: Kafkas Erzählung In der Strafkolonie im europäischen Kontext* (Stuttgart: Metzler, 1985), pp. 80–7.
17. Malcolm Pasley, 'Semi-Private Games', in Angel Flores (ed.), *The Kafka Debate: New Perspectives for our Times* (New York: Gordian, 1977), pp. 188–205.
18. Malcolm Pasley, 'Franz Kafka. Der Proceß. Die Handschrift redet', *Marbacher Magazin*, 52 (1990), p. 21.
19. See Stanley Corngold, *Franz Kafka: the Necessity of Form* (Ithaca, NY: Cornell University Press, 1988), pp. 228–49; Mark M. Anderson, 'The Ornaments of

Writing: *In the Penal Colony*', in *Kafka's Clothes: Ornament and Aestheticism in the Habsburg Fin de Siècle* (Oxford: Clarendon, 1992), pp. 173–93.

20. J. P. Stern, 'Introduction'.
21. Max Brod, *Franz Kafka: a Biography*, tr. G. Humphreys Roberts and Richard Winston (New York: Schocken, 1973), pp. 82–4.
22. 'Letter to his Father', in *Wedding Preparations in the Country and other Posthumous Writings*, with Notes by Max Brod, tr. Ernst Kaiser and Eithne Wilkins (London: Secker and Warburg, 1954), p. 181.
23. Anthony Northey, *Kafka's Relatives: their Lives and his Writing* (New Haven and London: Yale University Press, 1991), p. 96.
24. Dodd (ed.), *Kafka*, pp. 171–88.
25. The former in Max Brod, *Franz Kafka*, pp. 84–5, the latter in Baxendall, 'Kafka and Radical Perspective', pp. 78–9. Subsequent quotations are from Brod's biography. The German text can be found in *BB*: 221–3.
26. *Kafka-Handbuch*, vol. 1, p. 506.
27. On Kafka's awareness of Kropotkin, see Dodd, *Kafka and Dostoyevsky: the Shaping of Influence* (London: Macmillan, 1992), p. 27; also Glišović, *Politik im Werk Kafkas*, pp. 25–7.
28. For a fuller account, see Orlando Figes, *A People's Tragedy: the Russian Revolution 1891–1924* (London: Pimlico, 1996), pp. 241–4.
29. The passage is quoted here in the now rather dated translation by the Muirs, *The Metamorphosis and Other Stories*, tr. Willa and Edwin Muir (Harmondsworth: Penguin, 1983), p. 79. The paragraph containing this passage is omitted from Malcolm Pasley's translation on the grounds that it was deleted in the manuscript. The relevant paragraph of some twenty-eight lines directly precedes the paragraph beginning: 'If one were to conclude from such phenomena' (*GWC*: 68).
30. Adorno, 'Notes on Kafka', p. 245.
31. Elias Canetti, *Kafka's Other Trial: the Letters to Felice*, tr. Christopher Middleton (London: Caldar and Boyars, 1974), p. 80.
32. Herbert Kraft, *Mondheimat. Kafka* (Pfullingen: Neske, 1983), p. 204.
33. Gilman, *The Jewish Patient*, pp. 66–8.
34. Elizabeth Boa, *Kafka: Gender, Class and Race in the Letters and Fictions* (Oxford: Clarendon, 1996), p. 149.
35. Stephen Dowden, *Kafka's Castle and the Critical Imagination* (Colombia: Camden House, 1995), p. 95.
36. Giuliano Baioni, *Kafka: Literatur und Judentum*, tr. Gertrud and Josef Billen (Stuttgart/Weimar: Metzler, 1994), p. 146. Baioni is here taking issue with a contrary view put forward by Binder, *Kafka-Handbuch*, vol. 1, p. 505.
37. Baioni, *Literatur und Judentum*, p. 268.
38. Walter Benjamin, 'Notes from Svendborg: Conversations with Brecht', in *Understanding Brecht*, tr. Anna Bostock (London: New Left Books, 1973), pp. 105–21, here 31.VIII.34, p. 110.
39. Kraft, *Mondheimat*, pp. 74–82.
40. Ibid., p. 82.
41. See, for example, Robertson's argument that Pascal in his reading of 'In the Penal Colony' 'seems to be foisting his own liberal views on to Kafka' (*Judaism, Politics and Literature*, p. 155).

FURTHER READING

Adorno, Theodor W., 'Notes on Kafka', in *Prisms*, tr. Samuel Weber and Shierry Weber (London: Spearman, 1967), pp. 245–71.

Baxandall, Lee, 'Kafka as Radical', in Angel Flores (ed.), *The Kafka Debate: New Perspectives for our Time* (New York: Gordian Press, 1977), pp. 120–5.

Deleuze, Gilles and Felix Guattari, *Kafka: Toward a Minor Literature*, tr. Dana Polan (Minneapolis: University of Minnesota Press, 1986).

Gilman, Sander L., *Franz Kafka: the Jewish Patient* (London and New York: Routledge, 1995).

Hughes, Kenneth (ed.), *Franz Kafka: an Anthology of Marxist Criticism* (Hanover and London: University Press of New England, 1981).

Kraft, Herbert, *Someone like K.: Kafka's Novels* (Würzburg: Königshausen and Neumann/Amsterdam and Atlanta, GA: Rodopi, 1991), tr. R. J. Kavanagh.

Morris, Tom, 'From Liblice to Kafka', *Telos* 24 (1975), 163–70.

Pascal, Roy, *Kafka's Narrators: a Study of his Stories and Sketches* (Cambridge: Cambridge University Press, 1982), pp. 60–89.

Sokel, Walter H., 'From Marx to Myth: the Structure and Function of Self-Alienation', in Harold Bloom (ed.), *Franz Kafka's The Metamorphosis* (New York: Chelsea, 1988), pp. 105–16.

Stern, J. P., 'The Judgement: an interpretation', *German Quarterly* 45 (1972), 114–29.

'Introduction', Kafka, *The Trial*, tr. D. Scott and C. Waller (London: Pan, 1977), pp. 7–16.

9

IRIS BRUCE

Kafka and Jewish folklore

Kafka's trials and animal metamorphoses are very common motifs in Jewish folklore; he also rewrote ancient myths and legends and frequently used a mock-midrashic, rabbinic discourse. Of course, many folk elements discussed in this chapter are not restricted to Jewish folklore but share characteristics with other folk traditions. What is of interest is the way Kafka recreates folk motifs and legends within a modern Jewish cultural framework and thus gives them new meaning. Folk elements, whether Jewish or non-Jewish, never exist for their own sake but rather merge with the author's own imagination. Thus, the nineteenth-century writer Mendele Moykher Sforim (c.1836–1917) has a downtrodden mare represent the Jewish people in Exile. Yudl Rosenberg (1860–1935) writes a story about the Prague Golem, pretending that the sixteenth-century Rabbi Löw created this humanoid monster 'to wage war against the Blood Libel' ('ritual murder') – the anti-Semitic charge according to which Jews needed Christian blood for their Passover rituals and slaughtered Christian children in order to obtain it.[1] Rosenberg knew full well that his version of the Golem legend was historically incorrect. The Golem, a creature made from clay, was supposed to help in times of persecution, but no legend had ever connected it with the scandal of blood libel. Still, when Rosenberg was composing his story, charges of ritual murder were ubiquitous. For this reason he used a prominent motif from Jewish folklore to recreate for *his* time a superhuman folk hero who could help fight injustice.

Unlike these Yiddish writers Kafka rarely integrates folk elements into an overtly Jewish narrative. Yet one cannot ignore the ritualistic murder of Josef K. in *The Trial*, given that this novel was written in the aftermath of the Beiliss affair in Russia (1911–13), which left its mark arguably on 'The Judgement' too. In view of Kafka's increasing interest in Zionism it should also not be surprising that he blends Zionist concerns with folk motifs. This is the case with 'Investigations of a Dog', which, in many of its anecdotal digressions, resembles the world of the Russian-born Jewish painter, Marc

Chagall (1887–1985), whose brightly coloured surrealistic canvasses teem with human and animal motifs from the culture of the East European shtetl. In response to Walter Jens's assertion that Kafka's readers encounter 'a Chagall world, the scenery of Jewish folklore', Gershon Shaked replied: 'But Kafka's abstract world is very different from Chagall's world of concrete Jewish symbolism. Had Kafka used the material he collected in his diaries, he might have created something like the world of Chagall.'[2] Neither of the two critics is entirely wrong; the truth lies somewhere in between. 'Investigations of a Dog' combines abstract reasoning with concrete animal symbolism.

Kafka's confirmed interest in Judaism began in 1911 when he was introduced to the Yiddish theatre group from the far-flung Austrian province of Galicia. His fascination with Yiddish culture became a catalyst for learning more about Judaism in general. In January 1912 he read Meyer I. Pinès's *L'Histoire de la littérature judéo-allemande* (*D1*: 223). Pinès devotes much space to folk and Hasidic tales, which are infused with cabalistic thought and symbolism, including metamorphoses. Moreover, when Kafka wrote 'The Metamorphosis' from November to December 1912, he was also already familiar with the writings of Martin Buber (1878–1965), who had started collecting Hasidic tales in the first decade of the twentieth century. The concept of metamorphosis is, according to Gershom Scholem, an 'integral part of Jewish popular belief and Jewish folklore'.[3] In the Hasidic tales of Rabbi Nachman of Bratslav (1772–1810), whose work Kafka knew through his reading of Buber, the protagonists are shown to undergo several metamorphoses as they move through the cabalistic cycle of transgression, punishment, exile, and trials in the hope of deliverance and redemption. For instance, in 'The Prince Who Thought He Was a Rooster', a prince takes off all his clothes, sits under the table, and refuses to eat anything but cornseed. No one can cure him of his delusion until a wise man also pretends to be a rooster and sits under the table with him. Step by step, the wise man convinces the prince that a rooster can wear clothes if he wishes, that he can eat human food and still be a good rooster, and that there is no reason why a rooster should not walk about. The 'moral' is: 'After he began dressing like a person, eating like a person, and walking like a person, he gradually recovered his senses and began to live like a person.'[4] It is not hard to recognise that the creator of Gregor Samsa inhabited the same cultural, if not mental, landscape as this tale. Transformations in Jewish folklore are generally inflicted as punishment for transgressions. Gregor's metamorphosis, too, is related to man's first transgression, which represents the root of all evil: the Fall or Original Sin. The connection with the 'Fall' is clearly established at the end of Part II, when his father (the patriarch in the familial and religious sense) 'punishes' Gregor by bombarding him with apples.

In the middle and late nineteenth century, with the rise and growing popularity of the Jewish Enlightenment (the *Haskalah*), religious and biblical references lost their devotional function for the most part and took on a secular meaning. Metamorphosis is treated in a humorously ironic fashion, for example, in the tales of I. L. Peretz (1852–1915), particularly in 'Thou Shalt not Covet'. Peretz suggests that the cycle of transgression and punishment could be endless, particularly if we are dealing with ordinary sinful mortals. In fact, he shows through the trials of a great rabbi that even 'saints' are only 'ordinary mortals'.[5] Having lived a virtuous and strict life according to the Commandments, the rabbi has never really 'lived' and enjoyed life. Now the time has come for him to be rewarded in heaven, but the Angel of Death has to struggle to make the soul leave the body. All the individual parts of the rabbi's body revolt and his agony is so great that he wishes for an easy death. But a Jew is not allowed to covet anything, not even an easy death. Thus a new cycle of metamorphosis begins. In his new life the rabbi is once again very virtuous, but just before he has completed his cycle, the evil spirit tempts him again. As he is standing in the cold, his attention is caught by an inn across from him. He enters and sees peasants sitting by a warm stove, 'drinking liquor, wiping it down with herring and pickles and talking obscenities'.[6] Only for a split second he envies them and wishes he could do the same. But this brings about his downfall and so the cycle is repeated once more. Peretz satirises the strict religious laws by underlining the all too human nature of the rabbi's transgressions which are 'some trivial matter, a mere nothing'[7] and out of proportion with the punishment he receives.

If metamorphoses can be treated humorously in Jewish literature, why should Gregor Samsa's be an exception? At the outset, the mood in 'The Metamorphosis' is not one of terror; nor does Gregor view himself as a horrible monster. His attempt to hold back his boss from entering his room starts up a chain of comic reactions that is distinctly Chaplinesque. In terms of his split personality, Gregor the vermin could be seen as a *dybbuk*, an evil spirit from Jewish folklore, which enters and possesses people. However, when the experience of turning into vermin becomes increasingly 'real', when Gregor is rejected and physically attacked by his father, the humour stops: 'now this was really no joke any more' (*M*: 19). From now on, his metamorphosis becomes increasingly a symbol of degradation and humiliation.

Metamorphosis also expresses 'the reality of Exile'.[8] In Mendele's novel *The Mare* (1876), the Wandering Mare states that she has been in this peculiar shape '[a]s long as the Jewish Exile!'.[9] There are even different *degrees* of 'inner' exile because 'banishment into the prison of strange forms of existence, into wild beasts, into plants and stones, is regarded as a particularly dreadful form of exile'.[10] This description allows us to see many of the animals in Kafka's stories, ranging from vermin ('The Metamorphosis') to apes ('A Report to an Academy'), jackals ('Jackals and Arabs'), a marten-like creature ('The Animal in the Synagogue'), dogs ('Investigations of a Dog'), and mice ('Josephine, the Songstress or: the Mouse People'), even the peculiar Odradek, half creature, half object ('The Cares of a Family Man'), as signifying different degrees of exile. Gregor could represent a particularly dreadful form of exile when he reaches the height of impurity in the third part of the story: 'he too was completely covered with dust; he dragged around with him on his back and along his sides fluff and hairs and scraps of food' (M: 48). However, it is not just Gregor who becomes increasingly impure, everyone is associated with uncleanliness after the apple scene, thus after the connection with the Fall is established. The father's uniform turns and remains 'dirty' (the German *fleckig* carries associations of *befleckt*, 'tainted') 'in spite of all the mother's and sister's care' (M: 41).

In Jewish mysticism any transformation is also regarded as 'part of the process of restoration',[11] and a crucial motif in Hasidic tales is the mystic longing for redemption. Atonement can here be reached only by going through the ritual stages of punishment, in other words, according to the principle 'descent for the sake of ascent'.[12] In another of Peretz's stories, 'Devotion Without End' (discussed by Pinès), a youth is cursed for his transgressions and finds that the way to redemption is through punishment and humiliation: 'But I must suffer, Rabbi, I should suffer, and the more I am shamed the sooner will my curse be lifted.'[13] In this context, Gregor's family's increasing degradation and impurity can be seen as necessary stages that have to be passed through in the quest for atonement. Furthermore, the music of the violin that Gregor and his family are drawn to is a key tragic motif which is associated with the longing for redemption. Both Gregor and his family have reached the depths of impurity and humiliation at this point but, significantly, they can respond to the music while the three tenants cannot.

There is a similar relationship between personal debasement and increasing readiness for attaining the realm of the divine in Peretz's 'Cabalists' (discussed by Pinès). A Yeshivah student imposes a penitence fast on himself and achieves different degrees of revelation until he finally hears 'a kind of music ... as if I had a violin within me'.[14] The clear sound of the violin symbolises the purity of the divine in contrast to the impure environment. And Gregor, too, has been fasting. When he hears the music, he feels 'as if the way to the unknown nourishment he longed for were coming to light' (M: 49). Fasting thus becomes a means for gaining spiritual nourishment through the divine. Gregor fails to reach redemption. But such 'failure' is inherent in most trials. Even the Yeshivah student in Peretz's 'Cabalists' does not find it.

There can be little doubt that Kafka frequently makes use of motifs that have grown out of mysticism. This is abundantly clear when we look at Kabbalah symbolism, which so permeates, for example, the Hasidic tales – with their palaces and chambers, the heavenly courtroom, the scales of justice, penitents' trials, divine radiance, as well as metamorphoses. Many scholars have pointed out these metaphors in Kafka, most prominently in the famous parable 'Before the Law', a central part of *The Trial*. Trials in Hasidic folklore are trials of ordinary humans who have committed no serious crimes. In Peretz's 'Thou Shalt Not Covet' the rabbi's transformations are called 'the saint's trial'.[15] This indicates a likely connection between Gregor's 'trial' and that of Josef K., whose transgression is also related to Original Sin. In a Yiddish translation of this novel, the Hebrew word *gilgulim* (transformations) is used to describe the 'trials' which merchant Block has suffered.[16] The translator, Melech Ravitch, also translates the title of Kafka's 'Metamorphosis' as 'der gilgul' (*Prozes*, p. 237), thereby establishing the previously outlined context of transgression, punishment, and continual striving for redemption in both texts.

Merchant Block and the many other accused willingly submit to the conditions laid out by the law and allow themselves to be humbled and humiliated. In contrast, Josef K. not only does not *believe* in the law but is quite *ignorant* of it. Like the man from the country, he is an *am ha-aretz*, someone who is ignorant of Scripture, that is ignorant of the law.[17] By associating K. with this folk figure, Kafka intimates that K.'s quest for justice is bound to fail. His ironic use of folk motifs (such as doorkeepers, heavenly courtrooms, and the failed mystic ascent) further underlines this defeatist message. Kafka is caricaturing Josef K., the man who is ignorant of the Scripture and the law contained within it, the *am ha-aretz*, who becomes lost in the commentaries on the parable, the 'exegesis of the legend' (13.XII.14; D2: 63). The logic of the 'halakhic and talmudic reflection which stands out so forcibly in the "doorkeeper before the law"'[18] is foreign to K.: '[it] led him into unaccustomed areas of thought' (*TT*: 223). Talmudic discourse is easily recognisable in the following explication:

> he's well aware of the importance of his office, *for he says*: 'I'm powerful'; he respects his superiors, *for he says*: 'I'm only the lowest doorkeeper'; when it comes to fulfilling his duty he can neither be moved nor prevailed upon, *for it says* of the man 'he wearies the doorkeeper with his entreaties';...; he can't be bribed, *for he says* of a gift...   (*TT*: 218, my emphasis)

In rabbinic fashion, every interpretation is followed by the citing of a proof-text from the original legend, always introduced by phrases such as, *for he says*. Moreover, a priest who talks like a rabbi is surely a comic subject.

Here we have Kafka the parodist. One may think of Max Brod's comment:

> When Kafka read from his work, this humour became especially obvious. Thus we could not stop laughing, for example, when he read out the first chapter of *The Trial*. He himself laughed so much that he could not read on from time to time. – This is surprising considering the terrible seriousness of the chapter. But this is what happened.[19]

Walter Benjamin recognised Kafka's ability 'to extract the comic aspects from Jewish theology', that is his *modern* appropriation of traditional, rabbinic narrative forms.[20] One passage from the first chapter parodies Josef K.'s loss of authority in a mock-rabbinic fashion. K. is asked by the Inspector whether or not he is surprised by the train of events that morning. He then has to qualify individual utterances until they are transformed, distorted or turned into their opposite. The narrative is marked by continual reversals, antithesis following antithesis, all of which creates ambiguity. Suddenly we start questioning the meaning of 'surprised' and 'by no means greatly surprised' (*TT*: 13) or other clichéed expressions. The narrative features show similarities with midrashic technique, which is concerned with 'the smaller units of Scripture, verses, phrases, single words'.[21] With its twisting and turning of meaning, the humour in Josef K.'s linguistic predicament exposes the trial from the outset as a farce.

K.'s lawyer Huld recounts an anecdote which represents the absurdity of this court with its 'petty lawyers' in a very humorous fashion. It describes how '[a]n elderly official, a decent, quiet gentleman, had studied a difficult case, rendered particularly complex due to the lawyer's petitions'. Out of frustration, trying to prevent the lawyers from coming into court, 'he went to the outer door, waited in ambush, and threw every lawyer who tried to enter down the steps'. As they desperately needed admittance to the court, 'because each day missed at court is a day lost', the lawyers decided that their best course of action would be to tire him out. By taking it in turns, they rushed up the stairs, '[o]ne lawyer at a time', so that the elderly official could throw every single one down to the bottom again 'where he would then be caught by his colleagues. That lasted for about an hour, then the old gentleman . . . grew truly exhausted and went back into his office' (*TT*: 118–19).

The lawyers' Sisyphus-like activity reads like a Jewish joke from Chelm, the town of fools from Jewish folklore. In one such story the Chelm Jews decide to build a synagogue at the bottom of a hill. But the trees which they need to cut down are at the top of the hill. So they climb up the hill, cut the trees off, and then carry them all the way down. However, there is one wise man in Chelm, who asks: 'Why are you doing this? Is it not much easier to roll them down?' So they carry all the beams up the hill again, one by one, in order to roll them down. The anecdote of the 'petty' lawyers in *The Trial*, who willingly let themselves be thrown down the stairs in order to reach their goal, caricatures their insatiability and reduces the serious court proceedings to farce.

In the Yiddish translation of the novel, the artist Yossl Bergner has illustrated these humorous scenes. One drawing is based on a further court anecdote related by lawyer Huld. In order to open K.'s eyes about the nature of the court, Huld tells K. about a big hole in the floor of the law offices which makes the lawyers trip over, while the accused beneath them, sitting on benches, are looking up to the ceiling at a leg which is sticking out (*Prozes*, p. 118). Another illustration shows the painter Titorelli twirling a hunchback around his head, a gesture which is reminiscent of the *kapora* ritual on Yom Kippur where a sacrificial chicken is circled around someone's head before it is slaughtered in atonement for everyone's sins. An originally religious ceremony thus becomes a folkloristic motif in *The Trial*. More than that, Josef K. is sacrificed in a similarly brutal and senseless fashion. On the one hand, his ritualistic death in the quarry evokes the age-old anti-Semitic accusation of ritual murder, most recently revived in the Beiliss trial; at the same time, it is also reminiscent of ritual slaughter. One could therefore call it a mixed metaphor which links ritual murder and ritual slaughter. Like the innocent Mendel Beiliss (1874–1924), K. has been circling from one authority to another, feeding on 'belief sustaining fictions',[22] but never making any progress in his 'case'. As an *am ha-aretz*, he is abandoned by the law as well as by society.

While neither Gregor Samsa nor Josef K. survive, not many of Kafka's heroes who do live to tell their tales prosper. The talking jackals in 'Jackals and Arabs' (1917) are a case in point. Their desperate attempts to preserve their cultural identity make them adopt a self-satisfied and self-righteous stance, turning them into very disagreeable creatures. Kafka is caricaturing the concept of the Chosen People who appear as intolerant of Arab culture as Arab culture is of them. Worse still, caught in a farcical cycle of oppression and punishment (they are constantly whipped by the Arabs), the jackals have literally become 'wild' animals inside. The psychological consequences are scorn and hate. The Arab's last comment testifies to this as well: 'Wonderful creatures, aren't they? And how they do hate us!' (*TOS*: 170). The jackals have managed to survive in the face of oppression, but they have paid a very high price. The great irony of the situation is that they are caught in a dilemma to which there is no solution: on the one hand, observance of the law is their only way of keeping their cultural identity; on the other hand, this is 'killing' them as it has made them hopelessly out of touch with the modern world and psychologically sick.

The ape called Rotpeter in 'A Report to an Academy' (like 'Jackals and Arabs' published in Buber's *Der Jude* in 1917 as well as *A Country Doctor* in 1919) fares no better, though he chooses the path opposite to that of the jackals. Rotpeter decides to assimilate into the dominant culture. Kafka knew the metaphor of the 'trained animal' for the assimilated Jew from Mendele's 'The Mare', while the figure of the ape appears in Zionist publications which he owned. Mendele's mare sees the process of assimilation as 'pure theatre!'[23] and resents this 'monkey business' which means being taught 'some trick or other': 'What's the use of lovely harnesses, expensive decorations...all these rewards for clever performance?' (pp. 618–19). And she sneers, 'Dance, little animals, dance!' (p. 606). The fate of Kafka's ape illustrates that the mare is right. Rotpeter has renounced his own nature and has become a performer, making a living as a freak on a 'variety stage' (*TOS*: 194). Over the years he has been so successful that he is now even invited to report to the learned academy. But Rotpeter is very aware of being put on display and feels resentful. He describes his assimilation as being 'driven forward through the successive stages of my development' (*TOS*: 187) and, according to one critic, knows that he did 'his best to meet this strange universe on *its* terms rather than on his own'.[24] Herein lies precisely his problem: not only is Rotpeter aping his environment (cf. the German *nachäffen*), but he attempts to internalise the values of the dominant culture. Renouncing his own nature ever more, he becomes increasingly masochistic and projects society's stereotypes onto other members of his group.

Richard Lichtheim, in *Das Programm des Zionismus* (The Zionist Programme, 1913), describes this phenomenon as follows:

> The systematic aping of foreign manners, anxious glances in the direction of the 'others', the artificial covering up of anything that could be seen as distinctively Jewish, this becomes the Law of Life. Already we have a Jewish anti-Semitism which attempts to demonstrate, in a comic and repugnant fashion, justifications for anti-Semitism and Jewish inferiority. Zionism wants to lead us out of this spiritual wasteland.[25]

Moreover, we can see Rotpeter's uneasiness in public in his relationship to his chimpanzee wife, whom he does not wish to see during the day. Rotpeter is a caricature of the Jewish assimilationist, the successful social climber who despises his origins and is over-sensitive about drawing attention to his 'true' identity.

The survival of Odradek in 'The Cares of a Family Man' is an almost painful thought. This story was published not only in *A Country Doctor* but also in the Chanukkah issue of the Prague Zionist newspaper *Selbstwehr* (19.XII.19). Here it has its place among other Chanukkah stories, and is immediately followed by a little story on the *Trenderl*, the German term for *dreydl* which means spinning top, a toy for children. Odradek himself is as elusive as his name: he is and is not a *dreydl*. He represents what Theodor W. Adorno, in his insistence on the importance of 'literalness' in Kafka, called an 'association joke',[26] that is when Kafka takes words, idiomatic expressions or common phrases literally and makes them appear as personifications in his texts. Odradek is also described as a 'star', but this Star of David lives alone, has no purpose, and certainly no religious or cultural significance. What bothers the family man who narrates the story is that an existence such as Odradek's, without meaning, empty and hollow as his laughter, seems set to survive everyone.

A further theme of survival is played out in Kafka's only story with specifically Jewish subject matter, 'The Animal in the Synagogue', which he wrote the following year, 1920. Here, a marten-like creature has for centuries called a synagogue its home. Its favourite spot is high up, close to the women's section, towering above the men. Many small synagogues in Eastern Europe had animal pictures on the walls. Though there is no evidence that there were any drawings in the synagogues in Prague, Kafka would not have had to travel far to see them in the country. It is quite plausible that he created this story from such a motif on the wall and made the animal come alive. The text says that the animal's colour 'does resemble that of the paint inside the synagogue, only it is a little brighter'.[27]

Considering the Second Commandment against graven images it is not surprising that the animal has continually been threatened with expulsion:

> There is evidence, however, that at that time the question whether the presence of such an animal might be tolerated in the house of God was investigated from the point of view of the Law and the Commandments. Opinions were sought from various celebrated rabbis, views were divided, the majority were for the expulsion of the animal and a reconsecration of the house of God.[28]

The rabbis considered such animal pictures a distraction to prayer. However, despite many attempts to remove them, animal wall paintings survived as part of the folk tradition and remained a popular art form in synagogue decorations.[29] In Kafka's story the 'graven' image is freed from its fixed – 'graven' – position, takes on a life of its own and escapes when in danger. Furthermore, the narrator enables the animal to survive by eliminating narrative situations which pose a threat to its existence, employing his mock-midrash as a tool. The animal lives in constant fear of being expelled, even though it has survived the rabbinic decision until now. On the one hand, this might mean that the rabbis' decree to remove it was never carried out and the danger is over. On the other hand, if it has not been carried out yet, then the expulsion might still occur. However, the narrator immediately eliminates this danger, interjecting that even if they still wanted to carry out the decision, a practical question needs to be solved first: the animal has to be caught. As with Odradek (who is 'exceptionally nimble and refuses to be laid hold of', *TOS*: 176), this is hardly possible: 'in reality it was simply impossible to catch the animal, and hence it was also impossible to drive it out for good'.[30] The lack of closure on the thematic level is echoed on the narrative level. The movement of the narrative goes in spirals and is potentially endless as possible interjections allow for continual narrative expansion. Thus, we hear that even though no one has obviously ever succeeded in driving the animal out, this does not necessarily mean that no *attempts* have been made in the past. At this point there is room for even a longer story, the recounting of a legend which the narrator says exists in the folklore of his people. But as soon as the legend begins, the narrative breaks off. It breaks off because this type of reasoning could go on forever and the narrator finally stops it. Fragmentary narratives such as these are typical of the genre *aggadah*, a commentary on the Scriptures in the form of legends.

Kafka wrote a great many fragments of this nature, fragments which have been generally ignored by critics and under-represented in editions of his work because they were considered 'incomplete'. Until recently the German–English bilingual edition, *Parables and Paradoxes*, was the only edition which included 'The Animal in the Synagogue'. In this collection we see Kafka rewrite in a mock-midrashic fashion not only myths of ancient Israel, but non-Jewish myths as well. His fragmentary texts have had a hard time gaining literary status; one, the Golem fragment of 1916, was never included in any edition of his *literary* texts and has now even been eliminated from the latest, 'critical' edition of his diaries on the grounds that Kafka had apparently crossed it out. The creation of the Golem is generally clouded in mystery and secrecy, but in Kafka's reworking of the legend everything is open for everyone to see. Usually the Golem's body is depicted as a monstrosity and associated with fear, but here there is no fear, everything is allowed in the rabbi's house, even the tasting of the clay becomes part of the ceremony. The clay tastes bitter and Kafka at this point opens up the possibility for a narrative digression, a whole new narrative seems to hinge on the word 'bitter'. But he abandons this idea and immediately proceeds with rewriting the creation story in Genesis. There is no snake, no deceit in the rabbi's house, this is the optimal space, the rabbi the perfect creator, throwing his mind and body fully into the act of creation.

'Investigations of a Dog' (1922) employs folklore elements for social satire. In January 1922, before writing this story, Kafka felt that his involvement with Zionism had been detrimental to his writing: 'All such writing is an assault on the frontiers; if Zionism had not intervened, it might easily have developed into a new secret doctrine, a Kabbalah' (*D*2: 202–3).[31] In the light of contemporary Zionism, the dog metaphor satirises the 'dog's life' many Jews led in the Diaspora, which is characterised by 'an endless aberration' (*Irren* – *GWC*: 162). *Irren* in the sense of *umherirren* ('wandering around confusedly') brings to mind the myth of the Wandering Jew, as well as the phrase *sich irren* (to make an error): the dogs' wandering is thus presented as the result of an erroneous decision, and from then on 'Error' seems to mark their whole existence. For instance, like many Zionists, the narrator dog believes it cannot be right that the dogs are 'obeying regulations that are not those of the dog community as a whole, indeed if anything opposed to them' (*GWC*: 143). He is bothered by this, and wants to question and speak up where the others 'seem content with silence' (159).

The dog's rebellion begins in his youth when he starts investigating and questioning the dog community's obsession with *Nahrungswissenschaft* ('the science of nutrition'), which has 'occupied us since the earliest times, it is the chief object of our reflections' (*GWC*: 149). Kafka's humorous word combination can be taken to refer to Jewish dietary restrictions and by extension to the commentaries in the Talmud where volume upon volume discusses the suitability of different kinds of food from the point of view of religious ritual. Truly, the rabbinic commentaries surpass the understanding of most 'dogs':

> it has become a science of such vast dimensions that it is not only beyond the grasp of any single scholar but beyond all scholars collectively, it is a burden too weighty for all save the entire dog community, and even they groan under it and cannot bear it completely. (*GWC*: 149–50)

The narrator therefore questions the need for this 'science': 'And all this endless labour – to what end? To none save to bury myself ever deeper in silence, so deep that no one will ever be able to drag one out of it again' (161). Thus, the dogs' own laws, the Scriptures themselves, are seen as furthering a defeatist attitude within the community, and the narrator even implies that the dogs want this. These charges are typical of Zionist discourse in Kafka's time. Ahad Haam, for instance, said, 'that the Jews are no longer the people of Scripture but the slaves of Scripture'.[32] And Kafka's school friend Hugo Bergmann (1883–1975) insisted that 'The Jews want the *Galuth* [Exile].'[33]

Towards the end of his life, Bergmann defended the story when it was published in Hebrew in 1971 and readers criticised Kafka for applying the dog metaphor to Jews. Bergmann argued amongst other things that it contained 'many allusions to the Zionist dream of Jewish life'.[34] Though this is correct, Zionism is not represented as an alternative. The Zionists, too, are concerned with 'the science of nutrition' and they are particularly obsessed with 'preparation of the soil' (*Bodenbearbeitung* – *GWC*: 164). Many of the Zionist publications that Kafka read dealt with practical matters such as land preparation in Palestine. His pun, which primarily refers to the dogs' constant preoccupation with marking their territory, gives the satire of Zionism away. In addition, the innumerable volumes of Zionist publications from this period seem just as inexhaustible as the many volumes of the Talmud. The Zionists' rebellion against tradition has led to an excessive intellectualism, which interferes just as much with the pursuit of a spiritual regeneration of the Jewish people as traditional dogma had done before. The dog is neither religious nor Zionist: 'I swallow down my food where I find it, but it does not seem to me to merit the slightest preliminary methodical examination from an agricultural point of view' (*GWC*: 150).

Against those who insist that agricultural considerations matter most, the dog argues that the law has at all times included a spiritual dimension. He refers to tradition itself, to the 'supplementary improvement-process in the form of incantation, dance, and song' (165). This spiritual dimension is less concerned with 'the ground nourishment in the narrower sense, [it] serve[s] principally to draw down the nourishment from above' (165). His description of traditional ceremonies where dogs jump in the air and 'wail the ancient folk-songs at the sky' (166) is very playful. So too is his vision of how traditional practices would look if the Zionists were right: 'it is to the earth that all the whispering, all the singing, and all the dancing should be addressed' (165).

'Investigations of a Dog' is no linear narrative; it is highly associative and contains many narrative breaks that are filled in by humorous anecdotal commentary which resembles anecdotes in rabbinic texts. For instance, there is the narrator's first encounter with the 'music dogs', who sing without producing a sound. Critics have pointed out that Kafka here alludes to his love of the Yiddish theatre, but he is also alluding to Jewish mysticism.[35] There are then the famous 'air dogs' (*Lufthunde*), a play on the Yiddish term *Luftmensch* ('air people'), a metaphor which is normally applied to unfortunates who have no income and must rely on the community for support, but which was also used in Zionist discourse to criticise those Jews. However, the narrator dog takes their side. To those who ridicule them, he replies that their criticism is uncalled for because they simply do not exist: as much as he has tried, he has never even managed to see a single one who exhibited such negative characteristics. Thus he continues to believe in them, albeit in a different fashion: 'no prejudices restricted my mental capacity' (156). And he annuls the criticism directed against them by rendering it humorous, once again by taking the metaphor literally. The depiction of the dogs soaring in the air is a comic device, and Kafka uses it in order to transform the air dogs' supposedly senseless existence into a meaningful one. Their strength lies in their survival and he admires them because their stubbornness shows that:

> despite what seem to our mind insurmountable obstacles, no species of dog, once extant, and however curious it may be, ever dies out, or at least not easily, at least not without there being something in every species which puts up a long and successful resistance. (158)

Moreover, the narrator is in search of fellow dogs he can relate to and the tenacity of the *Lufthunde* implies at least the possibility that one day there might also be more like him. Suddenly the dogs appear to him entirely wonderful: 'far more *wonderful* to my mind is the absurdity, the silent absurdity of these curious individuals' (156; my emphasis).

In his youth, the narrator dog performed many experiments to prove the validity of the spiritual dimension. These anecdotal episodes illustrate the challenge which Kafka's narrative reversals represent for tradition, convention, or political dogma. Benjamin was the first to point this out:

> [Kafka's writings] do not modestly lie at the feet of doctrine, as aggadah [legends, anecdotes] lies at the feet of halakha [law]. When they have crouched down, they unexpectedly raise a mighty paw against it.[36]

Seven years earlier Scholem had called Benjamin's secular interpretation a 'presumptuous supposition', comparing it to the blasphemous nature of an attempt to paraphrase in words the quest for a divine judgement.[37] But such an attempt is indeed depicted in 'Investigations of a Dog' when the little dog succeeds in showing that food is actually attracted to someone who is hungry. Again, the midrashic technique is to take the metaphor 'spiritual food' literally: the dog imagines what it would be like if 'the food were then to descend of itself from above, and without paying any attention to the ground were to come knocking at my teeth for admittance' (168). Here we have a parody of a biblical motif ('Manna' in the wilderness descending on man) and of a mystical motif (the doorkeeper). The description of the experiment is ludicrous: the narrator's fertile imagination has produced a kind of *Luftnahrung* ('air food') which pursues the little dog from above and ridicules any kind of religious quest.

A subsequent anecdote further supports Benjamin's argument. Having been told that his experiments are not convincing, the little dog turns to traditional practices where the way to redemption is through self-negation and fasting. Again the narrator exploits this anecdote for creative storytelling. Before he started on his fasting experiment, the little dog had actually made sure that his point of departure was according to the law. He knew that in a famous disputation a sage at one time wanted to prohibit fasting. But another sage intervened and answered, significantly with a question, in good Talmudic fashion: 'But who will ever think of fasting?' (*GWC*: 171), implying that it would never occur to anyone in his right mind to do such a thing. The first sage found this answer so convincing that he no longer saw any need to prohibit fasting. But, the narrator intervenes, this does not solve the problem; since no law had been formulated, the question still needs to be asked: 'Is not fasting forbidden after all?' (171). The function of this parody of Talmudic reasoning is to satirise the seriousness and naiveté of the young dog: desperately in search of a straightforward 'law' that he can apply to his present circumstances, he eagerly reassures himself that fasting is not forbidden and goes ahead with his experiment. Naturally, the results are catastrophic. He is starving, has spells of delirium, and suddenly comes to realise that the commentators' views had been downright wrong.

Kafka's secular perspective is clear: the dog himself admits that his 'work was really an attempt to undermine the science of nutrition' (169). His experiments show that he has reduced the law to a mere functional, literal level. This becomes increasingly obvious in the little dog's final 'assault on the frontiers', when he stubbornly persists in his fasting and pushes the situation to its very limit. At the climax he experiences what Scholem described to Benjamin as 'the nothingness of Revelation' (20.IX.34; *Correspondence*, p. 142): 'what faced me here and now was earnest, this was where research could have proved its worth, but where had it gone? Here was only a dog snapping helplessly at the empty air' (173). This is the 'presumptuous supposition!!' which Scholem perceived and objected to in Benjamin's reading of Kafka. But Benjamin is proven right in that Kafka's dog here is raising a big paw against *halakha*. Moreover, observance of the law is ridiculed in the immediately following episode with the hunting dog who insists that the little dog *must* get out of his way. The little dog challenges this new *halakha*, 'nothing but musts. Do you understand why we must?', and receives the reply, 'No . . . but there is nothing to understand about it, these are self-evident, natural things' (174). The humour of the situation lies in the pun on the German *müssen* which in formal speech means 'to have to' in the sense of 'must' and, more prosaically, 'to urinate'. This is what leads to the misunderstanding. The little dog does not see the play on words, and the hunting dog reacts ironically: 'My dear little dog, do you really not understand that I must? Don't you understand what is self-evident' (175).

The anecdotal encounter with the hunting dog has the function of providing final liberation. The dog's singing frees the little dog from himself, his self-imposed restraints, and he 'went bounding off in the mightiest of leaps with the melody at my heels' (175). The hunting dog is certainly no 'death hound', as Winfried Kudszus believes.[38] Kafka is not drawing on Wagner. This singing dog, like the earlier singing dogs, evokes the cabalistic music from Jewish mysticism. In fact, the hunting dog who sings has stepped right out of the world of contemporary fairy tales. He is what we might call a sort of 'Bambi Kabbalah dog'. *Bambi* (1923; published in late December 1922) was written by Felix Salten (1869–1945), a contemporary of Kafka's, and well known to him as a Zionist. Salten's deer world, an allegory of Jewish history with a Zionist message, finds an equivalent in Kafka's dog universe. Though there is no ironclad proof that Kafka knew this text before it was published, the similarities are far too striking not to attract our attention. We know how concerned Kafka was about Jewish educational matters, especially after the founding of the Jewish Elementary School in Prague in 1920, and how eagerly he had been collecting Jewish children's literature ever since the establishment of the Jewish *Volksheim* (People's Home) in Berlin in 1916 when he helped his fiancée Felice Bauer find appropriate instructional materials for the refugee children she was teaching. His interest in Jewish children's literature does make it at least plausible that he knew *Bambi* (or parts of it) before it was published – possibly through his Zionist friends who were friends with Salten. In any event, the sudden appearance of Bambi's father, when Bambi is lying on the ground in a pool of blood, incapable of going on, is strikingly similar to the scene in 'Investigations of a Dog'. The narrator dog, also lying in his blood, is comparable to Bambi; the hunting dog to Bambi's father.

The description of the hunting dog suggests a deer as much as a dog: 'He was lean, long-legged, brown with a patch of white here and there, and had a fine, strong, piercing glance. "What are you doing here?" he asked. "You must go away from here"' (173). In Salten's novel the eyes of Bambi's father are always remarkable: they are dark, deep, penetrating, kind and proud. The father also uses very similar words when he commands his son to get up and come with him. Moreover, the eroticism which manifests itself in Bambi's love and admiration for his father is transformed in Kafka's story into the hunting dog's (incipiently erotic) advances. Then the incredible happens: the hunting dog begins to sing and the little dog is literally carried away by the melody, which seems to exist independently even of the hunting dog, soaring in the air and coming towards him, existing for him alone. This melody gives the little dog the necessary strength to 'fly away' (in the original German) as in a fairy tale. In this 'happy' ending there seems to be no irony. In hindsight, the narrator comments that even if this experience was 'an error it was not without a certain grandeur; it remains the sole reality, if only an apparent reality, that I have carried over into this world from my time of fasting' (175). These anecdotes, and especially the scene with the Bambi Kabbalah dog, are not just 'beginnings' for a new kind of writing, the new type of folkloristic Kabbalah, which Kafka said existed already in his earlier work. Rather, Kafka has created his own imaginary world out of the contemporary discourses (traditional, Zionist, mystic, children's literature) available to him. It is a clear interdiscursive construction.

Within the folkloristic cultural framework, a new voice has emerged which has liberated the narrator from his dog life and removed him not to a Zionist world but to an imaginary one which resembles the associative fantasies in a Chagall painting. Does not Kafka's entire representation of the Jewish world in 'Investigations of a Dog' evolve out of a humorous play on the Yiddish term *Luftmensch* (air person)? Here, *Luftmenschen* are transformed into dogs of various strange breeds: Zionists with their *Lufthunger* (air hunger), the spiritualists with their *Luftnahrung* (air nourishment), the incredible *Lufthunde* (air dogs) themselves, the ecstatic *Musikhunde* (music dogs) – not forgetting the Bambi Kabbalah dog. These imaginary creatures pursue many strange activities: mostly *Nahrungswissenschaft* (the science of nutrition) and *Bodenbearbeitung* (the cultivation of the land), but those of a more spiritual orientation go as far as practising the art of *Musikwissenschaft* (the science of music).

In this dog universe characterised by metamorphosis and error, a little dog undertakes his 'assault on the frontiers', in a manner not unlike Josef K.'s struggle or the travails of the ape Rotpeter. Along the way he encounters *halakhas* (laws, rules) of various kinds, challenges them and exposes them as errors. Metamorphosis shows its presence in fluid linguistic structures and shifting ideological formations. Real miracles occur when the Golem's creation becomes a mystical experience, or when 'meaningless existences' like 'air dogs', or the little dog himself, are transformed into something 'wonderful'.

But let us not be taken in by fantasies and miracles. Josef K. may think he has an important position at the bank, yet his world – and this too is like a Chagallian painting – comes tumbling down and soon he himself is no more than a *Luftmensch*. The reality of *The Trial* is that the accused are degraded and treated like dogs: merchant Block is Huld's 'dog' and Josef K. is killed 'like a dog'. These human characters share the fate of Kafka's animals because they all live out their lives alone, amongst the garbage, on staircases, in the desert, in a variety show, or, like the mice in 'Josephine, the Songstress', always very tired. Kafka's imaginary animals and characters do have a place in Chagall's allegorical and mystical landscape. The synaesthesia of eyes and song, vision and sound, memory and melody creates a Chagallian magic realism. One might object that the beauty of Chagall's vivid colours lasts, and that Kafka's brief flights into fantasy end only too soon. But the colour of memory (of the music dogs and the Bambi Kabbalah dog) gives the little dog the strength to endure life amongst his dislocated 'brothers and sisters' in their worlds of exile and alienation. And it is also this memory of a simple 'folk' tradition which gives the singer Josephine the strength to carry on and cling to her art until her last breath.

NOTES

Some sections of this chapter have appeared in earlier versions in previous publications: 'Elements of Jewish Folklore in Kafka's *Metamorphosis*', in M: 107–25; 'Aggadah Raises its Paw against Halakha: Kafka's Zionist Critique in *Forschungen eines Hundes*', *Journal of the Kafka Society of America* 16.1 (1992), 4–18; 'Der Proceß in Yiddish, or "The Importance of Being Humorous"', *TTR (Traduction, Terminologie, Rédaction)*, 7:2 (1994), 35–62.

1. Yudl Rosenberg, 'The Golem or The Miraculous Deeds of Rabbi Liva' (1809), in Joachim Neugroschel (ed./tr.), *Great Tales of Jewish Fantasy and the Occult*, p. 162.
2. Walter Jens, 'Ein Jude namens Kafka', in Thilo Koch (ed.), *Portraits deutsch-jüdischer Geistesgeschichte* (Cologne: Du Mont Schauberg, 1961), pp. 179–203, here p. 186; Gershon Shaked, 'Kafka, Jewish Heritage, and Hebrew Literature', in *The Shadows Within: Essays on Modern Jewish Writers* (Philadelphia: The Jewish Publication Society, 1987), pp. 3–21, here p. 9.
3. Gershom G. Scholem, *Major Trends in Jewish Mysticism* (New York: Schocken, 1961), p. 283.
4. Rabbi Nachman, 'The Prince Who Thought He Was a Rooster', in *Gates to the New City*, here p. 458.
5. I. L. Peretz, *Selected Stories*, pp. 29–33, here p. 29. This text is included in Peretz's *Volkstümliche Erzählungen* (Berlin: Jüdischer Verlag, 1913), which Kafka sent to Felice Bauer in 1916.
6. Peretz, *Stories*, p. 33.
7. Ibid., p. 29.
8. Scholem, *Trends*, p. 281.
9. Neugroschel, *Great Tales*, p. 557.
10. Scholem, *Trends*, p. 282.
11. Ibid., p. 283.
12. Arthur Green, 'Teachings of the Hasidic Masters', in Holtz (ed.), *Back to the Sources*, pp. 361–401, here p. 392.
13. Peretz, *Stories*, p. 122.
14. Peretz, 'Cabbalists', in Howe and Greenberg (eds.), *A Treasury of Yiddish Stories*, pp. 219–23, here p. 222.
15. Peretz, *Stories*, p. 30.
16. Franz Kafka, *Der Prozes*, tr. Melech Ravitch, illustrations Yossl Bergner (New York: Der Kval, 1966), p. 194.
17. Kafka recounts an anecdote about an *am ha-aretz* in his diaries (29.XI.11; D1: 166).
18. Gershom Scholem in *Benjamin über Kafka*, p. 79.

19. Max Brod, *Franz Kafka: a Biography*, tr. G. Humphrey Roberts and Richard Winston, 2nd edition (New York: Schocken, 1960), p. 178.
20. Letter to Gershom Scholem, 4.II.39, in *The Correspondence of Walter Benjamin and Gershom Scholem 1932–1940*, ed. Gershom Scholem, tr. Gary Smith and Andre Lefevere (New York: Schocken, 1989), p. 243.
21. David Stern, 'Midrash', in A. A. Cohen and P. Mendes-Flohr (eds.), *Contemporary Jewish Religious Thought* (New York: Scribner's, 1987), pp. 613–20, here p. 615.
22. Henry Sussman, *Franz Kafka: Geometrician of Metaphor* (Madison, Wis.: Coda Press, 1979), p. 110.
23. Neugroschel, *Great Tales*, p. 617.
24. Leo Weinstein, 'Kafka's Ape: Heel or Hero', *Modern Fiction Studies* 8 (1962/63), 75–9, here p. 78.
25. Richard Lichtheim, *Das Programm des Zionismus* (Berlin: Zionistische Vereinigung für Deutschland, 1913), p. 22. Kafka owned this book.
26. *Assoziationswitz*: 'the literalness is driven to the point of a pun', Theodor W. Adorno, 'Notes on Kafka', in *Prisms*, tr. S and S. Weber (London: Spearman, 1967), pp. 243–71, here p. 248. Cf. also Hartmut Binder, 'Common Sayings and Expressions in Kafka', tr. D. and I. Bruce, *TTR* (*Traduction, Terminologie, Rédaction*) 5.2 (1992), 41–105.
27. *Parables and Paradoxes*, ed. Nahum Glatzer (New York: Schocken, 1961), p. 49.
28. Ibid., p. 57.
29. See Shalom Sabar, 'Synagogue Interior Decoration and the Halakhah', in Rivka and Ben-Zion Dorfman (eds.), *Synagogues Without Jews* (Philadelphia: Jewish Publication Society, 2000), pp. 308–17. I am grateful to the editors for sharing their information with me, also to Michael Greenstein who first discovered the animal in Toronto.
30. *Parables and Paradoxes*, p. 57.
31. I have modified this and some of the translations to follow.
32. Cited in Adolf Böhm, *Die Zionistische Bewegung: eine kurze Darstellung ihrer Entwicklung*, vol.2 (Berlin: Welt-Verlag, 1920), p. 5. Kafka owned this book.
33. Hugo Bergmann, 'Jawne und Jerusalem', in *Jawne und Jerusalem: Gesammelte Aufsätze* (Berlin: Jüdischer Verlag, 1919), pp. 33–42, here p. 36.
34. Bergmann, 'Franz Kafka und die Hunde', *Mitteilungsblatt der Irgun Olej Merkas Europa* 34/35, 3.IX.72, p. 4.
35. 'The Hasidic Niggun', in *Encyclopaedia Judaica* 12 (Jerusalem: Keter, 1972), pp. 637–9, here p. 638.
36. Letter to Scholem, 12.VI.38, *The Correspondence of Benjamin and Scholem*, p. 225.
37. Letter from Scholem to Benjamin, 1.VIII.31, quoted in *Benjamin über Kafka. Texte, Briefzeugnisse, Aufzeichnungen*, ed. Hermann Schweppenhäuser (Frankfurt aM: Suhrkamp, 1981), p. 64.
38. Winfried Kudszus, 'Musik und Erkenntnis in Kafkas *Forschungen eines Hundes*', in M. Woodmansee and W. F. W. Lohnes (eds.), *Erkennen und Deuten: Essays zur Literatur und Literaturtheorie. Edgar Lohner in memoriam* (Berlin: Schmidt, 1983), pp. 300–9, here pp. 306–7.

FURTHER READING

I. Jewish literature

Buber, Martin, *Tales of the Hasidim: the Early Masters* (New York: Schocken, 1947/75).
Tales of the Hasidim: the Later Masters (New York: Schocken, 1948).
The Tales of Rabbi Nachman (Bloomington: Indiana University Press, 1956).
Greenberg, Eliezer and Irving Howe (eds.), *A Treasury of Yiddish Stories* (New York: Schocken, 1973).
Holtz, Barry W. (ed.), *Back to the Sources: Reading the Classic Jewish Texts* (New York: Summit Books, 1984).
Neugroschel, Joachim (ed./tr.), *Great Tales of Jewish Fantasy and the Occult* (New York: The Overlook Press, 1987).
Peretz, I. L., *Selected Stories*, ed. Irving Howe and Eliezer Greenberg (New York: Schocken, 1975).
Salten, Felix, *Bambi*, tr. Whittaker Chambers (New York: Grosset, 1929).
Schwartz, Howard (ed.), *Gates to the New City: a Treasury of Modern Jewish Tales* (New York: Avon, 1983).

II. Kafka and Judaism

Alter, Robert, *Necessary Angels: Tradition and Modernity in Kafka, Benjamin and Scholem* (Cambridge, Mass.: Harvard University Press, 1991).
Baioni, Giuliano, 'Zionism, Literature, and the Yiddish Theater', in Mark M. Anderson (ed.), *Reading Kafka: Prague, Politics, and the Fin-de-Siècle* (New York: Schocken, 1989), pp. 95–115.
Beck, Evelyn Torton, *Kafka and the Yiddish Theater: Its Impact on His Work* (Madison: University of Wisconson Press, 1971).
Gilman, Sander L., *Franz Kafka: the Jewish Patient* (New York: Routledge, 1995).
Grözinger, Karl Erich, *Kafka and Kabbala*, tr. Susan Hecker Ray (New York: Continuum, 1994).
Isenberg, Noah, *Between Redemption and Doom: the Strains of German-Jewish Modernism* (Lincoln and London: University of Nebraska Press, 1999).
Jofen, Jean, *The Jewish Mystic in Kafka* (New York: Peter Lang, 1987).
Robertson, Ritchie, *Kafka: Judaism, Politics and Literature* (Oxford: Clarendon, 1985).
Spector, Scott, *Prague Territories: National Conflict and Cultural Innovation in Franz Kafka's Fin de Siècle* (Berkeley: University of California Press, 2000).

10

DAGMAR C. G. LORENZ

Kafka and gender

Kafka configures gender roles in both familiar and unexpected ways. His characters, despite certain conformities with the stereotypes of his age, are in flux, calling to mind Otto Weininger's scale of masculinity and femininity.[1] Gender boundaries in Kafka's writings of all periods are indistinct as are boundaries between species. For Kafka one is not born male or female, to paraphrase Simone de Beauvoir, one becomes one or the other or sometimes a mixture of the two.

As a recent critic has pointed out, his approach to gender was tied up closely with Jewish thinking on the subject.[2] A close look at earlier and later works will reveal also that he did not revise his concepts of gender relations over time, contrary to Klaus Theweleit's assertion that by 1922 Kafka had achieved an understanding of women based on individuality, but rather that he 'de-essentialised' gender all along. Kafka derived gender models from a variety of sources all of which he approached in a critical, detached way. The diversity of the available models allowed him to recognise the relativity of each and, as Theweleit notes, to escape the exclusively heterosexual model which admits 'only victors and victims...(not men and women)'.[3] Contrary to Heinz Politzer's findings, gender in Kafka is used in anything but a stereotypical manner.[4] Configuring Kafka as anti-feminist would be as limiting as foregrounding the homosexual traits in his works at the expense of the heterosexual.[5] His women characters, often seductive and lascivious, lack the exotic appeal of other *fin-de-siècle femmes fatales* and even his most fragile female characters are self-sufficient and surprisingly resilient. Furthermore the positions Kafka the letter writer assumes towards his female correspondents are determined not only by gender but by factors of culture and class. Whether a woman is Jewish and eligible as a marriage partner plays an important role.

Most of the protagonists of Kafka's literary texts are male and have certain biographical attributes in common with him, hence the frequent associations between Kafka and his characters made particularly in early Kafka scholarship. In biographical studies Kafka's texts are typically treated as parables about his own troubled life – thus his avoidance of marriage and his inability to establish a mature heterosexual relationship loom large. The cultural, heterosexual, and Freudian biases are obvious. For Christian authors who remained single or married late in life – such as Goethe, Grillparzer, or Nietzsche – bachelorhood has rarely been problematised to the same degree as for Kafka, whose early critics (Brod, Politzer, Sokel), all writing from exile in the United States or Israel, shared his Habsburg-Jewish background.

Kafka's representation of gender and sexuality is inspired by the culture of Prague. His father had originally spoken Yiddish, then Czech, then German. Kafka wrote in German and was proficient in Czech, to which he frequently resorts in his letters to Milena Jesenská. He also had knowledge and an appreciation of Yiddish. In his social sphere cultural and religious expressions coalesced with secularised Jewish culture, Jewish orthodoxy, and popular Hasidic tradition. At the end of the nineteenth century Jewish gender role expectations were heterogeneous but distinct from those in Christian culture. With so many different models present no social paradigm remained unquestioned. Kafka furthermore witnessed fundamental social and cultural changes. Gender roles shifted as they had never before as new educational and employment opportunities for women opened. Socialism and women's movements worldwide undermined established patterns of behaviour. The First World War, the new nation-state republics which emerged from the postwar settlement, and women's suffrage marked the end of the old order.

Kafka's texts do not merely mirror these circumstances, they examine them critically. 'The Metamorphosis', for example, problematises the concept of the male provider (albeit a son and brother rather than a father and husband), a modern concept of Gentile origin, by foregrounding the working man's isolation and alienation from his family and community. Kafka also reveals the precarious situation of women once they lose the traditional protection of their families. Vulnerable to unwanted sexual advances from powerful men, they put their social standing and livelihood in jeopardy if they reject male advances, as is the case with Amalia in *The Castle*. But Kafka also shows the potentially liberating aspects of female employment. Single female characters such as Frieda (*The Castle*) and Fräulein Bürstner (*The Trial*) live away from their families. Their independence, in part expressed by the way they follow their erotic desires, in part by their pursuit of entertainment, are virtually unparalleled in other literature of the time. There is a clear sense in Kafka's fiction that changing women's roles affected all segments of society. The throng of unattended children in the Tintorelli episode of *The Trial* point to the problem of child care and education in the modern world. Nowhere is a mother or father to be seen and the little girls approach the painter and K. precociously aware of their sexuality. The few traditional families he portrays are distinctly troubled: Gregor Samsa, the modern provider in 'The Metamorphosis', reduces father, mother, and sister to a parasitic existence. After Gregor's demise, the rest of the family, including mother and daughter, take responsibility for their lives and prosper. Kafka's textual strategies underscore the disorientation caused by social and intellectual paradigm changes. Reader expectations are constantly foiled by the fast-changing perspectives, unreliable narrators, information gaps, and the destabilisation of basic categories such as time and space, as well as gender.

Kafka, the product of a multicultural society in transition, thus had to contend with complex and disparate gender models. His attitude towards his first fiancée, Felice Bauer, a Jewish woman from Berlin, professionally active and financially independent, differs from that toward Milena Jesenská, considerably younger than him, a journalist and an intellectual of Christian Czech origin. The conflicts Kafka addresses in his letters to women reflect the specific parameters of each relationship. There is no need to explain his Jewishness to Bauer, but he feels compelled to describe to her the importance of his writing and his unconventional lifestyle. In his letters to Jesenská, on the other hand, he addresses his Jewishness numerous times. He wants to explore her feelings regarding race and culture so that he can gauge the possible effect they might have on their friendship and position himself towards her accordingly. Other issues are their respective native languages, hers Czech, his German. At times he uses his background and her youth and marital status to maintain a distance. While he courted Bauer as a man courts the woman he has decided to marry, Jesenská was already married, and Kafka seems to have had a certain admiration for her Jewish husband, the writer and journalist, Ernst Polak. For various reasons, including Kafka's tuberculosis, living together with Jesenská on a permanent basis was out of the question.

Yet it is surprising how many of Kafka's letters to women are similar in tone and sentiment. Regardless which woman he writes to, in practical and intellectual matters his attitude is that of an equal partner. He gives straightforward advice to his sister Ottla, trying to assist her in making the appropriate choice regarding her education; he has a frank exchange on Martin Buber with Bauer; and he deliberates on editorial decisions and language with Jesenská.

The gender constellations in Kafka's letters and his fiction undermine the social and ideological hierarchies of the dominant culture. At the same time his texts show an affinity to concepts embedded in *fin-de-siècle* Central European Jewish culture, such as the motif of transformation – *Verwandlung* – and the interdependence rather than the opposition of male and female, also favourite motifs for Hermann Broch and Elias Canetti. Kafka's characters as well as his self-representation lack the psychologising features to come across as 'rounded'. They are distinct from the 'case studies' of his contemporaries, Gerhart Hauptmann, Thomas Mann, Arthur Schnitzler, or Robert Musil. Yet there are similarities between his characters and those of other writers exploring their Jewish identities, such as Else Lasker-Schüler, Claire Goll, Gertrud Kolmar, and Elias Canetti.

The complexity that baffles Kafka readers in general is particularly striking in his representation of gender. Notions of gender identity and role are destabilised by the competing Gentile and Jewish paradigms. Recent studies which have foregrounded Jewish paradigms in Kafka's work have brought to the fore distinct methods of assessing status by valorising specific activities in Jewish and German culture (Boyarin, Gilman, Biale, Grözinger).[6] For example, Judaism has traditionally excluded women from learning scripture and participation in the synagogue, limiting them to the religious duties associated with motherhood and the domestic sphere, including the laws of ritual purity. Yet Jewish women were expected to be involved in the family business and were usually knowledgeable in trade and finance. Daniel Boyarin cautions not to misread these patterns as promoting a 'kinder, gentler' patriarchy since 'male domination was firmly in place' despite the greater economic mobility of Jewish women.[7] Christians may have considered the role of Jewish women masculine, but this was not the case. Male high-status positions were inaccessible to Jewish and Christian women alike.

Critics who have contextualised Kafka's writings within European modernism are all important for an understanding of his configurations of gender. Jewish, Christian, and secular Christian cultural narratives coalesce in his writing as they do in other modernists of Austro-Hungarian background. However, Kafka does not synthesise Eastern and Western paradigms. On the contrary, he lays open the tensions between Austro-German and Czech traditionalism and modernism, as also between the narratives of the classical languages and those of the modern Western world. He shows discrepancies and asynchronicities, making the incongruities between the mutually enhancing as well as mutually exclusive paradigms transparent. Romantic love, for example, a dominant feature of German Romantic and post-Romantic literature, is conspicuously absent in his work. Reader expectations are occasionally led in that direction because of certain character constellations or plot lines, but the expectations remain unfulfilled. In *The Man who Disappeared*, for example, tension is created by the introduction of Pollunder's daughter Klara who Karl Roßmann leaves his uncle to meet, thereby neglecting his commitments. When Klara materialises, she is bold, athletic, apparently promiscuous, and not at all to Karl's liking when she wrestles him to the ground. Something similar occurs in 'A Country Doctor' with its initial constellation of an unmarried older man and a young female servant.[8] Yet rather than uniting the potential couple, the plot separates them for ever in a tragicomic manner when the doctor is summoned in the middle of the night to attend to a patient, leaving Rosa to the mercies of the horse handler, whose violent appetites might somehow be manifestation of the doctor's own desires.

Episodes involving two unattached males do not result in erotic encounters despite the tension and desire present in them. Similar to much of the largely de-sexualized but highly erotic fiction of Leopold von Sacher-Masoch they are left open-ended and ambivalent. When he meets his rich uncle, Karl Roßmann abandons the stoker into whose bed he had climbed earlier. While the advocate Huld inspires feelings of revulsion and fascination in Josef K., the encounters between the pair take place in Huld's bedroom. K. develops also a momentary sense of solidarity with a fellow defendant named Block, to whom he feels close. Huld's ritualistic humiliation of Block in the presence of Leni, Huld's nurse, who is sexually involved with all three men, calls to mind sadomasochistic practices as thematised in Sacher-Masoch's *Venus in Furs* (1869).

Finally, Kafka undermines the traditional literary paradigm according to which a woman's sexual encounters end in marriage or tragedy. Rarely is marriage even discussed. The case of K. and Frieda in *The Castle* is an exception. Here the couple's uncertain position (he an uninvited land-surveyor, she a barmaid), not to mention K.'s distractionary interest in other characters, make a stable relationship, let alone marriage, highly unlikely from the start. Sexual encounters involving single women and married or unmarried men occur frequently in Kafka's fiction, however. These casual and at times businesslike relationships call to mind the pattern of the pornographic novel, such as *Josephine Mutzenbacher* (c.1900).[9] Usually the intimacy occurs spontaneously, as does Frieda and K.'s love-making on the barroom floor or the passionate kiss between Fräulein Bürstner and Josef K. At times coercion is involved: but in *The Man who Disappeared* it is the socially inferior woman who took advantage of the hero, who was less than half her age. Karl's recollection of this sexual encounter is one of

Kafka's most explicit sexual episodes. However, it is the female who takes the role of aggressor:

> Then she lay herself down beside him...listened to his heart, offered him her chest so that he could listen to hers but which she couldn't make him do, pressed her naked stomach against his body, searched with her hand, so disgusting that Karl shook his head and neck free from the pillows, between his legs, thrust against him a few times, it seemed to him that she was a part of himself. (DV: 36)

The reversal of the traditional roles reveals the arbitrariness of gender codes and pens a perspective from which men and women appear equally capable of violence and submission. Rarely in Kafka's writing do the partners express tenderness or feelings of obligation towards one another. In contrast to pornographic literature, however, and again similar to Sacher-Masoch, Kafka avoids graphic physical descriptions and obscene vocabulary.

Kafka's texts defy deciphering – they are not encoded. Informed by the great occidental systems of Hegel, Marx, or Freud, they do not reproduce them. Nowhere is this more obvious than in the representation of gender and sexuality. Male and female characters are configured as inseparable, even interchangeable, the same way world and mind, external and internal reality, subject and object, appear as one in his works. Clothes and names, the outermost layers, rather than physical or psychological coding, are the primary indicators of gender. Occasionally Kafka thematises cross-dressing or overdressing, for example in *The Castle*, where girls are mentioned wearing men's boots. On the other hand, Pepi's hyper-feminine adornments after her promotion to the position of barmaid strike K. as inappropriate, a caricature of femininity. Mark M. Anderson assigns clothes to the sphere of worldly business: 'chains with which the individual is bound to society'.[10] Clothes are indicators of urban society's unnatural relationship to the body. They provide protection and identity, including gender identity, but they are also material fetters and an incursion on the body's freedom. The bondage of women and the social constraints on them are signalled by the fact that female characters are often cast as victims of fashion. This is true for Brunelda, even though she is said to be rich, as well as for Pepi. Although both women possess a measure of material independence, they feel compelled to make themselves objects of male desire by dressing provocatively. In 'The Judgement' Herr Bendemann condemns his son's fiancée primarily because of the way she dresses. Excessively fashion-conscious characters turn themselves into images; images and attire can even replace a woman's physical presence completely. In 'The Metamorphosis' Gregor, having turned into an insect, crawls on top of the picture of a lady in furs, his prized possession which he wants to protect from being taken away, and presses his body against it as if in a sexual act. This is only one of many instances in Kafka's writing that masculinity or femininity are depicted in the absence of the appropriately gendered being.

Contrary to the explicit gendering through clothes and names, references to the body tend to be gender-neutral and somewhat vague. Primary or secondary sexual characteristics remain unnamed. At the end of 'The Metamorphosis', for example, it is only in conjunction with the word 'girl' that the epithets applied to Gregor's sister acquire gender specificity:

> While they were thus conversing, it occurred to Mr and Mrs Samsa almost at the same moment, as they gazed on their increasingly vivacious daughter, that in spite of all the sorrow of recent times, which had made her cheeks pale, she had blossomed into a pretty and full-figured [üppig] girl. (EL: 157–8)

In conjunction with a different referent they could be applied to a flower and even to a young male. Similarly the fantasy of intimacy in a letter to Milena Jesenská:

> Because I love you . . . I love the entire world and your left shoulder is a part of it, no, it was at first the right one, and therefore I kiss it if I want to and also your left shoulder is part of it and your face beneath me in the forest and my relaxing on your almost uncovered chest. (9.VIII.20; BM: 202)

The gender-neutral shoulder, the face, and the Brust (chest) rather than the female-specific Busen or Brüste (breasts) achieve gender specificity only if the addressee is known. Otherwise, the same text could also refer to a male partner. The same can be said of the episode involving physical proximity between Karl Roßmann and the stoker:

> 'Just lie down on the bed, you'll have more room,' said the man. Karl crawled inside as best he could and laughed out loud at his forlorn attempt to swing himself over . . . 'Just stay', the man said pushing against his chest quite roughly with one of his hands so that he fell back into the bed. (DV: 11–12)

The roughness of the older man, the enforced compliance of the younger, simulate male and female patterns in an all-male environment.

The fluctuating gender role constructs do not conform with the more predictably polarised qualities of masculinity and femininity that the fin-de-siècle majority discourse represented as innate. In Kafka male characters with few masculine, female characters with few feminine traits occur and vice versa. The hard-working Therese in The Man who Disappeared and the independent-minded Amalia in The Castle are reminiscent of traditional Jewish female models, but they also call to mind the strong female figures of Austrian *biedermeier* literature, for example Barbara in Grillparzer's *Der arme Spielmann*, a novella of which Kafka was particularly fond, and the independent women in Adalbert Stifter's *Der Nachsommer* and *Brigitta*. All these characters are self-sufficient and sexually inaccessible. The 'battle of the sexes', August Strindberg's foremost theme, is reflected in the physical fights between Karl and the amazonlike Klara, as well as in the psychological struggle of the narrator with his real or imagined female opponent in 'A Little Woman'. The favourite *Jugendstil* motif of the vamp is evoked by the father in 'The Judgement' when he describes how his son was lured by a loose woman into a serious commitment. Leni in *The Trial* recalls seductresses from the world of Undine (an elusive water sprite often configured in German folklore and Romantic literature as a companion for human males), who fail to keep her love and loyalty because of their innate human shortcomings, curiosity or possessiveness. Leni's physical deformity, a piece of skin connecting her fingers in a reptilelike fashion, is a sign of her connection to the animal-realm. Often Kafka's female characters call to mind the Christian polarisation of woman as whore or mother without completely fitting into that pattern, or the polarisation put forward in Weininger's *Geschlecht und Charakter* (Sex and Character). Strong female figures, such as the cook in *The Man who Disappeared*, the innkeeper in *The Castle*, and Frau Grubach in *The Trial*, may appear gender-neutral, but there is something loose and unpredictable about young unmarried working women. Josef K.'s lover Elsa is a waitress, who in her spare time receives gentlemen callers in her bedroom. Even the moral character of Fräulein Bürstner, who apparently holds a demanding and responsible position, is called into question by Frau Grubach. The ease with which she yields to K.'s unexpected advances suggests that she is accustomed to casual intimate encounters, whereas her avoidance of him thereafter seems to indicate the opposite.

Kafka explores the full range of male gender stereotypes, including the unheroic, irresolute, and effeminate configuration of Jewish masculinity – often complemented by competent, no-nonsense but uneducated female characters – and the rough male type, who reflects Gentile gender role expectations of male assertiveness. Karl Roßmann, although he is already a father, represents the submissive male, dominated by male and female characters alike. On the other hand, Josef K. and K. both display submissive or dominant behaviour, depending on the situation. In their ambivalence they embody the gender patterns of both Jewish and Gentile society.[11] The heroes of Kafka's two most famous novels can therefore be read as Jews in transition. They seek, but have not yet achieved, assimilation. In the highly condensed and rich symbolic short story 'A Country Doctor', Kafka presents many divergent models of masculinity. The doctor, unable to rescue his maid from a brutal intruder, ends up lost on a never-ending journey. Like Ahasver, the Eternal Jew, he is unable to settle down. After losing his female companion, he also fails in his profession since he cannot heal his young patient. The sick boy with the mysterious wound in his thigh – a possible allusion to the Gentile view of Jewishness as a disease – exemplifies the Gentile stereotype of the Jew as either effeminate (the suppurating wound is an horrific male vision of the vagina) or as diseased. The expectations of the villagers add to the gendering of two male characters as masculine and feminine respectively. The doctor is expected to lie down in bed with his youthful patient in order to heal him. Compared to the doctor and the boy, the horse-handler appears as the epitome of a male aggression. He appears seemingly out of nowhere, forces the doctor off his property, and presumably rapes the maid. Strong, brutal, ignorant or defiant of the law, he represents a 'goyish' kind of masculinity. Such brutish behaviour is not an isolated instance in Kafka's writing. The student's treatment of the court usher's wife in *The Trial* is similar, when he carries the woman off half against her will, half with her consent.

In the absence of extensive psychological commentary Kafka's characters appear fragmentary, even cartoonlike. Relationships between his minimalist literary figures are as hard to imagine as their self-sufficient existence. The erotic encounters between them are as open-ended as the quests they undertake. Conventional endings such as integration into a community or family do not occur – there is neither a 'happily ever after' nor real tragedy. Existing marriages are portrayed as problematic and seem to be beyond the narrators' grasp. A passage about Jesenská's marriage articulates the sense of mystery to which the letter writer is an outsider. Kafka surmises:

> that you are joined to your husband through a marriage, sacramentally speaking, quasi impossible to dissolve... and I through the same kind of marriage – I do not know with whom, but the glance of this terrible wife often rests upon me, that I do feel.
> (13.VIII.20; *BM*: 214)

In other words, for Kafka the concept of a marital commitment may or may not involve a human partner as his counterpart.

Generally the characters are caught up in their own perceptions and desires. They fail at communication and intimacy. The very existence of the other, be it the outside world or a second individual, is never quite certain. All perceptions are filtered through the narrators' consciousness. Factual knowledge is unattainable, so is any certainty about the thoughts and actions of either narrator or character.[12] Kafka deliberately constructs situations in such a way as to exclude interchange. The individual is a prisoner of the senselessly moving material world. There are no redeeming forces such as the Eternal Feminine or the opposite, woman as a demonic power. Any such notions on the part of the protagonists turn out to be illusory. While Roßmann, Josef K., and K. frequently turn to women to advance their cause, the women turn out to be less powerful and less interested in the protagonist's concerns than he imagines. Almost invariably the male character mishandles the relationship by betraying the woman's trust. Frieda loses her privileged position because of her association with K. This development leaves her unconcerned because she considers K. her rescuer who offers her the prospect of marriage. She seems to consider being his wife preferable to her position as the lover of a high-ranking castle official. K. does not show the same loyalty to Frieda but seeks the company of other women as well as the sexually ambivalent Barnabas. Roßmann takes up with less than trustworthy fellows, Delamarche and Robinson, against the warning of his friend, Therese. Josef K. recognises at one point that he networks primarily with women, stating that he enlists female support ('Ich werbe Helferinnen', DP: 114). It is apparent that he and K. have no genuine appreciation of the women they encounter: their interest is commensurate with the degree of influence with the higher authorities they attribute to the women. The attempts to advance themselves end for Kafka's protagonists in frustration because they project their own wishes and expectations on to the women. In effect, they construct their female counterparts according to their needs. This is illustrated in 'The Judgement' where the two female characters (mother and fiancée) are absent, like the distant friend. Both he and the temptress Georg's father refers to in his accusations are creations of the characters' imaginations.

The multivalence of gender in Kafka causes a pervasive sense of uncertainty; retreating into radical individualism offers itself as one way out of the dilemma of gender role confusion. Kafka himself vacillated between different models, including the health- and body-conscious modern man, the ascetic, the dandy, the intellectual, alternatives that presented themselves, differently contextualised, to be sure, to fin-de-siècle Jews and Gentiles alike. He was also aware of the implications of class and community although he did not conform to any of them completely. For Kafka, who did not define himself as an assimilated German Jew, a Zionist, a Socialist, a Jewish traditionalist or religious Jew, the self, even a fragmentary self, promised a measure of autonomy. In the absence of a strong sense of community, even a fragmentary, alienated self promised autonomy. Yet Kafka was aware of the price that he had to pay for being a Jew and a bachelor. Single life, considered desirable in many European traditions is nothing short of a curse from the point of Jewish society. Through his profoundly alienated characters Kafka expresses the irresolvable conflict engendered by the inability of the individual to come to terms with the competing concepts of community, configured as family, corporate membership, and marriage. All these undermine individual autonomy but promise acceptance, safety, and comfort.

In Jewish thought the unattached individual stands apart from the complete humanity of the couple. The latter is conceptualized in Yiddish by the fusion of male and female in expressions such as *tate-mame* (parents), and *husnkalle* (bride and groom). 'The Bachelor's Misfortune' reveals the degree to which Kafka's thinking is influenced by such notions. This short text enumerates the suffering that awaits an unmarried man in his old age: lack of dignity, loneliness when he is sick, isolation in a coupled society without role models for a single lifestyle and, finally, childlessness which excludes him from the life cycle altogether. A childless man has no *Kaddish*, no one to recite the prayer for the dead for him, and his name will be erased from the Book of Life. 'Unhappiness' reverberates with the same profound sense of loneliness. The apparition of a small child, a real or imagined dialogue, an imagined female ghost, and a fellow tenant's criticism precipitate the narrator's surrender: 'Now I could have easily gone for a walk. But because I felt so very alone I preferred to go upstairs and to bed' (*EL*: 36). The unmarried central figure of 'Blumfeld an Older Bachelor' contemplates acquiring a dog to fill the void in his personal life but fears the disorder and turmoil such a creature might cause. In his state of isolation he appears both tragic and pathetic.

There is a striking similarity between Kafka's father as he is portrayed in the 'Letter to his Father' and Georg's father in 'The Judgement'. Gilman argues that in the story Kafka reflects the stereotype of the Jewish male as configured by the dominant culture, characterising Herr Bendemann senior 'in terms of illness; unmanly appearance, like, but not identical to tubercular women'.[13] According to Gilman, Kafka viewed his own father as a sick Jew despite the fact that he had been generally in good health. In other words, by extension, as the son of such a father, he ascribed to himself stereotypically feminine traits although he had been strong and virile. In so doing, Kafka adopts the anti-Semitic stereotype of Jews as corrupt and sick. At the same time he takes up the notion that the intimacy between male Jews and a male god causes the Jewish people to become configured as feminine. 'The Judgement' is only one of the many instances where specifically Jewish concepts converge with Gentile ones in a way that makes the text accessible to 'Jewish' and a 'non-Jewish' readings.

The ideal Jewish male was the Torah scholar. The religious establishment, teachers and students, was a male hierarchy and excluded women from positions of rank and distinction. The homosocial structures of Hasidic society were counterbalanced by the emphasis on heterosexuality and the stigma attached to single life and childlessness. Yet, from the perspective of Gentile society, where aggression, physical strength, and heroic conduct are viewed as masculine, the '(ideally) gentle, passive, emotional' Jewish male appeared as a pseudo-woman.[14] The extreme sensitivity in Kafka's letters, his shy, non-aggressive demeanor in his photographs, and the cerebral approach to sexuality conform to the Jewish ideal. Similar notions occur in Weininger's *Sex and Character* which correlates Jewishness and femininity and endorses the Gentile gender and cultural bias.

Traditional teachings configured the female element as holy. The *Shekhina*, the female aspect of God, is said to consort with Yeshiva students who live separate from women.[15] It was believed that a man could establish a connection with the divine only through a woman, only through her could he participate in God's creative aspect. This is precisely what Kafka seems to have had in mind when he terms intercourse *Alchymie* and 'magic' (*Zauberei*) in a letter to Milena (9.VIII.20; *BM*: 202). However, his invocation of tradition is highly playful. Milena is a Gentile woman and in terms of Jewish law *Nidda* – impure. She is hardly the right partner for a Jewish man to achieve a mystical experience. Likewise, certain episodes in his novels, most notably *The Trial* and *The Castle*, reflect Jewish tradition without, however, validating it. For example, Josef K. is drawn to women who have access to the legal establishment. He concentrates on them to such a degree as to get sidetracked and offend the male officials. The same thing happens to K., whose encounters with women fail to bring him closer to the castle elite but create potential conflicts with the very powers he wishes to impress. The way that Kafka as well as his protagonists conduct their affairs with women make it likely that they will lose touch with the transcendental realm – if such a realm exists at all and if they believe in it. Of course, none of Kafka's works proceeds with any certainty regarding the existence or non-existence of the divine, or for that matter, a binding law. Hence the experimental character of all of the protagonists' quests, including their erotic adventures. More often than not the exploits turn out to be exercises in futility.

Some of Kafka's texts that portray the disenfranchisement of women do so by way of dynamic female characters, as is the case in the story 'The Married Couple'. The husband is a well-known businessman with far-reaching connections, a man on whose good will the narrator's livelihood depends, and the exclusive focus of his very active wife. While he is the centre of all of her activities, she seems incapable of communicating with anyone else. Completely absorbed in her marriage, she serves him like a maid or mother, taking off his heavy coat, dressing him in his nightgown and seemingly restoring him to life after his collapse. These are similar to the tasks that Georg Bendemann performs for his father. An outsider to the intimacy of the couple, the narrator can only guess at the meaning of the wife's gestures. When she kisses the hand of her seemingly dead husband, the narrator conjectures that it is a 'little marital game' (*DE*: 137), while in fact he may be witnessing a mystical revitalisation ritual. All the narrator understands, and that only partially, is the male-dominated sphere of work patterned after the modern Gentile paradigm. Other representatives of this sphere are the competitor and the senior businessman. In addition, the narrator is exposed to the realm of disease, the son and the doctor. In both spheres the misunderstandings and limited perceptions prevail suggesting that the male structures are flawed. Male power comes also under scrutiny in the account of the couple's interaction. In their inequality and difference man and wife complement each other: she lives for him, he through her. They appear linked in an almost mystical fashion, and he recovers from his near-death merely because of her touch. This incident reverses the initial impression of male dominance and female subservience. Not only does the episode call into question the doctor's art, it implies that even the most powerful man sustains life through a woman. The seemingly insignificant woman turns out to be the force on whom depends the welfare of all males in the story.

The detailed description of the wife's activities fails to provide the key to the meaning of her interaction with her husband. On the one hand, the modest industrious wife seems to possess the 'inscrutable power of women' discussed by Grözinger.[16] Kafka casts the woman in the traditional role which suggests that she is the pillar upon which the entire household and the family business rest. The text even mystifies the sources and function of the superior female powers by suggesting that they are different from those of men. Were it not for the protagonist's highly subjective perspective, his miscalculations, and his biased view of other men, the story could be read as an endorsement of traditional sexist myths regarding the spiritual powers of women. The unreliability of the narrative voice makes it impossible to draw such a conclusion.

Embedded in 'The Married Couple' are other concepts derived from Jewish mysticism, including the businessman's extreme dependence on his wife. According to Biale the *Shekhinah*, the feminine aspect of God's presence, is ambivalent. It represents both the Great Mother and a devouring Goddess. Gilman's theses on the role of the Jewish male as patient, as well as the mystical paradigms presented by Biale, illuminate the paradox of energy and vitality in a frail female body and the manifestation of disease in a powerful man and his son. Indeed, Kafka views power with extreme scepticism as an external show of force. The wife, on the other hand, the source of her husband's strength, does not require external status symbols. Her powers are manifest in his very survival; the status he achieves is her accomplishment. Ultimately, her concern for him is the interest of an entrepreneur in his investments and means of production. The questions remains, however, as to what benefit the wife derives from her position. Her lot resembles closely that of the gatekeeper in 'Before the Law'. Being constantly on guard and preoccupied with her husband, she lives in a complete symbiosis with him, one partner no less in bondage than the other.

If sexuality is the tool to bring about man's union with God and the empowerment of the male, the father in 'The Judgement' has achieved this goal. He states: 'On my own I might have had to give way to you, but in this way mother has passed on her strength to me' (*EL*: 50–1). This sentence corresponds to Kafka's assessment of his own parents' relationship in 'Letter to his Father':

> She loved you too much and was too devoted to you to be an independent spiritual force in the child's struggle for very long. A correct instinct on the part of the child, by the way, as the mother became more and more closely linked with over the years. (*ZFG*: 34)

The father's body in 'The Judgement' represents the joint male and female aspects of parental power as indicated by the scar of an old war wound in his thigh. The motif of the male wound also occurs in 'A Country Doctor' where it feminises the young patient in contradistinction to his literal gendering as male. The scar in 'The Judgement', uncovered and named, in conjunction with the phallus which remains unnamed, is the expression of the father's androgyny, his completeness. According to Elizabeth Boa, the central theme of 'The Judgement' is the unveiling of the phallus to the son, the violation of the biblical taboo that calls for the death of the transgressor.[17] However, the father's male genitals are not the issue: even they cannot but be exposed if he lifts his shirt high enough to show his thighs. Foregrounding the scar brings into focus the father's vulnerability and penetrability. As in 'The Married Couple', the husband/father would be the dying old man the son thinks he is without availing himself of the energies provided by the wife/mother. He draws his strength from her, calling to mind Kafka's description of his own parents' symbiotic relationship quoted above. Contrary to the biblical case, Georg Bendemann views both his father's and his mother's exposed genitals, but he does not do so voluntarily. The father flaunts his male and female nakedness before the son to render him powerless.

Having, as it were, absorbed the mother, the father is in constant contact with her and through her in touch with the divine. Thus he enjoys the power of both sexes. The equally monstrous as godlike *tate-mame* triumphs over his son: he prevents him from joining the community of men as a husband, father, and friend and from entering into a union with the divine. Having thus deprived the son of his basis for living in the here-and-now and the beyond, the father sentences him to death for a crime he himself has caused him to commit. To add insult to injury, the son, by yielding to the urge to commit suicide, upholds the very law that the father has violated. This course of events corresponds roughly with Kafka's own reproach in the 'Letter to his Father' 'that you, for me the so terribly authoritative person, did not keep to the commandments which you imposed on me' (ZFG: 20). It also may be a reflection of the role of Kafka's father in the sexual initiation of his son.

The destructive power of the paternal word is repeatedly documented in the 'Letter to his Father'. Yet, despite patterns reminiscent of traditional Jewish narratives, important elements in 'The Judgement' are fundamentally different. In cabalistic lore the verdict of the father is always justified and functions like a curse and comes true immediately. Kafka's narrative voice, on the other hand, lacks the certainty and piety of the popular Jewish moralist and the unambiguous narrative trajectory. Without these, a moral position in favour of either character, father or son, cannot be established. Kafka lacks the naiveté and faith Grözinger attributes to the 'simple and fearful mentality of the masses', the audience and propagators of cabalist popular tradition.[18]

Ultimately Bendemann's demise remains as mysterious as the father's actions. Both are open to multiple readings. A secular patriarchal society would consider the untimely death of a son tragic and a man preventing his son from fulfilling his destiny as a husband and father reprehensible. This is precisely what Kafka implies in 'Letter to his Father' when he writes: 'But since we are the way we are, marrying is closed off to me because it is of course your very own territory' (ZFG: 60). The father who foils his son's attempts at having a wife and children, of becoming spiritually whole by engaging in marital relations, who jeopardises the future of the family and that of Jewish life altogether, seems perverse, even criminal.

The notions of sin and punishment with which certain members of Kafka's family are said to have associated sexuality, some of which the author seems to have shared, prompt an alternative reading. Defining sin as sexual transgression problematises Bendemann's wish for marriage. His primary goal may indeed be to satisfy his sexual desires rather than producing learned sons. At least the father both in 'The Judgement' and in 'Letter to his Father' suggests that the son's reason to marry is less than respectable. Biale discusses the high stakes in love-making reflected in *Iggeret-ha-Kodesh* which he refers to as a 'sexual guidance book'.[19] While it was the husband's duty to satisfy his wife, he had to force his thoughts to be pure. Biale traces the hostility to pleasure during intercourse back to medieval Jewry. Indeed, he writes that the Baal Shem Tov held women responsible for male fantasies about women which he assumed to have been caused by telepathy. While in some traditions celibate marriage was considered a way out of the humiliation brought on by intercourse after the commandment to procreate had been fulfilled, the very idea of celibate marriage remained problematic in Judaism. Herr Bendemann infers that his son's marriage plans are a ploy to take over the role of head of the household and the family business while satisfying his lust with an undeserving and possibly immoral woman. According to the father, such acts bring shame upon the dead mother and constitute disloyalty toward the friend. The figure of the vamplike seductress, the fiancée, is already a stock character in the legends of the Baal Shem Tov. The father sees the supposed transgression against his authority as entwined with the son's sexual maturity, which calls to mind the story of Adam and Eve. There is no indication in Kafka's text that the father's interpretation of the son's state of mind is correct.

In a cabalistic framework Georg Bendemann's suicide rather than being tragic could also signify a redemptive process. The father, having absorbed the mother's energy, has already begun concentrating the scattered divine sparks into one. He has also won the affection of Georg's friend, a bachelor who is not involved in the cycle of procreation and does not contribute to the further atomisation of the divine sparks. Thus the father, endowed with both male and female genitals, figures as a symbol of the undivided Adam. The son's self-elimination ends the threat of creating new human or Jewish life. Indeed, notions of ending Jewish life and human life altogether were not uncommon in the early 1900s. There were times when Theodor Herzl and Karl Kraus advocated mass conversion to end anti-Semitism by eliminating Judaism, and Otto Weininger considered sexual abstinence and the eventual elimination of the human race preferable to the humiliating business of sexual intercourse and the exploitation of women it causes.

If, however, secular post-Shoah thinkers such as Günter Anders are correct and Kafka considered God, and by extension the father, the source of evil, 'The Judgement' must be interpreted as criticism and a caricature of the cannibalistic powers mobilised by the patriarch. The father annihilates and absorbs the individuality of everyone he comes into contact with. Under the circumstances, death is the son's only salvation from succumbing to the fatherly will or from perpetuating the system embodied by the father. Were the son to survive he would have no choice but to participate in an authoritarian society that he rejects. The traffic that flows across the bridge at the moment Bendemann jumps to his death expresses his final exclusion from the world of business, sex, and procreation.

My readings of 'The Judgement' show that the story does not lend itself to a unitary interpretation. Indeed, inconclusivity is the major characteristic of Kafka's œuvre altogether. In his letters, for example, he casts himself in all the gender roles available in his literary texts: as transgressor and victim, seduced and seducer, masculine and feminine. Vis à vis Felice Bauer, for example, he feigns ignorance and disinterest, even incompetence in matters of work and business, as his letter of 2 November 1912 shows: 'I cannot think my way properly into business... My office work... makes me so fidgety and senseless' (*BF*: 69) He also casts himself in the position of the wife in 'The Married Couple' when he writes to her that 'You, just you alone are my only real connection with people and *only you shall be that in future*' (12.VIII.13; *BF*: 443). He presents himself as *homme fragile*: 'I do not know whether you... comprehend my jittery senstivity which is always at the ready, but once lured away leaves behind like a stone' (8.II.12; *BF*: 81); and subsequently as potential perpetrator of awful deeds: 'You do not know me, in my dreadfulness you do not know me' (13.VIII.13; *BF*: 457). Conversely, he also attributes all these roles to the women. There is a sense of equal strength, of equality, between him and his letter partners, as he acknowledges after the first engagement has been broken off: 'I have found that we are both ruthless against each other; not perhaps because one of us is not sufficiently fond of the other, but we are ruthless' (25.I.15; *BF*: 624).

Gender for Kafka is a matter of positionality, not of biology, as is obvious in 'The Judgement' as well as in 'The Metamorphosis'. Both texts feature a son, who is a businessman and breadwinner. The father, a retiree, is initially configured in a feminine role, frail, homebound, and inactive. In 'The Judgement' a shift from masculine to feminine occurs when the businessman-son checks on his father and assumes the role of a care giver and nurturer. He notices the types of things a wife is expected to concern herself with, the father's state of neglect, his dirty underwear, and his ill health. For a short while the relationship of father and son resembles, as it were, that of a husband and wife. Gregor Samsa has emasculated the father by assuming the role of provider and head of household. The father is as dependent on him as the women, Gregor's mother and sister. When Gregor fails to meet the family's and his employer's expectations and loses his job, the ensuing decrease in masculinity is visualised as a loss of humanity altogether. He turns into a beetle, whose maleness becomes associated with filth and perverted sexuality rather than strength, as his clutching the picture of a lady in furs suggests. The sexual prowess that for a human male is a source of pride and self-confidence appears sordid and shameful in association with a male insect. Clearly, this is an allusion to the sexually charged anti-Semitic propaganda of the time. The sons' disempowerment in 'The Metamorphosis' and 'The Judgement' is proportionate to the renewal of the father's strength which culminates in the death sentence against the son. Running to his death without a will of his own, Georg Bendemann calls to mind the substance-less female as well as the Jew, the 'female among races' in Weininger's *Sex and Character*: 'The total woman has no Ego.'[20]

In contrast to Weininger, Kafka de-essentialises gender. The interdependence between male and female in 'The Married Couple' can also occur with reversed roles, as for example the Brunelda episodes in *The Man who Disappeared*. They feature a female character as the centre of attention of not one but three males: Delamarche, Roßmann, and Robinson. The men's subservience to her engenders an increasing dependence and willfulness on her part, while she becomes more and more incapable of controlling her woefully overweight body. The same is true with the fathers in the two stories.

Kafka even de-essentialises humanness and species belonging by thematising metamorphoses and transitional phases between human and animal of all kinds, for example in 'Report for an Academy' and 'A Crucifixion'. He also ascribes certain animal features to humans, such as Leni's webbed hand. Rather than signalling a state of spiritual imperfection by attributing animal features to humans, Kafka assumes no categorical distinction on the basis of species. In Kafka's writings gender and species are operative as positions of power and dominance rather than qualitative differences. Feminine and masculine positioning occurs regardless of whether the respective characters are designated human, male and female, or exclusively male, as in 'Before the Law', or whether all characters are animals, such as 'Josephine, the Songstress or: the Mouse People'.

Kafka's texts thus utilise elements from the divergent cultural discourses and codes to which the author had access, thereby showing all of them as relative. He undermines the basic categories such as gender and humanity and destabilises the assumptions and tenets inherent in Jewish and Gentile traditions alike. A profound agnosticism emerges from his texts as they uncover the unreality of appearances, gendered or otherwise, the unreality of reality.

NOTES

1. See Gerald Stieg, 'Kafka and Weininger', in Nancy Harrowitz and Barbara Hyams (eds.), *Jews and Gender: Responses to Otto Weininger* (Philadelphia: Temple University Press, 1995), pp. 195–206.
2. Susannah Heschel, 'Sind Juden Männer? Können Frauen jüdisch sein? Die gesellschaftliche Definition des männlichen/weiblichen Körpers', in Sander L. Gilman, Robert Jütte, and Gabriele Kohlbauer-Fritz (eds.), *Der schejne Jid.*

Das Bild des 'jüdischen Körpers' in Mythos und Ritual (Vienna: Picus, 1998), pp. 86–96.

3. Klaus Theweleit, 'Gespensterposten. Briefverkehr, Liebesverkehr, Eisenbahnverkehr. Der Zug ins Jenseits. Orpheus 1913 in Prag (KAFKA)', *Buch der Könige. Orpheus und Eurydike* (Basel: Stroemfeld/Roter Stern, 1988), pp. 976–1046, here p. 1035.

4. Politzer argues that Kafka rejects femininity and privileges masculinity and observes a positive affinity between Kafka and Weininger. Heinz Politzer, *Franz Kafka: Parable and Paradox*, 2nd edition (Ithaca, NY: Cornell University Press, 1966) p. 200.

5. The former argued by Boa, *Gender, Class, Race*, the latter by Patricia McGurk, 'Cracking the Code in *A Country Doctor*: Kafka, Freud, and Homotextuality', in Frederico Pereira (ed.), *Literature and Psychology* (Lisbon: Inst. Superior de Psicologia Aplicada, 1995), pp. 111–18.

6. Sander L. Gilman, *Franz Kafka: the Jewish Patient* (New York: Routledge, 1995); Karl Erich Grözinger, *Kafka and Kabbala*, tr. Susan Hecker Ray (New York: Continuum, 1994).

7. Boyarin, *Unheroic Conduct*, pp. 157, 160.

8. Edward Timms, 'Kafka's Expanded Metaphors: a Freudian Approach to *Ein Landarzt*', in J. P. Stern and John J. White (eds.), *Paths and Labyrinths: Nine Papers Read at the Franz Kafka Symposium Held at the Institute of Germanic Studies* (London: Institute of Germanic Studies, 1985), pp. 66–79.

9. Subtitled *Meine 365 Liebhaber*. This classic of the confessional genre is attributed to Felix Salten, the creator of Bambi. English versions include *The Memoirs of Josephine Mutzenbacher: the Intimate Confessions of a Courtesan* (Chatsworth, Calif.: Brandon Books, 1967) and *A Woman of Pleasure* (Carroll and Graf: New York, 1986).

10. Mark M. Anderson, *Kafka's Clothes: Ornament and Aestheticism in the Habsburg Fin de Siècle* (Oxford: Clarendon, 1992), p. 47.

11. Frank Möbus argues that Kafka belongs neither to Christian nor Jewish tradition but follows an eclectic theology, *Sünden-Fälle: die Geschlechtlichkeit in Erzählungen Franz Kafkas* (Göttingen: Vandenhoeck und Ruprecht, 1994), p. 148.

12. Lorna Martens argues that 'in Kafka's fiction, generally, the "other" in as much as it is imagined at all, becomes a purely self-reflective category, with none of the power, legitimacy, or beauty it had in earlier Austrian texts', *Shadow Lines*, p. 121.

13. Gilman, *The Jewish Patient*, p. 54.

14. Boyarin, *Unheroic Conduct*, p. 156.

15. Jody Myers and Jane Rahel Litman, 'The Secret of Jewish Femininity: Hiddenness, Power, and Physicality in the Theology of Orthodox Women in the Contemporary World', in Tamar M. Rudavsky (ed.), *Gender and Judaism* (New York: New York University Press, 1995), pp. 51–80, here p. 52.

16. *Kafka und die Kabbala*, p. 93.

17. Boa, *Gender, Class and Race*, p. 115.

18. Ibid., p. 150.

19. *Eros and the Jews*, p. 102.

20. *Geschlecht und Charakter*, p. 240.

FURTHER READING

Anderson, Mark M., 'Kafka, Homosexuality and the Aesthetics of "Male Culture"', *Austrian Studies 7: Gender and Politics in Austrian Fiction*, ed. Ritchie Robertson and Edward Timms (Edinburgh: Edinburgh University Press, 1996), 79–99.

Beck, Evelyn Torton, 'Kafka's Traffic in Women: Gender, Power, and Sexuality', *The Literary Review* 26:4 (1983), 565–76.

'Gender, Judaism, and Power: a Jewish Feminist Approach to Kafka', in Richard T. Gray (ed.), *Approaches to Teaching Kafka's Short Fiction* (New York: Modern Language Association of America, 1995), pp. 35–42.

Biale, David, *Eros and the Jews* (Berkeley: University of California Press, 1997).

Boa, Elizabeth, *Kafka: Gender, Class, Race in the Letters and Fictions* (Oxford: Clarendon, 1996).

Boyarin, Daniel, *Unheroic Conduct: the Rise of Heterosexuality and the Invention of the Jewish Man* (Berkeley: University of California Press, 1997).

Martens, Lorna, *Shadow Lines – Austrian Literature – Kafka – Freud* (Lincoln: University of Nebraska Press, 1996).

Robertson, Ritchie, 'Mothers and Lovers in Some Novels by Kafka and Brod', in Margaret Littler (ed.), *Gendering German Studies: New Perspectives on German Literature and Culture* (Oxford: Blackwell, 1997), pp. 97–112.

Stach, Reiner, 'Kafka's Egoless Woman: Otto Weininger's *Sex and Character*', in Mark M. Anderson (ed.), *Reading Kafka: Prague, Politics and the Fin de Siècle* (New York: Schocken, 1989), pp. 149–69.

11

ANTHONY NORTHEY

Myths and realities in Kafka biography

'We are reading a book. A novel, say, or a book of short stories. It interests us because it is new, because it is...novel, so we read on', says Sydney, the aspiring Kafka biographer in Alan Bennett's play *Kafka's Dick*, and continues:

> And yet in what we call our heart of hearts (which is the part that is heartless) we know that like children we prefer the familiar stories, the tales we have been told before. And there is one story we never fail to like because it is always the same. The myth of the artist's life.[1]

In fact, Bennett's play centres around one of the central myths of Kafka's life: the relationship with his father. But is the audience's myth-making due to the fact that Kafka's life, as Sydney goes on to maintain, 'conforms in every particular to what we have convinced ourselves an artist's life should be', or is it due to biographers who have over the years conditioned us to certain stories? To answer these questions this chapter will give a brief overview of Kafka biography and look at some of the larger and smaller myths about Kafka's life.

Bennett's Sydney could also have brought up the question of whether and, if so, how the life influenced the work, for that question lurks in every literary biography, especially in those devoted to Franz Kafka. It is indubitable that reality in the shape of stimuli from the outside world entered Kafka's work and I aim to shed light on the various ways this happened. It will become evident that Kafka used a multitude of real-life sources from the most ephemeral experiences to the most profound events either from his own life or from the lives of others and that he transferred these sources in a variety of ways into his work.

As an example of myth stands the contention that Kafka's 'Aeroplane in Brescia' represents the first published German text to describe the flight of an airplane. This is, of course, not true, but three major English-language Kafka biographies make the claim.[2] The truth is that no self-respecting Prague newspaper of Kafka's day wanted to appear behind the times. All carried regular columns devoted to those popular areas of technological breakthrough – photography, automobiles, and, of course, flying machines: airplanes or dirigibles, which all came under the heading *Aeronautik* or its German name *Luftschiffahrt*. And only a short time before a piece entitled 'The Eternal Heureka' ('Das ewige Heureka') had appeared in the *feuilleton*-section of the *Bohemia* written by the Prague poet turned journalist, Josef Adolf Bondy (somewhat older than Kafka), in which he described a flight by Orville Wright at an airshow in Berlin-Tempelhof.[3]

In some instances myth is too inflated a term to use; instead one can only speak of incorrect or incomplete biographical information that has made the rounds during the last sixty years – some of it traceable to Max Brod, some to other biographers. One such detail is the designation of Marie Werner, *das Fräulein*, as Kafka's governess and thus, according to one popular biographer, 'the most enduringly human presence' in the 'emotional desert' of his childhood.[4] Stirring words, but amusing, considering that she was about the same age as her infant charge and came to live with the family in 1911 by which time he was in his late twenties. Max Brod accords the Loewy uncles, Alfred and Josef, greater status than they in fact enjoyed in Kafka's life, although in this case it is perhaps indicative of the importance the family wanted to give itself.[5] Dora Diamant, who lived with Kafka in the last year of his life, was thought to be a very young girl in her teens when she met Kafka in the summer of 1923, but turned out to be somewhat older.[6] Much of what is told about Julie Wohryzek, Kafka's second fiancée – the contention that she was a seamstress by profession or that she died in a mental institution – is plain false information, not necessarily myth.

Brod's biography of his friend, first published in 1937, represents the first comprehensive view we have of Kafka's life and should be read in conjunction with his postscripts to the novels and of course his many other works about the Prague literary scene. Brod's views are influenced by two things: first, his strong belief in Zionism and Judaism. Thus for him much of Kafka's work, especially in the later period, becomes a continuous search for God. This, at least, is what other scholars and biographers, quoting his commentary, have stressed to the point of creating another myth. Surprisingly, other ideas of Brod's, his thesis of Kafka's infantilism for instance, never received comparable attention. The second influence on Brod's description was his extraordinary veneration for his friend. Kafka's uncompromising style, his purity of language, which eschewed cheap novelistic effects, emanates from the author's pure, uncompromising life. For Brod, therefore, the person and the work were one and the same. Kafka, the pinnacle of pure art, Kafka the man of impeccable character who made life complicated for himself because he refused to take the easy way out and rationalise his faults away. And the more the world began to take notice of Kafka and elevate him to the position of seminal twentieth-century literary figure, the purer Kafka became in Brod's eyes. After mythologising Kafka's pureness, he beatified him; and having travelled the highest of high roads, he expected all to do the same. An example of his influence is provided by a short poem his companion Ilse Esther Hoffe published in 1948, the first stanza of which reads:

> The name which hourly lips mention
> The friend of friend who burns wounds of longing
> Him do I wish to grasp in all his purity.[7]

No biographer has really taken up the challenge. Deep respect for Kafka has obscured some of his less pleasant traits and actions. In this connection I would mention his shabby treatment of Julie Wohryzek, whom he abandoned for Milena Jesenská and to whom he refers condescendingly in his correspondence with her as *das Mädchen* ('the girl').

With the rapid rise in Kafka's stock, especially after the Second World War, many who had known him, some only briefly, came forward with their reminiscences and anecdotes.[8] Most of them portrayed Kafka as the tall silent type who, when he spoke, always had something significant to say. Some of these people are responsible for stories which are difficult to verify. In a letter to Alexander Wolfgang Schocken, Grete Bloch, the close friend of Felice Bauer, intimated that she had borne a child by Kafka; his secretary, Fräulein Kaiser, that she and the author had been in love. It should be noted that both women told their stories to other people but did not publish them themselves. There is no evidence whatsoever for Bloch's claim, which is now disregarded by Kafka researchers.

In postwar West Germany Klaus Wagenbach wrote the next full-length biography of note; the first of a projected two volumes dealt with the author's life from birth until 1912. Although the second volume never appeared, he did issue a shorter complete account of the life in Rowohlt's ro-ro-ro series of introductory monographs. Kafka's family and friends had been decimated by the Nazis and much of the old Prague had disappeared, but Wagenbach still enjoyed the privilege of access to a few surviving friends and to relatives. Ida Bergmann, for example, had no memory of the author herself, but a wealth of information about the previous generation. The young Wagenbach, who was soon to become a prominent figure in left-wing literary life in the Federal Republic of the 1960s, gave greater attention than before to Kafka's participation in the Brentano circle and laid special emphasis on his social engagement, his purported association with the radical Michal Mareš, and his work for the Workers' Accident Insurance Institute.

Although Wagenbach and others had used literary archives, it was really the next two decades that saw the first serious archival research that endeavoured to throw critical light on the social background of Prague and Bohemia, to examine facets of Kafka's life that had gone unnoticed, and to collect what documents connected to Kafka that still survived (especially in Czechoslovakia). This was no mean feat during the reign of the Soviet-backed Communist regime which was hardly partial to its most famous modern writer. The central figure in Kafka biography since the early 1970s, someone whose work cannot be overestimated, is Hartmut Binder. In his two-volume *Kafka-Handbuch* as well as in numerous other books and articles, he has set about fine tuning our view of Kafka and his time. In more recent years this type of biographical research has led to closer study of various segments of Kafka's life, the trips that he took abroad, for example.

Efforts in the English-speaking world until the 1980s had been confined mainly to biographical sections of monographs on the author and his work.[9] Exceptions are *Franz Kafka: Man Out of Step* (1973) by Deborah Crawford, a highly inaccurate, even fanciful biography, and *Kafka in Context* (1975) in which John Hibberd gives a short, dispassionate but useful overview of the author's life, probably the most balanced and accurate of the English-language works to date. Ronald Hayman's *Kafka: a Biography* (1982) represents the first longer work in English and was followed by Ernst Pawel's *The Nightmare of Reason: a Life of Franz Kafka* (1985), a non-scholarly biography, and Peter Mailloux's *A Hesitation Before Birth: the Life of Franz Kafka* (1989). All more or less content themselves with a description of Kafka's life and work, although Pawel's *The Nightmare of Reason* benefits from the author's Central European origins and personal knowledge of the cultural background. In addition and more ambitiously Frederick R. Karl's *Franz Kafka: Representative Man* (1991) attempts to link Kafka to modernism in Europe, seeing Kafka as 'a repository of everything coming together in the arts at the turn of the century' (p. 99). As far as the basic facts of his life are concerned all these biographers borrow liberally from the archival research of others, especially Hartmut Binder – and sometimes with cursory or no acknowledgement. They add nothing in concrete terms to what was already known. What differentiates them from the older biographical work is attitude. Pawel, Mailloux, and Karl, far from endorsing his sainthood, have brought out his neurotic side: either the guilt he suffered for wishing the death of his brothers who died in infancy (Pawel); or his obsession with food and the alimentary tract as a tool to gain control (Karl). In fact, the image of Kafka as a manipulator emerges far more markedly in all of them. Much of this psychological ground was covered in greater detail and with reference to the schools of Freud and Jung by the chapter on Kafka's childhood in the first volume of Binder's *Kafka-Handbuch* (pp. 110–70).

Frederick R. Karl has spoken more recently of the almost irresistible temptation of seeing Kafka as 'the prophet of the Nazi state and the slaughter of Jews, among several other unwanted types'.[10] Karl, like Hayman and Pawel, seems to have been particularly struck and preoccupied by the incongruity of the Jew Kafka, much of whose family was annihilated by the Nazis, writing in the language of the oppressors, in fact becoming one of their greatest writers of the century, if not their very greatest. This irony was undoubtedly responsible in part for their questioning of Kafka's tie to German culture and the tendency to lay greater emphasis on his Jewish background, from Pawel's notion of everyday Jewishness in his upbringing to the more advanced theories that Talmudic or Hassidic thought, structures, and motifs formed and entered his work. Much of this can be attributed to wishful thinking. Notwithstanding the inadequacies Kafka might have perceived in his German education and even the German language from time to time, German literary tradition was the foundation of his development as a writer. If nothing else it differentiated him from his uneducated father.

Hayman and Pawel seem to have taken their cue from Christoph Stölzl's work on anti-Semitism in Bohemia and emphasise the stressful, tension-filled atmosphere in which Kafka grew up.[11] Impetus to this view has been given by the enormity of the Nazi mass murders of the Jews during the Second World War. While it is certainly true that Prague's Jewish population was under pressure from anti-Semites there, one cannot claim that the climate was more anti-Semitic than in other European cities. Indeed, one could argue that the paradigm of anti-Semitism at the end of the nineteenth century was provided by France in its Panama scandal and Dreyfus affair, to which Kafka, of course, had his own special connection. Kafka's uncle Alfred Loewy was for virtually all of his life the employee of Philippe and Maurice Bunau-Varilla, who were involved first in the Panama scandal, when Jewish financiers were blamed for the collapse of the project to build the Panama Canal resulting in big losses for small investors, and then in the Dreyfus affair.[12] In fact, in his discussion of the contemporary or near contemporary negative Jewish stereotypes Kafka internalised and tried to reject, Sander Gilman relies not merely on German but also heavily on French and English texts for his examples.

And, contrary to the myth among Kafka scholars, German Jewish intellectuals in Prague were not completely orphaned in 'swampy margins of civilization'[13] populated by Czech anti-Semites. They developed and cultivated an active German cultural life and tried in their small way to vie with Vienna, Berlin, and Munich, with whom they had close contact. This led the

Prague-born poet and journalist Emil Faktor to joke: 'For every ten Germans [in Prague] there are twelve literary talents.'[14]

When it comes to the question of whether Kafka's life entered into his work opinions differ widely, from Martin Walser's rather peremptory pronouncement that the more complete the literary text the less one needs to know about the author, to Malcolm Pasley, who considers him an *'Erlebnis- dichter* par excellence'. Pasley states that 'nothing really true or significant could be expressed except through the channel of personal experience, and that in this wide sense all his writing is autobiographical'.[15] Looking back on the biographical interpretation that preceded Walser's statement, one can perhaps see a certain justification for his exasperation. Scholars had focused repeatedly on certain central facts of Kafka's life to the point where they began to become myth and eclipse other valid nuances and eventually the validity of the central fact itself. No doubt Walser was reacting in part to things like the mythologising of Kafka's relationship to his father.

The strong pressure to reject the positivistic view that the events of life influence art has embarrassed those who search for possible sources for the work. But there can be no doubt that Kafka's fiction often draws upon life and it does so in a variety of ways, for both the superficial detail and for the more significant conceptual ideas, the inspirational spark to set it in motion. *The Man who Disappeared* serves as a good example. When confronted by it the reader might ask why Kafka chose to write about an adolescent male in a foreign land he never visited, nor expressed any desire to see. Kafka liked to travel, visited several European countries, talked vaguely to Hedwig Weiler of wanting to look out over 'Mohammedan graveyards' (October 1907; B2: 72), but never spoke of going to the New World, permanently or temporarily. We ask what impressions he relied on in fashioning his 'most modern New York' as he himself termed it in a letter to his publisher, Kurt Wolff (25.v.13; B1: 117). Certainly there existed a number of references to America accessible to all in German-speaking countries or specifically in the Prague of Kafka's time, ranging from literature for the young – James Fenimore Cooper, Karl May – to Arthur Holitscher, lectures by František Soukup, the visit to Prague by Thomas Edison, and numerous articles in the Prague German dailies, the *Prager Tagblatt* and the *Bohemia*.

Scholars, perhaps because their *métier* is books, have a predilection for ferreting out sources in the word – literary or philosophical – rather than in people and events. Binder argues convincingly that much of the author's description of city buildings and bustling city traffic does not stem from recorded secondhand information about New York at all, but from first-hand impressions Kafka gathered on his two visits to Paris.[16] In choosing names, Clayton in the Oklahoma chapter of *The Man who Disappeared*, for instance, was he guided by a deeper sense of what the 'clay' might have connoted in English ('lost land')?[17] Or is there a more prosaic explanation (which would not necessarily negate his ability to appreciate the nuance in the English language)? Often Kafka must have passed the Prague offices of the English firm Clayton & Shuttleworth Ltd, manufacturer of agricultural machinery, which was located within his daily walking radius at 11 Hybernská Street. In another case he seems to have used a similar source. The rather unusual name of the head waiter Isbary in the Hotel Occidental might have been inspired by Hlawatsch & Isbary, a firm which produced woven woollen and cotton goods in the Bohemian city of Graslitz and had a factory depot at 1 Panská Street in Prague. (An encounter with this firm during the course of his work at the Workers' Accident Insurance Institute is not out of the question either.)

While giving all the above listed sources for *The Man who Disappeared* their due, one must still acknowledge that a fact specific to Kafka's personal environment – his four adventurous cousins, who emigrated to the United States before 1910 – undoubtedly gave the main impetus for the novel. Karl Roßmann's story crystallised around features from their lives. Elsewhere I have described the many details these cousins could have supplied.[18] Despite Pawel's dismissal of 'psychological reductivism that laboriously traces plot, structure, and characters back to their purported inspiration',[19] one does well to follow the thread of obvious inspiration in Kafka's first novel, which points to its main focus. The salient fact in the occurrences that provided the real-life basis – beyond all detail – is that the four young men represented living examples of success. They had coped with a new country, new alien surroundings, and in some cases even (like Karl) at a very young age. As models they stand in contrast to Karl, who is actually much more like the author. In *The Man who Disappeared* Kafka puts his personality, or at least pieces of his personality, to this test in the person of his protagonist – and Karl, despite his energy and good intentions, is defeated. Franz Kafka's America and Karl Roßmann's emigration are metaphors. He represents a child thrust into the 'new' world of adult life. (One significant irony of his situation is his becoming a father before even understanding what sex is all about.) In this *Entwicklungsroman* (novel of development) the protagonist actually regresses, becoming 'smaller' and increasingly passive and like a child. He goes from a position of independence, admittedly tempered by his naiveté, to various forms of imprisonment which become increasingly severe.

The lives of people Kafka knew became a reality he could empathise with and one that influenced his work. The next piece of evidence suggests that even single incidents and individual images inspired him. The work is 'The Hunter Gracchus' ('Der Jäger Gracchus'). After an accident 1,500 years ago, a fall which otherwise would have been fatal, the protagonist has been condemned by a peculiar twist of fate to a state of limbo in between life and death, 'his death ship lost its way; a wrong turn of the wheel, a moment's absentmindedness on the pilot's part' (BB: 44). The tale centres around a striking image: the barge carrying the hunter's bier slowly drifting into the port of Riva on Lake Garda, one of the few times in Kafka's fiction when he actually names and describes a real locale. The roots of this singular image can be traced to an incident that occurred when Kafka visited Riva in September and October of 1913. At mealtimes in the Sanatorium of Dr von Hartungen he sat between a Swiss girl (who has since been identified as Gerti Wasner) and an army general, whom he mentions in a letter to Brod (28.IX.13; B2: 121). This man was undoubtedly Ludwig von Koch, a retired major general in the Sixth Regiment Hussars in the Austrian army, who on the morning of 3 October retired to his rooms, took out his Browning revolver, and shot himself in the chest and head. His body was laid out in the mortuary chapel of St Anna before being interred in a cemetery in Riva on 6 October. Presumably the chapel was accessible to those who wished to pay their last respects, and if Kafka did not witness the general lying in state he must at least have heard of the violent incident. Delving a bit deeper, one recognises that the story's motif is derived from the myths surrounding suicide: the soul that cannot find eternal rest. In previous centuries the bodies of suicides could not be buried in consecrated ground, as a symbol of this lack of finality, but were often interred at crossroads, where the executioner's gallows stood.

One piece of evidence that supports this theory about Kafka's source is that, in his otherwise true-to-life description of Riva, he has replaced the statue of St Nepomuck, that actually stood in the harbour square, with that of a sabre-wielding hero. Pasley has proffered numerous examples of Kafka's allusions to his own work in his fiction.[20] Here too he alludes to his source and also stresses that it is a source by the fact that the reader does not see the statue directly but is only aware of it through its shadow.

In the midst of this biographical œuvre one should not forget Kafka's own autobiographical statements in letters, his diary and the massive 'Letter to his Father'. Some of it appeared first, little by little, before the war, most of it in a much more comprehensive form from the 1950s onward. Reviewing this wealth of material, one has to conclude sometimes that Kafka is the originator of myths about himself, an unwitting originator perhaps, because he had no intention of publishing his diaries and letters. Take for example the autobiographical sketch in his diary and the 'Letter to his Father', both of which remain favourites with Kafka biographers. The Kafkas are depicted as robust and mercantile, the Löwys intellectual and religious, even mystical, the author seeing himself more a product of the latter. Most biographers have taken his perception and converted it to gospel without regard to the 'other hand', which would give a more balanced view. For, in fact, the Löwy family produced more apostates than the Kafkas. Rudolf, Alfred, and Josef all converted to Christianity (or were forced by circumstance to do so). Julie Löwy spoke of her very industrious and wealthy relatives who all converted and assimilated to the point of changing their name to Lanner, the most important of whom was Alexander, owner of a brewery in Košíř and mayor of that Prague suburb (and Rudolf Löwy's employer). And the Kafkas were not without their intellectual, religious side. Strong circumstantial evidence points to a connection with Angelus Kafka, chief rabbi of the district of Pilsen, whose daughter was the mother of another Prague poet, Hugo Salus.[21]

Pawel's remark quoted above is actually directed specifically at those who highlight the biographical foundation of 'The Judgement'. Yet one does well to recall not just the obvious father–son conflict, the central myth of Kafka biography, but all the real-life parallels, in order to penetrate the deeper significance of a work that Kafka considered one of his best, if not his very best. In 1911 he had entered into a business venture with his brother-in-law, Karl Hermann, and a scant two weeks before writing 'The Judgement' had made the acquaintance of Felice Bauer, unmarried and perhaps not adverse to maintaining future contact with him. Outwardly the two conditions to become a model son – marriage and a firm financial basis – seemed to have moved within his grasp. In fact, however, he had realised for some time that, although he might have wanted to please his father, working for the Prager Asbestwerke Hermann & Co. ran contrary to his whole nature. Marriage too was for him a highly doubtful proposition; only a year previously, on drawing up the contract for the partnership with Karl Hermann, the lawyer had spoken of the rights of future family members, and Kafka had despaired of ever producing any himself (8.XI.11; *TB1*: 184–5).

Thus, despite indications that outwardly everything in his life was miraculously falling into place, he felt that he was actually destined towards failure and loneliness and this dichotomy underlies the story. In it the showdown between outward possibility and intuited destiny occurs. On the surface everything is as tranquil as the spring day on which the story takes place, everything in Georg's life offers a closed front to the viewer like the row of houses in his street that he sees out of his window. It takes almost no time at all for Georg's perfect world to be made to crumble. But more is destroyed when the father finally condemns him to death by drowning. It is here where one must go beyond what biographical interpreters have observed to date.

Anthony Thorlby, naively or disingenuously, puzzles at not being able to find points of similarity between the successful businessman Georg Bendemann and Franz Kafka without considering that Bendemann represents not the real Kafka but the possible Kafka.[22] A dream too good to be true, Bendemann is the construct of Kafka's imagination, a fiction. Within the precincts of the story he is truly innocent. How can he be faulted for his normal development, his wish to marry, his unmitigated success in his father's business? However, as a fictional manipulation to circumvent what for Kafka was the certain future reality (failure on all fronts, business and marriage), he is devilish. Thus the generally accepted literary convention of the separation of the author's real life from his fictional persona as story-teller has to undergo revision in 'The Judgement'. What is ultimately being destroyed in this *papier maché* protagonist is literature itself. While creating fiction Kafka achieves its negation at the same time and thus really carries out what he sees as his own father's wish (his rejection of literature). Therein lies the possible reason why Kafka considered this story a unique success: it is literature that destroys itself, perfectly ambivalent. The dubiousness of any singular perfection, any work of art, be it an intricate machine of torture ('In the Penal Colony'), a labyrinthine burrow ('The Burrow'), fasting ('The Fasting-artist'), philosophical thinking ('Investigations of a Dog'), singing ('Josephine, the Songstress or: the Mouse People'), becomes a repeated theme in his fiction.

That bureaucracy formed one of the mainstays of the Austro-Hungarian empire at the end of its life represents a given in European history. Emperor Franz Joseph laid great stock in bureaucratic duty, his own and that of his civil servants. The Arbeiter-Unfall-Versicherungs-Anstalt für das Königreich Böhmen (Workers' Accident Insurance Institute for the Kingdom of Bohemia, to give it its full title) had been established by this government, but enjoyed a good deal of autonomy. No doubt the insurance company, the 'best-hated' organisation in the empire as it was popularly known, had been placed at arm's length from the government for good reason. It was positioned to take fire from both the workers and the employers, while the government under pressure from the industrialists of the empire set policy favourable to them and thereby undermined the institution it had created. There were few who worked at the Institute that did not realise its precarious position.

In describing Kafka's work for the Institute, biographical myth presents Kafka as the lone employee with a social conscience, 'the man who sided with the workers against his own organisation'.[23] There is no doubt from passages in his diary and from what Brod and Janouch reported that he felt for the common workers and saw that they were being shortchanged. Alan Bennett's *The Insurance Man* is clearly based on Kafka's comment that the workers, rather than coming cap in hand to the Institute, had every right to storm the building and demand their right. And the film *Kafka* by Steven Soderbergh, another popular interpretation of his life, does the same. In addition to relying on the Frankenstein and Golem legends and shots of mysterious Prague, the film offers a full five scenes (and several of them quite long ones) in Kafka's place of work. True to legend and perpetuating it, the film depicts the insurance company as the bureaucratic villain and the tyrannical oppressor of the young author.

But it is doubtful that Kafka enjoyed the independence to 'go it alone' in a crusade for the downtrodden. In fact he skilfully carried out policy set by the director of the Institute, Dr Robert Marschner, who appreciated the fact that Kafka could be relied upon to know his bounds and to stay within them. In the various positions Kafka held over the years from *Aushilfsbeamter* (temporary assistant) to secretary he had to fulfil several duties, but contact with workers did not actually figure all that prominently in his work. On the other hand, one of his primary tasks was to represent his employer in the battle with entrepreneurs who declared lower payroll expenses than they actually had in order to minimise their accident insurance premiums. On the basis of newly discovered documents Hartmut Binder has shown recently that Kafka did the 'leg-work', and prepared the documents which Marschner submitted under his signature.[24] Since the director of the Institute was ultimately responsible for what went forward to the courts and the ministries, there can be no doubt that he made sure that it reflected Institute policy. The annual reports appeared under Marschner's signature and that of Otto Příbram, the titular head of the organisation. And the 'sophistic' article that Kafka wrote anonymously for the *Tetschen Bodenbacher Zeitung* describing the cause for the chronic deficits of the AUVA does not represent freelance work either. It was undoubtedly commissioned by Marschner and had to be endorsed by Příbram. It was, after all, the second of two articles by the Institute and in it Kafka had to conform in style and tone to the first that had been written by someone else.

The Institute published annual reports, which besides giving an overview of statistics and administrative personnel, included sections on special themes. The job of addressing these special issues fell to Kafka and while no self-respecting biographer fails to mention them, none appear to have read them or read them very closely. Kafka's first article deals with accident insurance in the building trades, his second with insurance for private automobiles, not liability insurance but accident insurance for hired chauffeurs of trucks and automobiles. Rather than exhort employers to be honest and pay premiums commensurate with the risk of their employees' work in vain, the Institute saw it might be easier to try to get some of them in certain branches of industry to lower the risk through accident prevention. Thus Kafka was entrusted with the job of making accident prevention seem a sensible, logical alternative and he did so in articles about safety measures in woodworking machines and in quarries.

Reverence for Kafka again has led some to declare that the texts bear his inimitable style. Such powers of discernment are wishful thinking. The reports are all couched in the same style, the earlier ones before Kafka's time are just as lucid as his and contained the same flashes of gallow's humour. Kafka's article on safety measures in quarries, for example, was identified at a later date not on the basis of its stylistic uniqueness but because of reference to it in the letters to Felice.[25] Wagenbach did not include it in the reports he republished because the Felice letters in which it is mentioned had not been published at the time of his biography.

An accepted part of Kafkan mythology is that the bureaucracy, bureaucratic red tape, endless files, and even the woodworking machines, for which Kafka advertised safety features, went into the conception of his work. In the behaviour of the stone-quarry owner, Josef Franz Renelt, whose case Kafka handled, Binder has found a good model for *Verschleppung* ('indefinite postponement'), one of Titorelli's mechanisms to avoid conviction in *The Trial*, for by launching appeal after appeal at various levels of government over a period of eleven years, Renelt managed to avoid payment of penalties. Finally, to boot, he got out of paying most of the premiums he owed.

Scheinfreispruch ('ostensible acquittal'), Titorelli's other alternative, could well have been inspired by another event that Kafka wrote about in 'The Extent of Insurance Obligation in the Building Industry and Ancillary Building Trades'. In 1906 the Administrative Court had cut the Gordian knot and in a sweeping, but necessary decision stipulated that all work in the building industry had to be insured without differentiation between on-site and off-site activity. This, of course, provided a great boon to the Institute by simplifying its work. But in a subsequent ruling in May 1908 the same court – probably under political pressure from the building industry – took back what it had given and reinstated the previous more chaotic circumstances. Thus for a short time the Institute had enjoyed a *Scheinfreispruch* from bureaucratic red tape. It is also no coincidence that Kafka, the author of the piece on safety in stone quarries, should locate Josef K.'s execution in one. Of course, speaking more generally, the use of technical jargon and hairsplitting was the hallmark of the texts published by the ministries, the courts and, by necessity, the Workers' Accident Insurance Institute. It could well appear that, as Josef K. observes, the lie was made into the governing principle of the world.

However much Kafka might have wanted to disassociate himself from the bureaucratic world, he had to play his role in it. In another case which Binder has documented, the author – whether on his own initiative or at a higher official's behest is not clear – participated in bureaucratic stubborness. He tried (in vain) to have the firm Chr. Geipel & Sons in the town of Asch reclassified as a more dangerous cotton mill when it clearly spun cloth from wool and silk, a process which deserved lower premiums.[26]

The word *Beamte* (bureaucrat) covered a much wider field for citizens of the Austro-Hungarian empire in Kafka's time. Today's *Beamte* in German-speaking countries is definitely associated with government. The term is usually translated as 'civil servant'. The army of *Beamten* in Kafka's day, however, also took in what were known as *Privatbeamten*, who were closer to the present-day *Angestellten* (employees) or who more generally might even be termed 'white-collar workers'. Thus bank employees like Otto Pick, Ernst Polak (Milena's errant husband), or Max Brod's father Adolf Brod, along with Kafka in his semi-governmental Institute, all would be called *Beamte*. As in today's world they were viewed ambivalently by the rest of society, suspiciously and enviously on the one hand, but held in relatively high esteem by those who had to earn their living with their hands. Nowhere was this more apparent to Kafka than in his numerous sojourns in the country among country folk, especially during his lengthy stay in Zürau in 1917–18.

To gain a deeper understanding of what being a *Beamte* meant to Kafka one must go to a letter he wrote to Käthe Nettl, the sister of Julie Wohryzek, the woman he was engaged to briefly in 1919/1920. Here he places his idea of *Beamten* in context. He begins to address himself. His self-castigation culminates in the words:

> But you are no farmer, whose land feeds his children, and – descending to the last rung – not even a merchant, I mean according to your inner leanings, but – probably the dregs of European professional classes – an official and in that overly nervous, lost to all dangers of literature, of weak lungs, tiredly avoiding the little scribbling work in the office.[27]

The agitation over another failed marriage attempt obviously brought on a moment of heightened insight when Kafka tried to define his broken existence, not only to the Wohryzek family but to himself. He generalises and presents a new social division in the world, a new system of classes or 'estates' as it were: the farmer, independent, achieving honest work by the sweat of his brow, the businessman, much lower on the ladder, engaged in less commendable endeavours, but nonetheless free to make decisions about his own enterprise, and on the very bottom rung the *Beamte*, the white-collar employee, who is dependent on the salary paid to him and must carry out the orders of his employer. In addition to naming these estates, Kafka suggests that this lowest group is not just to be found in what was the old Austro-Hungarian empire, but that it is a Europe-wide phenomenon. And he has to be considered a member of this underclass because of an inner predisposition (*der Anlage nach*). He was, in other words, born to be nothing else but a civil servant.

The profound negative significance of bureaucracy, paradigmatic of an aimless, useless existence, leaves little room to see the seat of bureaucracy, his castle in the novel that bears that title, as a transcendental place of divine grace (Brod) or as a metaphor for his writing (Mailloux).[28] In his novel Kafka has again reversed polarities of valuation in transferring life into fiction. He has elevated bureaucrats to a caste that the village holds in awe and gives them an almost feudal dimension: like knights they descend from the castle to move among the lowly who always refer to them deferentially as *Herren*.

On the evening of his arrival K. looks up into the dark where he knows there is the structure called the castle, but very typically he does not see it. Only on his first day, as he sets out to reach it, is the building he strives toward described in any comprehensive manner. After the first and only depiction a shift in focus takes place away from the exterior of the castle to the persons who staff it. For Steven Dowden the meaning of the novel is summed up in this description, but the weakness of that interpretation lies in the fact that nowhere in the remaining 200 pages does Kafka lay any more weight on the exterior of the building.[29] By the end of the story the words *Beamte* and *Behörde* (authority) proliferate and one loses sight of the edifice. The word *Schloss*, when it appears, actually becomes synonymous with the officials that populate it. It is therefore ironic that scholars, biographers in particular, lavish so much speculation on what building in real life might have inspired Kafka's castle.

Why does K. want to reach the castle? Does he seek to enter merely in order to gain permission to stay in the village as a land-surveyor? We know that his claim to being what he says he is, is doubtful. Does he want to fight this class of respected do-nothings or does he want to insinuate himself into their ranks? In the same way one could ask whether Josef K. in *The Trial* does not belong to the same bureaucracy he so implacably opposes. He perceives the court, its corruption and sleaziness, as an entity separate from him, as an antithesis. (And so does the reader who views the events from his perspective.)

That the author's work can supply biographical information represents the corollary of the supposition that biography fed into art. Had Felice Bauer read 'The Judgement', the work that Kafka dedicated to her, more carefully, she might have realised sooner that their relationship was going to be problematic. Aside from the fact that the content of his works reflects crises in his life, a more formal aspect, a change in the pattern of narration signals a new insight, a new direction of personal development for the author. Concerning *The Castle*, John Hibberd notes: 'K.'s relationship with Frieda, in particular, has a dimension which was scarcely developed in the earlier novel, for the reader is almost able to identify with the girl as well as with the hero.'[30] This can happen because, contrary to the myth that Kafka's works are written from the perspective of the protagonist, Frieda is given monologues in which she develops her own feelings, her hopes and disappointments in contrast to a character like Leni in *The Trial* whose role is restricted to that of an informant about the court. In his last novel Kafka moves away from self-centredness and gives far more opinion from the female viewpoint than in any other of his previous works. In fact Olga's long monologue – hardly interrupted over the course of several chapters – offers (in part at least) a description of the relationship between the sexes in Amalia's rejection of Sortini, a member of the bourgeois, all-male club of bureaucrats.

This shift in attitude heralds a milestone in Kafka's biography. Now at the end of his life he empathises with that sex he had caused so much grief. Far from seeing the Milena episode as the sole model for *The Castle*, one should give much more weight to the influence of Kafka's failure with the other women in his life, especially Felice and Julie. They, after all, like Frieda, had held out the prospect of fashioning some semblance of family life, which he, too mindful of his quest, had spurned. The woman figures in *The Castle* stand as a fitting tribute to them.

NOTES

1. Alan Bennett, *Plays Two* (London: Faber and Faber, 1998), p. 112.
2. Mailloux, *A Hesitation Before Birth*, p. 138; Karl, *Representative Man*, p. 238. Crawford even turns the airshow in Brescia into 'the world's first such gathering', *Man out of Step*, p. 61.
3. *Bohemia*, 82. Jahrgang, Nr. 254, Mittags-Ausgabe, 14 Sept. 1909, pp. 1–2.
4. Pawel, *The Nightmare of Reason*, p. 17.
5. By Max Brod, *Kafka: a Biography*, pp. 7–8.
6. The forthcoming biography, *Kafka's Last Mistress* by Kathi Diamant (no relation), will clear up this misinformation. Meanwhile, see Yehuda Koren, 'Kafka's Doomed Love: the final chapter of a tragic romance ends next week in a London cemetery', 7 Aug. 1999, *The Guardian*, Saturday Review, p. 3.

7. Ilse Esther Hoffe, 'Vor dem Bild eines grossen Toten (Franz Kafka)', *Prisma* 17 (1948), 29.

8. Most of these anecdotes have been collected by Hans Gerd Koch (ed.) in '*Als Kafka mir entgegenkam . . .' Erinnerungen an Kafka* (Berlin: Wagenbach, 1996).

9. Anthony Thorlby, *Kafka: a Study* (London: Heinemann, 1974); Charles Osborne, *Kafka* (Edinburgh: Oliver and Boyd, 1967).

10. Frederick R. Karl, 'Writing Kafka's Biography', *Biography and Source Studies* 3 (1997), 19–37, here p. 34.

11. Christoph Stözl, *Kafkas böses Böhmen: zur Sozialgeschichte eines Prager Juden* (Munich: Edition text & kritik, 1975).

12. Northey, *Kafka's Relatives*, pp. 12–13.

13. Pawel, *The Nightmare of Reason*, p. 258.

14. Emil Faktor, 'Jabsiade', in a joke-edition of the *Berliner Börsen-Courier* published in 1926 for the fiftieth birthday of Josef Adolf Bondy. See my article '"Brot mit dem Rasiermesser geschnitten": das Leben und Werk Josef Adolf Bondys', in Hartmut Binder (ed.), *Brennpunkt Berlin: Prager Schriftsteller in der deutschen Metropole* (Bonn: Kulturstiftung der Deutschen Vertriebenen, 1995), pp. 21–71, here p. 22.

15. Martin Walser, *Beschreibung einer Form: Versuch über Franz Kafka* (Munich: Hanser, 1968), p. 11; Malcolm Pasley, 'Semi-Private Games', in Angel Flores (ed.), *The Kafka Debate: New Perspectives for our Times* (New York: Gordian Press, 1977), pp. 188–205, here p. 194.

16. Binder, *Kafka in Paris* (passim).

17. Elizabeth M. Rajec, *Namen und ihre Bedeutungen im Werke Franz Kafkas: ein interpretatorischer Versuch* (Berne: Peter Lang, 1977), p. 127. Alfred Wirkner connects it with the 'Clayton Bill' passed by the US Congress in 1914, Alfred Wirkner, *Kafka und die Außenwelt: Quellenstudien zum 'Amerika'-Fragment* (Stuttgart: Klett, 1976), p. 82.

18. Northey, *Kafka's Relatives*, pp. 51–67.

19. Pawel, *The Nightmare of Reason*, p. 273.

20. Pasley, 'Semi-Private Games,' p. 194.

21. Anthony Northey, 'Die Kafkas: Juden? Christen? Tschechen? Deutsche?', in Kurt Krolop und Hans Dieter Zimmermann (eds.), *Kafka und Prag. Colloquium im Goethe-Institut Prag 24.–27. November 1992* (Berlin: de Gruyter, 1994), pp. 11–32, here pp. 16–17.

22. Thorlby, *Kafka*, p. 32.

23. Karl, *Representative Man*, p. 61.

24. Hartmut Binder, 'Wollweberei oder Baumwollweberei. Neues vom Büroalltag des Versicherungsangestellten Franz Kafka', *Europäische Kulturzeitschrift Sudetenland, Böhmen, Mähren, Schlesien. Vierteljahresschrift für Kunst, Literatur, Wissenschaft und Volkskultur* 39:2 (1997), 106–60.

25. Northey, *Kafka-Handbuch*, vol. 2, pp. 573–5.

26. Binder, 'Wollweberei', pp. 148–58.

27. Klaus Wagenbach, 'Julie Wohryzek, die zweite Verlobte Kafkas', in Jürgen Börn et al. (eds.), *Kafka-Symposion* (Munich: dtv, 1969), pp. 31–42, p. 39.

28. Max Brod, 'Nachwort zur ersten Ausgabe', *Das Schloss. Roman, Gesammelte Schriften*, vol. 4 (New York: Schocken Books, 1946), p. 417; Mailloux, *A Hesitation Before Birth*, p. 524.

29. Steven Dowden, *Kafka's Castle and the Critical Imagination* (Columbia, SC: Camden House, 1994), pp. 47–54.
30. Hibberd, *Kafka in Context*, p. 210.

FURTHER READING

Binder, Hartmut, 'Leben und Persönlichkeit Franz Kafkas', in Binder (ed.), *Kafka-Handbuch*, 2 vols. (Stuttgart: Kröner, 1979), vol. 1, pp. 103–584.
Kafka in Paris: Historische Spaziergänge mit alten Photographien (Munich: Langen Mueller, 1999).
Brod, Max, *Franz Kafka: a Biography*, tr. G. Humphreys Roberts and Richard Winston, 2nd edition (Schocken Books: New York, 1973).
Crawford, Deborah, *Franz Kafka: Man out of Step* (New York: Crown Publishers, 1953).
Gilman, Sander L. *Franz Kafka: the Jewish Patient* (New York: Routledge, 1995).
Hayman, Ronald, *Kafka: a Biography* (Oxford: Oxford University Press, 1982).
Hibberd, John, *Kafka in Context* (London: Studio Vista, 1975).
Karl, Frederick R., *Franz Kafka: Representative Man* (New York: Ticknor & Fields, 1991).
Mailloux, Peter, *A Hesitation Before Birth: the Life of Franz Kafka* (Newark: University of Delaware Press / London and Toronto: Associated University Press, 1989).
Northey, Anthony, *Kafka's Relatives: their Lives and his Writing* (London and New Haven: Yale University Press, 1991).
Pawel, Ernst, *The Nightmare of Reason: a Life of Franz Kafka* (New York: Vintage Books, 1985).
Unseld, Joachim, *Franz Kafka: a Writer's Life*, tr. Poul F. Dvorak (Riverside, CA: Ariadne, 1997).
Wagenbach, Klaus, *Franz Kafka: eine Biographie seiner Jugend 1883–1912* (Bern: Francke Verlag, 1958).
Franz Kafka: in Selbstzeugnissen und Bilddokumenten (Reinbek bei Hamburg: Rowohlt, 1964).

12

OSMAN DURRANI

Editions, translations, adaptations

Manuscripts

The various bundles of handwritten pages that make up Kafka's literary legacy are remarkable for two antithetical qualities: a cryptic, idiosyncratic approach in combination with the almost childlike outward appearance of the surviving pages. The surviving manuscripts consist of notebooks in several formats, along with loose-leaf bundles and material in envelopes. These pages are covered in handwriting that varies from the neat and legible 'fair copy' to casual and messy jottings. Deletions and emendations are carefully executed, but the loose sides are rarely numbered. The author's handwriting changes noticeably over the years, and is sometimes replaced by that of another, most probably his sister Ottla, to whom Kafka sometimes dictated letters and messages. To describe the task of transcribing the manuscripts as daunting would be an understatement. It seems little short of miraculous that on these slender, unstable foundations rests a canonical œuvre of unrivalled power and authority.

Scholars accustomed to the labyrinthine meanderings of Kafka's prose have noted that a stark simplicity shines through the complexities of what has been written on the pages. The author's preferred medium is the school exercise book in its most basic form: the small octavo booklets that were used by countless high-school fledglings as *Vokabelhefte*, handy pads and jotters for vocabulary and note-taking, and the larger quarto size, reserved for the young scholars' exercises and homework. Sometimes, Kafka would avail himself of official headed stationery (*Kanzleipapier*). As we examine his method of composition, features reminiscent of classroom practice begin to stand out. His handwriting is only superficially neat. He ignores margins and never applies an eraser, preferring to strike out redundant text and to squeeze in his corrections however and wherever possible. He treats rules of spelling and punctuation casually and inconsistently and uses paragraphs sparingly. He often alternates modern and older orthographic features (*ging* beside *gieng*, as the simple past of *gehen* – 'to go or to walk') and has a preference for the obsolete. The antiquated *Proceß* Kafka used is now considered more appropriate than *Prozeß* as the original title of *The Trial*, although in fact Kafka tends to avoid using 'ß' in favour of 'ss'. Furthermore Kafka preserves idiosyncrasies of the Prague idiom and of South German dialect usage in formulations such as *paar Worte* in place of *ein paar Worte* ('a few words') and *trotzdem* ('nevertheless') in the sense of 'although'. Shorthand notation, which he learnt at school, crops up sporadically.

It is now recognised that the oddities of Kafka's manuscripts go beyond what one might expect of a provisional draft of a story or novel.[1] He seems to take delight in misspelling the commonest words (*Teater* for *Theater*) and place names ('Newyork'), as though they were trivial and required only fleeting attention. What matter whether the currency circulating in America is the dollar or, as Kafka has it, the pound sterling? The significance of these apparent 'lapses' is heightened by an awareness that he worked in the world of money and therefore certainly knew the 'correct' terminology. Non-standard spellings are not limited to his early works. Far from becoming more mature as the years go by, the outward presentation seems to deteriorate. Orthography and punctuation become more casual. He makes no attempt to number the chapters of *The Trial* as he had provisionally done in *The Man who Disappeared*.

When it came to preparing an edition, the easiest task was to decipher his handwriting, though that was hardly straightforward. It was incomparably more challenging to decide what to leave in its original form and which changes could or should be made. Successive generations of editors have approached this problem from different angles, but never to the complete satisfaction of all interested parties. It is for this reason that we now have three separate editions of Kafka's writings. The first was undertaken by his friend Max Brod, who combines the reputation of a 'Judas' with that of an 'Evangelist'. The second was produced by an international team of scholars along strictly 'academic' lines and is the standard edition. The most recent attempt was begun in 1995 by a small commercial publisher with the aim of empowering the manuscript in its 'raw' but authentic form. These editions will be described in more detail below, and are listed in the 'Further Reading' section at the end of this chapter.

The history of the manuscripts could be the subject of a full-length adventure novel or movie. Whatever Brod's shortcomings as chief editor and interpreter of his friend's literary achievements, he more than compensated for them by scrupulously collecting Kafka's papers in the immediate aftermath of his death. He then preserved them, at great inconvenience to himself, when he fled from Prague on the last train before the Nazi occupation in March

1939 and followed a circuitous route across the Balkans and the Black Sea to Palestine. From there, the bulk of the extant material was sent to Zurich in 1956 and eventually transferred to the Bodleian Library in Oxford in 1965. The manuscript of *Der Proceß* was not included in this donation, but passed on to Brod's secretary, Ilse Ester Hoffe, on his death in 1968. She was subsequently accused of selling off individual pages of these irreplaceable documents, a few of which were later discovered in auctions. Most of these appear to have been retrieved and are now in the keeping of the Deutsches Literaturarchiv in Marbach. Small collections of manuscripts are held in Yale University and by private individuals in Prague and elsewhere. But the losses are considerable. For example, Brod showed little interest in the fair copies Kafka submitted to publishers for typesetting purposes. One of these was found in an autograph dealer's shop in Marburg in 1971, others have more recently surfaced at auctions. Brod had also given away pages to friends and collectors. On 26 May 1994, a handsome set of page proofs turned up at Sotheby's, London, where they were auctioned for around £40,000.[2] The voluminous *Letters to Felice* were also auctioned (by the recipient's heirs) and are currently in the hands of an unknown purchaser.

Publications authorised by Kafka

Kafka is often viewed as an author who remained largely unknown to his contemporaries on account of a profound reluctance to expose his works to a readership beyond his immediate circle of friends. He famously gave instructions that his works were to be burned after his death. It is therefore surprising to note that publications approved by him during his lifetime were relatively numerous. Between 1908 and 1924, approximately seventy texts appeared in print, excluding obituaries, reviews and non-literary material. They range from newspaper items and stories of varying length in journals to self-contained collections of prose passages and chapters from his novels. A total of seven slim volumes was no mean achievement, but neither was it indicative of a runaway success. The recent edition of all works published during Kafka's lifetime fills a single volume of 447 pages.[3]

The image of Kafka as a reluctant author has been discredited by Joachim Unseld, who was able to demonstrate that Kafka went to great lengths to ensure that not just a selection, but all of his completed works appeared in print in editions of high quality. The journals in which Kafka's first works appeared were often costly de luxe editions, now ornate collectors' items. A proliferation of small newspapers and magazines created a relatively favourable climate for the publication of short prose works in the pre-war period. But Kafka's first attempt at publication, a short story entered for a competition, most probably at Christmas 1906, was unsuccessful, and the text, entitled 'Himmel in engen Gassen' ('Sky in Narrow Streets'), has been lost. However, the author's close friendship with Max Brod proved decisive. Brod was a man of tremendous energy who had himself published no fewer than nine volumes, including several novels, collections of poetry and short stories, and a comedy for the stage, by 1912.[4] They were an unequal pair: Kafka sought perfection, was shy, scrupulous, and self-critical, while Brod appeared to aim, with the confidence of a born extrovert, for maximum publicity, instinctively knowing that he would have to engineer his own success. Brod quickly realised that his friend was no ordinary talent, but a genius, and devoted time and energy to finding publishers and winning recognition for him. He also sensed that Kafka lacked self-discipline and that it would fall to him to provide support and encouragement.

Kafka's relationship with the publishers Ernst Rowohlt and Kurt Wolff dates from 1912. It has sometimes been represented as resulting from a lucky 'chance encounter' (*Zufall*) which was to lead to a perfect partnership; in fact, it was carefully orchestrated by Brod. Shortly after their first meeting in Leipzig on 29 June 1912, Kafka dispatched a thirty-three-page manuscript to Rowohlt's newly established firm, who, by dint of using a typeface so large that Kafka regarded it as more suitable for the dissemination of the Laws of Moses (8.XI.12; *BF*: 83), produced a bibliophile edition entitled *Betrachtung* (*Contemplation*) which ran to ninety-nine pages. Kafka's attitude to the technical production of his work was to remain ambiguous. On the one hand, he assured Brod that the text may well contain 'something idiotic', and informed Rowohlt that all authors express their individuality by 'concealing their faults in an individual manner' (14.VIII.14; *B2*: 167); on the other hand, when discussing an appropriate format, he voiced his preferences as regards typeface and appearance with confidence, politely yet firmly insisting on a particular type of binding and paper. A curious interplay of self-deprecation and eager attentiveness to detail subsequently characterised Kafka's relationship with his principal publisher, Kurt Wolff, and with journal editors.

Posthumous editions

On 31 July 1924, a mere fifty-six days after Kafka's death, Brod signed an agreement with the Berlin publisher Die Schmiede which committed him to producing a posthumous edition of the collected works. Brod may not, at the time, have realised that he was taking on one of the most challenging and thankless editorial portfolios in the history of publishing, but he could hardly have failed to be aware of several major pitfalls that awaited him. He would be accused by some of the unforgivable crime of breaking the confidence of his dying friend, who had made out two separate, though contradictory, testamentary dispositions according to which his surviving works were to be destroyed. Brod's defence was that when Kafka charged him with this task, he replied that he would not carry it out. Kafka apparently raised no objections when Brod found a firm that was willing to publish four stories during 1923, and was after all still correcting the proofs on his death-bed.

Brod must have known that he would be involved in legal wrangles with other parties, such as Wolff, who claimed the rights to some of the texts and who was later entrusted with printing the remaining novels. He would have to unscramble the intricate patterns of his friend's handwriting, in which the word *schon* (already) is all too easily misread as *schwer* (heavy or difficult). He would need to number pages and name chapters, imposing a form on loosely structured fragments and rough sketches, little of which had been prepared for publication and much of which had been written down in a manner incompatible with publishers' requirements. He would need to enter into the mind of a man who used his writing as a form of dialogue with himself. He tried unsuccessfully to obtain letters from Kafka's sisters and papers dating from Kafka's last months in Berlin. Dora Diamant refused to part with what remained with her and Brod respected her wishes; her papers were later destroyed by the Gestapo. The rewards were far from obvious at the time: Kafka's publications had not been selling well during the preceding years. The second edition of *Betrachtung* had sold only 427 copies in three years.[5]

Undaunted, Brod set about the task with efficiency and zeal, fully intending that the three novels should appear in chronological sequence. But Wolff clung to the rights to *Amerika* with some justification, since he had been entrusted with the first chapter, 'The Stoker', back in 1913. Brod's edition therefore begins in 1925 with the text of *The Trial*. It commended itself as the first volume of the series for a number of reasons. The manuscript had been given to Brod as a personal gift in 1920, and he could thus claim exclusive rights to it. The existence of a complete final chapter was another bonus. Brod deliberately excluded the fragmentary passages, assuring readers that they were not missing much by being given the finished material only. He conceded that additional material was still extant and promised to include it in what was planned as the final volume of his 'collected' Kafka. It is typical of Brod's methodology of 'defragmentisation' that he chose to relegate unfinished material to the end of a volume or to a supplement, rather than place it where it might have occurred within the narrative. He used the same method when he came to edit the diaries.

Initially, this approach was applauded by many critics. Recognised authorities, including Siegfried Kracauer and Hermann Hesse, played down the fragmentary quality and advised readers to view the text as 'almost complete' or as a collection of pieces that combine so well as to make up a self-contained totality. By the time *The Castle* appeared in a more self-evidently unfinished form in the following year, readers were able to appreciate its overall design as something not unlike an antique torso.

Both publishing firms entrusted with parts of the first edition, Die Schmiede and Kurt Wolff Verlag, were in serious financial difficulties by the time of the Wall Street Crash in 1929. Four volumes of a second edition, consisting of the three novels and the narrative prose published during Kafka's lifetime, were issued by Salman Schocken (Berlin) in 1935 just months before the company lost its 'special dispensation' (needed in Hitler's Germany to sell books by Jewish authors to Jewish clients) later that year. Two further volumes, containing prose fragments, and extracts from Kafka's diaries and letters, appeared with Mercy Sohn in Prague in 1936 and 1937. As a Jew and a modernist Kafka was unwanted by the Nazis: his books could only be published outside Germany. A third edition began to appear in New York from 1945, in the newly constituted firm of Schocken Books. Although virtually identical to the second, it did contain a new set of editorial postscripts in which Brod emerged as franker than hitherto on a number of points, admitting for the first time that he had relied on 'feeling' when it came to devising the order of certain chapters. He implies that, since Kafka read out the entire text to him, his 'feelings' in such matters could be trusted.[6] A fourth edition, begun in 1950 – the last to be overseen by Brod – contained further alarming admissions along these lines. Now, for the first time, the editor was moved to admit, somewhat casually, that it was possible that he had put the chapters of *The Trial* into the wrong sequence: his fifth chapter may well have been Kafka's second.[7]

Brod's editorial strategy was more complex than that of a bowdleriser or an obscurantist. He soon came to realise that the public's conception of literature was changing and that the growing body of Kafka's readers was far from uniform in its interests. By 1935, we find him admitting that he no longer felt obliged to exclude material that might have confused the unprepared minds of the previous decade. Kafka's readers were quickly becoming Kafka's interpreters, and Brod's second edition contained appendices with fragmentary and deleted passages that would be of value to specialists and enthusiasts. But there were many changes that Brod seemed unwilling to make. *The Trial* remained subdivided into incorrectly numbered chapters; it was shorn of regional vocabulary and other non-standard elements. Readers had to wait until 1946 to learn that the novel Brod had presented to them as *Amerika* Kafka had called *The Man who Disappeared* in his diaries. Yet critics who disparage Brod should note that the only major item processed by a different editor (Willy Haas) during Brod's custodianship of the manuscripts was *Letters to Milena* (1953). It is a more selective and very much less reliable compilation than anything he undertook himself.

Inevitably, the inconsistencies produced criticism among experts, which was fuelled by Brod's reluctance to grant them access to his sources. In 1957 Herman Uyttersprot proposed what he misleadingly called 'A New Ordering of Kafka's Works', cruelly deriding Brod for his incompetence.[8] Specialists such as Friedrich Beissner in Germany and Eric Marson in Australia (to whom the manuscripts were not available) began to compare Brod's own versions of the novels and found startling and unexplained discrepancies. The first and second editions of *The Trial* (1925; 1935) were shown to contain a grand total of 1,778 unexplained textual variations. It seemed hard to understand how Brod could claim authenticity for any of his work in the light of such disparities.[9] He had even revised works that Kafka himself had proof-read. His editorial failings were magnified in the eyes of those who objected to his religiously coloured interpretations, as seen in the penultimate chapter of his biography and in his volume on 'despair and salvation' in Kafka. His views were too prescriptive. He claimed sweepingly, for instance, that 'The castle...stands for divine guidance.'[10] In 1965, Wolfgang Jahn was able to demonstrate that Brod had deliberately manipulated the text of *The Man who Disappeared* with a view to reducing the effect of its pessimistic qualities.

Brod repeatedly described his labours as provisional and hinted that a new edition of Kafka along historical-critical lines was needed. For this reason, he agreed to place those papers which he had rescued (but not letters and gifts to himself) at the disposal of the academic community at large. 1969, a year after his death, saw the publication of the two manuscript versions of 'Description of a Struggle', but it was many years before the first volume of the new critical edition appeared. Paradoxically, this was the last of the three novels. A new Kafka emerged; now, in 1982, readers could discover what specialists had known for some time: that *The Castle* had been begun in the first person. It was possible to identify the precise point at which Kafka replaced *ich* with K. The chapters were placed in a new sequence, tenses were changed, and Kafka's regional idioms were restored. It was noted that the previous editions of the novels contained on average two substantive errors on each page.[11]

Unsurprisingly, the new, 'authentic' Kafka was not universally welcomed. Some readers preferred the less sanitised, familiar version; others would struggle with the non-standard spellings and punctuation. Editorial emendations were clearly signalled for the first time, but they could be difficult to track down via page and line numbers in separate volumes of commentaries.

Specialists, on the other hand, were quick to spot that the new version had ironed out some inconsistencies and modernised some spellings, while leaving others untouched. Deletions and variants were again relegated to an appendix or to a companion volume, as they had been by Brod.

When preparing his works for publication, Kafka always made strenuous efforts to correct his own mistakes and decode his abbreviations. He had even asked Brod to check his drafts and go over the proofs for him. This suggests that Brod's version might, in the end, look more like what Kafka would have published than the new edition over which the Germanists had laboured for many years. Malcolm Pasley, one of the editors, may have foreseen this when he reminded readers in the afterword that the new versions were addressed to the 'ear' rather than to the eye and that the manuscripts 'have something of the quality of a musical score' (DS: 390). This could, indeed, be the key to the seemingly deteriorating appearance of Kafka's writing. Increasingly, he wrote the texts down with a view to reading them out aloud: a very practical concern that provides a surprisingly simple explanation for the missing marks of punctuation no less than for the simplified spelling he used. The Castle, however, was written 'for the sake of the writing, not for reading' ('zum Geschrieben-, nicht zum Gelesenwerden'), and here, as Pasley has shown, the punctuation marks are applied differently.[12] It seems impossible to do justice to these conflicting factors on the printed page.

According to a more recent response to the historical-critical edition, not enough attention is paid in it to the author's creative method as revealed, particularly, by his handwriting. This indifference towards the manuscripts in their most basic form led the small publisher of Stroemfeld to take advantage of the end of the seventy-year copyright period and announce a new venture: a series of facsimiles, in which the calligraphic qualities of Kafka's writing would take centre stage. The trend had been started in the 1970s, with Dieter E. Sattler's publication of Hölderlin's manuscripts. Now, readers would find not only what Kafka wrote, but see how he wrote it. Graphologists would be able to draw their own conclusions from the thick lines with which the author crossed his 't's, capital 'a's and 'f's, and from the long down-strokes of the 'g's and capital 'k's and 's's, which have a habit of plunging recklessly into the next line. Stroemfeld's edition was intended to liberate Kafka's texts from the Kafkologists and to give the lie to those who advocate a laborious textual apparatus as the only means of representing his work on the page. The word as written by the author has a visual effectiveness that no philological treatise can hope to achieve. Other problems are effortlessly and elegantly resolved. The sequence of chapters in The Trial is left open by the sixteen sections that can now be rearranged at will. Readers are obliged to enter into a more dynamic relationship with the author and can try their hands not only at interpreting, but at editing the text for themselves. Only a few volumes of this enterprise have so far been produced.[13] The public's response was mixed. Stroemfeld's case was initially characterised by hostility towards the editors of the historical-critical edition, who were accused of gross negligence, and directed against Pasley in particular, who was blamed for attempting to restrict access to the manuscripts that were kept in Oxford.[14] After protracted negotiations involving the British Academy, the editors Roland Reuss and Peter Staengle now have unrestricted access to all holdings in the public domain and enjoy the support of an increasing number of specialists.

Translations

If none of the editions has found universal favour, the chances of preparing a satisfactory translation of an uncertain original into a foreign language are not good. There are compelling arguments for regarding Kafka's writings as utterly untranslatable. Modern theories stress the inevitable 'translation losses' inherent in any translation. George Steiner, for instance, describes authors and translators as collectively 'groping towards each other in a common mist',[15] and the idea that a 'translator' is little better than a 'traducer' has a long history. Kafka's scepticism about the extent to which language can be relied upon is well attested: 'My whole body warns me about every word' (15/17.XII.10; *B2*: 131) he writes to Brod, and to himself in his diary, 'My doubts form a circle around each word' (15.XII.10; *TB1*: 103). Language, he concludes, may at best be employed 'to indicate' (*andeutungsweise*) but not 'to compare' (*vergleichsweise*) (aphorism 57; *BK*: 237).

Given the problems thrown up by Kafka's texts, it is astounding to learn that his first English translators, Edwin and Willa Muir, applied themselves to the task as untutored amateurs, having learnt German unsystematically on their travels in the early 1920s. They claim to have found his prose 'less rigid, less clotted', and therefore 'much easier' to translate than that of other writers.[16] Their English rendering of *The Castle* appeared in 1930, in an edition of 500 copies. 'The Great Wall of China' followed in 1933, then *The Trial* (1937), *America* (1938 – or *Amerika*, as it was titled in the United States itself), and 'In the Penal Colony' (1948). When Brod released new material, this was appended in translations by Eithne Wilkins and Ernst Kaiser. The first translators had little option but to follow Brod's editions as best they could, and to look to Brod whenever they encountered difficulties. The Muirs went along, less dogmatically perhaps, with his view that Kafka was a seeker of spiritual truth and commended *The Castle* to the Anglophone reader as a modern-day *Pilgrim's Progress*.

The difficulties for the translator derive to some extent from Kafka's working practice and from the circumstances in which his writings were published. The question of titles and proper names is one that catches the reader's attention for obvious reasons. Sometimes there are several provisional titles for works in progress. The short story 'The Village Schoolmaster' ('Der Dorfschullehrer') was also known as 'The Giant Mole' ('Der Riesenmaulwurf'), and *The Man who Disappeared* was abandoned in 1916 without having acquired a definitive title. Brod called it *Amerika* instead of *Der Verschollene* at a time when neither he nor anyone else suspected that the public would seek or gain access to Kafka's diaries. The term *verschollen* denotes a person who has 'gone missing' and 'is presumed dead' and has associations with *Scholle* ('clod', 'soil'), which in turn suggests connections with the land-surveyor of *The Castle*. Brod defended his choice of title for many years on the grounds that Kafka talked of his 'American novel', and occasionally of 'The Stoker'. The Muirs' translation was marketed in Britain as *America*, but in the United States as *Amerika*, in order to highlight the element of foreignness.

Readers will easily spot that Pasley's 'A Fasting-artist' is the same as the Muirs' 'A Hunger Artist'. The latter is evidently a literal rendering of *Ein Hungerkünstler*; the former considers the artist's hunger as more of a devotional act. It is a commonplace that Kafka's writings are full of just such ambiguities. Some translations manage to achieve a widening of the original, a 'translation gain'; but most frequently, the result is a loss. The word 'metamorphosis', for example, opens up notions of evolutionary progress which the text does not fulfil. This is why Pasley chose the more modest-sounding noun 'transformation' for what, in German, is, at first glance, no more and no less than a 'change'. Yet *Wandlung* refers to a complete about-turn, a conversion, and even a 'transubstantiation' of a religious kind. Both titles are therefore liable to trigger associations that go beyond what Kafka intended, or do not go far enough.

The titles of *The Trial* and *The Castle* provide striking instances of loss. *Der Process* signifies a 'trial', but also a 'process', a 'procedure', and, in medical parlance, the 'progress' of an illness. *Das Schloss* is a 'castle', but also a means of 'closing' (*schließen*), a 'lock' or 'padlock'. The German has sinister overtones which its equivalent does not possess in English. The text of this novel makes use of vocabulary which, while still current in modern German, also possesses an archaic flavour. Key terms like *Bote* (messenger), *Gehilfe* (assistant), *Landvermesser* (land-surveyor) are stripped of most of these connotations in the English. In French, where in each of these cases there were clear choices to be made between archaic and current terms (*courrier* versus *messager*; *commis* versus *aide*; *arpenteur* versus *géomètre*), the translator regularly opted for the more remote form, giving the impression of a medieval saga.[17] The Italian reader of *The Trial* is fortunate in being able to make comparisons between three representative approaches. The earliest, by Alberto Spaini (1933), smoothes over unevennesses and attempts to render the work intelligible. More recently, Giorgio Zampa provided a literal version which follows Kafka rigorously, even in matters of punctuation, before the novelist Primo Levi undertook his version as a 'middle way' between the two. Even Levi, however, saw fit to 'take pity on the Italian reader and introduce some breaks', especially in the 'Advocate' chapter.[18]

Proper names often hold out the promise of a cryptic key to the author's intentions and are therefore particularly difficult to translate. A number of these are more or less intelligible in several languages – K. being the most obvious example; but it is worth noting that many translations tend to turn 'Josef K.' into 'Joseph' or 'Guiseppe K.'. J. A. Underwood changes 'Gregor' into 'Gregory' Samsa, but stops short of making 'Karl' into 'Charles' Rossmann. The associations of names such as 'Westwest' and 'Ramses' are relatively accessible. The English-speaking reader is actually at an advantage over many others when it comes to unravelling some of the American place names, such as 'Clayton' and 'Occidental'. The name 'Bendemann' produces a more precise notion in the Anglophone reader's mind than among speakers of German. But German names like 'Roßmann', 'Fräulein Bürstner', or 'Advokat Huld' (very approximately: 'Horseman', 'Miss Scrubber', 'Advocate Grace') have associations attached to them that take longer to explain. The names in *The Castle*, 'Klamm', 'Momus', 'Galater', 'Vallabene', and many others, are indicative of the author's multiple perspective and presuppose an almost encyclopedic range of knowledge.[19]

The new editions compel translators to make choices not only between competing theories but also between textual variants. Today's German readers have come to accept many linguistic peculiarities as a fair price to pay for access to the 'real' Kafka, but American readers are more likely to be irritated by his indecision about the correct spelling of 'New York' (Kafka writes 'Newyork' as well as 'New york'). Kafka's predilection for puns is not limited to the titles he chose. Relevant linguistic devices include the ambiguous word *verhaftet* in the first line of *The Trial*, which does not correspond neatly to 'arrested'. While 'to arrest' may signal a 'slowing down', 'stopping', or 'retarding' action, 'verhaften' suggests a 'clinging' or 'staining' process. Only laborious annotations would give a flavour of these multiple meanings. This was attempted by Claude David in the French *Pléiade* edition, which provides 215 pages of notes on *The Castle* alone.[20] The general reader will probably not have the patience to struggle through a labyrinthine meta-textual appendix, which in any case will never be complete.

One much-debated pivotal expression is the designation of the 'thing' that Gregor Samsa is turned into at the beginning of 'The Metamorphosis'. All the early translations assumed that the main character had become a kind of insect, something that is only implied but not stated in the original. Nevertheless, we find words such as 'bug' or even 'cockroach' used in some translations, even though this is blatantly at variance with Kafka's text, which is unspecific when it comes to identifying the type of 'verminous creature' (*Ungeziefer*) that Gregor recognises himself to have become. Even Pasley has Gregor turn into 'a monstrous insect', and J. A. Underwood writes, rather crudely, 'a giant bug'. Stanley Corngold has 'a monstrous vermin' (*M*: 3), which comes closer to the term Kafka uses. The monstrosity is underlined by translations such as 'un insecto monstruoso' (Spanish) and 'un insetto grosso' (Italian). Since we first encounter Gregor in his bed, several critics have assumed that he has become a 'bedbug': 'If Gregor cannot be taken seriously as a bedbug in the technical sense (*Cimex lectularius*), he is still, literally speaking, a bug in a bed since he wakes up that way one morning.'[21] Nothing could be more inappropriate. Kafka studiously avoided any reference to entomological terms – except in the cleaner's abusive 'dung-beetle' – and asked his publisher's illustrator not to place an image of an insect on the cover of the book. This request has been ignored by many, including the Penguin Modern Classics edition. Alexandre Vialatte renders the qualifying *ungeheuer* as *véritable*, highlighting the 'real' in place of the fantastic. This has, in turn, led to major errors in the translation of 'Die Verwandlung' into languages such as Persian, whose translators used the French version of 1938 as the basis of their work.[22]

Readers who are sensitive to Kafka's attempts to parody the literary styles of the past will miss many associations of this type. The early English and French translations of *The Man who Disappeared* reproduce the phrase 'Verflucht sei wer uns nicht glaubt!' as 'Down with all those who do not believe in us!' and 'Malheur à qui ne nous aura pas cru!'[23] The religious dimension is almost absent. Hofmann catches the flavour more accurately with: 'Accursed be anyone who does not believe us!'[24] Not all the recent translations are necessarily superior, as S. S. Prawer was able to show when comparing Underwood's banal 'even greater release' with the Muirs' 'heights of redemption' as a rendering of 'gesteigerte Erlösung' in 'Josephine, the Songstress or: the Mouse People'. The main point here, according to S. S. Prawer, is that while Underwood's versions admittedly correct some earlier errors, 'they make Kafka into a less elegant writer than he was'.[25] But there are dangers in seeking too many associations. When Titorelli is described as painting *Heidelandschaften*, it is not exactly self-evident that Kafka is 'clearly punning on the word *Heide*', 'a heathen', and that the subjects of these paintings are therefore not just heaths but also 'godless landscapes'.[26] Fortunately for non-German speakers, the rigorously philological line of approach is not the only one, and the pursuit of exactitude in such matters brings with it a host of new difficulties. Yet it is beyond doubt that one feature of Kafka's style, described by fellow novelist Martin Walser as 'speculatively subjunctive groping',[27] is almost impossible to reproduce effectively in a language that lacks a subjunctive mood.

The prison chaplain who confronts Josef K. with a seemingly unfathomable paradox in *The Trial* pronounces the most devastating assessment of the inexact science of interpretation when he delivers his observations on the parable 'Before the Law':

> 'Do not misunderstand me', said the clergyman, 'I am merely indicating the different opinions that exist in this matter. You must not set too much store by opinions. The written word cannot be altered, and opinions are often no more than expressions of despair at this fact.' (*DP*: 230)

In any translation, Kafka's words and phrases will necessarily diverge from the original, but generations of attentive readers the world over have demonstrated that their unsettling effect is not, or is hardly, diminished in a new medium. Translation losses may direct our thoughts away from some implications that seem obvious to speakers of German, but they will probably also provide new, previously unrecognised angles from which Kafka's writings may be approached. The chaplain recognises that all secondary discourse gnaws away at the source text, as fresh minds apply themselves to rewriting, transforming, or even to subverting a defiantly immutable original. This position is close in spirit to those modern translation theories that seek to liberate and empower the translator, claiming that all reading involves an element of misreading, and no one reading is better than any other. Hence 'all readings, potentially infinite in number, are in the final analysis equally misinterpretations'.[28] Kafka knew that all texts are manipulated by their monolingual readers no less than they are by translators and readers of translations.[29] The availability and continuing production of sensitively executed renderings into other idioms are a vital part of this process. They ensure that Kafka stimulates readers and researchers alike in countries far beyond the frontiers of the German-speaking world, even when the price that must be paid is a 'subversion' of the original. A brief consideration of reworkings of Kafka in other media will reveal the extent to which the frontiers of Kafka's art have moved far beyond the words he wrote.

Adaptations

Kafka's texts have inspired several generations of artists working in a wide range of media, including the visual arts, opera, theatre, and prose. Wolfgang Rothe claims that the features of Kafka's face have exerted a powerful influence on graphic artists. Ironically, in view of Kafka's instructions not to attempt depiction, the monstrous 'insect' from 'The Metamorphosis' proved a more popular subject than most of his other literary motifs. 'Odradek' (the object-cum-creature at the centre of 'The Cares of a Family Man') provided a topic for a competition among artists. Hans Fronius devoted himself to the task of illustrating Kafka's works. In 1937 Brod organised an exhibition of more than 100 woodcuts and drawings derived from Kafka's works. An exhibition entitled 'Kunst zu Kafka' was held in several European cities in the mid 1970s.[30] As recently as 1999, the Royal Academy of Arts displayed a painting by Mick Rooney of *Dr Franz Kafka Attending a Performance of 'Shulamith' in the Yiddish Café Savoy, Prague on 13th October 1912* (oil, 71 × 47 ins), a detail from which is depicted on the cover of this book.[31]

Musical settings begin with none other than Max Brod, who set a poem in 1911. He continued to work on music for Kafka's texts, producing in 1951 a setting of two passages from his diaries which he entitled, *Tod und Paradies* (Death and Paradise). Beside Gottfried von Einem's opera of *The Trial* (first performed at the Salzburg festival in 1953), a number of short texts have generated operas, including *A Country Doctor* (Hans Werner Hense, 1951) and *The Penal Colony* (Joanna Bruzdowicz, 1972). Successful reinterpretations include Gunter A. Schuller's *The Visitation*, which transfers the plot of *The Trial* to the USA, where the black Carter Jones is made to suffer at the hands of white persecutors led by a man called Chuck. A ballet, *The Report of Herr K.* was premièred in Ulm in 1977.[32]

Many dramatisations were produced in languages other than German, although attempts to recreate Kafka's style and even to complete his unfinished novels have also been undertaken by a number of German authors. Brod produced the first adaptations of *The Trial* and *The Castle* for the stage. The novelist André Gide and theatre director Jean-Louis Barrault saw themselves as 'Kafka's brothers' and began developing the idea of a dramatised 'Trial' in 1942.[33] It had a timeless quality ('Place: Everywhere. Time: Always') and was performed in many cities, although attempts to revive it in the 1960s were less successful. By then, the approach adopted by Orson Welles was felt to be more in keeping with the public's expectations. Huge, mechanised bureaucracies were to blame for Josef K.'s persecution, which took place against a backdrop of concrete bunkers and seemingly endless vaults and passages. Jan Grossman brought a Czech adaptation, noted for its visual puns and galumphing wit, to London's Aldwych Theatre in 1967. Steven Berkoff began his extremely successful dramatisations with a version of *The Trial* at the London's Round House in 1972, a feast of mime and dramatic invention, set among mirrors and door-shaped frames. Film directors now tend to avoid existentially timeless and tyrannically bureaucratic settings in favour of the more realistic atmosphere of Kafka's native city.

Although the term 'Kafkaesque' was coined by Englishman Cecil Day Lewis in 1938 as a byword for everything felt to be 'alien' and 'incomprehensible',[34] English-speakers will find some familiar territory in his works. One of his three novels is set entirely in America, and despite topographic and other dislocations, it contains a variety of apt, in some cases highly prophetic, insights into the increasing mechanisation and industrialisation of the New World. Kafka prepared himself by studying Arthur Holitscher's *Amerika heute und morgen* (America Today and Tomorrow), then the most up-to-date German source on life in the western hemisphere, and attending sociology lectures by František Soukup. There are satirical passages about technology, overcrowding, exploitation of workers, and inventions of weird gadgetry that would not have seemed out of place to a generation of cinema-goers brought up on Fritz Lang's *Metropolis* and Charlie Chaplin. Brod himself drew attention to the 'Chaplinesque' features in this novel,[35] and it is not difficult to identify such passages, for example, in the description of life in the lift-boys' dormitory of the Occidental Hotel.

After Philip Roth's exploration of neurotic sexuality in *The Professor of Desire* (1977), an English Kafka surfaces in two plays by Alan Bennett, who maintains that, as a vegetarian who was fond of the sun, 'he seems a familiar crank', easily imagined in too-large shorts, hiking with friends in Letchworth, muttering self-deprecatory platitudes ('Silly me!').[36] *The Insurance Man* traces the misfortunes of a man who wakes up one morning with an unsightly patch of skin which rapidly spreads across his body. He is referred to the state insurance company, a maze of intricate and illogically arranged offices, where he becomes convinced that only 'Dr Kafka' will be able to deal with him. Other insurance claimants are chased away under Kafka's very nose. Daniel Day Lewis in the title role was suavely off-hand about his clients' misfortunes, far removed from the image of Kafka as the tormented underdog. The upshot is that the 'real' Kafka was part of a bureaucratic machinery that, while dealing with victims of industrial injuries, failed to recognise, and still less to treat, precisely those neurotic ailments which critics have seen reflected in the author's fiction. The long-suffering victim, Franz, is eventually employed, with predictable consequences, in an asbestos factory part-owned by Dr Kafka himself.

A number of short stories have lent themselves to adaptations as one-man performances. One of the first to gain exposure in this form was 'A Report for an Academy', in which the difficult transformation from ape to human was suggested rather than accomplished on stage. Armed with a briefcase in one hand and a banana in the other, Klaus Kammer distracted audiences through clever visual antics in Berlin, 1962. Subsequent productions tended to involve two actors: the naïve and the mature ape, or the ape in the company of an interpreter.[37] Since then, there have been other dramatisations, most notably Berkoff's *The Metamorphosis*. Berkoff's account of his work, *Meditations on Metamorphosis*, is remarkable not least for the parallels it reveals between Kafka and modern dramatists such as Arthur Miller.

Several German poets and novelists have attempted to produce continuations of Kafka's works which reveal intriguing aspects of the originals in a new light. Dagmar Leupold's *Die gemästete Grete* (Stuffed Grete) takes the form of a monologue by Gregor Samsa's sister, now in her nineties, feeding cornflakes to the squirrels in a retirement home and reminiscing about the strange transformation of her now half-forgotten brother.[38] Eckhard Henscheid's *Rossmann, Rossmann* is an ambitious attempt to continue the plot of *The Man who Disappeared* in a light-hearted vein, albeit in a style that has numerous points of contact with Kafka's. In Henscheid's *Franz Kafka Makes a Film of his 'Country Doctor'*, the author is persuaded by a team of young schoolteachers to collaborate in the production of a film of his story on a sun-drenched Italian beach in the interests of generating powerful alienation effects. This perhaps explains why the horses become motor-cycles and the name of 'Rosa' is changed to 'Abigail'. Kafka, missing his room in the Alchemistengasse in Prague, is frequently moved to tears, though it remains uncertain whether his frustrations are triggered by the absence of one fondly loved Bürstl Karin or by the off-hand treatment of his text.[39]

No survey of this kind would be complete without reference to the World Wide Web, on which Kafka is increasingly well represented. In June 1999, the Altavista search engine returned no fewer than 12,591 Web pages in response to a query about 'Franz Kafka'. By June 2000, the number of hits had doubled to 24,360. These include a large number of factually informative sites with links to biographies, bibliographies, texts, and translations. There is also no shortage of 'imaginative' work with a Kafka component that can be accessed: *Kafka in the Labyrinth* is one such, as is *Kafka im Weltraum* (Kafka in Space). The former provides hyperlinks to other authors, such as Jorge Luis Borges, who have 'labyrinthine' interests. The latter is a text adventure game, devised by Linus Reichlin. Here, too, there is every indication that Kafka will continue to provide inspiration not just for readers, critics, and artists, but for the growing cyberspace community in the future.

NOTES

1. See especially Wolf Kittler and Gerhard Neumann, 'Kafkas Drucke zu Lebzeiten. Editorische Technik und hermeneutische Entscheidung', in Kittler and Neumann (eds.), *Franz Kafka: Schriftverkehr* (Freiburg: Rombach, 1990), pp. 30–74.
2. Hartmut Binder, *Kafka-Handbuch*, 2 vols. (Stuttgart: Kröner, 1979), vol. 2, p. 6; H. R. Woudhuysen, 'Kafka's Page-Proofs', *Times Literary Supplement* 20 May 1994, p. 29.
3. Wolf Kittler, Hans-Gerd Koch and Gerhard Neumann (eds.), *Franz Kafka: Drucke zu Lebzeiten* (Frankfurt aM: Fischer, 1994).
4. See Margarita Pazi, *Max Brod. Werk und Persönlichkeit* (Bonn: Bouvier, 1970), p. 170.
5. Ludwig Dietz, *Franz Kafka* (Stuttgart: Metzler, 1975), p. 74.
6. Postscript to the third edition of *Der Prozeß*, p. 322.
7. Postscript to the fourth edition, p. 326.
8. Herman Uyttersprot, *Eine neue Ordnung der Werke Kafkas? Zur Struktur von 'Der Prozess' und 'Amerika'* (Antwerp: de Vries-Brouwers, 1957).
9. Eric Marson, *Kafka's Trial: the Case against Josef K.* (St Lucia: Queensland University Press, 1975), p. 8; Friedrich Beissner, *Der Erzähler Franz Kafka* (Stuttgart: Kohlhammer, 1952), p. 46.
10. Brod, *A Biography*, p. 189.
11. Ritchie Robertson, 'Not by Brod Alone', *Times Literary Supplement*, 14 Oct. 1983, p. 1129.
12. Pasley, 'Zu Kafkas Interpunktion', in *'Die Schrift ist unveränderlich': Essays zu Kafka* (Frankfurt aM: Fischer, 1995), pp. 121–44, here p. 128.
13. Roland Reuss and Peter Staengle (eds.), *Der Process*. Four volumes have appeared to date (2001); approximately fifteen are in preparation.
14. The author witnessed an unsuccessful attempt to force the German P. E. N. Club to pass a resolution condemning Pasley (Künstlerhaus, Munich, 14 May 1998).
15. *After Babel*, p. 65.
16. 'Translating from the German', p. 96.
17. Binder, *Kafka-Handbuch*, vol. 2, pp. 683–5.
18. Franz Kafka, *Il processo*, tr. Primo Levi (Turin: Einaudi, 1983), pp. 253–5.
19. Inquiries into Kafka's names include Herbert Tauber, *Franz Kafka: an Interpretation of his Works* (London: Secker and Warburg, 1948), pp. 153–4. See also Elizabeth M. Rajec, *Namen und ihre Bedeutungen im Werke Franz Kafkas* (Berne: Lang, 1977).
20. Franz Kafka, *Œuvres complètes*, tr. Alexandre Vialatte, Marthe Robert, and others, and annotated by Claude David, 4 vols. (Paris: Gallimard, 1976).
21. Robert F. Fleissner, 'Is Gregor Samsa a Bed Bug? Kafka and Dickens Revisited', *Studies in Short Fiction* 22 (1985), 225–8, here p. 228.
22. Nasrin Rahimieh, '*Die Verwandlung* Deterritorialized: Hedayat's Appropriation of Kafka', *Comparative Literature Studies* 31 (1994), 251–69, here p. 256.
23. *America*, tr. Willa and Edwin Muir (Harmondsworth: Penguin, 1967), p. 246; Kafka, *Œuvres complètes*, vol. 1, tr. Vialatte, p. 235.

24. Hofmann (tr.), *The Man who Disappeared (America)*, p. 202. See also Jean-Louis Bandet, ' "Si la roue n'avait pas grincé...": imitation et parodie chez Franz Kafka', *Etudes Germaniques* 53 (1998), 339–64, here 342.
25. S. S. Prawer, 'Difficulties of the Kafkaesque', *Times Literary Supplement*, 14 Oct. 1983, 1127–8, here p. 1128.
26. Patrick Bridgwater, *Kafka and Nietzsche* (Bonn: Bouvier, 1974), p. 88.
27. Martin Walser, *Beschreibung einer Form: Versuch über Franz Kafka* (Munich: Hanser, 1961), p. 30.
28. Said, *The World, the Text, and the Critic*, p. 39.
29. Hermanns, *The Manipulation of Literature*, p. 237.
30. Binder, *Kafka-Handbuch*, vol. 2, pp. 841–51.
31. Michael Kenny (ed.), *Royal Academy Illustrated Catalogue 1999* (London: Royal Academy Publications 1999), p. 172.
32. *Kafka-Handbuch*, vol. 2, pp. 851–9.
33. Ibid., vol. 2, p. 825.
34. Ibid., vol. 2, p. 671.
35. Postscript to the first edition of *Amerika*, subsequently reproduced in the later editions, p. 359.
36. *Two Kafka Plays*, p. ix.
37. Binder, *Kafka-Handbuch*, vol. 2, p. 833.
38. Dagmar Leupold, *Destillate* (Frankfurt aM: Fischer, 1996), pp. 29–33.
39. Eckhard Henscheid, *Rossmann, Rossmann* (Zurich: Haffmanns, 1991).

FURTHER READING

Bennett, Alan, *Two Kafka Plays* (London: Faber and Faber 1987).
Berkoff, Steven, *Meditations on Metamorphosis* (London: Faber and Faber, 1995).
Cohn, Dorrit, 'K. enters *The Castle* – On the Change of Person in Kafka's Manuscript,' *Euphorion* 62 (1968), 28–45.
Crick, Joyce, 'Kafka and the Muirs', in J. P. Stern (ed.), *The World of Franz Kafka*, (London: Weidenfeld and Nicolson, 1980), pp. 159–75.
Gray, Ronald, 'But Kafka Wrote in German', in Angel Flores (ed.), *The Kafka Debate: New Perspectives for our Times* (New York: Gordian, 1977), pp. 242–52.
Harman, Mark, 'Digging the Pit of Babel: Retranslating Franz Kafka's *Castle*', in *New Literary History* 27 (1996), 291–311.
Hermans, Theo, *The Manipulation of Literature: Studies in Literary Translation* (London: Croom Helm, 1985).
Lev, Peter, 'Three adaptations of *The Trial*', *Literature/Film Quarterly* 12 (1984), 180–5.
Muir, Edwin and Willa, 'Translating from the German', in Reuben A. Brower (ed.), *On Translation* (Cambridge, Mass.: Harvard University Press, 1959), pp. 93–6.
Roth, Philip, *The Professor of Desire* (New York: Farrar, Straus, and Giroux, 1977).
Pasley, Malcolm, 'Franz Kafka MSS: Description and Select Inedita', *Modern Language Review* 57 (1962), 54–9.
Robertson, Ritchie, 'Edwin Muir as Critic of Kafka', *Modern Language Review* 79 (1984), 638–52.
Said, Edward, *The World, the Text, and the Critic* (Cambridge, Mass.: Harvard University Press, 1983).

Steiner, George, *After Babel: Aspects of Language and Translation*, 3rd edition (Oxford: Oxford University Press, 1998).

Unseld, Joachim, *Franz Kafka: a Writer's Life*, tr. Paul F. Dvorak (Riverside: Ariadne, 1997).

Primary texts in German

See also Maria Luise Caputo-Mayr and Julius Michael Herz, *Franz Kafka: International Bibliography of Primary and Secondary Literature*, 2nd edition (Munich: Saur, 2000).

Brod's first edition: *Der Prozeß* (Berlin: Die Schmiede, 1925); *Das Schloß* (Munich: Kurt Wolff, 1926); *Amerika* (Munich: Kurt Wolff, 1927).

Brod's second edition: *Gesammelte Schriften* (Berlin: Salman Schocken, 1935–37). 4 vols. (*Erzählungen und kleine Prosa* and the three novels). Volumes 5 and 6 (*Beschreibung eines Kampfes. Novellen, Skizzen, Aphorismen aus dem Nachlaß* and *Tagebücher und Briefe*) appeared in Prague: Heinrich Mercy Sohn, 1936–7. This edition includes fragments and revised postscripts, and further attempts by Brod to normalise Kafka's style.

Brod's third edition consists of volumes 1–5 of the second edition. New York: Schocken Books 1946, with minor alterations.

Brod's fourth edition (Frankfurt aM: Fischer, 1950–74) consists of 11 volumes, of which three were edited by others: vol. 4, *Briefe an Milena* (ed. Willy Haas), vol. 10, *Briefe an Felice und andere Korrespondenz aus der Verlobungszeit* (ed. Erich Heller and Jürgen Born), and vol. 11, *Briefe an Ottla und die Familie* (ed. Hartmut Binder and Klaus Wagenbach).

The historical-critical edition: *Schriften Tagebücher Briefe*, ed. Gerhard Neumann, Malcolm Pasley, and Jost Schillemeit was begun in 1982 and is currently in progress. The novels, short fiction, and diaries are available in paperback as *Gesammelte Werke*, 12 vols. (Frankfurt aM: Fischer, 1994). The first of five projected volumes of letters appeared in 1999.

Roland Reuss and Peter Staengle (eds.), *Der Process*, 795 separate sides of facsimile in sixteen parts and an accompanying CD-ROM, (Frankfurt aM: Stroemfeld, 1997). *Historisch-kritische Ausgabe sämtlicher Handschriften, Drucke und Typoskripte. Einleitung* (Frankfurt aM: Stroemfeld, 1995). *Beschreibung eines Kampfes* appeared in 1999.

Primary texts in English

Early editions

Willa and Edwin Muir (tr.), *The Castle* (1930), *The Great Wall of China and Other Pieces* (1933), *The Trial* (1937), *America* (1938). Ernst Kaiser and Eithne Wilkins (tr.), *In the Penal Settlement and Short Prose Works* (1949), *Wedding Preparations in the Country and Other Posthumous Prose Writings* (1954), all London: Secker and Warburg, reprinted New York: Schocken, sometimes under slightly different titles. These versions are still available, with minor revisions and supplements, published by Vintage Classics, London 1999.

Editions, translations, adaptations

Recent translations

Idris Parry (tr.), *The Trial* (1994); Michael Hofmann (tr.), *The Man who Disappeared (America)* (1996) and J. A. Underwood (tr.), *The Castle* (1997), based on the new critical German edition; Malcolm Pasley (tr.), *The Great Wall of China and Other Short Works* (1991) and *The Transformation ['Metamorphosis'] and other Stories: Works Published During Kafka's Lifetime* (1992), all Harmondsworth: Penguin Books.

The first volumes of a new series based on the restored texts appeared in 1998: Mark Harman (tr.), *The Castle*, and Breon Mitchell (tr.), *The Trial*, both subtitled 'A New Translation Based on the Restored Text', New York: Schocken, 1998.

13

MARTIN BRADY AND HELEN HUGHES

Kafka adapted to film

Die Bilder sind ja gut (The images are good of course)

Bertolt Brecht[1]

Seasickness on *terra firma*

Kafka's earliest surviving short story, 'Description of a Struggle', contains a passage often quoted in discussions of the relationship between words and images in Kafka's writing:

> I have experience, and I don't mean it as a joke when I say that it is a seasickness on *terra firma*. In essence you have forgotten the true names of things and now in haste pour arbitrary names over them. Quickly, quickly! But as soon as you run away from them you forget their names again. The poplar in the fields, which you have named the 'Tower of Babel' because you didn't know or didn't want to know that it was a poplar, sways namelessly again and you have to call it 'Noah, when he was drunk'.
>
> I was rather surprised when he said, 'I am pleased that I did not understand what you said.'
>
> Annoyed I replied hastily, 'The fact that you are pleased about it shows that you did understand it.'
>
> 'I did indeed show it, Sir, but you also spoke strangely.'   (*BK*: 89–90)

The narrator's sense of outrage at the linguistic quirks of the community is, as one commentator has put it, dismay at the 'confusion metaphor poses for nomination', the way in which each image substituted for the 'true names of things' leads further away from the object itself to a proliferation of meaning.[2] Certainly, the reference to the Tower of Babel implies that metaphorical substitution is an essentially arbitrary act. This is, however, clearly only one side of the coin. Whilst, taken at face value, metaphor may amount to a perilous 'slippage of signification',[3] it also – in the present instance, at least – produces images which are both ingenious and droll. It is certainly evident from the exchange which follows that the narrator's diagnosis is less comprehensive than he believed, and the linguistic problem he encounters more intractable.

The issue of arbitrary embellishment and metaphorical substitution faces any visual artist reckless enough to turn to Kafka for inspiration. Whilst the dilemma of the divergence of word and image is, of course, inescapable in all literary adaptation, it is particularly acute in the case of an author who systematically problematises this very relationship in his writing. As he wrote to Felice, 'Images are beautiful, we cannot do without images, but they are also a source of much anguish' (6/7.XII.12; *BF*: 164).

Few film-makers who have turned to Kafka for material to adapt or to stage – and there are many of them[4] – seem to have confronted this issue explicitly. For one thing that can be said about the majority of Kafka films is that they are conspicuously, often spectacularly, visual. They 'faithfully' envisage the experience of reading Kafka's prose – they supply visual substitutes for the text. In so doing they cheerfully endorse Brecht's remark on Kafka, 'die Bilder sind ja gut', and ignore Kafka's own reservations about the effects of 'moving images'.

Hanns Zischler, in his valuable study *Kafka geht ins Kino* (Kafka Goes to the Cinema), has demonstrated that Kafka was a keen cinema-goer. His book also reveals, however, a complex ambivalence towards the new medium. In a travel-diary entry, for example, the author refers to having enjoyed 'boundless entertainment' in the cinema. Even here the approbation is tempered by the term *maßlos* ('boundless'), which seems to suggest something immoderate and hectoring. A further example of this notion of cinema as overawing occurs in the opening entries (from the summer of 1909) of what was to become Kafka's diary:

The audience freezes when the train passes by.

'If he will keep asking me.' The 'a', separated from the sentence, flew away like a ball on a field.

(*TB1*: 11)

Although there is no obvious connection between these two notes, there is a notional link between the enforced paralysis of the spectator in the cinema and the disintegration of meaning if language becomes image (in this instance disconnected image fragments or 'graphemes'). Kafka is more explicit in a travel-diary entry following a visit to an Imperial Panorama (*Kaiserpanorama*) in the industrial town of Friedland. He compares this popular form of visual spectacle, consisting of three-dimensional panoramas viewed through special lenses, with the moving pictures of the cinema. He finds its still images more lifelike because they allow the gaze the stillness of reality, whereas 'cinema lends the restlessness of its own movement to what is seen, the calm gaze seems to be more important' (January 1911; *RT*: 16).

Prescient remarks in a letter to Felice of November 1913, following a visit to a Veronese cinema, neatly encapsulate Kafka's critique of cinema as a place where reality, in this case emotional, is consumed rather than experienced. They foreshadow, at least in implication, Adorno and Horkheimer's critique of the culture industry, in which cinema is a source of escapism and, simultaneously, a begetter of alienation:

> I encounter nothing that moves me in any deep sense. That is also the case when I cry, as was the case yesterday in a film theatre in Verona. I have been given the ability to enjoy human relationships but not to experience them.
>
> (6.XI.13; *BF*: 472)

Lost in transit

Returning to the issue of adaptation, it is not, of course, only directors of moving images who have translated Kafka. To commemorate the fiftieth anniversary of his death, an exhibition in Bonn in 1974 brought together prints, drawings, and paintings based on his stories and novels. Günther Nicolin provides a timely warning in the introduction to the catalogue:

> It is easy to illustrate Kafka's text in the traditional way, i.e. to draw each image of that wonderfully clear prose – Kafka himself feared as much – but nothing is gained by this, rather, attention is wrenched away from Kafka's diction.[5]

The problem of adapting Kafka's works to the visual media is neatly summarised in these remarks, which acknowledge both the attraction of the countless strong images to be found there, and the frustration of the loss that occurs in transit.

The Second Commandment
(*Thou shalt take unto thee no graven image*)

In fact the dilemma facing the illustrator keys into a paradox at the heart of Kafka's œuvre. On the one hand, there is the strongly visual use of language – metaphor, analogy, a meticulous naturalism in the description of architectural space and landscape, for example – and on the other, the restricted viewpoint of the protagonists. Together these make for the disconcerting world view generally labelled 'Kafkaesque' – they also present a cameraman, for example, with a veritable conundrum.

However, the most famous argument for caution in transferring Kafka's verbal images into visual representations comes from Kafka himself in the much-quoted letter to Kurt Wolff about 'The Metamorphosis':

> I have just had rather a…shock. Because…it has occurred to me that he might want to draw the insect itself. Not that, please not that!…The insect itself cannot be drawn. It cannot even be shown from a distance.
>
> (25.X.15; B1: 136)

Kafka's alarm has been interpreted psycho-analytically, analysed in terms of the peculiarities of his narrative technique, and defended with recourse to Jewish debates concerning the Second Commandment's prohibition of images.

Yet, despite all these pitfalls and admonitions, the straightforward appeal of the image has been strong enough for visual artists to disregard Kafka's qualms, making their illustrations, paintings, films, and videos controversial documents of that abiding interplay of text and image and the endless problem that is literary adaptation.

Excursus: biopics

A diverse range of film-makers have responded to Kafka's vision with feature film adaptations of the novels and short stories, profiles and biographies of the man himself, short films, experimental and otherwise, and animations.

Not surprisingly, given the well-rehearsed debates concerning the relationship between Kafka's life and his writings, a substantial proportion of these films – Steven Soderbergh's *Kafka* (1991) is only the most famous – are based on the author's biography. Again not surprisingly, given Kafka's canonical status, many have educational remits. These include Harold Mantell's *The Trials of Franz Kafka* (1973) and David Thomas's *Franz Kafka's 'The Trial'* (1988), along with numerous more-or-less essayistic productions for German television.

One of these 'biopics' deserves special mention. Zbigniew Rybczynski's experimental video film *Kafka* (1992) attempts to investigate systematically a method of employing the illusory capacity of film and video – the Méliès quality of cinema – to merge the biography with the fiction, to use technology to illustrate the complex relationship in Kafka's prose between realism and the fantastic. Rybczynski's film even has what one might term a 'Kafkaesque' perversity about its very production: the actors were required to learn to move and speak to fit in with the camera, rather than the more usual reverse relationship. It is a process which allowed the film-maker to introduce novel techniques for generating the illusion of free space inspired by the unexpected shifts in location experienced by Kafka's protagonists. For this reason alone, Rybczynski's film represents a noteworthy attempt to discover a film-specific analogy for an aspect of prose style.

The 'Kafkaesque' 1: Animated metaphors

Reviewing the 1981 British puppet film *Ein Brudermord* by The Brothers Quay, Richard Combs writes:

> All roads, not just for the Quays, but for the European puppet film, might lead through Kafka. First of all, puppet films are probably best qualified to give clear and accurate meaning to the notoriously generalised concept of the 'Kafkaesque'. With their concrete abstractions, their metaphors endowed with a startlingly literal life, they come close to the Kafka method. And that paranoiac vision which sees life as an endless, impenetrable, infernal bureaucracy is most nicely rendered in the 'found' materials of puppetry, a world of arbitrary bits and pieces where the tawdry, the pathetic, the strange and the intimidating freely intermingle.[6]

It can be asserted that certain special effects in film, especially animation, used to bring objects to life or render humans and other creatures strange are in some way 'Kafkaesque'. Despite the fact that they have not taken Kafka's texts as the basis for their films, directors such as the Czech animator Jan Švankmajer and the American maverick David Lynch have also habitually been labelled in this way on account of their creation of a profound sense of unease about everyday objects both animate and inanimate. It could even be argued that the visual tricks played by film-makers may constitute cinematic equivalents for the way in which Kafka takes idiomatic expressions in German and points to their disturbing and suppressed visual origins. However, although productive parallels can undoubtedly be drawn between, say, 'The Metamorphosis' and Lynch's *Eraserhead* (1976), or *The Trial* and Švankmajer's *Faust* (1994), there is a great danger here of blurring boundaries between Kafka's prose, Expressionism, Surrealism (Czech or otherwise), *Pittura Metafisica* (of de Chirico and others), Existentialism and *das Unheimliche* (the uncanny).

The 'Kafkaesque' 2: Surreal dictators

Such is the general currency of the concept 'Kafkaesque' that it is frequently also applied to political films which introduce a surreal element to the depiction of political dictatorships. The main ingredient of the societies described in such films is an all-powerful and incomprehensible authority which weakens the individual psychologically and physically. The characters in these narratives do not only experience the world as terrifyingly confusing, they also find their own actions to be guilt-ridden and inadequate. Good examples are the Czech film *Postava K Podpírání* (Joseph Kilián / A Sad Story, 1963) by Jan Schmidt and Pavel Juráček, which uses deliberately Kafkaesque motifs as the basis for an ironic parable depicting the absurdities of Stalinism, and Râul Ruiz's labyrinthine Chilean film *La colonia penal* (1971), which uses Kafka's 'In the Penal Colony' merely as its starting point. *Postava K Podpírání* contains all the ingredients of the Stalinist Kafkaesque – disappearing institutions, ringing telephones with no one to reply, waiting rooms, paper walls, and wandering bureaucrats, while *La colonia penal* depicts a newly independent island with a colonial history where news is manufactured, filled with polyglot soldiers, a poet pickpocket, an eccentric and suicidal President who is assassinated, superstitious natives telling bizarre fables, and a journalist who is suitably impressed by it all.

In postwar Germany two Existentialist films dealing with alienation and unseen dictatorial authorities belong to this catagory – Ottomar Domnick's sci-fi study of fear and misery in fifties West Germany, *Jonas* (1957), with a script by Hans Magnus Enzensberger, and Ferdinand Khittl's *Die Parallelstraße* (The Parallel Street, 1961), in which an imprisoned group of intellectuals makes hopeless attempts to solve the riddles of the intellectual adventure by rationalisation and exegesis. They pay for their failure with death at the hands of an unseen arbiter.

Hungry artists

It is worth noting in passing a rather self-conscious quirk of cinematic Kafka reception. While large numbers of Kafka's short stories and aphorisms have been the source for short films and animation, one appears to hold a special appeal for long-suffering or destitute avantgardists – 'Ein Hungerkünstler'. Film-makers attracted to it have included the Americans Fred and Mary Smith in 1976, the British director Bernard Rudden in 1995, and the 'Winnipeg Wacko' James Pomeroy in the same year.

All's Welles that Ends Welles

In what follows, two landmark adaptations of Kafka's novels will be examined in more detail – Orson Welles's *The Trial*, and Jean-Marie Straub and Danièle Huillet's adaptation of *The Man who Disappeared*. They represent two entirely different approaches to the awkward problem of putting Kafka's vision on the silver screen.

Although Orson Welles's *The Trial* (1962) is the most famous of all Kafka screen adaptations, and named by Welles himself as his favourite amongst his films, the initial reaction to it was not favourable. Whilst Kafka devotees bemoaned the liberties taken with the text, in particular with the parable 'Before the Law', journalists looking as ever for a second *Citizen Kane* were disappointed at its abstract quality and measured pace. Subsequently it has received the detailed critical attention it deserves, but remains controversial not least for the way in which the personality of Welles himself overshadows Kafka's novel. With the director taking on the role of the Advocate and providing the voice which introduces and closes the film, *The Trial* exhibits an unsettling yet striking symbiosis of author, character, and filmmaker. James Naremore has described Welles as 'something of a patrician, a man who has always been more interested in the psychology of the oppressors than in the anxieties of the oppressed'.[7] Gertrud Koch describes Welles as a showman creating a show trial whilst drawing on all the trends in interpretation that were fashionable in the 1960s: 'A little bit of religion, a little bit of the nightmare, cultural critique of mass society, and at the end the atomic threat as an existential condition'.[8]

Welles's staging of the arrest towards the beginning of the film is where Kafka's text and the director's interpretation mesh most easily. Indeed it is in the legal scenes which punctuate the film that Welles follows the original text most closely. It is perhaps hardly surprising in the wake of McCarthyism, and at the height of the Cold War, that concepts such as civil liberty, accusation and defence, and emotions of guilt, helplessness, and confusion are eminently transferrable from the context of a native of Prague born before the First World War to the immediate concerns of an American citizen two decades after the Second. Welles achieves a fine balance of paranoia and surreal humour in juggling the awkwardness of a private space invaded with the corruption of the men arresting Josef K., and the protagonist's own confused feelings of guilt and outrage. Crucial to the success of this scene is the near-hysterical performance of Anthony Perkins as K.

Kafka's novel is repeatedly given specific historical and geographical connotations in Welles's film. The director's postwar sensibility draws out in particular the notion that the individual victim may and indeed should stand up for all victims:

> what has happened to me is after all only an individual case and as such it is not very important since I am not taking it very seriously, but it is an example of a procedure which is being carried out against many. I am standing up here for these many, not for myself. (DP: 64)

The manifest absurdity of these pronouncements, in the context of the novel, is substantially played down by Welles.

Diverse issues such as postwar collective guilt, the desolation of the modern metropolis and its brutalist architecture, the status of modern art, and even physical disability – in the form of a spurious but witty tirade delivered by an irascible 'cripple' – are introduced as substitutes for Kafka's observations inspired by Austro-Hungarian Prague. The painter Titorelli provides a neat, if incidental, example of Welles's method of actualisation and recontextual-isation. Whereas Kafka's Titorelli sells K. three identical heath landscapes – 'here were the trees, here the grass and there the sunset' (*DP*: 220) – Welles's character sells 'action paintings' of 'wild nature'. Most famously the film modernises and spectacularises the bank with a vast room of typists and adds a dialogue between the uncle and K. about the institution's central computer and its potential to answer the more profound questions posed by K.'s situation. Welles even provides a contemporary slant on the office by transferring some of the sexuality of the private sphere to the workplace.

The social environment, and in particular its architecture, is considerably shifted in Welles's film by the use of a vast housing estate of concrete slab blocks in Yugoslavia as equivalents for the tenement blocks described by Kafka:

> But the Juliusstraße…at one end of which K. stood for a moment, was a street of almost completely uniform buildings on both sides, tall, grey tenement blocks occupied by the poor. Now, on a Sunday morning, most of the windows were filled, men in shirtsleeves leaned out of them and smoked or carefully and tenderly held their small children on the sill. Other windows were piled high with bedding over which the tousled head of a woman would appear briefly. People shouted to one another across the passage, one such call was just then causing great mirth above K.'s head. (*DP*: 53)

There is none of the life and animation of this scene in Welles's film, which seeks instead to create the Stalinist atmosphere of the Cold War in which individuals are isolated by their environment rather than thrown together. As such, Welles's approach could be seen as the triumph of what we under-stand as the 'Kafkaesque' over Kafka himself, the phrase 'almost completely uniform buildings' being extended into a vision of lives that have become dwarfed within massive building projects and town planning. Kafka's vision of the modern bureaucratised society as organic, labyrinthine, a complex of individual networks, is metamorphosed into the grids and plans of the postwar modernist revival.

The contrast between Kafka's bureaucratised society and that of Welles is most apparent in the latter's adaptation of the parable 'Before the Law', which in the film is given added prominence by appearing both at the begin-ning and the end. Welles uses the story as an explanation for the film's lack of narrative logic, declaring, as the directorial voice, that the story has the 'logic of a dream, a nightmare'. The final line of the film, 'My name is Orson Welles', signals the triumph of Welles over Kafka at the end of a sequence which returns to the theme which obsessed the director from *Citizen Kane* to *F is for Fake*, the relationship between truth and fiction, and the substantiality of illusion, in particular cinematic illusion. If Kafka's text has been read as a metatextual critique of bureaucratised structures, language, and processes of interpretation, the final minutes of *The Trial*, a compendium of cinematic quotations and encyclopedia of filmic devices (incorporating deep focus, wide panoramas, shadows, silhouettes and projections, jump cuts, handheld camera, and freeze-framing), amount to a Wellesian mini-essay on the power, both positive and negative, of cinematic illusion. The fireworks of this denouement, however, and the bold assertion of the director's own presence, irresistably amount to an affirmation of creative energy over the demise of the protagonist (which is itself indeed by no means as explicit as it is in Kafka's novel). The sheer inventiveness and energy of this final sequence seems, perversely, to force one to the conclusion that indeed all's Welles that ends Welles.

Kafka's spine

Jean-Marie Straub and Danièle Huillet's 1983 adaptation of *The Man who Disappeared* – the film bears the provocative title *Klassenverhältnisse* (Class Relations) – is a dissection of its source material. According to its directors, stripping a text to its bare bones – 'what we are looking for is simply a spine, a skeleton'[9] – is the only way of ensuring that a literary adaptation does not slip away 'like shit on a sheet of plastic'.[10]

Not surprisingly, given the film-makers' reputation as the most intellectually uncompromising of *Literaturverfilmer* (literary adaptors), *Klassenverhältnisse* is entirely consistent with the materialist, Brechtian method of exploring literary source material developed in their previous films – critical anatomies of Böll, Bruckner, Corneille, Brecht, Mallarmé, Fortini, Pavese, and Duras. In an interview about the Kafka film, Straub commented on this method as follows:

> First of all, you have to know what interests you and what doesn't. Most people in the world today don't know that any more. And you have to know what relates to your own experiences, i.e. what affects you and what doesn't. Because you don't actually 'film' a book, you enter into a dialogue with it, you want to make a film out of a book because the book relates to your own experiences, your own questions, your own outbursts of hatred or your own declarations of love. The first thing I always do is to start copying things out.[11]

Elsewhere in the same interview Straub remarks:

> we didn't want to make a 'historical film', we had had it up to here with costumes – and: we wanted to put Kafka's text to the test: simply test it: 1920 and now, because in capitalist societies history does unfortunately repeat itself, perhaps not exactly, but there is a continuity.[12]

In *Klassenverhältnisse* Kafka's text is treated as a document of a particular time and place. Referring to the decision to shoot the film in contemporary Hamburg, Huillet has claimed that history cannot lie. This was in fact an eminently sound decision given that Kafka never visited America, and that Karl Roßmann carries the baggage of the old world around with him. According to Straub, a film camera should record and document, not illustrate:

> Film is, after all, not an instrument for illustration or description. Writers' descriptions are best left to the writers.
> There are a number of reasons for this. There had already been a Kafka film before ours, *The Trial* of Orson Welles. He tried to show what Kafka described. For example...: a room where forty girls sit and type. In our film there is just *one* lift. We wanted to do the opposite of what Orson Welles did; we didn't want to show in any way what Kafka described.[13]

It is also consistent with Straub/Huillet's Marxist credentials that they should read Kafka as a realist:

> He could not be less metaphysical and unrealistic. On the contrary, every relationship in his text is thoroughly realistic, everyday even. [...]
> The incredible thing about Kafka is that he was the first (and to date probably the only) writer of our so-called industrial society.[14]

Straub/Huillet's approach to translating Kafka for the screen – producing a metatext, an 'Interlinearversion' as Walter Benjamin uses the term – takes as its starting point Kafka's alleged definition of capitalism as a 'system of dependencies',[15] and also embraces the novel's fragmentary form. For their cinematic dissections, Straub/Huillet have tended either to select lacunary or unfinished texts – Schönberg's *Moses und Aron*, Brecht's *Die Geschäfte des Herrn Julius Caesar* (The Business Dealings of Mr Julius Caesar), Hölderlin's first and third *Empedokles* fragments – or apply their own dynamite to the material. The aim is to open up the text to scrutiny, to suspend and stall it. Their method is essentially a materialist historiography as defined by Benjamin:

> A constructive principle lies at the heart... of materialist historiography. Thinking does not consist exclusively of the movement of thoughts but also in bringing them to a halt. Where thinking stops in a constellation packed with

tensions, it deals it a shock through which it crystallizes out as a monad. The historical materialist only approaches a historical object where he encounters it as a monad.[16]

The aesthetic principles underpinning Straub/Huillet's reading or copying out of *The Man who Disappeared* are the cinematic equivalents of *Stillstellung* (bringing to a halt) and *Chock*: on the structural level, epic fragmentation and stasis alternating with abrupt montage; on the photographic level, non-diegetic framing and extreme perspectives; on the performative level, non-naturalistic acting and delivery; on the linguistic level, a breakdown of the prose into non-semantic 'quotations'. To cite one example: a controversial aspect of the film has proved to be the subdivision of the dialogue into discrete blocks separated by artificial pauses. Examples include:

I have here a | cap for you.
Wait I will | make | it a little more comfortable for you
You see Robinson | we gave him our | trust have for a whole day | dragged him around with us and lost at least half a day in the process |

The result is in fact nothing more mysterious than a form of linguistic estrangement. Just as the narrative of *The Man who Disappeared* changes direction unexpectedly – the abandoning of the stoker for example – so the caesuras in the dialogue of Straub/Huillet's film suggest a linguistic bifurcation. The halting pace allows the viewer to become aware of the construction of meaning and leaves sufficient space for an anticipated meaning to be fleetingly registered before being contradicted. A given statement could simply branch off in another direction at each artificial pause. Those who speak without pausing – Uncle Jakob for example – are simply those whose position of absolute power extends to, or rests on, language. Uniquely amongst film-makers, Straub/Huillet have invented an oral equivalent for the celebrated polysemy of Kafka's prose:

This has first and foremost to do with contents, nothing else. And then these contents become rhythms...
   Contents, where one attempts not to establish a *single* content; to leave it open to the viewer and listener so that he can decide for himself how to deal with what is spoken.[17]

Straub/Huillet have often cited Cézanne as a source for their own method of uncovering the backbone of their chosen source material, and it is useful to reiterate the visual analogy in the context of *Klassenverhältnisse*. Their process of translation echoes Cézanne's rendering of Mont Sainte Victoire as a constellation of abstract volumetric shapes: 'May I repeat what I told you here: treat nature by the cylinder, the sphere, the cone, everything in proper perspective.'[18]

The result of this process when applied to Kafka's novel is a kind of cinematic *Lehrstück* (learning play) in the Brechtian sense and a thoroughgoing de-mystification of the text. The dissection shows the novel 'in proper perspective'. Moreover, the atomisation of narrative and language, coupled with the startling beauty of the film's black-and-white photography, in fact open up *The Man who Disappeared* to a lucid, thoroughly non-'Kafkaesque', even optimistic reading. As Straub rather laconically put it:

> Perhaps Karl is heading at the end to somewhere where a utopia exists which we will only have reached in three hundred or three thousand years; but it could also be that he is heading somewhere entirely different – into oblivion, away with him...

'But I do believe that he *is* a rebel – just as he is. That is how he is in the film. But that was always the strength of Kafka's story.'[19]

The Tower of Babel

Cinematic literary adaptations abide in a complex relationship with their source material. In the transfer from page to screen they are engaged in a process of translation, substitution, and interpretation, and the material thus displaced essentially stands in a metaphorical relationship to the original text – the Tower of Babel to the poplar. In his essay 'The Task of the Translator', Walter Benjamin argues that the process of interlingual transfer can elevate the original text closer to 'the language of truth – true language'. He defines the intent of the author's text as 'naive, primary, graphic', that of the translator's as 'resultant, ultimate, ideational'. The role of the translator, he concludes, is 'to free in the rendition that which is imprisoned in the original'.[20] This must also be the paramount objective of any serious film-maker who chooses to adapt literary source material.

This chapter has concentrated on *The Trial* and *Klassenverhältnisse* as paradigms of Kafka adaptation. Neither, as we have seen, attempts to discover a direct stylistic equivalent for Kafka's prose. This has been attempted by other Kafka films meriting serious attention. A particularly fine example is Michael Haneke's *Das Schloß* (The Castle, 1997), which space has not permitted us to engage with at length. Haneke's film constitutes a middle ground between exegesis and dramatisation. It readily admits a debt to the materialist aesthetic of Straub/Huillet, whilst attempting to discover a more fluid, less cerebral form of realism, one which does not shy away from staging modest visual equivalents for character and setting. The result is perhaps closest to the style of the last films of Robert Bresson, the Tolstoy adaptation *L'Argent* (1983) in particular. Welles and Straub/Huillet show fundamental differences in their approach to translating words into images. Welles stages his reading as a sequence of spectacular Kafkaesque visions, culminating, during the director's orotund credits, in the image of the locked door from Kafka's 'Before the Law' encapsulated by a camera lens. It is an image which suggests, one presumes inadvertently, that Kafka's text has been paralysed and subjugated to the monocular vision of cinema.

This is not, of course, to say that Kafka's prose is in any way intrinsically unsuited to translation to screen. In a letter to Benjamin, Adorno went so far as to argue that his novels represent 'the last, disappearing texts connecting literature to silent cinema (which not by chance disappeared at almost exactly the same time as Kafka's death)'.[21] The farcical Keystone-Kops-style policemen in *Klassenverhältnisse* may indeed be an acknowledgement of this cinematic echo in Kafka's prose. The problem, as we have seen, is to find a cinematic method of translation which is appropriate rather than faithful.

Kafka's prose exploits to the full the capacity of language to shape discourse as it develops. Language can do this because it is compelled to segment thoughts into discrete elements which are then sequentially modified. The following passage from 'Description of a Struggle', the story with which this chapter began, was extracted by Kafka for separate publication in 1913 under the title 'Die Bäume' ('The Trees'):

> For we are in fact like tree trunks in the snow. They appear simply to rest on the surface such that one could push them away with a light touch. But no, one cannot, for they are firmly fixed to the ground. But look, even that is only apparently the case. (*BK*: 110)[22]

Here, the initial metaphor is problematised in each of the three sentences that follow. The first of these provides a much-needed explanation for the analogy, thereby implying that it lacks the self-evidence of a 'true' image. The second confirms this lack of transparency by demonstrating that the metaphor is dependent on an awareness of the real state of things (the rootedness of the tree). The third then destabilises the equation again by questioning the rootedness of the tree and, by implication, also of the metaphor. The result in this case is physical and linguistic slippage.

The slippage is not, however, as extreme as it might appear. Just as the narrator relies on the existence of the 'true names of things' in 'Description of a Struggle', so there are also examples of 'true images' to be found in Kafka's writing. In *The Man who Disappeared*, for example, the protagonist finds solace in a photographic image of his mother:

> How could one possibly gain from a picture so completely the incontrovertible conviction that here was revealed a hidden emotion of the person depicted...The picture slipped from his hands, he then laid his face on the picture, its coolness felt good on his cheek and with a pleasant sensation he fell asleep. *(DV: 135–6)*

The reassurance Karl gains from the picture is based on its stillness, which allows contemplation, and its truthfulness. It is these two qualities which are the guiding principles of Straub/Huillet's method of Kafka adaptation. In rejecting the claim that Kafka's writings are either metaphysical or allegorical, Straub has quoted a remark by the author which he and Huillet had written on their shooting script: 'Metaphors are one of the many things that make me despair of writing.'[23] Straub/Huillet's first principle, as we have seen, is 'copying out', a pre-translational exercise; the subsequent process of translation to film entails observing the minutiae of rhythm and pause in Kafka's prose.

Film is, by and large, consolidatory in its synthesis of images, words, and sounds. When confronted with a form of language use that emphasises the discrete and the separate, as in the case of Kafka, a film-maker is forced either into monocularity or into using film in a radically different way. In either case the reader-turned-viewer is obliged to observe how metaphors work differently from images, and how experiences brought together in words are not the same as events bracketed together in time. In a striking remark on the Imperial Panorama, following those quoted above, Kafka himself conceived of a cinema which would do away with that incessant movement which drains cinema of 'the calm of reality': 'Why is there no union of cinema and the stereoscope?' *(RT: 16)*

Klassenverhältnisse, in our opinion, is unique among Kafka films in that it not only maintains a critical distance between Kafka's text and the film-makers' images, but also achieves the author's calm of reality. The dialectical relationship between words and pictures that results opens up space for a complexity of meaning commensurate with that of Kafka's prose.

NOTES

1. Walter Benjamin, 'Notes from Svendborg: Conversations with Brecht', in *Understanding Brecht*, tr. Anna Bostock (London: New Left Books, 1973), pp. 105–21, here 5.VIII.34, p. 110.
2. Allen Hoey, 'The Name on the Coin: Metaphors, Metonymy, and Money', *Diacritics* 2 (1988), 26–37, here p. 26.
3. Ibid., p. 27.

4. The authors compiled a list of forty Kafka films in researching this article at the British Film Institute.

5. Günther Nicolin, *Kunst zu Kafka: Ausstellung zum 50. Todestag* (Bonn: bücherstube am theater, 1974), p. 5.

6. Richard Combs, 'Ein Brudermord', *Monthly Film Bulletin* 630 (1986), 219–20, here p. 219.

7. Naremore, *The Magic World of Orson Welles*, p. 199.

8. Gertrud Koch, ' "Nur von Sichtbarem läßt sich erzählen". Zu einigen Kafka-Verfilmungen', in Wolfram Schütte (ed.), *Klassenverhältnisse*, pp. 171–8, here p. 173.

9. Wolfram Schütte, 'Gespräch mit Danièle Huillet und Jean-Marie Straub', in Schütte (ed.), *Klassenverhältnisse*, pp. 37–58, here p. 54.

10. Straub in interview with Harun Farocki, 'Einfach mit der Seele, das gibt es nicht', *Filmkritik* 317 (1983), 242–7, here p. 246.

11. Schütte, 'Gespräch', p. 46.

12. Ibid., p. 45.

13. Straub in interview, 'Wie will ich lustig lachen, wenn alles durcheinandergeht: Danièle Huillet und Jean-Marie Straub sprechen über ihren Film *Klassenverhältnisse*', *Filmkritik* 333/334 (1984), 269–78, here p. 272.

14. Schütte, 'Gespräch', p. 39.

15. Ibid., p. 39. Straub's quotation appears in the discussions with Kafka published by Gustav Janouch. The authenticity of these discussions is now generally doubted, and they have therefore been disregarded in this chapter. They do, however, contain some pithy remarks on cinema which have gained common currency within film studies, although Hanns Zischler rejects them wholesale. (Gustav Janouch, *Conversations with Kafka*, 2nd edition, tr. Goronwy Rees (London: Deutsch, 1971), pp. 146–9 and esp. 160.

16. Walter Benjamin, 'Theses on the Philosophy of History', in *Illuminations*, ed. and with intro by Hannah Arendt, tr. Harry Zohn (London: Cape, 1970), pp. 255–66, here pp. 264–5. Translation modified.

17. Schütte, 'Gespräch', p. 54.

18. Paul Cézanne, letter to Emile Bernard, 15 April 1904. Quoted in H. B. Chipp, *Theories of Modern Art* (Berkeley: University of California Press, 1968), p. 19.

19. Schütte, 'Gespräch', pp. 42, 58.

20. *Illuminations*, pp. 69–82, here pp. 76–7, 80. Translations modified.

21. Letter from Adorno to Benjamin (17.XII.34), in Theodor W. Adorno and Walter Benjamin, *The Complete Correspondence 1928–1940*, ed. Henri Lonitz, tr. Nicholas Walker (Cambridge: Polity Press, 1999), pp. 66–73, here p. 70. Translation modified.

22. For the conference in Prague which preceded publication of this volume, Martin Brady made a short experimental film based on this text (*Kafka Hora*, 1999, colour and b/w, 4 mins.). In front of a background of looped footage of birdprints in the snow, a small model tree starts to spin at 78rpm, framed so that the trunk is cut off just above the roots. The tree is freeze-framed every six frames, which gives it a halting movement. The film opens with Kafka's text on screen and the spinning tree is accompanied by Klezmer music (a lively Hora). This music stops as the tree comes to a standstill.

23. Schütte, 'Gespräch', p. 40.

FURTHER READING

Byg, Barton, *Landscapes of Resistance: the German Films of Danièle Huillet and Jean-Marie Straub* (Berkeley: University of California Press, 1995).

Naremore, James, *The Magic World of Orson Welles* (Dallas: Southern Methodist University Press, 1989).

Schütte, Wolfram (ed.), *Klassenverhältnisse: von Danièle Huillet und Jean-Marie Straub nach dem Amerika-Roman 'Der Verschollene' von Franz Kafka* (Frankfurt aM: Fischer, 1984).

Welles, Orson, *The Trial* (New York: Simon and Schuster, 1970).

Zischler, Hanns, *Kafka geht ins Kino* (Reinbek bei Hamburg: Rowohlt, 1998).

14

IRIS BRUCE

Kafka and popular culture

Kafka has inspired numerous artists in their creative work: in poetry, fiction, drama, film, painting, even music. Susan Sontag aptly observed that he has 'attracted interpreters like leeches'.[1] Out of the vast material available, I have selected a few texts from three genres: comic book, science fiction, and film. By referring to Kafka as an 'inspiration' for these artists, I do not mean to suggest that they were merely 'influenced' by him. On the contrary, reading Kafka through them will show how they have left their mark on Kafka, inasmuch as their readings contribute to the ways in which we read his texts. In his famous essay, 'Kafka and His Precursors', Jorge Luis Borges stated: '[Every writer's] work modifies our conception of the past, as it will modify the future.'[2] A similar relationship can be said to exist between Kafka and the artists who followed him.

'The Metamorphosis' clearly serves as an intertext for Woody Allen's comic film *Zelig* (1983). After a round of medical experiments Zelig ends up walking on the walls of his room.[3] The film is set in America (and Europe) in the interwar period. Leonard Zelig, the central character, is a 'human chameleon', who takes on the personal and physical characteristics of individuals whom he encounters. Thus he is found in Chinatown as a 'strange-looking Oriental' and arrested, but when he emerges 'incredibly, he is no longer Chinese but Caucasian'.[4] Zelig becomes a great celebrity, a freak, and a performer – a movie is even made of him, called *The Changing Man*. The public goes Zelig-crazy, they make him perform with 'a midget and a chicken',[5] put him into a room with two overweight men and wait for Zelig to puff himself up, or show how 'in the ... presence of two Negro men, Zelig rapidly becomes one himself'.[6] Even the reporter seems to suggest that this is a little too much: 'What *will* they think of next?'[7]

Both Kafka and Allen make 'visible' dehumanising conditions in early twentieth-century society. For Kafka, this visibility is achieved largely through visual or figurative language, such as animal metaphors. But Kafka wanted these metaphors to remain ambiguous, to exist, as Stanley Corngold put it, in a 'solitude of the indecipherable sign' (M: 89). As we know he expressly asked his publisher not to depict Gregor Samsa on the cover. Unlike Kafka, Woody Allen makes racial stereotypes quite explicit, manipulates them, and more obviously deflects them humorously or ironically. Read within the fascist and anti-Semitic discourses of the late 1920s, Zelig's statement, 'I used to be a member of the reptile family, but I'm not anymore',[8] alludes to a common racist stereotype used against the Jews. Allen highlights the humorous side by making it 'visible' in the new dance *Doin' the Chameleon*, which 'sweeps the nation',[9] thereby projecting the stereotype back on to the society which created it in the first place: the Jews were also said to have no fixed cultural or individual identity as they took on the characteristics of whichever host culture they lived in. By moving not only beyond racial boundaries but also beyond North America, the joke is not on Zelig any more but rather on the whole world.

But Allen goes beyond making explicit what is implicit in Kafka. He also 'reads' Gregor's or Zelig's 'unstable make-up' very critically in relation to the rise of fascism. As a Jew who lacks a personal identity, Zelig is a perfect case study for an individual drawn to fascism. Initially, he tries to define himself by becoming like individual people. Then he identifies with a whole cultural set of values, the 'American Way'. Finally he defines himself by identifying with a large political movement. It is a small step from his beginnings to his drowning in a fascist collective identity. Trained to be a commodity with no soul of his own, he follows fascism as if it were the newest fad society had to offer.

David Cronenberg's *The Fly* (1986) and *Naked Lunch* (1991), notable for their combination of horror, fantasy, and science fiction, exploit the grossness of the insect metaphor for the thrill which accompanies the shock effects on the viewer. In *The Fly*, Seth Brundle is a rational scientist who tries to overcome the boundaries of biological determinism by transporting himself into other spatial dimensions through teleportation. The movie seems less a commentary on Kafka than on the dangers of modern science and technology and the disastrous consequences that can result from human error. For in a fit of jealousy and alcoholic delusion, Seth abandons his rational faculties, is careless when he tests the experiment on himself and does not notice the presence of a fly in the transporter. The merging of their molecules leads to the creation of a human-animalistic 'metamorph', the Brundle-Fly.

What is Kafkaesque here, though, is Cronenberg's exploration of deeply rooted anxieties, which include the fear of losing control over one's body, of succumbing to irrational animalistic impulses, of being entirely at their mercy. More importantly even, Cronenberg's 'reading' of the unsettling and threatening possibilities in the insect metaphor includes a humorous dimension.

When one considers how many postwar readers of Kafka have missed the humour and playfulness in his work, Allen and Cronenberg are rare exceptions. Cronenberg especially stands out as one of the few who sees humour even in gruesome scenes.

Naked Lunch (1991) transforms the metamorphosis metaphor within a postmodern framework. The leitmotif of the movie is, 'Exterminate all rational thought'. We are about to embark on a journey into irrationality and enter the worlds of 'Interzone' and 'Annexia', where different laws apply. The protagonist, Bill Lee, introduces himself as 'Exterminator': he is a pest control man by profession. His wife, Joan, is one among many who is addicted to insect poison, or bug powder, and 'Interzone' authorities, who control the insect powder addiction business, pronounce her non-human. The representative of 'Interzone' who pronounces her death-sentence is none other than 'Gregor Samsa'. Gregor also appears in connection with writing: there are even live insect typewriters, and typing on them is depicted as an addictive, erotic, and parasitical activity.

'Otherness' in this movie is not a racial or social issue but a gender issue, which is not deconstructed and presented critically. Women are killed or eliminated (at one point a female insect typewriter is brutally crushed by a male typewriter), while traditionally repressed homosexuality is celebrated. In addition, the protagonist needs to 'exterminate' his wife every time he enters a new zone of experience. In the end the women turn out to be identical (they are also killed in the same fashion), which reveals the movie's underlying circular structure. This circularity, where endings and beginnings are arbitrary, is characteristic of postmodernism. The people in 'Interzone' become not only addicted but also the victims of their own libidinal desires: *eros* and *thanatos*.

The 1990s continued to display a fondness for marketing the horrible and ugly. David Mairowitz and Robert Crumb's comic book *Kafka for Beginners* (1993) is a critique of modern consumer society, demythologising Kafka by poking fun at the Kafka industry in academic circles and popular culture. They appropriately end with an ironic representation of the booming Kafka industry in Prague now: here we have Kafka T-shirts, Ghetto-Pizza, McKafka Hamburgers, a Metamorphosis Beauty Salon, etc. However, *Kafka for Beginners* itself aims for popular consumption and it is striking how many cartoons focus on magic, mystery, the fantastic, sexuality, and particularly on gruesome details such as Kafka chopping off part of his head with a butcher's knife on the very first page, graphic depictions of a sadistic ritual murder scene, of the stages of torture in the 'Penal Colony' and of the hunger artist's suffering. It seems that we cannot do without scenes of violence and humiliation, that we must exploit them for the market potential they contain.

Yet for all this comic-book gore, rendered by the artist who brought us such underground cult classics as Fat Freddy's Cat and the Freak Brothers, *Kafka for Beginners* is a serious and well-researched book, intended to reach out to students and others generally interested in literature. Crumb's cartoon images are matched by Mairowitz's lively and incisive commentary. The end result is part educational, part entertainment and brings out the affinities between Kafka's more extreme imagery and popular gothic forms; that it is also a re-mythologisation of its subject goes without saying.

We see a similar mix of humour and brutality in the short 'science-fiction' story by David Gerrold, 'Franz Kafka, Superhero!' (1994).[10] Gerrold draws on 'The Metamorphosis' but also alludes to 'The Judgement' and 'The Vulture'. He playfully integrates a host of mythical figures from popular culture into the narrative – Superman, Batman, Dracula, and even the Teenage Mutant Ninja Turtles. Kafka himself transforms into 'Bug-Man', a vampire-like insect, who is preparing for his battle against the monster 'PsycheMan', the last evil outpost in the dark underworld of Austria. 'PsycheMan' is in fact the evil doctor Sigmund Freud who terrorises victims by making them fight their own fears, upon which they lose their identities and destroy themselves. During their battle, 'Bug-Man' loses because he begins to doubt himself, but Kafka takes over and outfreuds Freud at his Oedipal game. Like Georg Bendemann with his father, Kafka takes up old Freud in his arms to lay him to rest and suddenly, in a final transformation, he plunges vulturelike at his enemy's throat and drinks his blood. Gerrold thus mixes elements of horror with psychological realism to produce an excellent mini Kafka thriller.

Kafka's writings are a good example of how iconic texts that used to belong to 'high culture' can be 'reborn' in popular culture in generically different formats. All of the above artists have engaged in a dialogically creative exchange with Kafka's work and placed him within a modern and postmodern context. Kafka's phenomenal rebirth is in itself a stunning metamorphosis. Here we have a writer who has successfully bridged the gap between high and popular culture, whose name is recognised by people who have never read one of his novels: the word 'Kafkaesque' has entered into everyday speech and taken on iconic value. However, this success has come at a cost. Perhaps this is part of our cultural inheritance after a century of Holocaust, wars of genocide, and the threat of mutually assured nuclear destruction; perhaps this is simply an example of capitalism's endless ability to transform important ideas and images into 'catchy' popular icons for the thrill-hungry public. The unsettling and threatening possibilities inherent in the insect metaphor, for example, derive from deeply rooted anxieties, primal and contemporary at the same time; not incidentally, they also offer up new images for consumption in the insatiable cultural marketplace. Woody Allen goes in an altogether opposite direction by exposing the Kafkaesque protagonist as a perfect puppet in a totalitarian system, as the ultimate conformist. Kafka's fate in our time is indeed a mixed one.

NOTES

1. Susan Sontag, 'Against Interpretation', in *Against Interpretation and Other Essays* (New York: Dell, 1961), p. 18.
2. Jorge Luis Borges, 'Kafka and His Precursors', in *Labyrinths* (New York: NDP, 1962), pp. 199–201, here p. 201.
3. See Woody Allen, 'Zelig', in *Three Films of Woody Allen. Zelig – Broadway Danny Rose – The Purple Rose of Cairo* (New York: Orion, 1987), pp. 1–141, here p. 42.
4. Ibid., pp. 15–16.
5. Ibid., p. 29.
6. Ibid., p. 30.
7. Ibid., p. 30.
8. Ibid., p. 94.
9. Ibid., p. 35.
10. David Gerrold, 'Franz Kafka, Superhero!', in *By any Other Fame*, ed. Ike Resnick and Martin H. Greenberg (New York: Daw, 1994), pp. 114–29. Many thanks to Geoffrey Winthrop Young for alerting me to this story.

INDEX

Index

Index

Index

Index

Index

Index

CAMBRIDGE COMPANIONS TO LITERATURE

CAMBRIDGE COMPANIONS TO CULTURE